T0333376

'This wrenching and inspiring tale of violence and courageous resistance, told through the eyes of a remarkable Palestinian family, vividly portrays a living example of what Adam Smith memorably called "the savage injustice of the Europeans".'

Noam Chomsky

'Fida Jiryis's story, which at times reads like a thriller, has a unique trajectory which she negotiates with intelligence and eloquence, simultaneously illuminating profound and painful subjects about home and belonging.'

Raja Shehadeh, author of *Going Home: A Walk Through Fifty Years of Occupation*

'This is a beautiful and searing book. The inhuman interrogations, the torment of the vulnerable, the "slow eviction" of an entire people should be understood by all in whose name the impunity of Israel and Zionism is given, year after year. I salute you, Fida Jiryis.'

John Pilger, award-winning journalist, scholar, and documentary filmmaker

'An impressive account of an important period in Palestine's recent history. Part history, part personal narrative, the author skilfully entwines the details of her life with that of her eminent father, and shows the power of Palestinians writing about their own lived experience. Highly recommended.'

Ghada Karmi, author of *Return: A Palestinian Memoir*

'A tale of resilience and incredible courage, this powerful memoir fuses Jiryis's personal recollections with the narrative of her homeland and its people. This is a frank and moving story of humanity and steadfastness, giving real content to the sacred Palestinian right of return.'

Ilan Pappé, Professor of History, University of Exeter,
and author of *Ten Myths About Israel*

'Since 1948, many Palestinians were born and raised in neighboring Arab states; others have lived and studied in the West; some managed to remain in their ancestral villages in Israel; still others have resided in West Bank cities that, since Oslo, are administered by the Palestinian Authority. Fida Jiryis is one of the very few Palestinians who have had *all* of these experiences and, as such, she is able to narrate her people's diverse modern history from a uniquely personal perspective. Passionate and provocative, Jiryis's is a story of tragic loss, hope and disappointment, homecoming and alienation.'

Jonathan Gribetz, Associate Professor of Near Eastern Studies,
Princeton University, and author of *Reading Herzl in Beirut: The PLO's
Research on Judaism and Israel*

'More than just an intimate memoir chronicling the tragedy of Palestinian history, *Stranger in My Own Land* is a finely detailed rendering of how love of family commingles beautifully and essentially with love of country.'

Moustafa Bayoumi, author, scholar, and *Guardian* columnist

'Fida Jiryis describes the spiritual damage to herself and her loved ones with ferocious honesty and precision. An essential story and a remarkable achievement.'

Philip Weiss, founder and co-editor of Mondoweiss

'Palestinian steadfastness stands out in this compelling book, in which Fida Jiryis artfully interweaves her family's history with that of her colonised homeland and people. Devoid of demonisation and sloganeering, it is a necessary, sobering testimony to Israel's systemic cruelty.'

Amira Hass, journalist, *Haaretz*

STRANGER IN MY OWN LAND

FIDA JIRYIS

Stranger in My Own Land

Palestine, Israel and One Family's Story of Home

HURST & COMPANY, LONDON

First published in the United Kingdom in 2022 by
C. Hurst & Co. (Publishers) Ltd.,
New Wing, Somerset House, Strand, London, WC2R 1LA
Copyright © Fida Jiryis, 2022
All rights reserved.

Printed in Great Britain by Bell and Bain Ltd, Glasgow

The right of Fida Jiryis to be identified as the author of
this publication is asserted by her in accordance with the
Copyright, Designs and Patents Act, 1988.

Distributed in the United States, Canada and Latin America by
Oxford University Press, 198 Madison Avenue, New York, NY 10016,
United States of America.

A Cataloguing-in-Publication data record for this book
is available from the British Library.

ISBN: 9781787387812

This book is printed using paper from registered sustainable
and managed sources.

www.hurstpublishers.com

To my father, Sabri; my mother, Hanneh; and my uncle, Geris

Racism's ultimate logic is genocide. Racism is a myth of the superior and the inferior race. It is the false and tragic notion that one particular group, one particular race is responsible for all of the progress, all of the insights, and the total flow of history, and that another group or another race is totally depraved, innately impure, and innately inferior.

Martin Luther King Jr.
'The other America' speech, Stanford University, 1967

CONTENTS

Partial family tree of individuals mentioned in the book
(Spouses and children have not all been included in other instances)

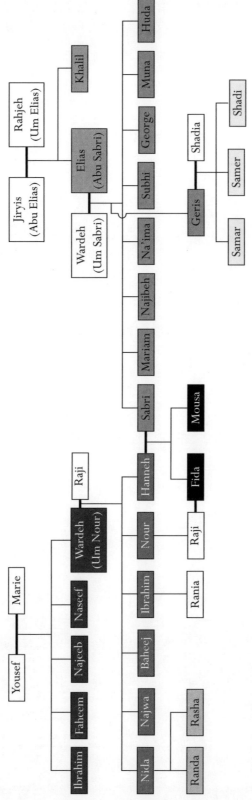

Note: *Siblings shown in the same shade.*

ACKNOWLEDGEMENTS

This book began ten years ago and was my own journey into a deeper discovery of my family and our history. It would not have been written without the hours of interviews and discussion that unearthed so much of our personal and collective story, as a family and a people. My heartfelt thanks go to my father, Sabri Jiryis, and my uncle, Geris Geris, for their input and unrelenting support. I also thank my aunts and uncles—Muna Jiryis, Najibeh Hadid, Nida Shaheen Jiryis, George Jiryis, and Shadia el-Mutasem—for opening up about difficult chapters in their lives. Thanks to Mousa Jiryis, my brother, for listening to me rant about this book as I worked through the thick of it.

The support, guidance, and valuable insight of my dear friend, Sam Bahour, was with me every step of the way. Sam watched this book progress from an idea to successive drafts and its final form, and helped in every way possible. I am eternally grateful.

I sincerely thank Anne Germanacos, of the Germanacos Foundation, who was an angel throughout this process and who funded the writing of this book. Thank you for your support and belief in me and my writing, and for being my dearest friend and mentor.

Thanks are due to Cordaid International for their funding of the initial research, and to a friend and great fighter, Trees Kosterman, for making it happen. I also thank the Rockefeller Brothers Fund and Ariadne Papagapitos for their funding support.

A special thanks to Katia Pistou, my shining light throughout this journey and every other, and to the Maltese writer and poet Immanuel Mifsud, who gently encouraged me towards the final full stop.

Huge, heartfelt thanks and appreciation to my wonderful editor, Alice Clarke, and to the team at Hurst for bringing this book out into the world. To the many friends and relatives who have encouraged me throughout this journey, especially Ahlam Hadid, Njoud

ACKNOWLEDGEMENTS

Daoud, Rowida Assy, Sawsan Khoury, Nimer Assy, Anna Mentsl, Athina Christoforides, Maan Abushawish, Manal Issa, Nidal Rafa, Najwa Mubarki, Sonia Kashou, Faten Khoury, Urieb Samad, Nouran Nassief, Hala Saadani, Jonathan Cook, Lori Lake, Ramzy Baroud, Ephraim Lavie, Sarah Ozacky-Lazar, and Mahmoud Muna, I am indebted to you all for your support and kindness.

To Ian Black, Norbert Goldfield, Ghada Karmi, Louise Steinman, Moriel Rothman-Zecher, Ayelet Waldman, Sam Sussman, Salim Tamari, Alexandra Pringle, Jess Row, Allison Malecha, and Göran Rosenberg, thank you for your help and support. To my dearest Ariana Melamed, thank you, with all my heart, for everything.

Fida Jiryis
July 2022

LIST OF ILLUSTRATIONS

Section 3

GLOSSARY OF COMMON TERMS

Arabic

al-Asifa   military wing of the Palestinian political party and militant group Fatah, jointly led by Yasser Arafat and Khalil al-Wazir (Abu Jihad), and active from 1965 until the 1990s

al-Ittihad   Arabic newspaper of the Israeli Communist Party, which had a predominantly Palestinian Arab membership

ammo   colloquial address for uncle or other older man; used by both uncles and nephews/younger people to address each other

arak   anise-flavored alcoholic drink, similar to ouzo

baklawa   traditional dessert of filo pastry, nuts, and sugar syrup

dabke   popular circle dance of the Middle East, performed by holding hands and moving in identical steps

dunum (dunam/donum)   a unit of land area used in the Ottoman Empire and still in use in the Middle East. 1 dunum = 1,000 square meters or 1196 square yards, about a quarter of an acre

effendi   a title of courtesy used in the Levant, including in Palestine during Ottoman rule and the British Mandate

fedayi/-yeen   Palestinian and Arab guerrillas in Palestine and neighboring countries who fought Israel from its founding until the 1980s

GLOSSARY OF COMMON TERMS

fellah/-in	peasants or agricultural workers
jiddo	similar to sidi/sido
knafeh	traditional dessert made with thin, noodle-like pastry or fine semolina dough, layered with cheese and soaked in sugar syrup
kubbeh	pâté of meat paste, bulgur wheat and spices
kufiyyeh	Arab headdress, either white or checkered white with red or black squares
labaneh	soft white cheese typical of the Levant
mukhtar (moukhtar)	traditional head of a village, town, or clan
sidi/sido, sitti	colloquial address for grandfather, grandmother; used by both grandparents and grandchildren to address each other
teta	similar to sitti
ustaz	Mister; also, teacher
wardeh	rose
za'atar	ground thyme and sesame, eaten as a dip with olive oil

Hebrew

kibbutz/-im	cooperative agricultural communities in Israel, traditionally established with a combination of socialism and Zionism. Many were established on lands seized from Palestinians during and after 1948
Knesset	Israeli parliament
moshav/-im	similar to kibbutz/-im
Shabak (Shin Bet)	Israeli General Security Service

BIOGRAPHICAL NOTE

My story begins in the 1940s, many years before I was born, in Fassouta, a small village in the mountains of the western Galilee, near the Lebanese border. My father, Sabri, was born in 1938, and witnessed the Nakba when he was ten years old. His parents, Elias and Wardeh, had a large family: three other sons—Geris, Subhi, and George—and five daughters—Mariam, Najibeh, Na'ima, Muna, and Huda.

Sabri's paternal grandparents, Jiryis and Rahjeh, also lived in the village and he was close to them, especially as he was their eldest grandchild.

My mother, Hanneh, was also born in Fassouta, in 1946. She lost her father, Raji, when she was nine years old. Her mother, Wardeh (Um Nour), was left with six young children, including Hanneh: the boys—Nour, Ibrahim, and Baheej—and two other daughters—Najwa and Nida.

My parents met in 1962, when my father was studying at the Hebrew University in Jerusalem, and my mother was sixteen and thinking of enrolling there after high school. In 1965, they connected again at the wedding of her aunt, Sarah, and were married in 1968.

My father's work as a lawyer and political activist led to him being voluntarily exiled from Israel in 1970. His younger brother, Geris, had also left during that year, when a resistance operation he was taking part in was foiled. He ended up in Beirut, and my parents caught up with him there. I was born in Beirut in 1973, and my brother, Mousa, in 1977.

This book tells my story, and that of my family and homeland.

NOTE ON NAMES AND PLACES

The material in this book is factual, but the names and identifying characteristics of some individuals have been changed.

Throughout this book, the word 'Israel' denotes the country today, but 'Palestine' denotes the same place as Palestinians refer to it: historic Palestine, part of which was colonized in 1948 and turned into Israel. Palestine also includes today's Palestinian territory: the West Bank, including East Jerusalem, and the Gaza Strip, militarily occupied by Israel in June 1967 and accorded by the United Nations, as the 'State of Palestine', non-member observer State status on 29 November 2012.[1]

INTRODUCTION

'Where is this Palestine you're talking about? There's no such thing as Palestine!'

Those were the words of an Israeli policeman to my father, detained in 1970. And, indeed, overnight, Palestine had been wiped off the map.

The disaster had been more than a century in the making. Political Zionism, an exclusivist movement, had emerged in the second half of the nineteenth century among the Jews of Eastern Europe, where the majority of world Jewry lived. Russian and Romanian Jews faced repression under czarist rule, with violence, massacres, and economic strangulation.

For 2,000 years, the Jews had been scattered as religious communities all over the world. Very few had sought to return to a supposed biblical destination—a situation that persists to this day. Israel was a religious concept, rather than a physical entity. To fulfill its project, however, Zionism, which was a non-religious movement, used Jewish religious sentiment towards a political goal: the founding of a 'Jewish state' in the 'Land of Israel', or historic Palestine.

In 1897, Theodore Herzl, an Austro-Hungarian Jew and the founder of modern Zionism, led the First Zionist Congress in Basel, Switzerland. The congress formulated a Zionist platform, known as the Basel Program, and founded the Zionist Organization (to become the World Zionist Organization in 1960). Its aim was to create a Jewish state, or 'Jewish national home', in Palestine. It capitalized on anti-Jewish sentiment in Europe and, according to Israeli author and journalist Ari Shavit, 'want[ed] this Arab land to be confiscated by Europe so that a European problem will be solved outside the boundaries of Europe',[1] by forming an enclave for European colonization in the heart of the Arab region. As US-based author and journalist Brett Wilkins explained:

1

From its earliest days, Zionism, which is at its core a settler colonial movement of white Europeans usurping Arabs they often viewed as inferior or backwards, propagated the myth of 'a land without a people for a people without a land'. Theodore Herzl, the father of modern political Zionism, argued that a Jewish state in Palestine would 'form a portion of a rampart of Europe against Asia, an outpost of civilization as opposed to barbarism'.[2]

In 1901, the Zionist Organization formed the Jewish National Fund (JNF, or Keren Kayemet le-Yisrael), with the aim of acquiring land in Palestine for Jewish-only use, to be worked by Jewish-only labor. Palestine was then under Ottoman rule and had a tiny Jewish community of less than one per cent of its population of Palestinian Arabs.

To acquire land, the JNF spared no means, whether persuasion, bribery, or deception. Although some Zionist intellectuals advocated the idea of peaceful coexistence between Jews and Arabs in Palestine, JNF bulletins showed 'indignation' at the very presence of Arabs who worked the land, and 'the sense that the company's highest aim was to uproot and wipe out all trace of these people to make room for Zionist settlers'.[3] JNF officials did not refer to 'buying' or 'acquiring' land; they used terms like 'liberating', 'emancipating', and 'redeeming' it to convey the idea that the land was 'captive' in the hands of the indigenous Palestinians.

In its final days, the Ottoman Empire's debts had risen, and with them the interference of foreign debtors in its affairs. The European consuls in it played a vital role in Zionist settlement in Palestine through facilitating the entry of Jewish nationals from their countries and helping them to acquire land and construction permits.

Under Ottoman rule, the rights of the Arab peasants, or fellahin, to the land had been granted by their working it. As the empire struggled with debt, it levied high taxes, despite the poverty that the peasants lived in. When they were unable to pay, the Ottoman authorities seized their lands and sold them in public auction. In this way, many lands were given to rich families in or outside Palestine. The authorities also pushed all landowners to register their properties at the *Tabo*,[4] the Ottoman land registry. Many peasants were afraid that, by making their ownership official, they would be targeted for taxation. They chose a dangerous route: to register their lands in the names of the large effendis, the feudal lords, who could pay the taxes, while the peasants paid them what they could. But they could not keep up. The land thus became unprofitable to the wealthy owners, and the Zionists moved to buy it, for large sums of money. Many of the owners lived outside the country, in Syria or Lebanon, such as the Lebanese Sursuq family, which sold the Zionists large swathes of land in various areas of Palestine.

Early Zionist settlers had come to favor employing Arabs over Jews, for Arabs worked harder and accepted lower pay, but the second wave of settlers had hostile attitudes of 'conquering the land' and instilling 'Hebrew labor'. Thousands of Palestinian peasants were driven off the lands where they worked, losing their homes and meager livelihoods. Clashes began with the Zionists, but the peasants had no property ownership. Yitzhak Epstein, a teacher and writer, speaking at the Seventh Zionist Congress in Basel, in 1905, described their wretched fate:

> When we come to take over the land, the question immediately arises: what will the Arab peasant do? … The Arab, like any man, has a strong bond with his homeland … I can still hear the dirge of the Arab women on the day their families left their village of Ja'una, today Rosh Pina, to settle in Hawran, east of the Jordan. The men rode asses and the women walked behind them, bitterly weeping, and the valley was filled with their keening. From time to time they would stop to kiss the stones and the earth … We must not uproot people from land to which they and their forefathers dedicated their best efforts and toil.[5]

During the First World War (1914–18), Britain promised to help the Arabs gain independence if they backed it in the war against the Turks. But, as the Arabs fought alongside Britain, it signed the contradictory Sykes-Picot Agreement with France and Russia to divide the Arab countries between them at the end of the war. The Zionists found an ally in Britain, which promised to help them with their designs if they, in turn, put pressure on the other Allies to allow Britain to have the mandate over Palestine. On 2 November 1917, in an infamous letter that came to be known as the Balfour Declaration, British Foreign Secretary Sir Arthur James Balfour conveyed to Baron Walter Lionel Rothschild, a leader of the Anglo-Jewish community, a message approved by the British Cabinet:

> His Majesty's Government view with favor the establishment in Palestine of a national home for the Jewish people, and will use their best endeavors to facilitate the achievement of this object, it being clearly understood that nothing shall be done which may prejudice the civil and religious rights of existing non-Jewish communities in Palestine, or the rights and political status enjoyed by Jews in any other country.[6]

On 11 December 1917, the Allied Forces, led by British General Edmund Allenby, entered Jerusalem after the surrender of the Ottomans. Arab relief at the demise of four centuries of Ottoman rule was short-lived: Britain clamped down on Palestine, Iraq, and Transjordan (later Jordan), while France took over Syria and Lebanon. The borders of these countries, hitherto collectively known as 'Greater Syria', were newly defined.

On 25 April 1920, Palestine came under official British mandate. Sir Herbert Samuel, a Zionist and the first practicing Jewish minister in British government, was appointed High Commissioner. At the time, Jews were only about 6 per cent of the population and owned less than 1 per cent of the land. But Britain began to deliver on its promises to the Zionists by allowing large numbers of Jews to immigrate to the country. The waves of Jewish immigration (1881–1904, 1904–14, 1919–23) were brought about by bad living conditions, disasters, and repression in Eastern Europe, which the Zionist movement used to fulfill its goals. It formed Keren ha-Yesod (later, the United Israel Appeal) and the Jewish Agency to work towards Jewish immigration and settlement in Palestine, and began to establish business and civic organizations in the country. In 1920, the Haganah, a Jewish paramilitary organization, was secretly formed.

Palestinians had been under four centuries of backward Ottoman rule and were beleaguered by ignorance and poverty. Most were illiterate. Clashes between them and the Zionists erupted in 1920, 1921, and 1929. Arab leaders met British officials, and many Palestinian delegations were sent to Britain to induce it to stop the Zionist designs, but to no avail. Some restrictions were put in place on Jewish immigration, but it continued, illegally at times.

Most immigrants came from Russia, Poland, and Germany, spurred not only by Zionism, but by the Great Depression and anti-Semitism. The rise of Nazism was probably the strongest factor that led to the realization of the Zionist plans and the founding of Israel.

In Palestine, the Mandate authorities gave the Zionist settlers preferential economic treatment, entrusted the country's natural resources to them, and appointed several of their supporters in key administrative positions, particularly in the judiciary and immigration departments. The Zionists worked in every worldwide community that they could reach to import Jewish immigrants and funds to Palestine, where they formed settlements, institutions, and political movements.

Palestinian resistance was rising. In 1933, protests broke out, with a general strike, and were violently curbed by the police. The British authorities had supplied a number of Jewish settlements with ammunition, weapons, and a network of roads and communication devices, and had set up police stations in the largest of them. British and Jewish business owners replaced their Arab employees with Jews, fueling Palestinian anger. The Jews presented the notion of 'Hebrew work' as a progressive, socialist model, but it discriminated against and excluded Palestinians. As author and journalist David Hirst explained in his 1977 book:

> As a recent immigrant [to Israel], [Israeli politician and Haganah member David Hacohen] was embarrassed on an overseas trip in explaining his inability to allow Arabs to join his [labor] association, the Histadrut, and how he and his friends guarded vineyards to prevent Arabs from reaching or working in them, how they poured gasoline over Arab tomatoes in the market and attacked Jewish housewives to smash the eggs that they had bought from Arabs.[7]

In 1936, Palestinian fury erupted in the Great Arab Revolt. It began with strikes and civil disobedience, then morphed to armed attacks and riots as the British authorities responded with extremely harsh measures. They used Defence (Emergency) Regulations to carry out arrests and expulsions, impose mass fines and curfews, blow up homes, and mete out death sentences in military tribunals. Tens of Palestinians were executed by hanging.

The Haganah worked closely with the British forces to quell the rebellion and win Britain's support. An offshoot of the Haganah, the Irgun Zvai Leumi (National Military Organization, or Irgun in short), carried out terrorist raids against Palestinians, spraying bullets at passersby and at buses, and setting off bombs in markets.

The revolt lasted for three years. The British authorities contained it, expelled the Palestinian leadership, and shredded their political parties. With the beginning of the Second World War, however, Britain changed its policy in order to appease the Arabs and win their support in its war on Germany. After all attempts to reach a Jewish–Arab agreement had failed, including a proposal to divide Palestine, which neither side accepted, the British initiated an independent policy to preserve their interests. In May 1939, British Secretary of State for the Colonies Malcolm MacDonald issued a White Paper to clarify his country's policy: conditional independence of a Palestinian state in ten years, governed by Arabs and Jews; restricting Jewish immigration to Palestine to 15,000 people annually, for five years; and protecting Palestinian property rights from Zionist acquisition.

The Zionists then turned against Britain, their former ally, and called for liberation from its control in order to establish their 'Jewish state'. Zionist militias in Palestine, such as the Irgun and Lehi (also known as the 'Stern Gang' and which split from the Irgun in 1940), began attacking the British. They took and killed hostages, carried out assassinations, dynamited buildings, raided banks, and attacked military targets. In 1945, the British Mandate authorities expanded the Defence (Emergency) Regulations in response. The regulations gave the authorities excessive, unchecked power. The High Commissioner had the right to bring anyone before a military court, detain or expel people from their homes or the country, seize property, and impose fines. His orders could 'amend any law, suspend the operation of any law, and apply any law with or without modification'.[8] People could be imprisoned for years without trial. The British authorities imprisoned many Jews and sent tens of them into exile in the African colonies.

The Zionist enterprise, however, had become a 'state within a state', an almost independent entity in Palestine. The militias raised their attacks on Palestinians, planning to throw them out of the country. Joseph Weitz, a Jewish National Fund official, had captured this in a chilling statement in 1940:

> Among ourselves it must be clear that there is no place in the country for both peoples together ... No other way but to transfer the Arabs from here to the neighboring countries; transfer all of them, not one village or tribe should remain.[9]

By 1948, with successive waves of immigration, the number of Jews had risen to around 650,000,[10] about 30 per cent of the population of Palestine. Despite the intense efforts of Zionist organizations for almost three-quarters of a century, however, they had acquired only 5.5 per cent[11] of the land in the country, albeit it was mostly fertile land. Most Palestinians refused to sell or leave their property. However, the Second World War and the Holocaust provided the impetus for the Zionist movement to manipulate the postwar powers. On 29 November 1947, the newly formed United Nations General Assembly voted, through a Partition Plan, to divide Mandatory Palestine into two states, one Jewish and one Arab, with special, international administration of Jerusalem.

There was an outcry among Palestinians, and fighting broke out in the country, with tens of Arabs and Jews killed. The Zionist militias were well organized, while Palestinian resistance was weak and fragmented, exhausted by British repression and Zionist violence. In March 1948, the American administration proposed to the United Nations Security Council to place Palestine under United Nations trusteeship[12] to reach a truce and guarantee the peace at the end of the British Mandate—although the intent was seemingly to coerce the Palestinians into acceptance of the Partition Plan. But the war raged on. The same month, Haganah commanders drew up Plan Dalet (D) to seize more areas than those allocated to the proposed Jewish State in the UN Partition Plan. They aimed to take hold of as much territory as possible before the end of the British Mandate, when the Zionist leaders intended to declare their state. Plan Dalet used terms like 'tihur' (purifying) and codenames such as 'Matateh' (Broom) and 'Biur Hametz' (Passover Cleaning). It aimed to expel the Palestinians:[13]

> Mounting operations against enemy population centers ... Destruction of villages (setting fire to, blowing up, and planting

mines in the debris), especially those population centers which are difficult to control continuously … In the event of resistance, the armed force must be destroyed and the population must be expelled outside the borders of the state.

In every region, a [Jewish] person will be appointed to be responsible for arranging the political and administrative affairs of all [Arab] villages and population centers which are occupied within that region.[14]

Communist Czechoslovakia supplied the Jewish militias with arms, which contributed to their victory. They carried out a trail of massacres, terror, and ethnic cleansing, emptying towns such as Jaffa, Lydda, Ramle, Haifa, Acre, Tiberias, Safad, and Bisan of most or all of their Palestinian inhabitants and depopulating hundreds of villages.[15]

On those ruins, Israel was founded. On 14 May 1948, the British Mandate expired. The Jewish People's Council gathered at the Tel Aviv Museum and, led by David Ben-Gurion, unilaterally declared the establishment of the State of Israel in the country. As Palestinian researcher Salman Abu Sitta noted in his foreword to a 2010 book by author and journalist Ramzy Baroud:

He [Ben-Gurion] in fact announced the victory of 65,000 well-trained Haganah soldiers, led by World War II officers, over defenseless Palestinian villagers who had tilled their fields and lived on their land for thousands of years.[16]

Armed forces from five Arab states moved in to intervene, but they only comprised irregular regiments of Palestinian and Arab volunteers. With insufficient numbers and old, failing ammunition, they were quickly defeated. In a matter of weeks, about 750,000 Palestinians were expelled,[17] more than half the Arab population of the country. Most fled with nothing except the clothes on their backs and the few belongings that they could carry. About 276,000 took refuge in the West Bank, 180,000 in the Gaza Strip, and about half were forced out of the country: an estimated 100,000 crossed into Lebanon, 100,000 to Jordan, 90,000 to Syria, 10,000 to Egypt, and 4,000 to Iraq.[18] Fawaz Turki, a Washington-based author and journalist who was a child on that journey, described the trauma that never left him in adulthood:

Like the apocalyptic images that my mind would dredge up, out of nowhere, of our refugee exodus twenty years before, as we trekked north on the coastal road to Lebanon, where pregnant women gave birth on the wayside, screaming to heaven with labor pain, and where children walked alone, with no hands to hold.[19]

The expelled Palestinians believed that they were going away for a short while until the Jewish attacks died down and they could return. But they never did. In a matter of weeks, they lost everything: their houses, belongings, lands, fields, money, and livelihoods, and became lost refugees. Of the Palestinians who remained in Israel, a quarter, 40,000, became internally displaced persons and were forbidden to return to their homes. By the end of the war, the Zionist militias had captured 78 per cent of Palestine: the portion allocated by the Partition Plan to the Jewish state and half of the portion allocated to the Arab one. This was the Nakba (Catastrophe), the most traumatic event in recent Palestinian history. In the wake of the Second World War and its horrors, the Jews received international sympathy and support for their efforts to create their 'national home', such that their onslaught on Palestine went unchallenged. Any Jew in the world could immigrate to the State of Israel and claim instant citizenship in it, while very few of the exiled Palestinians were allowed to return.

1

A HOMELAND IS LOST

The man looks dead to me ... It's like being dead to lose a home overnight, a black night like this one, and be condemned to wander Allah knows where.

Anton Shammas
Arabesques[1]

I

'We're leaving.'

'Leaving?' my grandfather, Elias, echoed.

'The Jews have gotten closer. We've decided to leave, until things calm down and we can return,' his friend, the old shepherd, replied.

In two days, they were gone. They took everything: their clothes, blankets, pots and pans. They even took their chickens.

Elias' son, Sabri, a boy of ten at the time, knew this because he went to their village. Riding his father's donkey, he made his way to the Deir, as it was locally known. Deir el-Qasi was five times larger than Sabri's village, Fassouta, and had been teeming with life. He had often seen its peasants carrying produce home from their fields.

But, on that day, as he approached it, nothing moved. There was no human or animal in sight. He urged the donkey forward through the alleys. Its steps echoed in the eerie silence, broken only by the rustle of the wind through the trees. 'The entire village, with its houses, gardens and paths, was empty,' he recounted, years later, 'wind blowing through it and windows creaking ... I've never seen a more depressing sight. The image continues to haunt me, when I think of the war.'

Desolately, he turned the donkey around. As they made their way back, he spotted a lone chicken pecking at the ground and suddenly felt sorry for it.

Back in Fassouta, he left the donkey and rushed to his grandfather's house. There was quite a commotion. Tens of people were gathered outside. They were not from the village. Some had blankets and others carried bundles, too heavy for their backs or heads. Babies were crying and children stared with frightened eyes.

Cautiously, Sabri pushed in between them, making his way into the house. Some of them had gone inside. He searched the faces fervently until he found his grandfather. Jiryis stood near the kitchen, issuing orders to his wife as more people crowded in.

'Sidi,'* Sabri panted, squeezing through the crowd and edging up to him. 'What's going on?'

'Quiet, boy!' Jiryis turned back to his wife, Rahjeh, who was laying a loaf of bread on the table. She opened a large clay pot, filled to the rim with balls of a soft white cheese, labaneh. Deftly, she spooned one out and spread it onto the loaf, rolled it, and handed it to the nearest man. 'Eat!' Jiryis urged him. 'Please, this is your house!'

The man looked pained as he took the food and mumbled his thanks. Sabri looked up at his grandfather. 'Sidi, who are these people?'

'Quiet!' Jiryis said, more impatiently this time. 'Go out and play. Come back later!'

But Sabri snuck into a corner and waited. Suddenly, a little boy of about his age stared back at him. He was holding his mother's hand. Sabri wanted to talk to him, take him outside to play, but, somehow, it did not seem right. He looked back at his grandmother, who seemed to be feeding the entire crowd, and felt a slight panic. What if she ran out of labaneh and could not make him her tasty sandwiches anymore?

Finally, an old man in a white headdress stepped up to Jiryis. 'Thank you, brother,' he said, gruffly. 'May God repay you with every good. We should be on our way.'

Jiryis nodded. Beads of perspiration gathered on his brow. He wiped them with the edge of his headdress. Voices of thanks were heard, hollow, cheerless voices, and the crowd began to shuffle, gathering their things. Led by their elder, they began a long trail out of the village. The little boy held his mother's hand and stole one last look back at Sabri. 'Sidi! Where are they going?' Sabri blurted out.

'North ...' his grandfather mumbled. His wife had come out of the house to join them and stood next to him. As they watched the receding figures, she lifted her apron to wipe a tear from her cheek. Jiryis, seemingly on the verge of doing the same, cleared his throat

---

* *Sidi/sido, sitti* (Arabic): colloquial address for grandfather, grandmother; used by both grandparents and grandchildren to address each other.

roughly and instructed her to go inside. They moved into the house as a chilly breeze picked up in the late autumn sunset.

'Come, sidi,' he muttered to Sabri, sitting down, wearily. He took out his tobacco and rolled a cigarette.

Sabri sat next to him and waited. He looked from one grand-parent to the other. 'I was in the Deir today …' he said, finally. 'There's no one there.'

Jiryis nodded and took a deep puff. Rahjeh retreated to the kitchen.

'Where have they gone, sidi?' Sabri persisted.

'To Lebanon.'

'Them, too?' The boy struggled to understand. 'Those people just now, are they from the Deir, too?'

'No, they're from Tarshiha.'

'Why are they leaving?'

'The Jews!' Jiryis said, in sudden anger. 'They will destroy the country!'

Sabri was a child, yet his habit was to sit in his elders' gatherings. The adults knew that a United Nations resolution had divided Palestine, that there were battles and people were expelled. They had heard of the fate of Haifa, Jaffa, Safad, and Tiberias. In the spring, news had reached them of the massacre at Deir Yassin, west of Jerusalem. On 8 April 1948, Abd al-Qadir al-Husseini, leader of the Palestinian resistance, was killed at al-Qastal, near the city. The next day, commandos of the Zionist militias, the Irgun and Lehi, attacked Deir Yassin. They went from house to house, throwing grenades inside before storming the homes and spraying survivors with bullets. More than 100 people were killed, including women, children, and the elderly. There were reports of rape and muti-lations. Twenty-five male villagers were loaded onto trucks, paraded through the Zichron Yosef quarter in Jerusalem, then taken to a stone quarry and shot dead. The villagers who survived were forced out of their homes and driven to East Jerusalem.[2]

The massacre was a major factor in the expulsion of the Palestinians from their land. Jewish militias approaching Arab villages gave instructions to leave immediately or face a similar fate. They often broadcast, over loudspeakers, recordings of shrieking women from Deir Yassin.[3] Haifa saw even more killings and a large exodus. In May, the State of Israel was unilaterally declared, and some of the Zionist militias, mainly the Haganah and its strike force, the Palmach, became the new Israeli army. News of massacres came from Abu Shusha and Kabri, and nearly 200 Palestinians were killed in Tantura, near Haifa.

In July, after Zionist forces conquered Lydda (today, Lod), near Tel Aviv, they massacred 250 people inside a mosque. Tens of thousands were forced out of the city in what became known as the Lydda Death March. Those who strayed off the path were shot. One survivor of the attack on Lydda, Fouzi el-Asmar, later recounted his experience in a 1978 book:

> The Jews put us in trucks and took us to some city, Tel Aviv apparently. There were crowds of men there—happy people, dancing in the streets. They danced around us a number of times without forcing us to get off the truck. Each time, we heard shouts and screams and sometimes we were even spat upon. We felt ourselves humiliated, but we had no possibility of retaliation.[4]

The massacres continued throughout the summer, forcing thousands to flee their homes. Many died of thirst or exhaustion on terrifying trails without food or water. Others drowned as waves of people tried to escape by boat from seaside towns such as Haifa and Jaffa. On their flight, they were under fire from Zionist militias. Families were separated, losing parents, children, and siblings, and some were never reunited. The survivors found themselves in makeshift refugee camps hastily set up in the West Bank, Gaza, and neighboring Arab countries. In 2010, author and journalist Ramzy Baroud recounted the experience of his father, who was a child at the time:

> When Mohammed Baroud, a ten-year-old boy from the now-distant village of Beit Daras, removed a dirtied blanket that served as a door to his family's tent, the world outside was entirely different from what he once called home. There was little promise here, no lush farms in the distance, and no green meadows to serve as playgrounds. Instead, an awesome and terrifying sight greeted him; tents scattered as far as the eye could see, thousands of new anxious faces ... He was overwhelmed with fear and indecision, and quickly snuck back to lie down by his parents' side ... The violent uprooting that took place in a matter of days and weeks, turning the boy's world upside down, was yet to sink in.

He stared at his sleeping family, covered in dust, with bleeding feet and swollen ankles. It may have all been a most convoluted nightmare, the kind that is stirred by the devil.[5]

Fassouta, in the western Galilee, saw the end of the war; it was October before the area was captured. As the Israeli army advanced, many people left in fear from the surrounding villages, especially those that had helped the resisting Arab Salvation Army. In Fassouta, people had taken no part in the fighting. They stayed put, but a thick fear hung in the air.

Sabri's grandmother brought in cups of tea on a tray, as he sat with his grandfather in silence. He smelled the fresh sage picked from the nearby mountains. 'Shall I bring you some labaneh with your tea, sweetheart?'

He nodded. 'We still have some?'

'Don't worry, I'll always have labaneh for you!' She smiled and padded back to the kitchen, returning with bread, a plate of the cheese, and olives. His grandfather sat and smoked, lost in his thoughts.

'Sidi, don't you want to eat?'

'No, you go ahead.' Jiryis got up to light a fire, seemingly looking for something to do.

'You should be getting home, little one. Your parents will be worried,' Rahjeh murmured a short while later, wiping her hands tiredly on her apron.

'Let him be ...' Jiryis said, stoking the wood. 'They'll know he's here.'

It was true. The first place to look for the boy, should anyone be missing him, was his grandfather's house. Sabri was the firstborn of Jiryis' eldest son, Elias, and held a special place in his grandfather's heart.

An urgent knock broke their thoughts. The neighbor burst in. 'I heard there were people in your house!'

'Yes. They left.'

'Have you heard the news? There was a battle with the Jews in Tarshiha!'

Jiryis winced. The elder of the crowd had told him that a battle was unfolding between the Israeli army, encroaching from the south, and the Arab Salvation Army. This all-volunteer mission had

17

been formed at the beginning of the year by the Arab League and was led by a Syrian, Fawzi al-Qawuqji, to stop the advance of the Zionist militias until the Arab states could organize their armies and send them in. About 5,000 fighters volunteered for the Salvation Army, but it was a tragically deficient, if heroic, endeavor. It lacked training and weapons, did not know the terrain, and fought without any support, losing one battle after another and suffering heavy casualties. Palestinian peasants could only help with simple weapons that were no match for the militant Zionist advance. 'Tarshiha has fallen!' the neighbor gasped. 'Suhmata, as well!'

Jiryis stood up in agitation. 'I was out, grazing the goats, and I saw this crowd walking north. I knew some of them; they were from Tarshiha.'

'Why did you bring them here?'

'To give them food. They have at least a day to walk. God knows where they'll go when they get to Lebanon!'

Sabri's eyes opened wide. He was used to running to his grand-father's house from school, at the church house just up the road, and grabbing something to eat several times a day. He tried to imagine how anyone could last on a sandwich for a day, and be walking, at that.

'What will happen to us?' The neighbor's face was white with fear.

'I don't know.' Jiryis turned to his grandson. 'Go home now. Tell your father to come to me in the morning!'

Sabri nodded and ran off. At home, the same question rang in his ears. 'What will happen to us?' his mother, Wardeh, asked as she cradled his brother, Geris. The baby had arrived after three daughters and was named after his grandfather.*

'I'll go see what's going on in the morning,' Elias frowned. 'And you!' he turned sharply to his son. 'You make sure you're home before sunset from now on, you hear me?'

Over the last weeks, some fedayeen† from the Salvation Army had made stealthy stops to ask for food and water, and the villagers

---

* Spelling 'Geris' as used by the character in question, the author's uncle.
† *Fedayi / -yeen* (Arabic): Palestinian and Arab guerrillas in Palestine and neighboring countries who fought Israel from its founding until the 1980s.

were terrified. Intermittent gunfire had been heard, scaring people and livestock. As Sabri stood before his father, another round went off in the distance, startling them both. 'Go to bed!' Elias ordered. 'And stay home tomorrow! I don't need to be out looking for you!'

Wardeh lowered the kerosene lamp to a flicker, and Sabri snuggled under the sheepskin covers on the thin mattress, laid out on the cement floor. His three sisters were asleep next to him. The baby was asleep, too. But the boy continued to turn the events of the day over in his mind.

Unknown to him, he was seeing the Nakba.

II

Elias threw his covers aside after a restless night. It was not yet daybreak, and, feeling the chill, he added a couple of logs to the dying embers of the fire and sat on his straw stool opposite.

Fassouta was a small village of about 650 people, nestled in the mountains of the upper Galilee, just south of the border with Lebanon. It lived on agriculture, like most Palestinian villages at the time. Its peasants grew wheat, lentils, and olives. The area also provided quality tobacco, and, during the British Mandate, they grew this plant for sale. Most kept their own chickens, and some raised goats, cattle, or sheep. A few who were better off owned a camel or bull for ploughing. The village was poor, but self-sustaining. Much of the food came from plants in the area and from vegetables that were grown: okra, zucchini, eggplant, peppers, and tomatoes. Some were dried in the summer for winter use. Meat was eaten on Sundays, when the butchers slaughtered a few goats. The biggest indulgence was the occasional bottle of arak* or a box of Turkish delight from Lebanon. Sabri would go with his father or grandfather to nearby villages in South Lebanon, such as E'ita el-Sha'ab or Rmeish, for trade. The borders were seamless; there were friendships and marriages between those villages and Fassouta, and people from each side ploughed land they owned on the other.

In the village, fabrics for tailoring or clothes were bought from a few peddlers, or on special trips to Acre, the nearest seaside town.

---

* *Arak* (Arabic): anise-flavored alcoholic drink, similar to ouzo.

Electricity and running water would only arrive two decades later. People used kerosene lamps and fetched water on their heads or on donkeyback from nearby springs. By early evening, the village would quieten down into a tired slumber.

Elias and Khalil, his brother, were the two butchers and made a good living. Elias owned a small herd of livestock given to him by his father, which he was diligently growing. Though he had had no schooling, he had a sharp acumen and keen business sense, and he kept excellent relations with the shepherds of nearby villages, his trading partners. Elias was a no-nonsense man who kept his money rolled carefully in an old jar and focused on raising his family. As his earnings grew, he bought a few plots of land around the village to secure their future. When he heard people discussing the goings-on in the country, he remained mostly silent. The declaration of the State of Israel five months previously had not directly affected his life, other than the sudden removal of his friends from the Deir, whom he sorely missed. But then Suhmata followed suit, and half of Tarshiha, and frightening news poured in of the downfall of tens of others: Bassa, Birweh, Damon, Manshiyya, al-Nahr, Ruways ... Rumors flew about the expulsion of people, and the names kept coming: Sumayriyya, Kuwaykat, al-Tall, Amqa, al-Zeeb, Khirbet Jiddin, Mi'ar, Umm al-Faraj.[6] It was like the beginning of an apocalypse. Elias looked at his sleeping family in panic.

He thought of his friends from Deir el-Qasi and wondered where they were. They had traded livestock with him and shared a deep knowledge of the surrounding mountains and grazing areas. When their animals got sick or gave birth, they had helped each other out. For years, Elias had mediated between their families when fights broke out over animals or other grievances. As a Christian, he was seen to be a neutral party by the Muslim clans, and his opinion carried significant weight.

Nothing had prepared him for their sudden exodus like this. Had they rushed in their decision? But they had been afraid. 'The Jews, they might spare you,' they had said. 'But we're Muslims and won't stand a chance.' Elias did not know how true this assessment was. There had been nothing but bad news for months.

In fact, the Israeli onslaught had targeted all Palestinians—Christians and Muslims. In their ghost towns, masses of Jewish settlers and soldiers took part in a campaign of looting Arab homes and shops. Fouzi el-Asmar, in his 1978 book, described what he and other children had seen when they had sneaked back into their hometown, Lydda:

> I was shocked ... by the sight of this large city completely deserted, the houses open, the shops broken into and the remaining merchandise rotting. We were afraid of the trucks which were working every day without a break. The men who had come with the trucks would go into house after house and take out any article of value such as beds, mattresses, cupboards, kitchenware, glassware, couches, draperies ...[7]

The campaign continued throughout the summer. Israeli army and senior government sources would later speak of the terrible 'pogrom' that had occurred against the property of the expelled Palestinians.[8] In a 2020 book, Israeli historian Adam Raz revealed many Jewish testimonies from the time. One was from Yair Goren, a resident of Jerusalem:

> The hunt for booty was intense ... Men, women and children scurried hither and thither like drugged mice. Many quarreled over one item or another in one of the heaps, or over a number of items, and it reached the point of bloodshed ...[9]

Netiva Ben-Yehuda, a Palmach fighter, gave her grim interpretation:

> Such pictures were known to us. It was the way things had always been done to us, in the Holocaust, throughout the world war, and all the pogroms. Oy, how well we knew those pictures. And here—here, we were doing these awful things to others.[10]

Elias dressed with the first rays of dawn and hurried out to see his father. The neighbors were already gathered and Jiryis was handing out coffee when a young man rushed in. 'Abu Elias,'* he panted, 'the mukhtar† has asked for you and the elders to come to his house at once!'

---

* In the Arab world, it is customary to call people 'father of' (*Abu*) and 'mother of' (*Um*) followed by the name of their eldest son, in deference.
† *Mukhtar*, or *moukhtar* (Arabic): traditional head of a village, town, or clan.

STRANGER IN MY OWN LAND

Jiryis nodded. He was generally unimpressed with hollow figures of authority. The previous mukhtar, in the Mandate days, had failed to help him when Jiryis was defending his fellow villagers from raids on their livestock. The area was so remote and so few figures of governance made it up there that occasional theft was inevitable. In that incident, some villagers from the Deir had attacked shepherds from Fassouta and tried to steal their livestock. Jiryis, known for his strength and fearlessness, had intervened and pelted the intruders with rocks, hurting several of them badly before helping the shepherds round up their herds and go home. The next day, a delegation from the Deir had come to the mukhtar of Fassouta, complaining bitterly. The head of the village had caved in and drawn up an agreement with them, stipulating the grazing rights of each party on specific lands, then called the unsuspecting Jiryis to his house and given him a harsh reprimand in front of the delegation, pushing the agreement at him to sign. Flushing in anger, Jiryis had grabbed it and torn it up before the astonished crowd, saying: 'This is not worth the paper it's written on!' before storming out. He knew these pacts never lasted.

But the Deir was now gone. Cutting his musings short, he turned to his son. 'Elias, come with me.'

Sabri, who had awoken and followed his father, made to scamper after them, but he felt a hand clamping down on him. 'Home, I said!' Elias glared, hurrying down the road with the men. But, as they crowded into the mukhtar's house, the boy squeezed in, trying to hide behind some elders.

The mukhtar broke the news. The Israeli army had occupied the last part of the western Galilee. The Arab Salvation Army had collapsed and people were left to defend themselves or surrender. 'The soldiers are coming on Saturday,' he finished, grimly. 'They asked that we submit peacefully.'

A thick silence filled the air. The men of the tiny village could hardly hope to fight an invading force that had taken over the country. They were also enclaved: by the army coming from the east and south; by the sea to the west; and by the Lebanese border to the north, where there were only the straggling militias of the Salvation Army, most of whom had been killed in their retreat. The men in the room eyed each other in fear. Their only hope was that they would be spared and be able to stay in their homes, like those in other villages that had survived.

Three days later, at 2:00 pm, the elders, led by the mukhtar and the priest, walked to the entrance of the village, carrying a white flag and the flag of the church. They stood near Elias' house and waited. Three Israeli jeeps rolled into Fassouta, carrying three soldiers each, with submachine guns and ammunition belts. They stopped at the sight of the procession and disembarked, greeting the villagers casually, as though on a visit. The elders escorted them to the priest's quarters, adjacent to the church. All the children were shooed away and Sabri had to leave.

Instructions were curt. Each man who had arms or ammunition was to place them, that night, in the courtyard of the mukhtar's house. 'With that,' the commander said, 'no one shall be harmed.'

Sabri heard this from the men afterwards. The next morning, he awoke early and ran to the mukhtar's house next door. Three guns lay on the ground. The soldiers returned and picked them up, marking the official handing over of the village. The surrender was as calm as it was surreal.

Other villages were not so lucky. The army moved on through 'Operation Hiram' and committed more massacres in Deir el-Assad, Majd el-Kuroum, and Bi'neh. The people of nearby Mansura, Sa'sa, Nabi Rubin, Arab al-Samniyya, Khirbet Iribbin, Suruh, Meiron, Ras al-Ahmar and Tarbikha were expelled, and the army trucked many of them to the Lebanese border. The killings continued in Dawayima, Saliha, Safsaf, and Jish before the remaining villagers fled in panic.[11] In Eilaboun, soldiers rounded up twelve young men and shot them, three by three, then expelled its people to Lebanon. Weeks later, they were allowed to return, after the archbishop of Acre intervened, but it was to an empty shell of a village, their belongings and livestock gone.

As the refugee crisis grew, Israel switched to expelling Palestinians internally rather than forcing them across the borders. Before arriving in the area of Fassouta, the army had occupied the northern border with Lebanon and closed it to prevent people from leaving, unlike in other places, where it had committed massacres and left one side open that led out of the country.

Only later would it become evident that the number of expelled refugees from the western Galilee could have been higher, had not circumstances played a part. By and large, things had moved according to Israel's plan: to 'get rid of' the Palestinians, who would be 'absorbed' into the neighboring Arab countries such that Israel was free to be the new and exclusive state for the Jewish people. But, in the summer of 1948, before the Israeli army occupied the western Galilee, the refugee crisis was at its peak. Swedish Count Folke Bernadotte, the United Nations Mediator in Palestine, put forth another scheme to redo the partition of the country and possibly hold off the establishment of the Arab and Jewish states that had been proposed. In September, the Zionist group, Lehi, assassinated Count Bernadotte in Jerusalem. He had been appointed four months earlier to bring peace to the region. Count Bernadotte had negotiated the release of about 31,000 prisoners from German concentration camps during the Second World War, including thousands of Jews.[12] After his assassination, Israel destroyed more Palestinian villages in the Galilee and expelled their people, then stopped, wary of mounting international pressure. Hence, most of the 100,000 Palestinians in the western Galilee stayed in their homes. The remainder of the Galilee had been heavily depopulated.

In the center of the country, a few thousand Palestinians remained in Jerusalem, Ramle and Jaffa. In 1949, the Israeli armistice agreement with Jordan included an exchange of land, provided that its inhabitants were allowed to stay on it. Jordan handed over an area known as 'the Triangle'[13] to Israel, and 35,000 Palestinians remained in their homes.

A third group of 15,000 Bedouin stayed in the Naqab (Negev) desert in the south. Thus, by 1949, three Palestinian concentrations remained in Israel, totaling about 160,000 people, or 13 per cent of the changed population.[14] They were mostly peasants and farmers, as the majority of professionals and intellectuals had been forced out during the exodus from the cities.

A man named Tu'meh, from the nearby village of Iqrit,[15] arrived in Fassouta to take shelter with a relative. The army had occupied Iqrit on the same day as Fassouta, with no resistance from the villagers. But, six days later, the village's inhabitants were ordered to leave. 'The soldiers want to clear the area, make sure the border is quiet,' Tu'meh told Elias. 'They gave us locks and keys for our homes. They put everyone on buses to Rameh, but they told us to take only a few things. We're going back soon.'

'Going back?' Elias asked.

'Yes. They did the same with Biram. Its people went to the olive groves.'

Panic spread that Fassouta's turn would come. Some villages had surrendered, but had still been depopulated by the army as part of an Israeli policy of 'an Arabless border strip'.[16] Two weeks later, Tu'meh heard the news from Biram. 'It began to rain. The villagers sent some people down to the village to ask the soldiers if they could go back. But the soldiers have looted their homes! They chased them off and said the land doesn't belong to them anymore!'

In November 1948, the new Israeli authorities conducted a first census of the country, and the Palestinians who had remained in it were given Israeli identification cards. A month later, the United Nations General Assembly passed Resolution 194 (III), stating that

> The refugees wishing to return to their homes and live at peace with their neighbors should be permitted to do so at the earliest practicable date, and that compensation should be paid for the property of those choosing not to return and for loss of or damage to property.[17]

Israel persisted in barring any such return. The creation of the state was applauded as a victory and reparation for the suffering of the Jews; Jewish immigrants from the world over poured in and celebrated its 'independence', and Palestinian dispossession seemed invisible. In a matter of months, hundreds of thousands were strewn all over the country and in surrounding countries in a humanitarian catastrophe. The New York-based Peoples Press wrote of their ordeals:

> The winter of 1949, the first winter of exile for more than 750,000 Palestinians, was cold and hard ... Families huddled in caves, abandoned huts, or makeshift tents which tore, were patched, and tore again as the cold rains pounded the ancient material ... American eyewitnesses in Jordan told of swarms of children with matchstick arms and legs and protruding bellies produced by progressive starvation and of babies dying because there was no milk ... Many of the starving were only miles away from their own vegetable gardens and orchards in occupied Palestine—the new state of Israel. Months

before, in July of 1948, David Ben-Gurion had stated the Zionist policy toward the refugees: 'We shall do everything possible to ensure that they never return.'[18]

In January 1949, a few weeks after news of the fate of Biram had reached the villagers, a fearful cry sounded in Fassouta. Israeli soldiers had come and gathered all the men that they saw in the streets. 'They're grabbing everyone they find! Stay home!' a neighbor urged Elias. About a hundred men were held in a nearby field under the aim of an automatic rifle mounted on an army van. The soldiers seemed unsure of what to do and were waiting for instructions. A female soldier spoke on her walkie-talkie as another lined them up. Sabri snuck up curiously and stood with them. Suddenly, though, he remembered the accounts he had heard of people being killed in this way, and he ran off. Behind him, he heard the soldiers saying: 'You have two days to leave the country. Anyone staying here or going south will be shot!'

Sabri thought of Deir el-Qasi and Tarshiha. He dashed home to find his mother gathering his siblings. 'Leave the baby!' a neighbor told her, in fright. 'How far do you think you can carry him? Leave him and take the older ones!'

Sabri looked at her in horror. Wardeh cried out and held on to her child as Elias shouted: 'Go where? I'll stay and die here!'

In a panic, Sabri grabbed his school satchel and put some bulgur wheat, bread, and a few books in it. But fate intervened. The head of one of the large village clans, who had his own connections, managed to speak to the Israeli military commander in Tarshiha, and the order was rescinded. Half the villagers had reached Rmeish, the nearest village in South Lebanon, before others hurried after them to call them back.

In February, the soldiers returned, rounding up a few men and telling people they had to go. Again, frantic communications flew around and the expulsion order was cancelled. The villagers were lucky. A few days earlier, the people of Kafr Anan, near Acre, had been expelled together with hundreds of refugees from Kafr Yasif, who had fled there from nearby villages during the fighting. Most were loaded onto trucks and forced to cross into Jordan.

Weeks later, a third attempt was made on Fassouta. Then, the soldiers stopped and never came back. The villagers took this as final indication that they would stay in their homes and breathed a sigh of relief.

But their troubles were just beginning.

2

THE ALIEN STATE

These people have walked off with our home and homeland, with our movable and immovable property, with our land, our farms, our shops, our public buildings, our paved roads, our cars, our theaters, our clubs, our parks, our furniture, our tricycles. They hounded us out of our ancestral patrimony and shoved us in refugee camps. They so thoroughly destroyed our villages that nothing was left of them but the wind that now blew through them. And they even robbed us of our name.

Fawaz Turki
'Reflections on Al-Nakba'[1]

I

Overnight, the remaining Palestinians in Israel found themselves under military rule, or martial law. This system had originated under the British Mandate, which had used Defence (Emergency) Regulations to quell the Great Arab Revolt of 1936–9 against Britain and the Zionists. The regulations were part of the harsh British response that had sentenced people to death, expelled thousands, confiscated their property and blown up their homes. At the time, Jewish voices had cried out in protest. Göran Rosenberg, a Swedish journalist and author, described the extent of this outcry:

> Leading Jewish attorneys condemned the regulations as 'legalized terror'. Ya'akov Shimshon Shapira, later to become Israel's attorney general, protested that 'the system established by the defense laws in Palestine is unprecedented in the civilized world. Not even Nazi Germany had anything like it ... There is really only one kind of regime reminiscent of what we have now—that of an occupying power ... It is our duty to tell the world that the defense laws implemented by the British government in Palestine undermine the foundations of justice in this land.'[2]

Yet, when the State of Israel was established in 1948, it quickly adopted the 1945 British Defence (Emergency) Regulations against the Palestinians who remained in it. Many of the former Jewish voices of protest went silent and helped to implement the laws, which sanctioned arrests, expulsion, isolation of villages, and destruction of property without a court order. Palestinian villages were grouped into areas and any movement between them required a permit from the military commander. Any Palestinian found to be travelling without a permit was called to appear before a military court and subject to imprisonment. The commander could withhold these permits without reason, and his powers were endless. He could impose curfews, oblige people to justify their movements, interfere in their employment, forbid them from changing jobs or moving house, and impose restrictions on social activities. The permits could even forbid their bearer from entering Jewish communities on the way to their destination.[3]

The commander could also place people under house arrest or expel them to any part of the country. Worse, he could imprison anyone under 'administrative detention', a practice that did not entitle the victim to a trial, and that could be renewed indefinitely. Detainees were tried in military courts where the judges were army officers, and the courts made decisions dictated to them by the military government. The detainee was sent out of the room while the court heard the charges against them; they could not even know what they were being accused of, nor reply in their own defense, for reasons of 'security'. Even their lawyer was denied access to these secret files.[4]

The military government ruled over Palestinians only, not over Israeli Jews. It quickly became an absolute power in the areas that it controlled. The only way to challenge it was to appeal to the Supreme Court, but the Court made it a rule not to interfere with the military government when its actions were based on 'security', not even to question its reasons. People could be imprisoned for years without knowing their charges. The words of Jewish figures who had formerly opposed these laws now applied, to the letter, to their enactment against the Palestinians:

> Are we all to become victims of officially licensed terrorism or will the freedom of the individual prevail? ... As it is, there is no guarantee to prevent a citizen from being imprisoned for life without trial. There is no protection for the freedom of the individual: there is no appeal against the decision of the military commander, no means of resorting to the Supreme Court ... while the administration has unrestricted freedom to banish any citizen at any moment. What is more, a man does not actually have to commit an offense; it is enough for a decision to be made in some office for his fate to be sealed.[5]

One of the first and most damaging consequences of the regulations was the loss of Palestinian property. In towns from which Palestinians were expelled, the state gave their homes to Jewish immigrants. In rural areas, it gave Palestinian land to new Jewish farming communities and arrested Palestinians who picked fruit from their own lands. Desperate to cultivate their trees, even when they had been taken from them, many peasants sought work from the new Jewish 'owners' of the land. But the state cracked down on this employment and forbade it.

The government moved to seize the lands of the refugees that it had displaced, whether internally or outside the country. It declared many villages and the lands around them 'closed areas', which meant that people needed permits from the military commander to access them. When these permits were denied, the villagers could not, despite their repeated attempts, return to their homes or get to their lands to till them. In October 1948, the state passed a law to declare any land left untilled for more than a year 'abandoned' and to seize it.[6] The government also proclaimed large swathes to be 'forest' or public lands, including the lands of many Palestinian villages, preventing peasants from grazing their livestock or collecting firewood. Eventually, it changed the status of these to state lands and began building Jewish settlements on them.

Another law prohibited Palestinian farmers living near the borders from getting to their lands, under the pretext of their being closed military or 'security' zones. In these zones, the defense minister, under the Defence (Emergency) Regulations, had the power to expel people permanently from their homes. Thus, their lands were eventually seized. More than one million dunums[*] of land belonging to Palestinians who remained in Israel were seized after 1948.

In 1949, armistice agreements were signed between Israel and its neighboring Arab countries: Lebanon, Egypt, Jordan, and Syria. The Gaza Strip came under Egyptian administration. By the end of that year, the new Israeli state had captured most of Palestine.

In March 1950, the government passed the 'Absentee Property Law' to formally seize the land of refugees. All property belonging to the refugees who had fled or were expelled was turned over to a 'Custodian of Absentee Property', a state official under the military regime. This included more than four million dunums of land,

---

[*] Dunum (dunam/donum): a unit of land area used in the Ottoman Empire and still in use in the Middle East. 1 dunum = 1,000 square meters or 1196 square yards, about a quarter of an acre.

73,000 rooms, and 8,000 stores and offices.[7] It was enough for the Custodian to declare that a person or group were absentees for them to be considered so, and he could rely solely on the witness of a state agent or co-opted mukhtar to determine this, without being questioned on his sources. Habib Qahwaji, a teacher and poet from Fassouta, later summed this up:

> The job of the Custodian of Absentee Property is the theft and loot-ing of Arab property in Israel, and the job of the highest legislative power in the country is to organize that theft and looting.[8]

These decisions were rarely revoked later, even if it was proven that the property owners were not absent at the time the decision was made.[9] Thus, this law also applied to internally displaced persons, about a quarter of the Palestinians who were still in the country but were prevented from returning to their lands.[10] They were termed 'present absentees', meaning the state considered them 'present in Israel but absent from their lands'. At an infamous court hearing, a frustrated Palestinian dashed up to the judge and took his hand, put it on his arm and exclaimed: 'Feel this! I'm here, aren't I? I'm a person standing here, in front of you, living and breathing! How am I an *absentee*? Why are you taking my land?'

But, for these individuals, their properties had to be 'released' from the Custodian after they had proved their ownership. This was a long and arduous process whereby the state meticulously examined each scrap of paper, resorted to delays, extorted the owners with high taxes, and tried to persuade them to sell the properties—before eventually, in most cases, seizing them anyway. From the Palestinians remaining in Israel, the Custodian stated that he had taken over 223,000 dunums of orchards, including '85,000 dunums of citrus plantations and ... 80,000 dunums of olive groves, 15,000 dunums of vineyards, 14,000 dunums planted with fig trees and smaller areas of almond and apricot orchards and banana plantations.'[11] Urban property included 25,416 buildings consisting of 57,497 residential apartments and 10,729 stores and light industry workshops.[12] Moshe Carmel, an Israeli commander, described the looting in Haifa:

> There were so many houses in ruins, and smashed furniture lying amid the heaps of rubble. The doors of the houses on both sides of

the street were broken into. Many objects from the houses lay scattered on the sidewalks ... On the threshold of the house was a cradle leaning on its side, and a naked doll, somewhat crushed, was lying next to it, its face pointing down. Where is the baby? Which exile did he go into? Which exile?[13]

Even international commitments were ignored. Half of the seized Palestinian land was from the Triangle, the richest and most fertile area in the country, although the armistice agreement with Jordan stipulated Israel's duty to protect the rights of the inhabitants in the areas it had annexed.

Eventually, the ownership of the seized properties was transferred from the Custodian to the development arm of the Israel Land Authority—changing hats under the same state apparatus—which then allocated them to various state sectors. The result was always the same: Palestinian villages were destroyed, their land was planted with trees or used for Jewish settlement, while urban homes and businesses were given to Jewish immigrants.

The severing of ties between Palestinians and their land was one of the most painful collective blows that they endured. Their connection to it ran very deep; the land and its trees were revered and guarded with life and limb, seen as a source of security and sustenance and tended to carefully to pass onto future generations. Some of the most heartrending accounts of the Nakba speak of the orchards left behind, the pain of destitute peasants pushed out of their fields and forbidden to return, sometimes while their lands were still within view. Some sneaked back to their groves, in the weeks following expulsion, to care for the trees. Desperate refugees, trekking the country without food, risked death to make their way to fields left behind to pick fruit on which to survive. Their bodies were sometimes found, riddled with bullets from Jewish snipers.

At the end of 1949, the United Nations finally acted. It set up the United Nations Relief and Works Agency (UNRWA) to administer more than sixty refugee camps. UNRWA's mission was to provide 'relief of the Palestine refugees ... to prevent conditions of starvation and distress among them'.[14] It barely managed to keep people alive. Hasan Amoun, a doctor who was a child at the time and was exiled to Lebanon, wrote of these conditions:

Ein el-Helweh, the camp, lies on a low plain at sea level, southeast of Sidon. That year saw a very hard winter, with snow falling even on the plains. UNRWA distributed cloth tents to people, who erected them on the mud; there was no base or cement to put them on. When the snow fell on the tents, water began to seep through. Each morning, we heard people beating thousands of tents with sticks to bring the snow down. It was a horrifying noise; the earth had turned into a spring of water, water from below and water from above ... My sister and I were young children. UNRWA distributed rations per person, sugar and flour, and families used to take us and pretend we were theirs, so that their measly allowance would be increased.[15]

The camps in neighboring Arab countries became permanent and housed generations of refugees, over decades. In Israel's subsequent wars on the Palestinians and in regional wars, many of those refugees were further displaced, time and again.

In December 1949, in violation of United Nations resolutions and its own commitments, Israel declared Jerusalem its capital and moved its parliament (Knesset) and government offices to West Jerusalem, which it had captured during the war.

The expulsions did not stop. After the founding of the state, the Haganah and other Zionist militias had merged into its new army, the Israel Defense Forces (IDF). Throughout 1949–50, the IDF went on to destroy another 268 Palestinian villages and expel their people. In many villages, it expelled several dozen men, usually the breadwinners and heads or eldest sons of large clans, in the hope that their families would follow.[16]

Palestinians were divided, with closed borders between them and no way to reunite. People lost parents, children, siblings, and friends. For many, it took years to track each other down, and many never did. In the next few years, some refugees 'infiltrated' the borders of Israel and returned to their homes, but they were often caught and killed, or expelled again. Others came back under an Israeli 'family reunification' program, but they were very few. Some of the remaining Palestinians in Israel stayed in their towns, others in about seventy villages that had survived, like Fassouta.

In April 1950, per agreement with Israel, Jordan annexed the West Bank. The armistice line, known as the Green Line,[17] was established between Israeli and Jordanian-Iraqi forces. The armistice lines with neighboring Arab states became the de facto borders of Israel. The new geography was fixed, and the deed was done.

II

'Father! Come, quick!'

A thick cloud of smoke, visible across the few miles, was seen over Iqrit. *'What the——?'* Elias gasped.

After their evacuation, the people of Iqrit were stuck in Rameh, between Acre and Safad. Some went to live with relatives in Lebanon until things calmed down. They held on to the Israeli army's promise that they would be allowed back to their homes, but a few weeks turned into months, and all their appeals to the authorities were ignored. A year and a half later, they filed a suit against the Israeli defense minister and the military commander. In July 1951, the Supreme Court ruled that the villagers must be allowed to return 'as long as no emergency decree existed against the village'. Predictably, the military government was quick to issue such a decree. The villagers turned to the appeals committee, but it ratified the expulsion order. Once again, they appealed to the Supreme Court, and a hearing was to be held in February 1952. Meanwhile, the village elders went back to the soldiers and asked if they could return. To their surprise, the commanding officer told them that they could go back to their village on 24 December 1951, after the soldiers had pulled out.[18] Father Elias Chacour, a Palestinian archbishop and author from neighboring Biram, described the ensuing events:

> On Christmas! What an incredible Christmas gift for the village. The elders fairly ran across the hill ... to spread the news. At long last they would all be going home. The Christmas Eve vigil became a celebration of thanksgiving and joyful praise. On Christmas morning ... bundled in sweaters and old coats supplied by the Bishop's relief workers, the villagers gathered in the first light of day ... Father, Mother, Wardi, and my brothers all joined in singing a jubilant Christmas hymn as they mounted the hill ...[19]

But, on that day, Israeli troops took the mukhtar of Iqrit, Mbada Daoud, to the top of a nearby hill and forced him to watch as they blew up the Christian village house by house. Father Chacour went on to describe the village's end:

At the top of the hill their hymn trailed into silence ... Why were the soldiers still there? In the distance, a soldier shouted, and they realized they had been seen. A cannon blast sheared the silence. Then another—a third ... Tank shells shrieked into the village, exploding in fiery destruction. Houses blew apart like paper. Stones and dust flew amid the red flames and billowing black smoke. One shell slammed into the side of the church, caving in a thick stone wall and blowing off half the roof. The bell tower teetered, the bronze bell keeling, and somehow held amid the dust clouds and cannon fire ... Then all was silent—except for the weeping of women and the terrified screams of babies and children.

Mother and Father stood shaking, huddled together with Wardi and my brothers. In a numbness of horror, they watched as bulldozers plowed through the ruins, knocking down much of what had not already blown apart or tumbled. At last, Father said—to my brothers or to God, they were never sure—'Forgive them.' Then he led them back ...[20]

From a hill in Fassouta, Sabri and his father stood watching the thick clouds of smoke in the sky. 'Merry Christmas ...' Elias muttered. He turned on his heels and walked home.

Alone, Sabri found his way to where Tu'meh was staying and knocked on the door. The man opened it and smiled at him.

'Iqrit ...' the boy began, his voice trembling.

'What about it?' Tu'meh asked, in alarm.

'It ...' The bile rose in Sabri's throat. 'They destroyed it!' he blurted.

Tu'meh broke into frantic tears. 'What?'

'Father and I just saw it. Over there ...' Sabri gestured helplessly to the horizon. Tu'meh was bent over in pain. The boy ran off, his grandfather's words suddenly replaying in his mind.

'They will destroy the country.'

III

'Don't hit your brother! Let him play with you!' Wardeh scolded.

Sabri, a teenager, wanted to roam the village with his friends and did not want his five-year-old brother on his heels. He had tried to shoo him away, yelled at him to go home, but to no avail. Finally, he had smacked Geris and stomped off. The little boy had run home, wailing.

'Your brothers and sisters are your support! Stick together and never hurt each other. Don't let strangers come between you!' his mother persisted.

Her children would grow up hearing this, and nine siblings would be as one, never fighting as they walked their paths through life. Wardeh's father had died when she was an infant. Her mother had remarried and given her daughter to her aunt to raise. After young Wardeh had married, she had no one to turn to if she ran into trouble. And this she often ran into with Elias, who had a very different character and whose temper often shook the house. But there was no brother or father of hers to intervene, no family to stand up on her behalf. Wardeh's children, and her sons, in particular, held a special place in her heart. As they got older, they were the peacemakers and supported her when the problems with their father got out of hand.

Sabri was annoyed at his brother for stealing his moment. 'I came first!' he said, brandishing the red star on his shirt.

Elias beamed. The rivalry between Sabri and Hatim, the mukhtar's son, was intense. Each year, the two friends competed fiercely at school to be top of class, a position that swung between them as their fellow pupils looked on. Elias always waited for the result. When he saw the red star, the proud father would tell everyone that 'the shepherd's son beat the son of the mukhtar!'

Wardeh smiled as she turned up the flame of the stove outside the house. The family was boiling their freshly harvested wheat to prepare bulgur. This coarse grain was a staple food in various dishes: kubbeh, a pâté of meat paste, bulgur, and spices; tabbouleh, a Middle Eastern salad; and mjaddara, a lentil dish, among others. Some wheat was further boiled and ground to make flour for the family's bread throughout the year. Sabri fidgeted impatiently. It would take all day to get to the end of the boiling, which was the bit he was waiting for. They would then take the wheat out of the cauldron and he would climb up on the roof to spread it in the sun to dry, but not before his mother began to bake oursa, a special pie with onions and peppers, on the double-ringed stove. At the very end, she would make flatbreads and lather them with butter and sugar, passing them out to eager little hands. This was a major treat and about as far as desserts went, for there were no confectionary shops near the village, and it would take a special trip to Acre or Haifa to bring back knafeh* or baklawa.†

Mariam and Najibeh, his younger sisters, bustled around. The house was like a beehive. With a few hundred animals, and crops of wheat, tobacco, and olives, everyone had to work: grazing the animals, milking them, cleaning the pens, and picking the harvest. At home, Mariam and Najibeh lent a hand with baking, cooking, making cheese, and the endless cleaning up. Even Na'ima, at seven, was given a few tasks. But life was good in the quiet, beautiful landscape of mountains and sunshine. The children brimmed with health, fed an organic diet and moving around all day. When they had a break, they played in the fields, running at will and climbing trees, and the most they had to worry about was the priest, who was their schoolmaster, and a teacher or two. On hot summer days, Sabri and his sisters would take shelter under the large fig trees, clambering up to pick their ripe, sugary fruit.

But Sabri had just finished elementary school. 'I want to go to Nazareth,' he said, turning to his father.

Few children in the village could study beyond Grade 8 in the humble schoolhouse at the church hall. The nearest high schools were in Kafr Yasif and Nazareth, transport was scarce, and most parents could not afford tuition and expenses. But Elias could. Hatim was set to go to the Terra Sancta College, a Catholic school in Nazareth, and Sabri wanted to join him. The school was the only one with a boarding arrangement, and it appealed to him. He hated preparing food and had no idea how to do it.

---

* *Knafeh* (Arabic): traditional dessert made with thin, noodle-like pastry or fine semolina dough, layered with cheese and soaked in sugar syrup.
† *Baklawa* (Arabic): traditional dessert of filo pastry, nuts, and sugar syrup.

Elias smiled. He felt immense pride in his firstborn and was tickled by the prospect of his son becoming a learned man, like the priest and the few teachers in the village. In September 1953, the two boys and three of their classmates were sent off to Nazareth.

IV

Fifteen minutes into the journey, near the village of Mi'ilya, the bus stopped. A policeman climbed on board and asked for their permits. The boys looked at him, crestfallen. No one had thought of that. They were told to disembark.

It was Sabri's first awakening. He wondered why, at fifteen years old, they needed permits to get to school. But military rule forced all Palestinians to have them. Their villages were under curfew at night, and, in the day, people could not work, study, even see a doctor a few miles away without a permit. The Israeli police would stop traffic on the roads and check. Those without permits would be arrested and taken to prison, then to a military court. Dozens, sometimes hundreds, would be convicted each month of having broken the restrictions. Israeli Jews were free to move at will, without any permits.

Hatim told the officer he was the son of the mukhtar. Even with his father's contacts, it took more than an hour to issue the permits.

After a long journey, the boys found themselves at the entrance of the imposing grounds and tall, stone buildings that would become their home for four years. One of many Christian missions in Palestine, the Terra Santa College prepared students for the British General Certificate of Education. The boys' school was run by Franciscan monks; the adjacent girls' school, by nuns, with a regimented routine of studies and prayer. To their dismay, the boys had to be in church every morning. By the time he graduated, Sabri had decided that he had attended enough masses to last a lifetime, and he stopped going to church altogether.

Outside the walls of the quiet school with its luscious gardens, the Palestine that had existed was in ruins. By the mid-1950s, the Palestine Question in the United Nations General Assembly had slowly morphed into a problem of refugees, then into 'the situation in the Middle East'. Palestine had all but disappeared from the Arab world and the world at large. The refugees were gone, forbidden from returning. Over 400 Palestinian villages had been depopulated; many were razed to the ground and Jewish communities built on their remains. The authorities carried out raids on Arab villages to catch what they called 'infiltrators': refugees in surrounding countries who crossed the borders, desperate to return.[21] An early Israeli law allowed security officials to shoot them.[22]

Internally displaced refugees could not go back, either. Many lived in ramshackle dwellings in towns and villages to which they had been expelled. From owning their homes and orchards, entire families had gone to sharing single rooms, which they could barely afford after losing their livelihood. They crowded into damp basements or unprotected shacks, where parents, children, and grandchildren slept, cooked, and subsisted. At school, Sabri met Anis Shaqqour, a new classmate from Biram. 'It's been five years since we were expelled,' Anis told him. 'We're stuck in Jish. And we finally won a suit in the Supreme Court to go back to our village.'

'And?'

Biram's fate was like Iqrit's. On 16 September 1953, the people of Biram watched from a nearby hill as the Israeli infantry and air force leveled their village to the ground. In an act of 'religious sensitivity', the churches and cemeteries of the two villages were left standing. The government then seized their land: 15,650 dunums from Iqrit and 11,700 from Biram.[23] New Jewish communities— Even Menachem, Shlomi, and Shtula—were built on them. The church of Iqrit was turned into an animal pen, while the site of Biram became Baram National Park, and a kibbutz* with the same name was set up near its land.

The village of Kafr Anan, near Acre, suffered the same fate. When some if its expelled people, who had managed to remain in the country, filed a request to the Supreme Court to be allowed to return to their village, all of its houses were destroyed by the Israeli army.

---

* *Kibbutz/-im* (Hebrew): cooperative agricultural communities in Israel, traditionally established with a combination of socialism and Zionism. Many were established on lands seized from Palestinians during and after 1948.

'Our village was blown up, too.' Hussein Hlehel, in Sabri's class, was from Qadita. The village had been destroyed in 1948 after it was emptied of its people. 'We ended up in Akbara, a small village near Safad. We're living in the place of the people of Akbara, who were thrown out of the country.'

Sabri battled with questions. There was a Palestine, there were Palestinians, and suddenly it was filled with Zionism and these settlers. Who were these people, this enemy? Where had they come from?

Zionism had used the rising threat of Nazism in Europe to justify the aim of creating a Jewish homeland in Palestine. When Nazism then declined, Zionism again made use of it: in 1952, a Reparations Agreement was made for West Germany to pay Israel for the costs of resettling Jewish refugees and to compensate individual Jews for losses in livelihood and property as a result of Nazi persecution. Israel never made reparations to Palestinians for livelihoods and property lost during the Nakba.

The Nakba was far from over. In the mid-1950s, Palestinian shock began to wear off as they understood their plight and began to fight back. There were strikes and protests in Palestinian towns. The Israeli authorities responded with killings, expulsions and home demolitions. In the refugee camps of the Arab countries, Palestinians turned to armed struggle as the world ignored their suffering. Small numbers of fedayeen, fighters from the West Bank and Gaza Strip, carried out attacks inside Israel. A special commando unit of the Israeli army, Unit 101, was created to counter Palestinian resistance. It made frequent raids into neighboring Arab countries, committing massacres, shelling crowded refugee camps and dynamiting public buildings. Thousands of Palestinians were killed.[24]

Barely a few weeks into the term, in October 1953, Sabri heard about Qibya, a village in the West Bank. Unit 101 committed a massacre that left sixty-nine people dead, two-thirds of them women and children. 'They made them stay in their homes and blew them up!' Hussein said. 'The news said there were bullet holes in the doors.'[25]

'In August, before we came to school, there was another massacre in al-Bureij,' Anis replied. 'A refugee camp in Gaza. They went through the camp and came out the other side, and they killed more than forty people.'[26]

Unit 101 also targeted Palestinians in Israel to drive them away. The Israeli *Haaretz* newspaper described how this was done to the Bedouins in the south of the country:

> The army's desert patrols would turn up in the midst of a Bedouin encampment day after day, dispersing it with a sudden burst of machine-gun fire until the sons of the desert were broken and, gathering what little was left of their belongings, led their camels in long silent strings into the heart of the Sinai desert ... And Moshe Dayan [who was commander of the southern region] came from Tel Aviv to congratulate them ... on their victory.[27]

Once a month, the school principal had to issue the boys permits so they could go home. On their bus rides, they saw some of the empty villages that had not been destroyed, standing there eerily, silent shells of what was once a life. But their turn would come. The Israeli government launched its project to 'clean up the natural landscape of Israel' by removing the remains of depopulated Palestinian villages.[28] It declared many of them 'closed areas' and used some for Israeli army training to prevent their people from returning. An official of the Jewish Agency, a body that worked to bring Jewish immigrants and settle them in Israel, oversaw this process:

> 'I plowed Palestine into earth by ordering the demolition of 300 abandoned Palestinian villages from the Negev to the Galilee,' said Ra'anan Weitz, the director of the Jewish Agency's Settlement Department in 1948, adding that he 'leveled them joyfully'.[29]

One day, as the bus rattled past Suhmata, a village near Fassouta, the passengers were startled by the sight of bulldozers. Sabri craned his neck to see. A bulldozer tore into one of the houses, knocking down a wall and raising clouds of dust. Then, a forklift maneuvered one of the large stones, characteristic of the sturdy Palestinian homes, onto the back of a truck. A man sitting in front of Sabri remarked to the other: 'They're taking them to use in paving the road ...'

The bulldozer rammed into the next house. No trace of Suhmata would remain when they were done, save for two or three bits of wall that would survive to bear testimony. Three Jewish communities: Tzuriel, Hosen and part of Ma'alot, were founded on Suhmata's land.

The destruction of Deir el-Qasi began, but some of its houses were spared. Sabri saw some movement in the village, people milling about, and asked his father when he got home.

'The Jews they brought to live there are from Yemen,' Elias replied. 'They like the Arab homes.'

'But what about the Deir? Its people?'

'It's called Elqosh now,' said Elias, flatly.

'What?'

'They changed its name to be after the town they came from. Al-Qosh, they said it was called.'

V

Curiously, the newcomers befriended the people of Fassouta. Yemeni Jews spoke Arabic and were closer in culture to the Palestinians than they were to the European Jews. The new people of Elqosh began to form friendships and do some small trade with the villagers.

The landscape was changing faster than anyone could keep up. In 1949, the Israeli government adopted a 'Judaization of the Galilee' project to increase the Jewish population of the Galilee, which had still managed to keep a Palestinian majority, despite the Nakba. In the early 1950s, the Jewish Agency, Israeli army and Interior Ministry began to coordinate their efforts to raise the number of Jews living in the Galilee, through various subsidies and incentive schemes, and by illegally seizing large areas of Palestinian land and allocating them for Jewish settlement. Thousands of legal disputes flared as Palestinians desperately tried to save their land from the hands of officials, who used military rule and the maze of state laws to confiscate it.

The state handed the land to kibbutzim and moshavim,* new Jewish collectives that were set up, and ordered all Palestinians to stay out of them, including those where they were being employed. Many Jewish settlers, far from being attached to the 'land of their forefathers', and, despite the financial incentives by the state to

---

* *Moshav*/*-im* (Hebrew): similar to *kibbutz*/*-im*.

lure them to farm work, had left the land to be worked by Palestinians, who had the real attachment to it. This was profitable for the settlers, who received a share of the harvest while they moved to find jobs in the cities.[30] The government soon cracked down on this practice.

Palestinians who remained in Israel lost more than half of their land,[31] a heavy blow for a people who lived off agriculture. The state gave them no financial assistance and levied higher taxes on them. Their earnings were less than half of those of Jewish farmers.[32] Farming became unviable for Palestinians, and many peasants became manual laborers. They were driven across the country to work in quarries and on construction sites, building towns and settlements in their homeland for Jewish-only occupants. Elias' house was on the main road leading into the village, and he saw the men gathering each morning. 'At the crack of dawn, they stand out here like sheep, waiting for the big cars to take them,' he told Sabri.

'Where?'

'To work. In building and I don't know what!'

The laborers returned in the evenings, exhausted and covered in dirt, with low pay that barely made ends meet. Some kept doing day jobs, when they could, in Jewish collectives, but they were eventually fired for not being organized in the labor unions, which were closed to them. In the first ten years of Israel's founding, the Histadrut, its trade union federation, refused Palestinian membership. This was under the pretext of 'Hebrew labor', one of the slogans of the state. Only in 1959 did the Histadrut open its doors to Palestinians, and then they had to join a separate Arab department. At the same time, the Histadrut fought any independent initiatives to form clubs or societies among Palestinians and created its own to counteract them. Once the independent initiatives were reduced and dwindled, the Histadrut ones ceased to exist and were renewed only for propaganda.[33]

Palestinians held the most menial, exhausting, and poorly paid jobs in the state. They worked in cleaning, picking produce, or any service jobs that they could scrounge in Jewish towns—waiters, dishwashers, cleaners, welders, and mechanics. In times of unemployment, the military government withheld movement permits to prevent them from reaching their workplaces and to ensure work for Jews.[34] Most office work was closed to Palestinians. They were barred from public posts or government jobs, except for teaching. In private business, the authorities placed obstacles for them to license shops and imposed heavy taxes, lifting them in return for cooperation and certain services, usually to the ruling party.

Even when they had the same jobs as Israeli Jews, Palestinians received lower pay and benefits and were suppressed as they progressed professionally. Though their families were larger, they also received much less in social benefits.

Elias was suffocating. The grazing areas around the village were reduced to a bare minimum, through seizure or by declaring them closed military zones, and he had a hard time with his sheep and goats. The authorities hounded the shepherds and cracked down with fines each time they overstepped the permitted areas, all of which had sprung up randomly and left him seething. 'Wide open hills, and they're on my heels at every tree stump!' he sputtered.

'Father, what happened with the police?' Sabri asked. Hatim had told him about an incident that had taken place in the village. He had heard this from his father, the mukhtar.

The military police had waged a sudden raid on the outskirts of Fassouta, arresting several peasants and shepherds who were ploughing the land or grazing their animals in 'closed areas'. They were tied to each other with ropes, then to the police car. The car began to move, and the entangled men had to stumble to keep up with it. Then it stopped, suddenly, and most of them fell forward. This was repeated several times until they were all bleeding. They were then loaded into the car, which began to move. Many of the villagers watched the scene, and their shouts brought others rushing over. The car drove a short distance before a crowd of men surrounded it. It finally stopped and the men were released, before it sped off.

Sabri, at seventeen, stared at his father in shock. Elias had been among those taken. The incident left Sabri with deep mental scars. At this point, he made up his mind to study law. He was certain that everything that was happening around him was wrong, and he was groping for a way to do something about it.

Elias found his tin box, in which he kept his money, and handed fifty pounds to his son for school fees and expenses.[35] Despite the hassle from the authorities, Elias managed to do well. He had acquired an excellent trading reputation; he could buy thirty or forty heads of livestock only on his word, and pay for them after he had sold them. He knew everyone in the surrounding area and well into South Lebanon, where the borders were still open and he could trade. Before 1948, he had also brought back arak to sell, but this had dwindled after the war, when it was forbidden.

Elias' relations with others affected his children, for he dealt with everyone as equals and did not discriminate based on religion or otherwise. 'They say *Allahu Akbar*, God is great,' he said of his Muslim friends. 'Is there anything greater than God?'

After lunch, Sabri stepped out to see his grandparents. Rahjeh took five pounds out of her apron pocket and handed them to him. 'Don't tell your father!' she said, as she did every month. 'He'll take them out of what he's giving you. These are extra, to spend as you please!'

Little did she know that, with her ritual, she was putting her grandson on the first steps of his path. He used this money to treat himself to falafel from the shop outside the school, but also to get his day school friends to buy him newspapers on their way in.

VI

Raji, who lived a few streets away from Elias' house in the village, rushed home from the fields for his cousin's wedding. He called to his wife to see if she and the children were ready. 'Go ahead!' she replied. 'I still have to dress these two!'

Impatient, he took one of his sons by the hand and made his way to the party, now in full swing. In local custom, someone was firing rounds of bullets in celebration. One of them ricocheted off a wall, hitting Raji and killing him instantly.

His wife, Wardeh, as was also her name, was left with overwhelming grief, six young children, and a black, gaping hole of fear.

Two years earlier, in 1953, Israel had enacted the National Insurance Law. Widows, like Wardeh, were entitled to a life pension as long as they did not re-marry, and allowances for their children until they turned eighteen. But Raji had not registered nor paid into the plan. Her claim for allowances was turned down.

'We will help!' Faheem said to his sister, as he sipped black coffee with one of the children on his lap. Her eyes filled with tears as she nodded.

'Dear, you have to be strong!' her brother urged, putting the infant down. 'Your brothers are standing by you. Don't worry! We'll make sure you'll not want for anything!'

But worry was all she could do. Her eldest child, Nour, was eleven; her daughter, Hanneh, was nine; and Ibrahim was seven. Baheej and Najwa were infants, and the baby, Nida, was just two months old. Raji's mother had suffered a stroke at her son's death and become partially paralyzed, and she lived with them, together with her unmarried daughter, Noura.

Nine mouths to feed.

Raji had been 36 years old. In an instant, Wardeh had turned from the wife of a well-to-do farmer to a widow, in a country in turmoil. In 1955, the harsh conditions of life in Fassouta had been amplified by the Nakba. The government was handing out basic food rations, but they were barely enough. The villagers continued to grow their food on the little land they had.

Wardeh had no time for grief. When the days of mourning were over, she rushed to the fields. In the plot she had tilled with her husband, she did a full man's work, ploughing, planting, and harvesting. When the older children were off school, she took them with her to help. They planted tobacco and wheat, selling them to middlemen that came to the village, and they kept a few chickens, goats, two cows, and a donkey. They had little means to buy anything. Occasionally, they would slaughter a chicken or a goat, but they lived mostly on beans, lentils, vegetables, and milk from the animals, which Wardeh also made into cheese. At night, after putting the children to sleep, she stayed up to knit woolen caps by the light of a kerosene lamp, selling them for a few pence to a Jewish trader who came to the village. The villagers respectfully began to defer to her as 'Um Nour', in reference to her eldest son.

Her brothers were true to their word. Naseef, the youngest, was still a student. But her older brothers were working. Faheem taught at the village school. He dropped in to see her early each morning and accompanied her to the fields to help as much as he could before going to work. After school, he returned to check on her and run any errands she needed. Ibrahim, her other brother, was teaching at Mghar, some 25 miles away. In the holidays, he would visit and bring food supplies and clothes for the children. Her sister-in-law, Noura, cooked and looked after the little ones while Wardeh was in the fields. Slowly, the panic lifted, though it would take years of toil to raise her family.

VII

At his young age, Sabri was already feeling watched. Although the Israeli government was occasionally lax in applying some aspects of its military rule, Palestinians were still controlled in their movement, monitored, and killed. Nazareth saw the strongest protests, and the state cracked down. Its first tool was its system of permits. Speaking up in any way was grounds to be denied a permit and to face arrest and intimidation. Israel had recruited a large network of informers in Palestinian towns and villages, including the mukhtars, who had to cooperate to keep their positions. Soon, these collaborators held many of the key positions in Palestinian communities. The government leased absentee land cheaply to them, and they could, in turn, rent it to the peasants for a high price or take a share of the harvest. The state also made the mukhtars responsible for sourcing laborers for construction projects and the like, and made them the 'go-to' people for solving any village problems. They were allowed to carry pistols, as a clear indication that they were the government's men. The villagers who were discontent with all of this were intimidated and stayed silent, for fear of bringing down the military government's wrath on them and their families.

The authorities used the 'carrot and stick' approach, encouraging people to work with them and relay information in return for special privileges. 'They're all giving reports!' Elias said in disgust. Sabri was dismayed when he went home to visit. 'They give them easier permits, drop their taxes ...' his father continued. 'And they promise them jobs, for them and their relatives. Of course they'll give reports!'

The 'reports' could be insignificant: a visit between people, an everyday conversation, even a meal at someone's home. But the military government collected these tidbits to make people feel constantly watched. It worked with the support of the police and the security service to spread the myth that it knew everything. 'They called me in the other day,' Elias said, 'and they asked where I got the money to get these new goats. It was the day after I had bought them! It was him ...' he gestured towards the neighbor's house. 'I know he watches, night and day!'

The authorities' meddling did not end there. They worked hard to deepen divisions between families and sects by encouraging them to nominate separate candidates for local council elections. When conflict broke out, the police turned a blind eye until it escalated. The authorities fought and incited against anyone who worked for the good of a town or village or expressed nationalist sentiments.

Sabri had just finished Grade 11. He was an avid reader and had begun to understand terms like imperialism and colonialism, and to link them to Zionism, the alien force that had taken over his country. Many of his peers were the same. The situation around them forced them to grow up early, to understand concepts that most of their parents did not know.

Since 1949, the armed truce between Israel and the Arab countries, enforced in part by the United Nations, had been punctured with raids and reprisals. Israel continued to strike against civilians, and Palestinian guerrilla attacks from the West Bank and Gaza Strip grew. At the same time, Arab states across the region were awakening to their national aspirations and seeking independence from colonialism. The star was Gamal Abdel Nasser, one of the two leaders of the 1952 Egyptian Revolution and Egypt's second president.

Nasser had been an officer in the Egyptian army in 1948 and was stationed in Fallujah, north of Gaza, to defend what remained of Palestine. His troops were insufficiently armed and had no clear directives. To his horror, it turned out that many Egyptian army units had been supplied with faulty weapons. He held on with a few soldiers in the Fallujah pocket for weeks, in ardent resistance. After the defeat, he returned to Cairo. Four years later, with other army officers, he overthrew the Egyptian king and his government, citing Palestine as a key reason. To Nasser, the loss of Palestine signified the deterioration of Egypt under King Farouk and his regime. The king had been condemned for his corrupt governance and the continued British occupation of Egypt, including the joint British-

French ownership of the Suez Canal, one of Egypt's most important assets.

Nasser ushered in a period of revolution and called for pan-Arab unity. Sabri and his peers saw in him a beacon of hope and rallied around his leftist political ideology, which spread like fire throughout the Arab world. The Algerian independence war from France was in full throttle. African and South American countries were striving for their freedom. Liberation movements were taking root everywhere, and Palestinians yearned for their own. The Israeli authorities felt the danger of the nationalist tide launched by Nasser and its awakening of those feelings amongst them, and cracked down on his followers.

The West turned hostile to Nasser and blockaded Egypt in money and arms. The World Bank retracted its pledge to contribute to the construction of the High Dam in Aswan.

'*The president will deliver an important speech tomorrow.*' On summer break in Fassouta, Sabri heard the repeated radio announcement. The next day, 26 July 1956, there was a flurry as everyone gathered at the homes of those with radios. In Palestinian towns and villages, when Nasser was set to speak, the streets were empty. Everyone was listening, despite the fear. The Israeli authorities could not arrest them all.

The speech was long. Nasser spoke in a measured, but angry, tone to thousands in Manshia Square in Alexandria. Finally, to his shocked listeners, he announced Egypt's nationalization of the Suez Canal. The Arab world went wild. No one had expected such a daring move. Britain and France, seeing it as a threat to their trade and military routes, were quick to retaliate. On 29 October, with Israel, they launched a tripartite attack on Egypt.

In Israel, the border police were stationed along the eastern frontier as part of an Israeli plan to expel the Palestinians of the Triangle if war broke out with Jordan as well.[36] The army ordered a curfew on all Palestinian villages near the border from 5:00 pm to 6:00 am. Anyone seen on the streets was to be shot. The mukhtar of Kafr Qasim, one of the villages, told the Israeli forces that nearly 400 peasants were working outside the village in the fields and were unaware of the curfew. It made no difference. As they made their way home, on bicycles or in mule carts or lorries, the Israeli border police began stopping and shooting them. Within an hour, forty-eight people—nineteen men, six women and twenty-three children—were killed.

In the south, Israel invaded the Gaza Strip, killing hundreds of Palestinians, and pushed forward into the Sinai Peninsula. British and French forces bombed Port Said and stormed the Suez Canal.

Eventually, the aggressors withdrew amidst international pressure. Despite the military defeat of Egypt, the Suez Crisis gave it a political victory. Nasser's popularity soared among the Arabs. For Sabri, the crisis was a turning point that set him firmly on his future path.

At school, he got some news.

'You're doing very well, son!' Father Hand, the Irish monk who directed the Terra Sancta College, smiled.

'Thank you, sir.'

'What are you thinking of studying?'

'Law,' Sabri answered.

'I'm looking into an opportunity for you to go abroad, to a Catholic university,' Father Hand continued. 'In Washington, possibly. There may be a scholarship for you.'

Sabri paused. 'Thank you very much, sir, but no ...'

The monk looked at him in surprise.

'I don't want to emigrate. I want to go to Jerusalem,' Sabri explained.

'Why?'

'To know my enemy.'

Father Hand raised his eyebrows. After a pause, he nodded, slowly. 'I wish you the best.'

Elias was somewhat amazed when Sabri was accepted into the Hebrew University. He gazed at his son through narrowed eyes as he showed him the letter. 'What does it say?'

'They're offering me a place on their law program and I have to pay the initial fees.'

'It says that?' Elias asked, in disbelief.

'Yes, and if you don't believe me, take it to your friend the priest to read it.'

3

RESISTANCE

They take our land. Why? For security reasons! They take our jobs. Why? For security reasons! And when we ask them how it happens that we, our lands and our jobs threaten the security of the state—they do not tell us. Why not? For security reasons!

Walter Schwarz
The Arabs in Israel[1]

I

'I can't move ...' Sabri groaned. He was running a fever and his legs felt like jelly.

He had felt weak and congested when he had left the village that morning. Anis and Hussein, his friends from high school, were going to university with him. The three had arranged to meet in Haifa to take the bus. When he arrived at the station, Sabri felt worse. On the four-hour journey, his eyes began to tear, his body ached, and he shivered in misery.

'We'll carry your bags!' they said, when they arrived in Jerusalem. They asked for directions to the Salesian Sisters convent, where they had rented their rooms. Sabri shuffled along, the village already worlds away. Only twelve of his peers there had finished high school, and he was the first to go to university. Hatim would go two years later.

Little had prepared the young men for the alienation they would feel in Israeli society, in which they found themselves for the first time. In 1957, the Hebrew University was the only one in Israel. Less than fifty Palestinians were admitted among hundreds of Jews, who largely ignored them. Palestinian communities suffered from poverty and government neglect of their education system. Very few of their children made it to higher education.

Then there was the Hebrew. Most Palestinian high schools had not taught it; it had been marginal before the Nakba. After the founding of Israel, Hebrew had risen, overnight, to become the language of the state. In his first year, Sabri was exempt from English, which he had done at school, and sent to study Hebrew with new immigrants.

At the end of the first week, as he and his friends stood in line at the cafeteria, they were feeling the strain. 'Get some bread!' Hussein hissed. Each of them took several slices. Sabri stood with his tray, eyeing the food as the server looked at him impatiently. Other students were pushing behind him. Reluctantly, he pointed to a serving dish, and she ladled some fish on a plate. 'Potatoes or rice?' she asked.

'Both.' He probably could not eat the fish, he figured, so he needed all he could get.

At their table, they made a little pile of bread for Hussein. He was an athlete who trained hard. The food portions did nothing for him.

'This is revolting!' Sabri exclaimed at the first bite.

Anis made a face. 'Does it have ... *sugar* in it?'

'It does,' Hussein muttered, swallowing a mouthful and following it with a slice of bread in two, quick bites. The boys were alien to the Eastern European cuisine that the Jewish immigrants had brought with them. Sabri thought of his mother's food. She would throw all of this to the chickens—who would possibly not eat it.

The journey to Fassouta took a whole day, and he could only visit every few weeks. On his first trip, Wardeh prepared a large glass jar filled with balls of labaneh in golden olive oil. 'To make a sandwich when you're studying. And here, some za'atar* ...' She tied a plastic bag of ground thyme and sesame. Spinach pies, bread, and date cookies followed.

'Mother, enough. I can't carry all this ...' But, in truth, he did not mind lugging the heavy bags for the relief of having snacks on hand.

The next morning, he awoke early, prepared his things, and was out of the house by 7:00 am. The bus did not come to Fassouta; he had to walk about 2 miles to get to the Safad-Nahariya road. At 8:00 am, he would catch the bus, which would take an hour to get to Nahariya. He would then catch another bus to Haifa, arriving at 10:30 am, and wait for the noon train to Jerusalem. Arriving at 4:00 pm, he would take a bus to the city center, then wait for the university bus to take him to the student dormitories.

On the bus journey to Haifa, he hoisted his suitcase onto the overhead shelf and propped the jar of labaneh, in a cloth bag, next to it. The bus began to move as he sat down, thinking of his friends' delight when he showed them the goodies. He glanced up at his things.

---

* *Za'atar* (Arabic): ground thyme and sesame, eaten as a dip with olive oil.

He froze.

The jar had tipped, slightly, as the bus moved. A tiny stream of oil was making its way, in a slow drip, onto the collar of a policeman seated in front of him.

A sudden sweat gathered on Sabri's brow. He watched in horror as a hand came up and felt the damp collar. The man looked around him in sudden alarm. Then his eyes shot upwards. 'What's this! Whose is this?' he shrieked, jumping from his seat and pointing angrily at the jar.

Sabri's heart was hammering. He kept his gaze fixed out the window, trying to appear nonchalant.

'Whose is this?' the policeman yelled, again. People looked at each other. Sabri rang the bus bell. When they came to a halt, he stood up, grabbed his suitcase and scurried off. His friends would long lament the lost jar of labaneh.

II

Um Nour led the donkey, laden with firewood, slowly towards the village. She paused, catching her breath. The dew had just cleared, and the mountains fell before her, covered in a thick blanket of green forest.

Pushing on, she led the animal slowly towards the house. She would unload this lot, then return for another. Her elderly neighbors could not go out to cut firewood, and she sold it to them for much-needed income.

'How many times have I told you not to go alone?' a sudden cry jolted her. She looked up to see her father, Yousef, sitting near the well outside her house.

'Father ...' She rushed up with the donkey.

'Why didn't you tell me to go with you?'

'I left early. I didn't want to wake you!' In truth, she hated asking for help. Um Nour appreciated all the assistance her brothers and family were giving her. But firewood, she could cut alone. Why wake her father before sunrise to drag him with her?

Tears rolled down his cheeks. It pained her. She did not want pity. 'Father, I'm fine! I'm going to give these to our neighbor. Come inside and have some coffee.' Her plan to return to the fields would have to wait.

III

Sabri had enrolled to study law. After settling in, he found time, whenever he could, to sit in on lectures in other programs on the history of the Jews. He wanted to hear it firsthand, as told by them. What had brought them to his country? Only a handful of Jewish students talked to him at university, and none came close enough to be friends. Palestinian students were so few at the time and their problems were so starkly different that they struggled in their own world.

Israel's dealings with its small, remaining Palestinian population were equally dismissive. They were not allowed to organize politically nor to form an independent party. Their options were limited to the only non-Zionist party, the Israeli Communist Party. But this was of marginal standing and could not make a dent in the hawkish policies under which they suffered. The party itself was also a target of the military government, which clamped down on its Palestinian members but allowed it to exist to prevent them forming their own organizations.

The state pushed its mainstream election lists into Palestinian localities, using the military government as its tool. The 'carrot and stick' methods that Sabri had seen in his school days had become entrenched: the government promised movement permits, jobs or benefits, help in getting trade licenses or loans, leasing pieces of 'state land' or absentee property, or easing of measures such as road plans not passing through people's land. Conversely, it threatened punishment: withholding permits, imprisonment, house arrest or internal expulsion, or blackmailing people with false accusations to force them to vote.[2] The military government interfered in local council elections in Palestinian communities and in their political or social activities.

By 1958, the oppression had reached its peak, enough to make the most docile victims revolt. The government had seized vast amounts of Palestinian land, yet had restricted movement permits so that Palestinians could not get to the cities to work. There were disappearances and killings. Bombs began to go off in Palestinian areas, a scare that lasted from 1956–8. The Israeli army conducted training and maneuvers near their villages, killing and injuring people.

In the ten years since the founding of the state, its remaining Palestinians had constantly expressed their anger and frustration through meetings or small clashes, yet things had only deteriorated. But meanwhile, Nasser's ideas for pan-Arab unity had taken root. On 22 February 1958, Egypt and Syria came together as the United Arab Republic, with Nasser as president. When the declaration was made, Sabri smoked his first cigarette in celebration with his friends. It was a turning point for Palestinians in Israel. They saw themselves as part of their greater Arab nation, thwarted from their natural place in it. They had huge hopes for its revival and freedom.

That year, Israel planned to celebrate ten years since its founding and to display its 'progress' to the world, including that 'enjoyed' by its Palestinians. It pressured them to take part in these celebrations, forcing their local councils to spend thousands on preparations when they were underfunded and neglected, unable to improve the harsh living conditions of their communities. The Communist Party issued a strong statement in protest:

> A people will not celebrate whose villages are destroyed, whose land is stolen, whose workers are fired because they are Arabs and refused any union protection, whose intellectuals and merchants are prevented from making a living, whose children are forbidden from studying their national culture, whose free movement is prohibited in their homeland, who are under humiliating military rule while their refugees sleep in tents, forbidden from returning, and whose basic right of self-determination is trampled.[3]

On 1 May, Labor Day, Palestinians came out in angry protest. In Nazareth, demonstrators clashed with the police and scores of civilians and policemen were injured. Hundreds of protesters were arrested. Two days later, clashes continued in Umm el-Fahem, in the Triangle, and spread to other villages. Voices were rising that something had to be done. There was a need for a Palestinian body focused on addressing its people's dire situation. On 14 July, despite pressure from the authorities, two founding meetings were held for the 'Arab Front in Occupied Palestine'.

It was odd to have two meetings, at the same time, in Acre and Nazareth. But it was the only way past the restrictions of military rule, so that those who could not make it to one could reach the other. The name 'Arab Front' was rejected by the district governor, who claimed it was 'racist'—though most of the state institutions had the words 'Jewish' or 'Land of Israel' in their names. The name was changed to the 'Democratic Popular Front', shortened to 'the Popular Front' or 'the Front'.

The Front included Palestinians of all social classes and political views. It was heavily influenced by the Communist Party but moved to address Palestinian grievances, demanding an end to military rule and oppression. The authorities were livid. Again, dozens of expulsion and detention orders against sympathisers of the movement were meted out. But the Front resisted. Based in Haifa and Nazareth, it campaigned for the return of the refugees, a halt to the seizure of Palestinian property, and the restitution of confiscated property to its owners. It demanded equality between Jewish and Arab employees, the end of all discrimination, and the improvement of education for Arabs. Its mouthpiece was *al-Ittihad*, the Arabic-language newspaper of the Communist Party.

In September, Sabri finished studying Hebrew and began his first year of law. New friends joined his class. Mohammed Mi'ari was from Birweh, from which Mahmoud Darwish, who would become the famous poet, also hailed. The Galilean village was blown up in 1948 after emptying it of its people. Mohammed told Sabri his story. He was eight years old at the time and found himself on a trail of suffering with the bewildered villagers. He described the weeks of agony, the hunger, the roads full of people in a terrible state of confusion and fear. Birweh's people were scattered, some in the surrounding villages, others as far as Syria or Lebanon. Mohammed's family was split across the borders and could not see each other again.

Mohammed became Sabri's friend for their years of study and beyond. Hasan Amoun, a first-year medical student from Deir el-Assad, joined them. He shared a room with Sabri's friend from high school, Hussein Hlehel, who had moved to the al-Musrarah neighborhood in East Jerusalem. They were lucky to find a good gas cooker. Their friends began gathering at their place to escape the cafeteria food. The young men cooked huge portions of rice and vegetables, whatever they could afford on their student budgets. 'I have a suggestion,' Hussein joked. 'Each of you can mark a plate as his; then there's no need to wash them after we're done. You can just set them aside till the next meal!'

That year, the Arab Student Council was formed at the Hebrew University. In the first elections, Hasan Amoun was voted chairman and Sabri his deputy. Sabri did not want the post; he preferred to be free to work as he wished without the shackles of a position. During the elections, he ran off to Fassouta. But, on returning, he found out he had been elected in absentia. The university administration opposed the Arab Student Council and wanted them to belong to the general student council, but they stood their ground, for they had their own concerns which were very removed from those of Jewish students. The Arab Student Council spoke out against racist policies, calling for protests and struggling for Palestinian rights.

Sabri worked hard with the group, but he wanted to do more. With his friends, he joined the Popular Front and sought to recruit others. They worked against the tide. Everything was suspect. Voting for the Front, organizing any political activity, reading Arabic newspapers not approved by the government, speaking up or writing, even listening to the radio were grounds for hassle and arrest. People listened to Arab stations or read *al-Ittihad* under the blankets or in secret. The military apparatus hounded anyone who was active in the Front and kept some under house arrest for months. It interfered in planned meetings, so that they had to meet secretly. Zionist parties joined the campaign of fear and coercion, and distributed leaflets smearing the Front.

Writers and intellectuals who criticized government policy were also harassed. Students, peasants and laborers were all targets of intimidation and were denied movement permits. They were expelled from their hometowns, cutting them off from their jobs and families. People were dismissed from employment based on 'blacklists' drawn up by the authorities, including anyone who took part in social or political events not approved of by the military government.

With rising pressure against it, the Front reached out to the United Nations and to the international community. Locally, it mobilized Palestinians to challenge military rule by moving around without permits. It reached out with awareness campaigns among

Israeli Jews, whom the state kept in the dark about the plight of the Palestinians.

The Front worked hard in its first year, but the end of the year saw a serious rift. A 1958–9 crisis between the communist-backed Iraqi leader, Abdul Karim Qasim, and the United Arab Republic, led by Nasser, reflected itself among Palestinians in Israel. The Nasserite current was increasingly frustrated with the Front and the Communist Party for their narrow outlook and blind allegiance to the Soviet Union, to the detriment of the Palestinian cause. The nationalist pan-Arab branch, of which Sabri was a member, felt a necessity to join the tide of Nasser, seeing it as the only hope for Palestinians and Arabs to attain freedom. Several nationalists from the Popular Front broke off to form their own group. Mansour Kardosh was one of them.

IV

Mansour's father, Tawfiq, owned a flour mill in Nazareth. Before the Nakba, carts and lorries from the villages below would snake up the long road to the town, carrying wheat to be ground. The mill also had a small ice generator and produced lemonade. Tawfiq had passed away in 1939, when Mansour was eighteen, leaving him to run the business and take care of his mother and seven siblings.

The young man had taken it in his stride. He had managed to obtain a license from the British Mandate authorities to be a certified producer of flour, and he continued to sell ice and lemonade in his shop. But, in December 1947, refugees began to flock to Nazareth. In April 1948, Haifa fell, throwing tens of thousands to the streets. Nazareth, from its high hills, watched the long lines of refugees fleeing on foot from the surrounding areas, carrying what little they could. On 15 July 1948, Saffuriyya and Mujaydil, the neighboring villages, also fell. Their people were expelled. When the army entered Nazareth the next day, Mansour and his family rushed from their house to a nearby convent to take refuge. They spent the night in darkness, with the power cut off, hearing automatic gunfire and voices over loudspeakers declaring a curfew.

Over the next days, they understood that their town had fallen. But they were spared from expulsion due to the special status of

Nazareth in the Christian world. The people of Saffuriyya and Mujaydil could not return to their homes. When some of them tried, the Israeli army drove them off. Later, it bulldozed their villages, changed Saffuriyya's name to the Hebrew 'Tsipori', and planted a forest in its place. The Ministry of Tourism put up a sign saying 'Tsipori National Park'. A Jewish farming community, Moshav Tsipori, was set up nearby.

Military rule was imposed on Nazareth. The commander was stationed near Mansour's mill. As the reality sank in, Mansour went to renew his license to produce flour. He was told that his equipment was outdated and that the mills in Afula, a neighboring Jewish town, would handle this task. Mansour lost his living and was forced to sell his mill equipment.

The military commander suggested dryly to Mansour that he continue supplying the new Jewish communities with ice, which was still used for food storage. The family invested in the ice-making part of the business. But, to leave Nazareth and distribute the ice, they needed a permit from the commander. The permits were delayed, day after day, such that the ice melted before they could get it to their customers. At the time, thirty-five refugees were sheltering in Mansour's house, having lost their homes and land. He began to think about activism when he thought they would all starve.[4]

It was not until 1953 that the government passed the 'Land Acquisition Law' to pay compensation for seized Palestinian land. It was intended to ensure that Palestinian owners signed away their rights and could not claim their property in future. The government also stipulated that it would appraise the land according to its value in 1948 and would pay compensation based on the value of the Israeli currency in 1950, which had since devalued. Thus, the price to be paid for the land, even if its owners were to accept, would only be a small fraction of its value. This 'compensation' was offered for tilled land only. Grazing lands, which were of vital importance to the villages, were considered 'public areas' and not compensated.

Most owners did not want to sell their land, seeing this as thinly veiled seizure. This refusal mattered little, however, because the state eventually seized their lands, as they battled in futile court cases. Hanna Naqqara, a Palestinian lawyer, recounted the experience of one of his clients:

When a peasant said to another official: 'What is this you are offering me? Only 200 pounds per dunum?' the official replied: 'This is not your land, it is ours. We are paying you your wages as a "watchman". You are only "watchmen"; you have "looked after" our land for 2,000 years and we are paying you your wages! But the land is ours!'[5]

In 1954, the state seized 1,200 dunums northeast of Nazareth, the area remaining for development of the city. The stated intent was for 'public use', to build government offices. But those steps were part of the 'Judaization of the Galilee' plan. The aim was to build an exclusively Jewish neighborhood,[6] and the first Jewish residents moved into Natzeret Illit (Upper Nazareth; now renamed 'Nof ha-Galil', View of the Galilee) in 1957. Palestinian laborers were prohibited from working there and had to commute to Haifa and other towns to find work.

In February 1959, the border policemen who had been involved in the Kafr Qasim massacre were brought to trial. They were found guilty and sentenced to prison terms, but they all received pardons and were released within a year.[7] Issachar Shadmi, the brigade commander who had ordered the massacre, was found to have issued a 'blatantly illegal' command to kill civilians,[8] but he was cleared of murder charges and instead found guilty of 'exceeding his orders' in specifying the hours of curfew. He received a punishment of a symbolic fine of ten *prutot* (cents) and a reprimand. His photograph, smiling and holding up the coin victoriously outside the court, showed Palestinians what their lives were worth in Israel.

Seeing these events, Mansour began to ask himself the same questions that had plagued Sabri. What was Zionism? Why was all this happening? He joined the Popular Front, until the rift within it caused him and his friend, Habib Qahwaji, to establish something new.

V

Habib was a teacher and poet from Fassouta who had taught at the Terra Sancta College in Nazareth and the Arab Orthodox College in Haifa. In April 1959, the two friends met in Nazareth at the home of a merchant, Hanna Mismar. With them were Toufiq Odeh, a laborer from Nazareth; Zaki Bahri, another from Haifa; and Mahmoud Srouji and Mohammed Abdul Rahman, merchants from Acre.

The group's second meeting, in July, was at Habib's home in Haifa. They were joined by many others, including Saleh Baransi, a teacher from the town of Taybeh in the Triangle, and Fouzi el-Asmar, a poet and journalist from Lydda. Habib recruited Sabri and his friend, Hasan Amoun, from the Arab Student Council at the Hebrew University. Sabri's classmate, Mohammed Mi'ari, joined them, as did Rashid Hussein, a poet from Musmus village in the Triangle, and Fakhri Jdai, a pharmacist from Jaffa.

The new group needed a name. Confiscation of their land was one of the greatest problems facing the Palestinians in Israel, and they chose 'al-Ard', The Land.

The young men shared a deep belief in Nasser and his ideas. Before him, they had battled despair and betrayal by the Arab states, and they had felt totally alone. When Nasser entered the scene in Egypt, and the Communist Party and Popular Front started speaking out in Israel, people began to break their chains. Nasser's message was far wider than the narrow demands of the Israeli Communist Party: he wanted to unify the Arabs to fight imperialism and to recover historic Palestine. He embodied the hope for liberation, change, the revival of the Arab nation, a better life. He cemented belonging and identity, nurtured hopes and dreams.

Al-Ard adopted a more pragmatic approach and acknowledged the United Nations Partition Plan and the State of Israel, but it stressed the right of the Palestinians to their own state, and the belonging of this state to the greater Arab nation.

Growing up in Israel, it had seemed to Sabri that the Palestinian people had all but disappeared after the Nakba. Refugees were scattered across the Arab countries, while those in Gaza were under Egyptian administration, the West Bank was ruled by Jordan, and the Palestinians in Israel were alone. Sabri felt that those who had remained in the country were responsible for reviving the Palestinian cause. With its closed borders, the country was hermetically sealed, leaving Palestinians unable to connect with any of their brethren in the wider Arab world. But the state's oppression strengthened their national feeling, and he wanted this small flame to remain, the name of Palestine not to disappear.

Saleh Baransi joined him in his fervent Nasserism. Mansour and Habib were older when they had witnessed the refugee crisis and were greatly affected by it. The four made up the central committee of al-Ard. Sabri, who had the best Hebrew in the group, became a sort of secretary and took on the correspondence with the authorities, of which there would be plenty.

Al-Ard applied for a license to publish a newspaper. Months passed with no answer, only evasion and delay. According to a law from the time of the British Mandate, any citizen could publish a single issue once a year without a license, as long as it was not a regular publication. Jewish organizations had resorted to this law before the establishment of Israel. Al-Ard decided to do the same. Its members would take turns publishing issues of their newspaper every few weeks under their various names, and would change the title, keeping the name 'al-Ard' in it so that the public would recognize it.

The newspaper was printed at an old press in Acre, al-Zeibaq, the only commercial press to agree to print it. Some of the group had good connections with Mapam, Israel's left-wing party, and Fouzi el-Asmar worked for *al-Fajr*, Mapam's Arabic literary magazine. Yet, although the party's printing press needed work in Arabic, it refused to print the newspaper.[9] Some issues of the paper were printed at the *al-Ittihad* press, but it too would sometimes refuse due to political pressure or the differences that existed between the Communist Party and al-Ard.

The first issue, in late 1959, was simply titled 'al-Ard' and published under Habib Qahwaji's name. Many young people waited at the doors of the press in excitement, and many volunteered, alongside the founders, to distribute the paper and collect donations. Two thousand copies were gone within a week. At the time, most popular newspapers sold less than a thousand copies per issue.[10] The paper spoke out against Israeli policies and made the following calls:

> Equal rights for the Arabs in Israel in all respects. The repeal of the discriminatory laws designed to destroy Arab identity, and the enabling of the Arabs to develop in the framework of their own customs and national character
>
> Recognition of the right of the Arab refugees to return to their homeland. No peace is possible while a million people are unable to return to their homes and are living on bread and water in tents

We do not ask for mercy for these refugees, nor do we play on the liberal conscience of humanity, for we believe that their problem is a political one.[11]

No sooner had the first issue circulated than a concerted smear campaign was launched in the Israeli press, accusing the founders of being anti-Israeli and of wanting to create a sabotage movement. But al-Ard's work was open and public. It distributed a letter stating its objectives to the Israeli press and to all members of the Knesset.

We demand:

1. The end of the military government
2. The return of plundered lands to their owners and an end to the seizure of lands and the Judaization of the Galilee
3. The raising of the standard of Arab schools in order to turn them into institutions in which one can have access to education
4. Equal rights for Arab workers
5. Aid to the Arab economy and the Arab peasant by helping them develop and not attempting to destroy them
6. The return of the Arab refugees to their villages. An end to the blowing-up of villages, whose inhabitants now go there on pilgrimages to cry over their lost land and homes (Biram and Iqrit)
7. A license for the newspaper.

There will be no peace without the return of the refugees, and this is their natural right ... We are part of a larger nation (the Arab nation). Why are we not allowed to express our opinion as to its future and fate?[12]

Al-Ard urged Palestinians to organize and handle their own affairs, calling for a boycott of the Israeli elections until the establishment of true democratic participation. Its call led to a 42 per cent abstinence rate among Palestinians in the 1959 Knesset elections. At the same time, it urged Jews and Palestinians to live in peaceful coexistence and saw this as the only option to move forward, with full rights for all.

That year, Israel lifted some curfews during the day, allowing large numbers of villagers to go to the towns and cities to work. One reason was the growing job market and the need for cheap labor. Another was, seemingly, to reduce the number of Palestinian youth who were secretly leaving for neighboring Arab countries, training, and returning to carry out resistance, or joining spy networks to help their brethren across the borders. Most of these youth had some schooling but could not continue their education due to the restrictions of military rule, and could only find work in manual labor. In fact, the obstacles placed on Palestinians in Israel, who found themselves without land or jobs, had been designed to quietly induce the remainder of them to leave.

They did not. With the easing of some aspects of military rule, after a decade of restrictions, Palestinians could move around again. They could see what was going on in the country, reconnect and recognise themselves as members of their larger community. Al-Ard developed branches in most Arab villages. Mansour was the leader in Nazareth; Habib, in Haifa and Acre; Saleh, in the Triangle; Fakhri Jdai, in Jaffa; and Sabri, in Jerusalem.

In September 1959, Sabri moved, with his friends, from the Salesian Sisters' convent to the dormitories on campus. He was relieved to have Mohammed Mi'ari living with him, who could cobble together a few dishes—nothing fancy, but it solved Sabri's problem, as he still hated preparing food. A little arrangement was made where he did the dishes if Mohammed cooked.

The two friends worked together in al-Ard. The Zionist groups on campus fought them as they had fought the Arab Student Council. But, soon, al-Ard drew in most of the Palestinian students at the Hebrew University. The group was made up of people with different, sometimes conflicting, leanings, and a large number who had no clear political path. Many Palestinians were looking for an independent organization, free from the constraints of the Communist Party, and they found this in al-Ard. Within a few months, it attracted tens of laborers, peasants, lawyers, merchants, writers, and poets.

Al-Ard was the first Palestinian movement in Israel to call for self-determination and a just solution to the Palestine problem. It fought on two fronts: the lifting of repression from Palestinian citizens and the granting of equal rights, making Israel a democratic state for all its citizens; and the Palestinians' right to their own state, as defined by the 1947 United Nations Partition Plan, where they could live in peace alongside the State of Israel. The group's leaders saw these aims as the only realistic options after the Nakba. They called for cooperation between Palestinians and Jews within a framework of justice and mutual recognition, and they were open in their desire to work with Jewish progressive and democratic groups.

Al-Ard was still waiting for a license to publish its newspaper. It applied again and again, and, despite the law stipulating an answer within a set period, there was no word from the authorities. It continued with its single issues. People encouraged the group and felt it belonged to them, and many made donations of five Israeli pounds, a good sum, each time they received the newspaper.

The paper reported news from the Arab world, particularly on Nasser, and anything that would bring the Palestinians in Israel out of their isolation. It exposed the problems facing Palestinians as a result of government policy: the lack of jobs and budgets for industry or agriculture, the persecution of those who spoke out, and the severe problems in their education system. Palestinian schools suffered from a debilitating lack of resources. The curriculum gave students few transferable skills for employment—if they could even hope to get a job upon graduating. Teachers were appointed not on merit but by the approval of the secret service, based on their willingness to cooperate and spy on their students and fellow teachers. Other teachers were intimidated by the threat of losing their jobs, and the Ministry of Education exercised tight control to prevent any mention of Palestinian history or identity. A tiny percentage of students managed to pass the matriculation exam to enter university, and, with widespread poverty, even less actually made it to higher education. Those who went to university often chose free professions, such as law, medicine, pharmacology, accounting, and engineering, because they would not be tied to government bodies in trying to find work. Jobs in public and many private enterprises required approval from the military administration or secret service, in return for political silence or cooperation.

Al-Ard protested this situation. The attacks in the Israeli press grew more intense. The group replied to them in its newspaper, defending the Palestinians' right to self-expression. After the sixth issue, the authorities began to crack down and consider the group's work illegal and a danger to state security. Most of its leaders were put under house arrest. But the newspaper continued, increasing its circulation four-fold.

These stirrings began to take shape outside the country, as well. In October 1959, the Palestinian National Liberation Movement, Fatah, was formed by Yasser Arafat, Salah Khalaf, and Khalil al-Wazir, all working in Kuwait. Arafat was a civil engineer born in Egypt to a Gazan father and a Jerusalemite mother, and was head of the General Union of Palestinian Students (GUPS) at Cairo University. His two colleagues had been expelled in 1948 from Jaffa and Ramle in Palestine. Other founders of the movement included Khaled Yashruti, the GUPS head in Beirut, and Salim Za'anoun.

The decade since the Nakba had shown the Palestinian refugees that the Arab countries had deserted them or conspired against them. These states paid lip service to the liberation of Palestine while their rulers colluded with Israel to protect their fiefdoms. Many small Palestinian factions had formed, but they were disjointed, lacked a central leadership and were under tight constraints in their host countries. Fatah brought many of them under its wing. It took a very different view to that of al-Ard: Fatah's goal was to liberate the whole of Palestine through revolution and armed struggle. The difference was expected, given their respective situations. Both worked against immense difficulties, and al-Ard, despite its more pragmatic approach, would face a harsh fate, all the same.

VI

In January 1960, Shmuel Divon, advisor on Arab affairs to the Israeli prime minister, held a press conference in Tel Aviv in which he launched an intense attack on al-Ard. He claimed that the group worked underground and was planning the destruction of the state. The press warned the Palestinians in Israel of the 'grave danger' that al-Ard posed to them due to its 'extreme' views, and the Communist Party itself joined the attack, in order to keep its standing as the sole political channel among the Palestinians. For the first time, Sabri, still a student, was summoned for interrogation. He was frank about what his group was doing, that it was a political movement trying to reach people through its newspaper, which the authorities had refused to license. He explained that they wanted to work through lawful, political means. But the authorities began a campaign against al-Ard's leaders. Three or four agents took turns trailing them and watching their homes at night.

Al-Ard managed to print twelve issues of its newspaper before the authorities intervened. Two weeks after Divon's public denunciation, the secret service offered the owner of al-Zeibaq press in Acre the equivalent of six months' profit if he stopped printing the paper. He refused, but agents returned as soon as the thirteenth issue was printed. They amassed all the copies and took them away. They then arrested Mansour, Habib, Saleh, and Sabri, together with Mahmoud Srouji and Elias Muammar, and searched their homes. The six were charged with publishing a newspaper without a license and given heavy fines of 1,000 pounds each and three months in prison. After appeal, they were able to suspend the prison terms and lower the fines to 500 pounds. But the ruling took a toll on their limited financial means, in addition to the legal and court fees they had to pay.

They needed another way, and they decided to register al-Ard as a company. This would allow them to print the newspaper as part of the company's commercial activities, as well as give them a base to continue political work and to receive funds. On the day of the court's ruling against them, Sabri filled in an application for 'al-Ard Limited Company for Printing and Publishing', and sent it to the registrar of corporations in Jerusalem.

The response was swift. A few weeks later, he received a letter that the application was rejected for reasons of 'public security and interest'. Meanwhile, many al-Ard members were placed under house arrest or had their movement permits revoked.

At the same time, a struggle was ensuing against a 'land consolidation' law proposed by the Knesset. Building on previous laws, the government would consolidate scattered pieces of land that it had seized and now 'owned' into contiguous units, in order to be able to use them for development—namely, to establish new Jewish settlements. To do this, it would give the Palestinian owners of the connecting pieces financial compensation or other land in return. On the surface, the idea seemed reasonable, but the prices offered for the land were, again, far lower than its market value, and the owners were offered plots far away, slowly eroding their ties to their villages. Often, the land offered was near Jewish settlements, endangering the peasants' access to it.

Palestinians began to mobilize in protest. In February 1961, al-Ard held a meeting. 'The proposed law can wipe us all out,' Mansour warned attendees. The urgency was not lost on the others. Most important, it seemed, was to unify the efforts to resist the law by various Palestinian bodies, which were all working separately. The group reached out to them. Quickly, Palestinians rallied against the law. The bill was finally omitted from the Knesset's agenda. It was a rare occasion on which Palestinian popular action, under military rule, managed to halt a proposed law. But, at the end of the year, the government announced that it had seized 5,500 dunums in the western Galilee belonging to the villages of Deir el-Assad, Bi'neh, and Nahaf, to build a new Jewish town, Karmiel.[13] The confiscated land included most of the villages' farmland and some of the finest stone quarries in the country, which were owned by Palestinians. The Judaization project also continued with the establishment of other Jewish communities in the Galilee and the Triangle.

In September 1961, Palestinian hopes in the Arab world received another blow. A military coup in Syria ended its confederation with Egypt as the United Arab Republic. The union had lasted just over three years.

At Habib's house in Haifa, Sabri was in tears. Their dream of Arab nationalism was shattered. Nasser's idea for pan-Arab unity had been strangled just after birth.

VII

The three little ones were perched on the front steps of the house, gazing intently into the distance.

'He's here!' Baheej jumped up. Their uncle, Ibrahim, was making his way towards them. 'Nida, go!' They were impatient to see if he had brought them presents, but too shy to ask. They pushed their youngest sister, the five-year-old, towards him. She bolted across the short distance and into her uncle's arms as he swept her up and kissed her.

'Did you bring things with you?' she breathed, eyes wide, looking at the bags he had put down.

'I did!' he laughed. 'But let me get to the house first!'

Chaos reigned as he made his way in and they pounced on the bags. There were new jackets and toys. Their mother looked on. 'Welcome, brother! Children, shh! Why did you trouble yourself again?' she fussed, looking at him.

'It's nothing!' He hugged her and sat down. 'Hello!' he said to Ibrahim, his namesake, as he rushed in to greet him. 'Where's Nour?'

'He's gone to work with Najeeb.'

Nour had just turned fifteen. His uncle, Najeeb, took him to work when he was off school. Najeeb worked in Solel Boneh, a construction company that hired Palestinian laborers. Um Nour was worried about her son, but their expenses were growing and she needed all the help she could get. The morning after school was out, she packed lunch for him and watched him get into the pickup truck with her brother.

'Make sure he goes to school, though,' Ibrahim cautioned.

'He is. He's only working in the holidays,' she nodded. She would help Nour save his money and send him to technical school, so he would get some vocational training. She did not want her children living the life of toil she had.

And Hanneh: she had blossomed into such a bright young girl. She rushed in now to greet her uncle. 'How's my sweetheart?' he smiled and hugged her. 'You just finished Grade 8, right?'

'Yes, Uncle.'

He turned to his sister. 'I want to take her with me, to Mghar. She can continue at school where I teach.'

'Mghar? But—'

'No "buts". She's very bright and she should finish school.'

'But, brother ...'

'Don't worry about expenses. I'll take care of it.'

'Where will she stay? And when will she come home?' Um Nour protested. This was very new.

'With me. I'll bring her to see you each time I come.'

Thus began Hanneh's journey out of the village.

VIII

Military rule was an ongoing problem for the Palestinians in Israel and a tool with which the state had dispossessed them and stripped them of their rights. Only minor changes had been made over the years, such as lifting some curfews during the day, more extended movement permits, and more channels to appeal the military government's decisions. But these changes were only made when the authorities felt that Palestinians had reached boiling point and were ignoring the restrictions or repeatedly protesting them. During David Ben-Gurion's second premiership (1955–63), a political battle raged in his leading party, Mapai, over the continued exercise of military rule. Ben-Gurion defended the policy and made constant slurs against the Palestinians and Arabs.

Opposition was reaching a peak. On 2 December 1961, Arabs and Jews marched in a joint demonstration in Tel Aviv. The Jewish-Arab Committee for the Abolition of Military Government was formed, comprising the Israeli Communist Party, al-Ard, the Arab Student Council at the Hebrew University, and Matzpen, an Israeli socialist organization, among others. The committee organized most of the mass rallies and other activities protesting the system. In February 1962, the authorities lifted the night curfew from the villages of the Triangle, which had lasted for fourteen years. But, in March, the residents of Deir el-Assad, Bi'neh, and Nahaf, after lodging a complaint against the seizure of their land to build Karmiel, called a protest meeting. The military commander responded by declaring their villages a closed area for the day so no one could reach them, and the meeting was canceled.[14]

Sabri was close to finishing his Master's in law. He wrote the synopsis of his thesis—'Military Government: System and Powers'—and took it to his supervisor, Benjamin Akzin, to sign off on it. The Russian-born professor had been secretary to Ze'ev Jabotinsky, a Zionist leader, and had served as the head of the political division of the New Zionist Organization, an extreme rightist entity founded by Jabotinsky, lobbying American support for a Jewish state in Palestine. In 1945, Akzin was secretary and political advisor to the American Zionist Emergency Committee.[15] Four years later, he emigrated to Israel and joined the faculty of law at

the Hebrew University of Jerusalem, eventually serving as dean—
which is when Sabri came to be standing in his office.

The dean took the proposal and perused it for a minute. He did
not look up. 'Has anyone else written on this?' he finally asked, still
staring at the paper.

'Not to my knowledge, sir,' Sabri replied, talking to the man's
bent head.

Still, the dean did not raise his eyes. Instead, he said: 'I have no
knowledge of the topic. I will refer you to another professor who
can oversee your work.' He wrote the new name, signed off and
pushed the paper back at Sabri, without looking at him.

The supervisor was Yitzhak Zamir, a Polish-born lecturer of public law who would later become the Israeli Attorney General, then
a judge at the Supreme Court. 'I don't get into politics,' he said.
'I'm concerned with the legal aspects, only. Write whatever you
want, as long as it's properly researched.'

Sabri was furnished with a document to enable him to meet officers in the army for his research. But several meetings, sent from
one to another, produced no information. He had expected this. He
would have to turn to any written laws he could find. He knew
quite a lot of the legal aspects already from his experience of living
under the regime. When he finished, a small news item appeared in
the Israeli press saying that an 'Arab' had written his Master's thesis
on military rule.

Al-Ard's battle continued. It appealed to the Supreme Court
against the decision to prohibit the registration of its company. The
Court overruled the registrar's decision, stating that his authority
did not extend to assessing national security interests,[16] and
approved the registration. But the judicial advisor to the government appealed the ruling. At the hearing, the registrar said that he
had rejected the application because the company intended to
engage in acts of 'incitement'. The judge replied: 'You cannot base
a decision on speculation. When they carry out incitement, you can
take legal action.' The court upheld its decision to permit the registration of al-Ard Company, Ltd. In early 1962, the company was
finally registered and its shares were sold to the leaders of the group
and a few of its supporters.

It was a small, rare victory. The next step was to apply for a license to publish its newspaper. Again, the authorities resorted to delays and evasion.

IX

The rhythmic chopping of the axe cut through the chirping of the birds and cicadas above. Um Nour was hard at work, wiping the sweat from her brow. Nida, Najwa, and Baheej were busy breaking off small twigs and collecting them in a large sack. They were for the young animals at home.

'Nida, come, take this to our neighbor, he'll unload it,' her mother panted, setting the final pieces of wood on the donkey's back.

Obediently, little Nida grabbed the animal's rope and began the walk home. 'I'll go with her!' said Najwa, hoping to escape the task at hand.

'No!' her mother said. 'She'll be fine!' The chopping resumed as the children's eyes followed their sister, wishing they, too, had a break. An hour later, she was back with the donkey, now relieved of its load, only to find another one waiting for it. Um Nour resumed piling the pieces of wood on its back as the children looked on, marveling at its patience.

'Right, off you go. Baheej, carry the sack between you and Najwa. Nida, lead the donkey again. Straight home. No dallying!'

The children, as though they had heard the bell for recess, took off as quickly as they could, dragging the bag between them. Their mother stayed behind to reap some wheat.

Back home, they heard the squawk of the hens as they laid their eggs. Their aunt was inside, cooking lunch. They dumped the bag they were carrying and, quickly, collected the warm eggs with their little hands, bundling them into the front of Baheej's shirt. Then they scurried out of the house and down the dusty roads of the village to their great-uncle, Hanna, in his shoe shop. Baheej showed him their treasure. 'Will you buy these?' he asked, eagerly.

Their uncle smiled. 'Of course.' Reaching into his pocket, he took out a few pence as the children laid the eggs carefully in a shoebox. No sooner had Baheej pocketed the coins than they ran off to the grocery shop of Botros Sha'er. With a bag of sweets, they trailed back home, chewing and licking happily.

Their mother made her way back to the village two hours later. As she passed her uncle's shop, he came out, grinning, and gave her the eggs.

'Hello, uncle ...' she greeted him. Her face fell. 'Oh, no!' She urged him to keep them, but he would not. Thanking him, she stormed home and found the three rascals. An ear-tweaking followed and their aunt rushed to intervene at their loud wails. But their mother knew they would do it again.

X

Naseef, the children's uncle and a friend of Sabri's, was also doing his Master's at the Hebrew University. He asked Sabri for a favor. 'My niece, Hanneh, is coming for a visit. She's in Grade 10, and she's thinking of enrolling at the university when she finishes school.'

'Yes, I think I know her. She's Um Nour's daughter, right? Her father died while we were at school ...' Sabri remembered his parents telling him the news, years earlier, when they had visited him in Nazareth.

Naseef nodded. 'They've struggled since then. But we're all pooling in to help. Hanneh is really bright.'

'That's great!' Sabri nodded. No girls from the village had made it to university; this was a first.

'But I have exams and I'm really tied up,' Naseef continued. 'Would you take her on a quick walk around the place?'

Sabri obliged. The young girl looked around the university in awe. 'How long have you been here?' she asked, shyly.

'Five years. I'm almost done,' he replied. 'You're in my sister Najibeh's class, right?'

She nodded. Sabri was hoping to convince his father to let Najibeh study. Mariam, his eldest sister, had no such designs and had married at seventeen. 'I heard you've very good at school,' he turned to Hanneh.

She blushed. 'Yes. I'm studying in Mghar, with my uncle Ibrahim. But I might go to Nazareth next year, for Grades 11 and 12. I want to continue to university.'

'What do you want to study?' he asked, in admiration.

They stopped in front of the faculty of science. 'I hope to come here,' she answered, looking at the building, then back at him.

XI

In June 1962, a small procession made its way to Jerusalem with Sabri, his parents, his brother and sisters, and several of his cousins. He had arranged for a bus to take them to the Hebrew University to attend his graduation.

Elias was in his glory. He did not understand much about higher education, but he knew his son had become the first university graduate in the village and the surrounding area. In fact, when Sabri graduated, there were still fewer than 100 Palestinian students at university. People asked Elias about his son, 'the lawyer', and he was having a hard time believing it.

Back at his parents' house, on a balmy summer night, Sabri lay on his bed and took out a book, *The Rise and Fall of the Third Reich*, by William Shirer. Conscious of his sleeping siblings crowding the two rooms, he turned down the light of the lamp, moving it close to him. He smiled as he looked at Huda and Muna, his youngest sisters. They were three and five years old, and he had intervened with his parents to name them after Gamal Abdel Nasser's daughters.

Wardeh was moving quietly about, checking up on her children. She stopped short at the sight of him. 'What are you doing?' she whispered.

'I'm reading, Mother.'

'Reading? Haven't you finished reading? Your eyes ...' she frowned.

'No, this is a book I'm reading outside of my studies,' he grinned.

'Right.' Wardeh looked unconvinced. 'Don't stay up too late!'

In the morning, Elias was heading to Nahariya with Subhi, one of Sabri's younger brothers. Sabri asked them to get him a copy of *Time* magazine, which was sold there. 'Subhi will show it to you,' he told his father.

In Nahariya, they finished their errands and Subhi had to continue to Haifa. Elias waited at the bus stop to return to Fassouta, magazine under his arm. The bus stopped and he climbed on board. Dressed in his sirwal, the baggy Arab pants with a drawstring, and his headdress, a white kufiyyeh, he drew a few curious stares from the Jewish passengers. Two of them, in religious attire, muttered something to each other as he sat down. Pretending not to notice, Elias casually flicked the magazine open and began staring intently into it. He looked at the photographs to make sure he had it the correct way upwards.

The passengers gaped. Elias played ignorant and turned the page, seemingly absorbed in a careful reading of *Time*. When he got home, he told the family, to their peals of laughter. 'They must have thought: "How the heck does this Arab peasant know to read a magazine? And in English, too!"' he chortled.

Na'ima passed around some crackers, which she had bought from the grocery shop, but Elias wrinkled his nose. 'Take this away,' he flicked his hand. 'I don't eat *sheknazi* food!' Try as they might, they could not teach him to say the word 'Ashkenazi', which referred to Jews who had come from Europe. But they knew his aversion to anything that came out of a box. To him, food was what he grew or raised. And, to him, the 'sheknazis' had brought this food with them and his children were falling prey to it.

'So, son, what are your plans?' he turned to Sabri.

'Look for a place to do my training,' he replied. 'I need to practice for two years before I can get my license.'

Elias nodded. 'Maybe you can help me with these scoundrels.'

'What?'

'They're bearing down on me with their taxes. Here ...' His father took a small sheaf of paper from the cupboard. 'See if you can make this out.'

'They want to make an estimate of your livestock for tax payment,' Sabri muttered.

'They already have. And I already paid. Four hundred pounds, they wanted. At this rate, I'll need half my stock for their taxes!'

Elias was well-off and did not need any favors from the authorities, which greatly irked them. Neither he nor his children had ever asked for anything; thus, they could not be pinned down by the military commander's aides. Elias could afford to pay for his son at university, which was the equivalent of the cost of a house—and which very few villagers could do. Thus, the authorities went after him with exorbitant taxes, overestimating what he owned to pile on the pressure.

'Pay to Caesar what is Caesar's, Father,' Sabri joked. 'We'll sort it out. I'll keep this with me.'

He made his way to his grandparents' house, remembering how often he had scurried up that road as a child. His grandfather hugged him in delight. 'Welcome! Congratulations, my boy!'

'Sidi, how are you?' Sabri asked.

'Not getting any younger,' the old man lamented. 'I can't see properly ... They made me these,' he took off his glasses. 'It was better for a while, but now it's gone all foggy again.'

'Can I see them?'

'Of course!' His grandfather looked at him in pride. He looked forward to Sabri's visits and often asked him about politics and events in the country. In fact, Sabri had acquired a bit of a following: when he came home on visits from university, a group of four or five older men would assemble to talk to him. In the evenings, he would make his way to one of their homes to 'have tea', and they would drill him on politics.

'Sidi!' Sabri said, in dismay, turning his grandfather's glasses over in his hand.

'What?' Jiryis frowned. 'They're not good? They cost me a fortune, you know! I'll go back and raise hell with him—'

'You need to clean them!'

'What?'

'Wash them!'

'Won't it destroy them?' the old man blinked.

'Grandma!' Sabri called out. 'Bring me some soapy water!'

Minutes later, his grandfather put his glasses back on and looked about him in awe. 'Bless you! Oh, what a hard time I was having!'

'You do this whenever they get dirty ...' Sabri laughed. 'I can't believe you didn't wash them all this time!'

'Your father giving you any trouble?' his grandfather asked, happy with his new-found vision.

'No,' Sabri grinned.

'Good. He was moaning the other day, going on about the goats and wanting you to be back and help him, and I said to him: "One word to that boy and you'll have me to reckon with!"'

'Sitti, are you still writing against the state?' Rahjeh asked, anxiously.

'Of course!'

She looked horrified. 'Stick to your work, son! We don't need trouble!'

Jiryis waved her away as he drew a puff on his pipe. When Sabri was younger, he had been charged with cleaning this, as well.

His grandfather's eyes clouded over in reminiscence. 'First, it was the Turks ...' he said. 'Then, the *engleez*.* And now we have these people. No one knows where it will end.' He looked at his grandson. 'Years ago, when the Turks were still here, it was their last battle, and they came and rounded up all the young men and took us to al-Arish, in Sinai, to fight. Yousef Shammas, my sister Nijmeh's husband, he was with me. When we got there, I was at my wits' end. I told him we would die a meaningless death, fighting the Turks' war!'

Sabri nodded. He knew the story, but it was his grandfather's favorite.

'I told him: "Let's escape!" He was too scared! He kept telling me: "No, they'll catch you and kill you!" But I kept nagging till he drew up a plan. You know what I did, sidi?'

He paused, savoring the climax. Sabri smiled.

'Shammas, he was a smart one. He pointed to the telegraph poles in the distance. They had begun to put them up. He said: "If you keep following those north, they'll take you all the way back to Acre." I tried to get him to come with me, but he was too scared. But I did it!'

Jiryis had managed to escape the camp and he walked for three weeks, keeping the poles in the distance to check his direction. He would hide and sleep in the day, when the Turkish soldiers were about, then walk by moonlight. He stopped at random houses to ask for food and kept going before anyone had a chance to tell on him, until he made it back to the village.

'And then,' Rahjeh said, 'he couldn't come home. They would come after him. He hid in a cave, and I took him food or sent it with

---

* *Engleez* (Arabic): the English or British people.

someone. But a few weeks later, they came to the house. Oh, I got a beating ...' she winced.

The Turkish soldiers had charged in and asked her about him. When she had feigned ignorance, they had thrown her on the floor, tied her legs to a pole, and given her a lashing. Poor Rahjeh's screams had brought the neighbors running to help. The soldiers had gone away, and Jiryis had waited for weeks before he had come home. His brother-in-law had returned a year later, as the Ottoman Empire collapsed. 'They always leave, sidi ...' Jiryis finished, with a deep puff on his pipe.

This time, Sabri was not so sure.

XII

The next day, he took the bus to Herzl Street in the Hadar, a busy commercial area of Haifa. There were many law firms along the road, and he walked into the first one. They had no openings. The second also turned him down. At the third, he saw a sign: 'Dr. Theodore Werzl'. Sabri asked to see him and introduced himself.

The man looked at him closely. 'What's your name, again?'

Sabri told him.

'You're an Arab?' the lawyer enquired.

'Yes.'

Werzl paused. Then he said: 'See that guy over there?' He pointed to another young man, sitting at a desk. 'He's an intern and he'll finish in three weeks. You can come in his place.'

Elias bought an apartment in Haifa for his children to live in. Na'ima and Geris came to live with Sabri and go to high school.

A few weeks into Sabri's training, Dr. Werzl received a visit from two men while his young charge was out of the office. 'Do you know who your intern is?' one of them questioned the lawyer.

'What about him?' he asked.

'He's involved in politics, printing newspapers, incitement ... How can you take him on?'

Dr. Werzl was a Holocaust survivor who had lost his wife to the tragedy. He looked at them for a long moment before replying: 'The Nazis used to ask us the same questions in Europe!'

His visitors got up and left. He did not share this story with Sabri until the end of his training, two years later.

XIII

Coming into wider contact with Israeli society, Sabri saw the extent of the news blackout on the situation facing his people. Externally, they were cut off from the Arab countries and heard accusations that they had become 'Judaized' and been co-opted into the Zionist project. Internally, all they endured was unknown to Jews in the state.

Sabri could not do much about the first, but he wanted to make a dent in the second. He began to expand on his Master's thesis in a book, *The Arabs in Israel*, in Hebrew. As he would later explain in an interview, the thesis, in particular, tackled military rule, which

> ... interferes with the life of the Arab citizen from birth till death, and is the ultimate decision-maker in all issues of laborers, farmers, professionals, merchants, intellectuals, on all affairs of education and social services; the registration of births, deaths and marriage; in matters of land; in the appointment and dismissal of teachers and public servants; arbitrarily, also, in political parties, social and political functions and affairs of local and municipal councils.[17]

Al-Ard was making contact with a number of Jewish circles. One was the Semitic Action Group, led by Uri Avnery, editor of the Israeli weekly *ha-Olam ha-Zeh*, who became a friend to the movement. Another was Mordechai Stein, a leftist lawyer known for his defense of Arab rights and for fighting Zionist policy. Stein formed a small political organization, The Third Force, which published *The Democratic Newspaper*.

Al-Ard had formed many cultural and sports clubs in Palestinian villages, mostly in the Triangle. But its application for a newspaper license had still not been answered. The group had applied with Saleh's name as editor. Stein offered to help. He would publish al-Ard's material through his newspaper and would not interfere in its content, nor put any political conditions on the group. Al-Ard was in discussion to take up his offer for a few months, until Sabri turned 25 and could apply for a license in his name, if Saleh's name was rejected. But the authorities threatened to close down *The Democratic Newspaper*.[18]

The contacts with influential Jewish figures helped garner opposition to military rule, and another demonstration was held on 19 February 1963, in Jerusalem. Prime Minister David Ben-Gurion retorted in a speech in the Knesset, determined to keep the military government:

> There are in this country two organizations which resent Israel, one called 'the Front' … a communist organization in disguise, and the other a nationalist group called 'al-Ard', both of which periodically distribute poisonous propaganda in the form of leaflets and pamphlets.[19]

He pointed to the alleviations that the government had made in the system of military rule. But these had, in fact, made things worse. Blacklists were drawn up of Palestinians who were deemed 'security risks', and they were forbidden to leave their towns or villages, day or night, without movement permits—when they had previously been allowed out in the day without any restrictions. Although the military government had relaxed some of the repressive measures imposed on the general population, it had devised a harsher system to target those individuals. Anyone who expressed dissent was put on this list.

Shortly afterwards, Sabri was placed under house arrest for the first time. The order was issued by the northern military commander, and its terms were:

> Not to reside outside the municipal limits of Haifa
>
> Not to change his place of residence in Haifa without police permission
>
> Not to leave the Haifa area without police permission
>
> To report to police headquarters at 3:45 every afternoon
>
> To return home no later than one hour after sunset and remain there until sunrise the next day.[20]

In the evenings, a policeman could arrive at any time, without warning, to check that he was home.

These administrative rulings, issued under the Defence (Emergency) Regulations still in effect, did not require justification nor

court approval, could not be appealed, and could be renewed indefinitely. Sabri found himself a prisoner in the city and, at night, in his
home. For his legal training, if he had to attend any court sessions
outside Haifa, he needed police approval. His friends were given
similar orders.

As he sat in his apartment, night after night, important developments were taking place in the Arab world. Fatah, the fledgling
resistance movement, had begun to establish bases in Algeria the
year before. Syria had shown support and Fatah had moved to
Damascus, where it began to organize, recruit fighters, and obtain
money and arms. By 1963, it had developed a commando-type
structure and formed its military wing, al-Asifa, which expanded to
hundreds of cells on the borders of Israel, in the West Bank and
Gaza, and in the refugee camps of Syria and Lebanon.

Palestinians outside Israel needed an independent leadership.
Though many were still committed to pan-Arabism and to Nasser,
they accused him of not doing enough for the Palestinian cause.
Nasser's creation of the Palestine Liberation Organization (PLO)
came in response. In January 1964, under his auspices, the Arab
League met in Cairo and called for a Palestinian body that would
express its people's demands. In May, about 400 Palestinian national
figures gathered in Jerusalem for the first meeting of the Palestinian
National Council (PNC). They announced the formation of the PLO
to represent Palestinians in exile and drew up its national charter,
calling for Palestine to be liberated through armed struggle, under
the banner of pan-Arabism. Ahmad al-Shuqairi was appointed the
first PLO chairman. In September, the Arab League met again and
established the Palestine Liberation Army (PLA), to be funded,
together with the PLO, by the Arab countries.

These developments would soon come to impact Sabri's life, and
that of his brother, Geris.

XIV

After months of waiting and back-and-forth correspondence, al-Ard
finally received an answer from the Haifa district commissioner,
who did not grant a license for the company to publish a newspaper
because the proposed editor, Saleh, did not fulfill a requirement of

the Israeli Press Ordinance of having a secondary school certificate. Al-Ard reapplied, giving Sabri's name as editor. When the commissioner saw that there was no further reason for refusal, he cited the Defence (Emergency) Regulations, which allowed him 'in his discretion and without assigning any reason therefore' to grant or refuse any permit.[21] Al-Ard appealed to the Supreme Court, but the court upheld the absolute powers of the district commissioner.[22] Without its newspaper, al-Ard could not reach people and its work was crippled.

The group decided to expose the situation on the international stage. In June 1964, they wrote a seventeen-page memorandum describing the plight of Palestinians under military rule and a list of discriminatory practices against them in all public sectors. They cited al-Ard's battle for legal means to publish its newspaper. The letter demanded equality for all citizens, the respect of basic freedoms, and the end of discrimination. It also called for Israel to recognize the 1947 United Nations Partition Plan and to allow the establishment of a Palestinian state.

It was one thing to write the letter, quite another to send it. Everyone knew that the Israeli postal service opened and censored letters at random. Sabri made forty copies and put them in different-looking envelopes. He gave them to his friends to post from various places in the country to increase the chance of a few, at least, making it. A copy of the letter was sent to all foreign embassies in Israel, members of the Knesset, the prime minister, and Israeli institutions, as well as to international newspapers and dignitaries abroad.[23]

At the same time, al-Ard decided on a different route: to register itself as a political party in order to work openly and express its demands. On 30 June 1964, the group met and drafted its by-laws,[24] which were signed by twenty-two founding members. They included:

Raising the levels of education, science, health and economy of the Arabs in Israel, as well as their political status

Seeking and achieving a true and just social equality among all social strata in Israel

Finding a just solution for the Palestine question, as a whole and indivisible unit, in accordance with the wishes of the Palestinian Arab people; a solution which meets its interests and desires, restores it to its political existence, ensures its full legal rights, and regards it as the first possessor of the right to determine its own fate, within the framework of the supreme aspirations of the Arab nation

Achieving recognition of the United Nations decision of 29 November 1947, which would provide a solution for the Palestinian problem, a just solution which would maintain the rights of both Israeli Jewish and Palestinian Arab peoples and would strengthen the stability and peace of the area

Support of liberation, unity and socialism in the Arab world by all legal means, recognizing the Arab national liberation movement as a decisive force in the Arab world, which Israel should regard positively

Acting for peace in the Middle East and in the world in general

Support of all progressive forces throughout the world, opposition to imperialism and support of all peoples who are trying to free themselves from its yoke.

Al-Ard stressed the need to establish a Palestinian Arab state:

It is true that the Arabs in Israel are not a nation, but they form part of a great nation. The Arabs of this country were and still are part of the Palestinian Arab people, who are indivisibly part of the Arab world … Their right to establish a Palestinian Arab state has been forcibly taken from them. If the Jews have a right to an independent state, the people of Palestine also have a right to an independent state.[25]

Sabri printed a copy of the by-laws and submitted it to the Haifa district commissioner for registration as a non-profit association, the legal entity for a political party. Two days later, the commissioner replied that al-Ard 'had been formed with the intent of violating the security and the very existence of the State of Israel' and that the registration was denied, based on the Defence (Emergency) Regulations in effect.[26]

Within weeks, the Algerian representative to the United Nations received a copy of al-Ard's letter and shared it with the members of the UN's General Assembly, including the Israeli representative. Some Arab representatives reacted to the report with great bafflement, as though they had just discovered that there were Palestinians in Israel. The Arab world's attention was on the refugees strewn across it; it was blind to those who had remained in their country, a situation that would persist for decades.

In Israel, the backlash came. The media reported the incident and launched another incitement campaign against al-Ard. They began to receive anonymous threats. The government spokesman announced that the Knesset had discussed al-Ard in its latest session, taking note of the district commissioner's decision, and that most of the ministers considered the formation of such a political party to be a 'grave danger' to the state. Levi Eshkol, prime minister and defense minister, consulted with his advisor on Arab affairs and with the security service on how to stop the group.[27] Israeli radio broadcast the news in its Arabic and Hebrew segments.

Al-Ard submitted another appeal to the Supreme Court against the denial of its registration as a non-profit association. In a long ruling, the court stated that the article of al-Ard's by-laws about the Palestinian people was 'an absolute and utter condemnation of the existence of the State of Israel',[28] and that the article on 'liberation, unity and socialism' in the Arab world supported 'the hostile attitudes [of the Arab world] toward Israel and the elimination of Israel by force'.[29] The court upheld the district commissioner's decision. Sabri, Saleh, Mansour, and Habib were again arrested, released, and placed under house arrest for three months. For the second time, the police raided their homes, though, on both occasions, they found nothing at Sabri's apartment. He was careful to keep all his sensitive documents hidden elsewhere. At Mansour's home, the police confiscated all his materials; even the text of the memorandum to the United Nations was seized and no copies were left. Prime Minister Levi Eshkol then used his powers under the Defence (Emergency) Regulations to declare al-Ard an illegal association. Shmuel Toledano, his advisor on Arab affairs, described the movement as a 'threat to the very existence of the state'. He added that the notion of 'Israeli Arabs' was a contradiction in terms because they belonged to 'another nationality'.

With this declaration, the al-Ard Company was terminated and all its assets were frozen. The movement's activities were banned, with the threat of ten years in prison for anyone who tried to continue. Saleh Baransi made their final statement.

We have worked ... side by side with other progressive and democratic forces in order to win for the Arabs their rights and equality.
We still feel that the world must hear the voice of our masses ...
crying out against oppression, discrimination, military rule, land
robbery, and demolition of houses, when we do nothing to impose
on the rights of others to live in peace.[30]

Their house arrest was extended for three months, then for
another six, bringing it to a year. Many al-Ard members and supporters were also placed under house arrest and had their movement permits denied.

XV

'Now what?' Geris, Sabri's brother, put the question to him at their
home in Haifa.

Sabri shook his head. 'We'll continue. We'll find a way.'

'You tried to print a paper; they closed you down. You registered a company; they didn't let you continue. You sent this letter
and they put you in prison! Is working the system getting you
anywhere?'

Sabri rolled his cigarette between his fingers, a habit he had when
he was thinking, before lighting it.

'The police come from Tarshiha and they close the village!'
Geris continued. 'People are afraid, no one goes out. Father was
out with the goats and he came near a piece of a land they called a
military zone. Every hundred yards they have a military zone. The
goatherds, they didn't know; the police came after them and they
were scared. They ran away, and so did the goats! The police
seized the goats!'

'I know ...' Sabri nodded. At seventeen, Geris was too young to
know the story of the villagers, including Elias, who had been tied
to the police car and dragged behind it—an incident that still
plagued his brother.

'They've stolen all the land! People are afraid to say anything.
When someone does something, they punish the whole village.
You, how many times have you been arrested?' Geris had worked
himself into a fury. 'You've just got out!'

Sabri looked down for a long moment. He still hoped there would be a legitimate way. 'Maybe we could go to the elections, get into the Knesset and change things from there,' he said.

'Really?' Geris scoffed. Unknown to Sabri, his younger brother and two of his classmates, Mousa Assi and George Matar, were seeking their own solutions. Mousa was from Fassouta. George's family had come from nearby Mansura, whose people were expelled in 1948. The three boys attended the Arab Orthodox College in Haifa, a private school where the secret service and the Ministry of Education could not interfere in staffing decisions. Some of the best Palestinian teachers were hired by the school, especially those who had been dismissed or hassled by the Ministry of Education for their nationalist stances. They spoke to their students about the situation in the country. The school prepared students for the Israeli matriculation exam but also used books from the Arab world to teach them the language and history, which were barely covered, if at all, in the Israeli curriculum. There were Arabic books on politics in the library, which Geris pored over. He pieced together more from the newspapers and radio, and was greatly affected by Sabri and their discussions. But he had not told his brother of his plan. Geris and his small group had begun to make contact with the Syrians, who were smuggling groups of fedayeen to Israel to carry out resistance.

On 1 January 1965, Fatah launched its military operations inside Israel. One of its men, Ahmad Mousa, was killed after trying to blow up a water-pump installation in Eilaboun, a Palestinian village in the Galilee. The pipeline was used by Israel to divert the course of the Jordan River towards Tiberias. Mousa was shot by Jordanian troops as he escaped to that country after the mission. King Hussein had given orders to clamp down on Palestinian guerrillas in order to reduce his country's tensions with Israel. But Fatah's operations continued, with most of its raids carried out from Jordan.

Geris and his friends began to ask, cautiously, how they could make contact with the organization.

4

EVERY PATH CLOSED

We view them like donkeys. They don't care. They accept it with love ...
To loosen the reins on the Arabs would be a great danger.

David Ben-Gurion
Israeli prime minister[1]

In February 1965, Sabri received his lawyer's license and found work with Hanna Naqqara, one of only two Palestinian lawyers who had remained in Israel after the Nakba. The other was Elias Kusa, who had retired.

Naqqara had begun to practice law in 1934 and was active in the 1936 revolt against the British. In 1946, he had joined the Arab Fund branch in Haifa, established to protect Palestinian land from Zionist confiscation. He was one of the founders of the League for National Liberation, a communist group that came together with Jewish communists in 1948 to form the Israeli Communist Party. After the Nakba, he was not allowed to return to Haifa. He went to Lebanon, from where he tried to return but was arrested and imprisoned in Israel until 1951.

In 1953, he opened a joint practice with Menachem Waxman, a Jewish communist lawyer. For twenty years, they specialized in defending Palestinians in land disputes with the state.[2] More than half of Palestinian land disputes were dealt with by their office.

Naqqara believed in joint Arab–Jewish work for justice. He was one of the initiators of the Arab-Jewish Conference in 1954 and 1956, demanding equality and citizenship rights for Palestinians and the end of military rule and land seizure.

When Sabri met him, the veteran lawyer was in his mid-fifties, a deep, calm thinker, courteous and given to logic and reason. He also had a sense of humor and a keen interest in literature, despite his sharp tongue and the battles he fought. Naqqara worked with a deep conviction, driven by a mission. He was generous and kind, and often reduced his fees or forfeited them for his poorer clients. He became known as the 'lawyer of the people' and the 'land lawyer', and he played an almost historic role in defending the rights of the Palestinians in Israel. Peasants whose lands had been seized flocked to his office. Some of the cases he battled through became part of Israeli basic law. Naqqara also fought for citizenship and family reunification. Sabri saw him as 'open-eyed in a country of the blind'.

In the early 1960s, the judicial struggle over land in the Galilee was at its peak. The government had finished the largest seizure of Palestinian land and needed to settle the issue of ownership rights to this land, much of which was not registered. The authorities continued devising measures to pressure owners to sell and used additional random laws to achieve their end. They based ownership rights on landscaping maps drawn in 1943, under the British Mandate. Land that had been cultivated since then was viewed in court as it had been twenty or thirty years before. Large plots of land that were not flat and workable for agriculture were not considered as one unit; the state divided them and seized some of them, chipping away at the land from inside and paving the way for further seizure through consolidation schemes. Large swathes of land were also seized based on the Defence (Emergency) Regulations.

Sabri worked with Naqqara on these cases, many of which reached the Supreme Court. But the court facilitated the seizure of land by entrenching laws that expanded the definition of state land and limited people's ability to claim title.[3] By April 1965, when Sabri finished his research for his book, *The Arabs in Israel*, the state had seized about two million dunums from Palestinians in the seventeen years of its existence. In an article he later wrote for the *Journal of Palestine Studies*, he explained the pretext by which the state justified this theft:

> When an [Arab] peasant said to an official of the Israel Lands Administration: 'How can you deny my ownership? This land is my property, I inherited it from my fathers and grandfathers, and I have a title-deed to it,' the official answered: 'We have a more important title-deed. We have a title-deed from Dan [in the north of Israel] to Eilat [in the south].'[4]

Naqqara also fought for the rights of Palestinian workers. Those were the first cases that Sabri handled, of laborers who were fired or harassed due to their political views or because they had not cooperated with the military government. At times, the authorities pressured the defendants to retract the power of attorney they had given Sabri, promising them a deal if they did. He urged his clients not to succumb and lose their rights. Occasionally, when the defendants were unable to pay the court fees, he paid them himself.

Naqqara also helped Palestinian prisoners. In the five years that he worked with him, Sabri visited every court and prison in the country. Each time, he needed a permit. He spent long periods of time under house arrest, which meant he could work during the day, but was only permitted to move around within the municipality of Haifa, where he lived. To leave the city, he had to request police permission two or three days before. In his university years, his movement permits had been issued annually. Now, they were only valid for a day or a week. He had to work, and things came up where he did not have time to chase after permits. He often traveled without them.

Many others were in the same boat. The poets, Mahmoud Darwish and Samih al-Qasim, also endured constant harassment. When they asked for help, Naqqara waved them to Sabri: 'They're your friends. You handle this!'

It was a depressing struggle, with few moments of relief. The three friends were all under house arrest for months on end, as well as the poets Tawfiq Zayyad, Rashid Hussein, and many other activists. Like Sabri, they often broke their confines and went out in violation of the orders, as life became suffocating. Alongside Mohammed Mi'ari, his friend and classmate, and a few others, they made up Sabri's small circle. They had very clear views and no other friends or communities. Those who did not want to get into politics or who wanted to walk a safe path did not go near them.

Most of their talk was on politics and culture. They identified with their wider Arab nation and followed its developments eagerly, but the news blackout by Israel kept them completely isolated. Very little information leaked out about them; the only means was through radio and by sending local Arabic newspapers in the post via some third country, which would take weeks. Once or twice a year, Sabri and his friends would hear that a newspaper, somewhere in the Arab world, had published an item about a demonstration in Haifa or Acre. The daily struggle they undertook, the dozens of nationalist Palestinians working in Israel, were all but invisible.

The little group would go to Iskandar or al-Umam restaurants in Haifa or to coffee shops on Jaffa Street, but they would not sit in one place all the time. They were under surveillance and were frequently called for interrogation. When they met, they would simply walk in any direction, find a place and sit down. Despite this, they were vulnerable to arrest, and if there was a planned demonstration or protest meeting, the authorities would forbid them from taking part.

At Easter 1965, Sabri was under house arrest in Haifa. He did not feel very festive, cooped up in the house alone. His mother called to tell him she was making kubbeh, the meat and bulgur pâté, his favorite. 'Can you come?'

Breaking his arrest, he got on a bus and was in Fassouta two hours later. His mother and sisters, buzzing with happiness, set the table. 'Do we have arak?' he asked.

Elias nodded, hastening to get a bottle from the wooden chest. 'How are you, son?'

'Could be better ...' Sabri sighed. 'They're on my case, won't leave me alone.'

'Well, there's a saying for everything ...' Elias said, quietly.

Sabri knew a jab was coming. 'What's that?' he smiled.

'Well ...' Elias cleared his throat. '"Turn your backside to the wasps, then call it fate!"'

His children burst out laughing as he added: 'It's not like you've left them alone, is it?'

'When they leave us alone, first ...' Sabri retorted, as Wardeh carried the big bowl of kubbeh to the table. It was followed by a piping hot saucepan of hoseh: a mix of onions and minced goat meat, cooked in olive oil and flavored with spices. Sabri speared a ball of kubbeh with his fork, spread it on his plate, and reached over for a large spoon of hoseh. The smell was heavenly. His mother handed him thin, freshly baked bread to scoop it up with. 'Cheers!' his father raised his glass.

A knock came at the door.

'Open it, Na'ima,' Wardeh said. 'Whoever it is, they're in luck!'

But two policemen stood there. 'Is Sabri here?'

Wardeh sprang up like she had been stung. 'He just came in! Let him eat! It's Easter; this is our holiday!'

'You've broken your house arrest. Come with us,' one of them said to him, ignoring her.

Wardeh opened her mouth again, but Sabri raised his hand. 'It's alright, Mother!'

He got up and walked out with them as the family sat, tears in their eyes, staring at the food.

1. Sabri at Terra Sancta College, Nazareth, in 2012, where he attended high school from 1953–7.

TERRA SANCTA COLLEGE-NAZARETH.........CLASS OF 1957

Front Row-L to R: Hanna Khoury, Rudolfo Palazzollo, Edmon Tabry, Hatem Khoury, Husein Heleihel, and Johnny Thomas.

2nd Row: Joseph Srouji, Raouf Abou Hatoum, Ziad Deeb, Sabri Giries, Pendelis Elios, Ismil Abunassar, Elie Shomar and Sammy Boushnaq

3rd Row: Jiries Hanhoul, Jiries Mazzawi, Aref Nashel, Kamel Badran, Maroun Zaher, Elie Nakhleh, Dimitri Gitanapolous, Shomar Shomar, and Anis Shakkour

WHAT HAS BECOME OF US??........ LET'S HEAR FROM EACH OF YOU....!! God Bless...

2. Sabri in the second row, fourth from the left, with his classmates during their graduation from Terra Santa College, Nazareth, 1957.

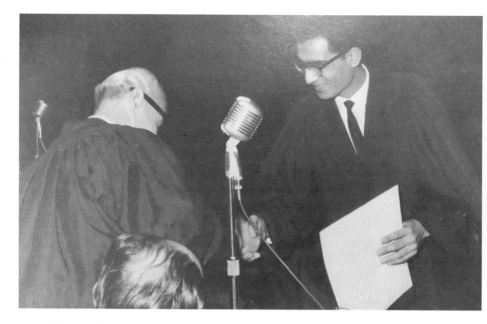

3. Sabri graduates in law from the Hebrew University, Jerusalem, June 1962.

4. Sabri and Hanneh, married in April 1968, Fassouta.

5. Hanneh with five-month-old Fida in Beirut, November 1973.

6. Hanneh with Fida in Beirut, 1975.

7. Sabri and Hanneh share a happy moment in Beirut, 1975.

8. Sabri and Hanneh at a friend's home in Beirut, 1979.

9. Sabri at home in Beirut, 1975.

10. Sabri and Geris on a summer night in Beirut, 1980.

11. Sabri and Hanneh with Fida and Mousa at home in Beirut, 1980.

12. Hanneh with Fida and Mousa in Beirut, 1980.

13. Fida with her uncle, Geris, at home in Corniche el-Mazra'a, Beirut, 1981.

14. Fida with the cat, Kojak, at home in Corniche el-Mazra'a, Beirut, 1981.

15. Sabri and Najwa, married in October 1983, Nicosia, Cyprus.

16. Fida and Mousa with Najwa in Cyprus, 1983.

17. Home in Strovolos, Nicosia, Cyprus, 1985–95.

18. Najwa in the garden at home in Strovolos, Nicosia, Cyprus, 1993.

19. Fida wearing thobe, traditional Palestinian dress, for a dabke dance at school in Nicosia, Cyprus, 1987.

II

Resistance was growing from beyond the borders. An increasing number of raids were carried out by Fatah, whose fedayeen sneaked in from Jordan through the West Bank. For months, Geris and his friends, Mousa and George, had been searching for a way to help them. In a risky move, the three boys decided to cross into South Lebanon, the closest option for them, to try and forge a link with the resistance. George's grandfather was the mukhtar of Rmeish, a nearby Lebanese village. They would go to him and ask for help.

On a hot night in mid-August, they slipped across the border via a circuitous route through the forest. George's grandfather was terrified when they told him what they wanted. 'I can't call anyone for you! The only way would be through the central operator, and the agents would listen in!' The boys asked him for money to go to Beirut and try to link up with the resistance there. 'There are roadblocks on the way!' he told them. 'If they find you, they have to hand you back to Israel! Go home!'

They argued with him, insisting that he give them a chance. But, by morning, the old man had sent them back. In Haifa, they found a pilgrim who was going to East Jerusalem and sent a message with him, to deliver to a contact he knew in Fatah. They said they were a group in Israel who wanted to engage in armed struggle and told the recipient how to reach them. But there was no response. It was hardly surprising, Geris told them. 'The first thing anyone would think is it's a set-up!'

In September, they went back to school. Geris did not tell Sabri about his escapade. But he knew that his brother was involved in secret work. They had many visitors, and, in those meetings, Sabri always kept his siblings away. Geris ached to get involved.

'How are we going to make coffee for all these people?' their younger sister, Na'ima, fretted one day, when every corner in the house seemed full.

'In a pan. Come with me.' Najibeh, her older sister, pulled her by the arm. The group was the largest to assemble in the house. Some had to sit on the floor. Others had brought little gifts of eggs or melons. Sabri closed the door, shooed his sisters away and told them to make coffee.

Najibeh was studying nursing in Nazareth, and she would come to Haifa on weekends to see her sister and brothers. Sabri did not share much with them, but they knew about al-Ard. Sometimes, he took Najibeh with him to see his friend, Mansour Kardosh, and his family in Nazareth.

'You can go to the celebrations, if you want,' he now told her, as she handed him the coffee for his guests. *To the Independence Day procession!* she thought, shocked at his suggestion. But she knew he was sending them out to protect them, did not want them to be involved in his work. They left shortly afterwards to give him privacy. But Najibeh was worried.

When they returned, everyone had gone, and he was smoking, quietly. She sat next to him. 'I didn't have a chance to tell you, something happened at the hospital ...' she began.

'What?'

'I did well in the exams, I'm sure I did, but they told me I didn't do well enough, and I have to repeat the year! I don't know what to do.' There was no way she had failed her first year, of that she was certain.

Sabri took a drag on his cigarette. 'It's probably to do with me, sister ...'

She looked at him in alarm.

'Just another way to hassle ...' he continued. 'But don't let it stop you. Go on.'

'Repeat the whole year?' she muttered, close to tears.

'Repeat it. You'll graduate a year later. Don't let them stop you!'

His words stayed with her as she drifted off to sleep. But she was woken in the middle of the night by a sound of shuffling footsteps. A few minutes later, she heard the apartment door open and close, quietly. She jumped out of bed, wide awake, and slipped out to the living room. A quick glance into his room confirmed that Sabri had gone. Probably to see Mansour, she thought. When Sabri was under house arrest and had to make these trips, he sneaked out in the night and came back before daybreak, before anyone saw him. Najibeh wrapped her shawl tighter around herself and sat on the couch, waiting.

III

Hanneh's young sisters put her clothes on and pranced around as she laughed. They loved it when she came home. She looked so worldly and beautiful, and they clamored to try on her skirts and dresses, far too big for them.

'Mother, I want to enroll for university in Jerusalem,' Hanneh said.

'What?' Um Nour blurted.

Hanneh turned to her uncle Naseef for support. He nodded to his sister. 'She'll make you proud!'

Um Nour stared. Only a handful of students from the village were at university, and none were girls.

Nida was clicking around in Hanneh's high heels and laughing when her mother snapped: 'Take those off and go heat the water for coffee!'

She turned back to Naseef. 'You're taking her away from me!' Hanneh had been away for five years. After finishing Grade 10 at Mghar, where her uncle Ibrahim taught, he had enrolled her for the last two grades at St. Joseph's School in Nazareth, where she had lived with the Salesian Sisters. Then she had returned to Mghar and worked for a year as a teaching assistant with him, to save some money. She was only coming home on holidays, blossoming into a young woman whom her mother barely knew.

Um Nour's heart ached on those visits. All the neighbors would come to see Hanneh, each bringing her a little something. That morning, their neighbor, Deeb, had come with a big basket of apples from the trees abandoned in Deir el-Qasi. Hanneh had been asleep, so he had tiptoed into the room and put the basket near her head. She loved the neighbors and made time to visit each of them when she was home, even if only for a few minutes. Her mother wanted her all to herself in the precious little time she was around.

And now, her daughter was going even further. 'When will she come home?' Um Nour asked, her voice catching.

But Naseef was stern. 'Whenever she can. She'll live next to me. I'm studying there and her room will be close to mine. You have nothing to worry about!'

Nour and Ibrahim, Hanneh's brothers, were studying carpentry in Nazareth and working with their uncle during their breaks. They travelled the country, joining hundreds of Palestinian laborers toiling to build houses, factories, and roads in the new state. In Tel Aviv, thousands slept in the stores and warehouses where they worked, or in shacks outside the city with no electricity or running water. In Jaffa, they lived in run-down homes in the Ajami neighborhood, where twenty or more people shared a room. They were frequently hassled by the police, and many began to use drugs. Um Nour saw her sons' exhaustion when they came home, and she was full of sorrow.

Hanneh would carve out a good future for herself, her mother thought. She was torn, proud of her daughter, yet missing her, painfully.

Naseef broke the silence. 'Tell you what! We'll take you to visit so you can see. How about that?'

Um Nour had never been to Jerusalem. They took her to the dormitories of the Hebrew University so she could inspect where her daughter would live. After that, she was at ease, and Hanneh was glowing when they came home.

Sarah, Um Nour's younger sister, was getting married that week. Hanneh was close to her aunt, and was overjoyed. On the wedding day, she changed her dress and hairstyle three times, dancing happily around the bride.

Someone took notice. Leaning across to Naseef, who had invited him, Sabri asked: 'Is this Hanneh?' He had not seen her in four years, since Naseef had asked him to take her on the tour of the university.

'Yes. She's starting university in September!' his friend smiled, pouring him a glass of arak. 'How are you?'

'I'm well. We're running in the next Knesset elections.'

'What?' Naseef put down the glass.

'Al-Ard. We're registering as the "Socialist List".'

'Are you serious?' Naseef blinked. 'But ... didn't they outlaw you?'

'They did, but that doesn't mean we can't run in the elections. We have nothing to lose. We can't work politically any other way.'

The sixth elections for the Knesset were set for November 1965, three months away. Naseef could not imagine that an Arab list would be allowed to take part. 'How do you plan to do this?'

'We're collecting signatures from voters. We need 750 to qualify.' In the long months of house arrest, the idea had crystallized in
the minds of the al-Ard group. If they could gain a seat and the
immunity of political office, it would be a breakthrough and they
could continue their work. They would set up offices in all Palestinian
localities and print their newspaper. In the Knesset, they could campaign for Palestinian rights and build opposition to racist laws.

'But ... will they let you do it?' Naseef asked, again.

'We're taking part in democratic elections.'

'But weren't you boycotting them so far?'

'So far, yes. But we're in a corner. They won't let us work any
other way. We've done everything. A company, a printing press,
an NGO ... They keep closing us down.'

Naseef nodded. Suddenly, they looked up to see Hanneh, dancing with a cousin. 'She's happy,' her uncle smiled, as Sabri gazed
at her.

Jubran Shammas, a close friend of Sabri's, was related to Hanneh,
and he became the trusted party for the little secret. 'Can you find
out more about her?' Sabri asked him, later.

'Sure,' Jubran chuckled. 'Should be easy enough. Thinking of
tying the knot, I see?'

'It's been four months since I started work. And I'm under thirty
and single, so I'm in the highest tax bracket.'

'Oh! So you want to do this to lower your taxes?'

They laughed. In village tradition, one's closest friend was sometimes referred to as his best man, and Jubran was Sabri's. He set to
work immediately and asked Fahoum, one of Um Nour's sisters. It
did not take much for her to put two and two together. Jubran came
back with two strange pieces of information: Sabri's object of affec-
tion liked to buy shoes, and, in clothes, she preferred the color blue.
'That, I can handle,' Sabri grinned.

Meanwhile, Fahoum was quick to tell Hanneh. Jubran paid a
seemingly innocuous visit to Um Nour's house to ask about the
family. During the conversation, he casually slipped in that his
friend was looking for a bride.

'We want to marry him off,' he said to Um Nour. 'I found two
or three girls and told him about them, but he hasn't given me an
answer.'

Hanneh blushed as her mother nodded, oblivious to the little scheme.

IV

By September 1965, al-Ard had collected 2,000 signatures for its list, well above the number needed to register. The electoral list included Saleh Baransi, Habib Qahwaji, Mansour Kardosh, Sabri, and six al-Ard supporters. Sabri had the books of signatures at his apartment in Haifa. He was back under house arrest. On 3 September, he went to the police to prove his presence, as usual, and asked for a permit to travel to Afula two days later, for work. The police told him to come back at 4:00 pm. When he returned, they asked him to wait. Almost two hours passed as the officers came and went, talking to him about many things, as if to pass the time. Finally, one of them handed him an internal expulsion order to Safad for three months. They had clearly been waiting for it to come through.

Sabri was dumbstruck. The order required him to prove his presence at the police station there, three times daily. He was being expelled from Haifa, from his home and work.

The police told him they would pick him up from his apartment two hours later to take him to Safad. In a daze, he went home to pack. He called Ya'acov Yeridor, a Jewish lawyer and friend of al-Ard who had represented the group in their legal cases. Then, he wrote a hasty letter and dispatched it to Mohammed Mi'ari. Mohammed was to keep a copy of the expulsion order that Sabri had attached. He was also to explain to the elections committee that Sabri had signed the nomination form, which the members of every list running in the elections had to do. If that was insufficient to proceed, and if the authorities tried to use Sabri's absence as a pretext for invalidating the list's registration, then Mohammed was to take Sabri's name off the list. 'Also, please check on my brother and sisters in Haifa, and give them money if they need it,' Sabri's letter finished.

The police were at the door. Sabri rushed into his room to pack. Thinking quickly, he stuffed the three books of voter signatures into his bag, underneath his clothes, and went back into the hall. 'I need to make a phone call to work,' he said. They nodded. He called Hanna Naqqara, told him to tell his family about the expulsion, and made his way out with them.

In the car, his mind was whirling. The books had to get to the group, otherwise the signatures would count for nothing and they would not be able to register for the elections on time. A policeman's voice cut into his thoughts. 'See? You're making all this trouble, and look at all the development. Look at this city being built!' He nodded in the direction of Karmiel, the new Jewish town that was springing up.

Shooting him a wry look, Sabri answered: 'Yes, and to do that, you've taken the land of three Arab villages, and to top it off, you won't let them live in your beautiful city when it's finished!'

They drove on in silence. At the station in Safad, they handed him to the officer in charge. He motioned him to sit down as he looked at his papers. 'It says three months,' he grunted. 'You have to find a place to stay.'

'Find a place? I don't know anything in this town!'

'Right,' the policeman sighed. 'Let me make some calls.'

A place was found for the lone Palestinian. 'You'll stay here tonight; the apartment will be ready tomorrow. I'll give you the address.'

Sabri spent the night in the police station. In the morning, he found himself having breakfast with the officers. He was then discharged with instructions not to leave the town without informing them, to be home every sunset and stay until sunrise, and to report to them three times daily—the rules he knew from house arrest. He signed and picked up his bag. 'Here's the address of the apartment,' the officer said.

Outside, on the main road, Sabri stood for a few minutes. When he saw a van of the electricity company approaching, he signaled for a ride. The van slowed down and came to a stop beside him. He squinted up at the driver: 'Haifa?'

'Sure. Jump in.'

V

'I don't have time! Make it quick!' One hour later, an urgent phone call was all he could afford before the police would find out. He

105

managed to deposit his valuable signature books with his friends. Then he heard the news. Mansour Kardosh was expelled from Nazareth to Arad; Saleh Baransi, from Taybeh to Bisan; and Habib Qahwaji, from Haifa to Tiberias. They had all been sent to distant towns with no remaining Palestinians and separated from each other so they could not organize and run in the elections. Other members of al-Ard, including Mohammed Mi'ari, were under house arrest.

Sabri stayed at his apartment in Haifa. Why bother looking for a ride to Safad when the police would come and get him? Barely an hour later, they were there. They took him to a military court, where he was sentenced to prison for twenty days for breaking his expulsion order. After that, he would be sent back to Safad. He tried to get them to change the expulsion to administrative detention in Haifa, because he could not work in Safad and he had to pay rent there. But his plea was rejected.

At Ma'asiyahu Prison in Ramle, the warden looked him over. 'Twenty days?' he grumbled. 'What task will I find for you in just twenty days?'

'You want me to stay longer so you can put me in meaningful employment?' Sabri retorted.

'Fine ...' the warden sighed. 'You see this garden out there? Each morning, you report to me at 8:00 am and you go out and water the plants. You can spend a few hours there, and we'll consider that your task.' He folded the papers, seemingly glad to have the trifling matter off his desk.

Sabri spent his mornings in the sun, thinking and smoking. That week, scores of young men were interrogated for their connection to al-Ard. The authorities claimed to have seized the signature books. They pressured those who had signed or donated to the list and many others who had not, whom they accused of doing so. Agents roamed the streets at night, knocking on doors, asking people to revoke their signatures and making threats. Habib asked his friends to get witnesses and file complaints. Al-Ard issued a memorandum in *al-Ittihad* newspaper and urged people to resist, to refuse to withdraw their signatures, and to stand in solidarity with the four who had been expelled.

Supreme Court Justice Moshe Landau, head of the Central Elections Committee, asked all parties to refrain from any action that violated the integrity of the election laws, and to attempt to convince their electorates, not intimidate them. He had, however, been on the panel that had outlawed al-Ard the year before.[5]

A media onslaught resumed against the group. 'Members of al-Ard temporarily expelled from their homes', wrote an Israeli newspaper, citing the reason as 'renewal of hostile actions towards the state'.[6] Another paper claimed they wanted 'to negate the existence of the State of Israel, from the Knesset podium' and accused the Socialist List of being 'a purely Arab list and a danger to the Arabs of Israel'.[7]

From prison, Sabri wrote to the Israeli Bar Association and asked them to intervene to revoke his expulsion order. He argued that al-Ard's acceptance of the UN Partition Plan and the group's decision to go to the Knesset refuted the claim that they supported the destruction of the State of Israel. They were trying to take part in democratic elections within the state. He wrote to the police and the military commander, asking them the same. If his expulsion were revoked, he hoped it would be for his friends, too.

Habib wrote to Mohammed, urging him to sign the nomination form on all their behalf and present the list to the Central Elections Committee. 'The immediate goal is the registration and confirmation of the list—do whatever it takes to make it happen!' He asked Mohammed to form a new leadership in each area to campaign for the list and find new members. 'If the list is confirmed by the Committee, write a strong statement of our goals and refute the allegations against us. Circulate it widely, to every home if possible. We need to reach each person at least once in our campaign.'

He also asked his friend to create a reserve leadership for al-Ard, a hidden one that could continue if the other leaders were placed under house arrest. 'I know you're tired,' he finished, 'but it's a battle and we must go on. We have plenty of time to rest later!'

On 7 September, Mohammed sent a letter to Sabri in prison. He told him that the lawyer, Ya'acov Yeridor, had submitted the list for confirmation by the Central Elections Committee. Yeridor had visited Mansour, Saleh, and Habib. Habib, expelled to Tiberias, had asked for a swimsuit and fishing hook so he could go to the lake. Sabri smiled. Mohammed also wrote that he had visited Sabri's brothers and sisters. He promised to write again and send him books and newspapers once Sabri had 'settled down' in Safad.

Mohammed was filling in for him at work, as well, and even checking the progress of his book with the state censor. Under the military government, all publications authored by Palestinian citizens had to go through censorship. Books were published with some pages left totally or partially blank and marked with a large 'X', where the censor had not permitted the content. Sabri hoped *The Arabs in Israel* would not suffer too much cutting, but he had his doubts.

He received no answer to any of his appeals. Sitting on the grass during his 'garden duty', he reflected on a statement a Bedouin had made, who had been held with him in administrative detention some months before. When the man had learned of al-Ard's efforts, he had frowned. 'Don't trouble yourself, brother. You won't get anywhere in this state!'

As soon as Sabri finished his twenty-day sentence and was sent back to Safad, the government instructed the Central Elections Committee to disqualify the Socialist List, on the grounds that it was 'an unlawful association, because its promoters deny the [territorial] integrity of the State of Israel and its very existence'.[8] Al-Ard went to the Supreme Court to dispute the decision. The hearing was set for 7 October.

In Safad, Sabri was lonely. Expulsion cut him off from his family and friends and made it impossible to work. Normally, under house arrest, he had to prove his presence at the police station once a day. Now, he was required to do so at 8:00 am, 1:00 pm, and 6:00 pm. From one hour after sunset, he was cooped up in his apartment until morning. In three months, he was never allowed to take a walk in the city at night.

His sisters sent him money and a radio with his friend, Hussein Hlehel. Geris came to visit. There was nothing Sabri could do and very little he could read. He asked his brother for Arabic newspapers and books; some took him no more than a few hours to finish. He received the manuscript of his book from the state censor with much material taken out. Sabri kept the whole text anyway, thinking of ways to publish it later.

In the daytime, he was glad to be out, but he soon became depressed. Safad had been ethnically cleansed of all its Palestinians in 1948. They were in refugee camps in Syria and Lebanon. As he walked the streets, their houses stared at him from every corner, taken over by Jewish immigrants. New constructions had been added to some homes, and they stood out in sharp contrast to the original structures. He found a small coffee shop to while away a few hours and read the papers.

One day, a man sat down on the empty chair at his table. Sabri looked up enquiringly.

'I'll be straight with you,' the uninvited guest said. 'I work with the Shabak,* and I'm the one tasked with keeping an eye on you.'

Sabri's eyebrows shot up. 'Welcome!'

'Am I bothering you?'

'Not at all.' Sabri motioned to the waiter and asked the man what he wanted.

'Coffee ...' he said. As the waiter retreated, the guest leaned forward and continued, quietly: 'They say you're a dangerous man.'

'Do they?'

The agent's face was a mix of curiosity and apprehension. 'You're working against the state, so they said.'

Sabri was glad for the diversion. He launched into a long discussion with him. 'Would you do it differently, if you were in my place?' he finished.

The man shook his head. 'But ... why do they say these things? You're actually a very nice, smart guy!'

'Thank you. Tell that to your superiors!' Sabri laughed.

'There is one matter, though,' the man continued, seemingly back from his reverie. 'I often see you talking from different phone booths. We can't trace your calls from these places. Who are you calling?'

Sabri laughed, again, louder this time. 'Do you think I would tell you?'

The man smiled and got up to leave. He signaled for the bill. 'Absolutely not!' Sabri waved him away. 'This one's on me!'

After his guest left, he folded his newspaper and got up, too. As he walked down a side street, a small bookshop caught his attention. Peering into the glass display, he came face to face with the works of the founding Zionists.

---

* *Shabak* or *Shin Bet* (Hebrew): Israeli General Security Service.

He walked in. The titles were by Theodor Herzl, Leon Pinsker, Moshe Hess, Moshe Lilienblum, Asher Zvi Ginzberg (Ahad Ha'am), Zvi Kalischer, and Max Nordau. Sabri bought one book, read it that evening, and came back the next day. The books were small and focused on the thought behind the movement. They were written before the First Zionist Congress in 1897. On the third day, he asked the shopkeeper: 'Can you sell me everything on this shelf?'

'In that case,' the man replied, 'I'll give you each for 15 cents instead of 20.'

Sabri bought more than twenty books. With nothing else to do, he spent his three months in Safad reading and taking notes. And he thought of Hanneh.

VI

On 7 October 1965, the Supreme Court heard the appeal of the Socialist List against its disqualification. Ya'acov Yeridor, counsel for the list, argued before Justices Shimon Agranat, Yoel Sussman, and Haim Cohn that the Knesset Elections Law did not empower the Central Elections Committee to invalidate lists because of their members' personal affiliations. The committee itself had admitted that it had no right to disqualify individual candidates, yet had disqualified a whole list solely on the basis of its composition, on the grounds that five of its ten candidates were members of the outlawed al-Ard movement. Yeridor then handed the court an affidavit stating that the list had no proposals against the existence or integrity of the State of Israel.

Attorney General Moshe Ben-Ze'ev, who appeared for the Central Elections Committee, reviewed the previous court decisions against al-Ard's attempts to register as an association and publish a newspaper. He quoted from a ruling by Justice Alfred Witkon that it would be 'foolhardiness to give the organization the power which it seeks'.

On 12 October, the Supreme Court upheld, by a 2:1 majority, the committee's ruling. The dissenting justice, Cohn, noted that 'in the material which was in front of the Central Elections Committee, and which was presented to us, too, there was nothing to justify, let alone mandate, the finding that there is a real or clear or present danger' posed to the state or to any of its institutions by the Socialist List.[9] The other judges did not dispute this, but argued that the grave issue placed before them justified diverging from the strict letter of the law, for the sake of 'defensive democracy'. Al-Ard's objection to the Jewish character of the State of Israel was tanta-mount, in their eyes, to objecting to the state's very existence.[10]

Justice Agranat wrote, in his decision: 'This is a realistic matter of a list of candidates aimed at achieving the elimination of the State of Israel.' Justice Sussman likened the proposed list to 'someone who wants to throw a bomb in the Knesset and cannot do so from the runway, so he wants to enter the hall through Knesset member-ship for this purpose'. He added that the state 'does not have to agree to be eliminated and wiped off the map'.[11]

Those statements had come in response to al-Ard's call for the implementation of the 1947 Partition Plan and the establishment of a Palestinian state alongside the State of Israel. It was this point, more than anything else, that eventually drove the authorities to eliminate the movement.

With this, al-Ard had exhausted all avenues in its battle for legiti-macy. In the five years of its troubled existence, its disputes had reached the Supreme Court six times.[12] The movement was con-sumed with trying to break the restrictions on it and to form an independent organization, to obtain some kind of legal standing so it could work openly. In the end, it could not achieve much beyond protest meetings and public lectures, and the clubs that it formed in Palestinian villages. Sabri later wrote: 'One of al-Ard's obvious mistakes was to trust in Israeli justice and democracy; another was to underestimate the Zionist concept of "security" and how widely it could be interpreted when convenient.'[13] For two decades after-wards, no independent Arab party would attempt to field a list of candidates in Knesset elections.

About 150 members or supporters of al-Ard were imprisoned, some under administrative detention, others for long periods on false charges of making contact with armed groups. The damage was far-reaching. Since the movement had the support of most young Palestinians in Israel, especially the intellectuals, the authorities could attack any Palestinian organization by saying it was a front for al-Ard. In this way, they sabotaged other efforts to create cultural clubs among Palestinians, and attempts by students or anyone else to organize.[14] In Kafr Qara, Taybeh, and Tira, some youth had formed sports clubs, mostly to try and find solutions to their problems, as the responsible Israeli departments ignored them. But the authorities viewed those as centers of nationalist gatherings and 'security risks' and put pressure on their members to close them.[15]

The elections were over, so Sabri's expulsion was over, too. On his last day in Safad, he sent a postcard to Mohammed with a picture of the town and Lake Tiberias (the Sea of Galilee) behind it. 'I don't know, of course, how many fish Habib managed to catch,' he wrote. 'You'll have to ask him.' Sabri was to return to Haifa the next day. 'I hope you can visit us in the evening!' he told his friend.

In Haifa, he reported to the police.

'What did you do in Safad all this time?' the officer asked, as he finished his paperwork.

'I read all the work of the early Zionist founders.'

'What?'

'Things I doubt you know,' continued Sabri. 'I had all the time in the world, so I used it to figure out how this mess began.'

The officer stared at him for a few seconds. Then he shook his head. 'If the military commander knew you would do this, he would likely have revoked the expulsion order ...'

5

BROTHERS IN ARMS

We ask for our rights, not charity; for justice, not mercy.

Al-Ard manifesto, 1965

I

In the same period, September 1965, Hanneh made it to the Hebrew University. She was studying economics with a minor in statistics. Palestinian students were still few in number. Due to the difficulties in being accepted onto courses in Israel, hundreds had gone abroad to study, especially in Eastern Europe. Many would not return.[1]

Hanneh was quiet and calm, usually deep in her books. It had taken her a lot to get there, and she was determined to succeed. She was not inclined to political work, though she took part in some student council activities. Her small group of friends were the Palestinian students in the university halls on Shprinsak 3, where she lived. They would go to lectures or to the cafeteria together, making sure she walked in front. 'We want to show them that we're forward and civilized, and that we educate our women!' Ali Rafa, a law student from Deir el-Assad, often said. Hanneh obliged, laughing. There were fewer than ten Palestinian women at the university.

In the spring, Sabri made his decision. He would go to Jerusalem to talk to her. Ignoring the permits, he got on a bus. As if on cue, he walked in through the university gate and suddenly saw her walking past in front of him. 'Oh, hello, ustaz!'* she stopped.

He could not believe his luck. 'Forget this about ustaz—my name's Sabri,' he smiled. 'Where are you going?'

'I was heading to lunch ...'

He was not hungry, but his chance was being handed to him on a plate. 'Great! May I invite you?'

In the cafeteria, she chose a sandwich. 'What are you doing?' he exclaimed. 'Get a proper meal!'

She smiled as he added: 'I'm a lawyer, you know, and I'm working. I can afford it!'

They got their food and sat down. When they began to eat, he cut to the chase. 'I want to ask you something.'

Her face went red.

---

* *Ustaz* (Arabic): Mister; also, teacher.

'Will you marry me?'

She smiled and said yes. His eyes opened in wonder as she added: 'I've known ...'

'You did? I thought it was my secret!'

'All your secrets are known to me ...' she laughed.

It must have been Jubran, he thought. He laughed, too. 'What should we do?' he jumped into the practicalities.

'I'm alone here, the only girl from the village. I don't want people talking. Go to Nazareth and tell my uncle Naseef that you asked me and I said yes. Then we can get engaged.'

II

'You have other suitors ...' Um Nour said. 'Why do you want this one?'

'What's wrong with this one?'

Her mother sighed. 'His work is bothersome, he's in politics and he's in and out of prison! Do you really want this life?' She looked at Naseef, willing him to interject.

Naseef had already had this discussion with his niece. He felt torn. Sabri was his friend, but he knew of the troubles he faced. 'He was expelled for three months last year, spent them in Safad ...' he said to Hanneh. 'Really, my dear, this could be a difficult life for you.'

But her mind was made up. As Hanneh left the room, Naseef said to his sister: 'Let her be ... It's her life. She's strong and educated; she'll take care of herself.'

Some weeks later, Sabri's aunt, Najibeh, lost her husband to kidney failure. He died in Rambam Hospital in Haifa. The elderly couple were childless and had no one to help. Sabri went to the hospital to get the body and take it to Fassouta for burial. He did not have time to get a permit.

In the village, he was shocked to see the police behind him. They followed him to church for the funeral, then to the cemetery. People stared. When the burial was over, the police trailed him back home and took him to the Tarshiha station on charges of violating his permit. He looked at them and said: 'My aunt's husband died and she didn't know what to do. I had to help!'

The officer behind the desk shifted in discomfort. They did not submit a charge sheet. But Sabri knew they had been there to intimidate him, to mark him out in the village.

A few days later, he received a letter of condolence from Hanneh. He was going to Jerusalem on the weekends to see her. On one of their walks in the city, he was stopped by a prosecution lawyer who knew him. Staring in astonishment, the man said hello, then leaned closer to Sabri and asked: 'So, in the end, you're going to marry a Jewish girl?'

The couple smiled. Hanneh had fair skin and hazel eyes. 'No, I'm an Arab ...' she said. The man smiled and nodded, as though all had become clear. She and Sabri walked away, shaking their heads.

'My book's finished,' he told her. It was ready to print. But he could not find a publisher in Israel. No one would touch the subject. Unknown to him, the highest levels of the security service were in discussion on how to prevent its publication. Yosef Harmelin, the director of the Shabak, said the following in a meeting—which was only revealed to Sabri more than half a century later, when the records were made public:

> Sabri Jiryis, one of the key people in this group that tried to form al-Ard, has written a book full of hatred and defiance ... on the rule of repression by the Jews against the Arabs in Israel. In my opinion, we must prevent the publication of this book. If it is not possible to prevent this with the usual methods that we are accustomed to until now, like censorship, and the current tools and law are not sufficient, we must dare to use something new that I am not fond of, but such are the state and its laws ... There are the Emergency Regulations, which prevent a person from publishing his views. This is not nice in a democratic country, but if we want to prohibit the publishing of this book, we have to use them.[2]

Finally, Sabri decided to print the book at his own expense, at the printing house of *al-Ittihad* in Haifa. In August 1966, *The Arabs in Israel* came out, in Hebrew. He gave it to a Jewish book distributor, Shlomo Ben-Shlomo, a tall, imposing character who had gone from being a Stern Gang member to a leftist. Ben-Shlomo began to circulate the book. A few weeks later, Sabri was surprised to receive a letter from the Israeli police, asking to buy two copies for their library. He duly sent them.

His friend, Ali Rafa, read the book and congratulated him. Ali was active in student life and had been a member of al-Ard. After graduating, he began to apply to law firms to do his legal training. Each time, they would check with the security services and turn him down. He finally found a lawyer who handled church business in Nazareth, who took him on. But, one month later, he told Ali: 'They called me from the defense minister's office and told me you're a communist and from al-Ard!'

Ali blinked. 'I can't be both! It's one or the other. Al-Ard are nationalists.'

'Well, in any case, I was given to understand that you're against religion and you hate others who are different, and that I have to let you go.'

In the pits, the young graduate finally found the number of Hanna Naqqara. 'Abu Tony, I'm not asking you,' he pleaded, 'I'm telling you that I'm coming to do my training with you!'

'Welcome!' the old lawyer replied. Ali turned up to share the small office with Sabri and another trainee, Walid al-Saleh. Ali, Walid, and Naqqara, all overweight, somehow had to share one chair between them—while each, Ali joked, needed three.

On 1 December 1966, Israel ended its military rule. Sabri had not known that, within four months of publishing his book, the regime would be dismantled. For eighteen years, military rule had 'settled in [people's] homes, nestled between the sheets of [their] beds, between father and son, man and wife, until everything seemed suspect', as Palestinian journalist Odeh Bisharat described.[3]

It was not a magnanimous response to years of popular struggle. The government had almost finished its seizure of Palestinian land, so there was no longer a need to limit people's movement.[4] They posed no security threat, nor could they usurp new Jewish settlements, which had become firmly implanted. The Jewish labor market was also experiencing a high demand, and the large number of Palestinians who were unable to leave their villages and find jobs, having lost their lands, was beginning to constitute a real social danger.

Movement permits were thus abolished. Sabri's relief, however, was short-lived. Just before the abolition, about one hundred Palestinians, including writers, poets, activists, lawyers, and intellectuals, were classified as 'security risks'. They received notice that the lifting of the law did not apply to them, and they had personal orders by the defense minister to stay in their places of residence and continue to request permits each time they wanted to leave. Every six months, the permits would expire and they would have to request new ones. The orders had previously specified wider zones, but now they restricted movement down to a town or village, or even a single neighborhood. Sabri was confined to Haifa, again, as were many of his friends.

Other limitations also remained in force. Despite the seeming abolition of closed zones and travel restrictions for the public, many areas, such as those near the borders or areas being developed for Jewish settlement, remained inaccessible. The sites of many destroyed Palestinian villages remained closed to stop their people from returning.

The 1945 Defence (Emergency) Regulations, on which military rule was based, remained in effect, and a special duties department of the Israeli police was formed to enforce them. This unit used fierce methods and was assisted by the entire police apparatus. It took very little, such as voting for the wrong party or showing any signs of protest, to provoke it. The unit targeted the wider population, such as peasants and workers, and extended its work to the 'mixed' cities where both Palestinians and Jews lived.[5] This had been rare in the days of the military government, which had worked in Palestinian areas, only. The term 'security' was used vaguely, as it had always been, and it took only an intelligence officer's word to accuse someone of espionage or contact with the resistance.

In the spring of 1967, Soviet intelligence confirmed Egyptian-Syrian suspicions that Israel was preparing for a major attack on Egypt. As the news began to circulate, some Jewish lawyers whom Sabri knew asked him, jokingly, to protect them if the Arabs were to occupy the country. But, by May, things were no joke. Nasser asked the United Nations Emergency Force (UNEF) to withdraw some of its units stationed between the Sinai Peninsula and Israel. The international force insisted on a full withdrawal. Egyptian forces were quickly deployed in its place. On 25 May, Nasser declared his intent to block the Strait of Tiran leading to the Israeli port of Eilat. A full-blown confrontation was only a matter of time.

III

On the morning of 5 June 1967, Ali came into the office wearing his swimsuit beneath his pants. 'I'm going swimming after work!'

'Haven't you heard?' Sabri replied. Young Israelis had been called to the army, and many businesses were shut down or were working in reduced capacity. Newspapers appeared in smaller issues, and fewer buses were running. Some Palestinians who worked in Tel Aviv went back to their villages, and many in the mixed cities locked themselves up at home.

Sabri was ill at ease and left the office. 'I'm going to see Mansour,' he told Naqqara's daughter, Lulu, who was the secretary. 'If the police come, tell them I went to court.' Abandoning the hearing he was scheduled to attend that morning, he got on the first bus to Nazareth.

Half an hour later, the police came looking for him in Haifa. 'He went to the Magistrates' Court,' Lulu told them.

'And Ali Rafa?'

'That's me,' Ali said.

'Come with us.' They took him to the police station, to the head of intelligence.

'Take your hands out of your pockets!' the man snapped. 'You're under arrest for forty-eight hours. Then we'll see.'

Ali was led out and came face to face with many of his friends. The policeman cuffed his wrist to that of Samih al-Qasim and began to lead them down the stairs to a cell. Suddenly, the whizzing of planes was heard overhead. 'Syrians!' the guards yelled. 'Get into the shelters!' The bewildered detainees were hurried into a bomb shelter until the noise subsided. Then, they were transferred to the Damon prison in Haifa, where they found other detainees from the Triangle.

Meanwhile, the police returned to Naqqara's office. 'We didn't find him in court!' they said to Lulu.

'That's where he was going ...' she shrugged.

When Sabri got to Nazareth, Mansour's wife, Yvonne, told him that Mansour had also been taken. 'Listen, no one knows you're here,' she added. 'They must be looking for you in Haifa. The upstairs apartment is empty. Why don't you stay there for a couple of days?'

The initial news was devastating. Israel had launched a massive aerial attack on Egypt and had struck all of its seventeen airbases. Within hours, the Egyptian air force was destroyed, its entire fleet still on the tarmac. The Egyptian army was exposed in the heat of the desert and thousands of soldiers were killed or captured. Sinai was filled with corpses and charred vehicles. In Gaza, Palestinian Liberation Army units lost all contact with their Egyptian superiors and fought helplessly using light arms, as civilians ran from the shelling.

Radio reports were muddled. Initial attempts by Arab stations to claim victory were soon exposed. Israel moved in full force against Jordan and Syria. Within twenty-four hours, their air forces were also destroyed.

Alone and frustrated, Sabri decided to return to Haifa. When he got down from the bus and made his way to his apartment, a voice stopped him. It was the brother of Salem Jubran, his friend. 'Sabri! Where are you going?'

'Home ...' he told him. 'I was in Nazareth.'

'Don't go back to your place! They came and took Salem! Here, take the key and go to his house. They won't come back there.'

Sabri nodded. Salem's house was close to his. Na'ima and Geris took turns bringing him food and newspapers, using different routes each day and checking carefully behind them. 'They've come for you so many times!' they told him.

On the evening of 9 June, in a heartwrenching speech, Nasser resigned. Millions of Arabs were reduced to tears. Demonstrations broke out, not only in Egypt but across the Arab world, beseeching him to remain. He did, but ruled over a humiliating reality. By 10 June, Israel had captured the Gaza Strip and Sinai Peninsula from Egypt, as well as the Golan Heights from Syria. While it lost 766 soldiers, tens of thousands of Arab soldiers and civilians were killed or wounded.

Sabri left Salem's apartment and headed to Tel Aviv. On the bus, he heard the news. Egypt had agreed to a ceasefire. *It's finished*, he thought. *And we're finished, for another ten years.* Nasser's standing fell like a house of cards in his mind. He had not only dashed everyone's hopes, but Sabri felt that Nasser must have been responsible, in some way or other, for this disaster.

He saw his friend, Ya'acov Yeridor, al-Ard's lawyer. Then he returned to Haifa. There was no sense in hiding any further. He went to the police, playing dumb about their quest for him, and asked for a permit to go to the Supreme Court in Jerusalem. The policeman was quick to pounce. 'I think you're wanted!' He sent him up to the offices of a special unit on the third floor.

'Sabri, we've been looking for you for days! Where have you been?'

'I was where I was ...' he shrugged.

'Well, there's an order for your arrest,' the policeman said. 'Sit down, and at noon we'll take you to your friends.'

The officers took him to a cell in the Damon prison, where there were tens of detainees, most of whom he knew. Saleh Baransi, Tawfiq Zayyad, Samih al-Qasim, Mahmoud Darwish, Salem Jubran, and Ali Rafa were there. Mahmoud had evaded the police, too, and finished preparing two issues of *al-Ittihad*, which he edited at the time, before turning himself in. But Sabri was the last to join them. They clamored around him anxiously. 'Sabri, how are you? Where were you? Is this true, what we've heard?'

'It's finished,' he replied, sitting down. 'It's all true.'

As he confirmed the outcome of the war, Saleh Baransi cried: 'These are lies! It can't be! It's not true!' Angrily, he turned to the others: 'He's a traitor; he doesn't know what he's saying!'

'You can choose to believe it or not; it's the truth,' Sabri finished, grimly. People had been betting on whether it would take twenty-four or forty-eight hours for the Arab armies to liberate Palestine. As the group huddled around the radio, the war was coming to a close. Israel was occupying the West Bank and East Jerusalem from Jordan. Within days, it seized three times more territory than it had in 1948 and created a second wave of displacement, uprooting more than 250,000 Palestinians, nearly half of whom were already refugees.[6] They were expelled, mostly to Jordan, but also to Egypt and Syria. In Jordan, six new 'emergency' camps were set up, thus named to distinguish them from those created in 1948. Amos Kenan, an Israeli writer and artist who was a reservist soldier and took part in the fighting, wrote the following in his account of the events:

They said that they were being expelled from every place, and they were not allowed anywhere, and that they had been walking for four days without food or water. They requested permission to return to their village, saying that if not, they would prefer that we killed them … On the horizon we could already see the next envoy … There were more old people, more women and children, and they dropped exhausted where we told them to sit down … The children were crying and some of our soldiers, too, burst into tears … We stopped a military vehicle which had in it a colonel, two majors and a woman. We asked the officers, 'Why are the refugees being sent to and fro, expelled from every place?' They told us, 'It's good for them. Let them walk.'[7]

At Damon, each time a new victory was announced on the radio, the Israeli guards raised the volume and cheered loudly. 'Nablus is in our hands! The old city of Jerusalem! The Golan!' They brought oranges for the detainees as a special dessert, which they refused, listening in horror. One detainee angrily pulled the radio's wire and snapped it.

They had relief for a couple of hours, but then began to get anxious. 'What have you done?' the prisoners chastised him. 'We want to know what's going on!'

They called the guard and explained. 'It's not my problem,' he said. 'Do any of you know how to fix it?' The man who had cut the wire said he did. The guard got them a ladder, and they reconnected the radio to the antenna outside.

They felt like an earthquake had hit them. Most of them had been too young during the Nakba, but now, they were living this nightmare. Dubbed the 'Six-Day War' or Naksa (Setback), this blow crushed people's morale and sent shockwaves through the Arab world. Since 1948, Egypt had taken the lead in the political and military struggle against Israel, but it had failed. Nasser's promises of victory and emancipation, on which the hopes of so many Arabs had rested, were completely discredited, and a wave of frustration and despair swept over the masses.

In the cell, several detainees cried. As he asked around, Sabri noticed that all the orders for administrative detention had come out on the morning of 5 June, when the war began. About forty people were held, all working in *al-Ittihad* or members of the Popular Front or, previously, al-Ard. But they were all writers, poets, and lawyers; none of them had military backgrounds or had been involved in 'subversive' actions, as Israel labeled them. In Nazareth and the Triangle, the authorities had done the same, rounding up anyone thought to have connections with the Palestinian liberation movement. There were no charges against them. No one interrogated them. They were arrested to preclude the possibility of any trouble and to intimidate others.

In the corner of the cell sat a Bedouin from Arab al-Aramsheh, in the western Galilee. He looked very agitated, and one of the men whispered: 'Seems they didn't find anyone there, so they dragged this poor chap, who has nothing to do with it!'

'It's OK, brother,' they tried to reassure him. He remained silent, looking around him in fear, seemingly both of them and the authorities.

Within two weeks, people began to be released. 'It's over,' Ali said. 'They know we can't do anything. No point keeping us here ...' But Sabri was kept until the end of the month, when he was discharged with another order of house arrest.

The apartment was empty. The police had revoked his siblings' permits and they had gone to Fassouta. His friend, Habib Qahwaji, had been dismissed from his teaching job and imprisoned, with his wife, on charges of connection to Syria. Mohammed Mi'ari was under house arrest in Makr, his village, and could not reach the law firm in Haifa where he worked.

Sabri sat alone, smoking, thinking. Nasserism had come to an abrupt end. The once-powerful appeal of pan-Arab nationalism had collapsed. Now, many Palestinians felt that the Arab nations could not be relied upon to help them and that they had to take their fate into their own hands.

The first police order that Sabri received was a prohibition from entering the newly occupied areas, including East Jerusalem. But he had stopped caring about orders or procedures. The next day, he got on a bus. On his previous visits to Hanneh, they could only walk around the west part of the city. Now, he told her: 'Let's go!'

'Where?'

'The old city.'

There was no fear, no soldiers. The war was over. People were walking around the markets, but they seemed bewildered and subdued, Sabri and Hanneh even more so. They visited the Church of the Holy Sepulcher and al-Aqsa Mosque, which they had not been able to do. They could not believe that they were in a Palestinian city with Palestinian inhabitants. Before 1967, the borders with East Jerusalem and the West Bank had been closed. Even if connections were made between Palestinians there and those in Israel, they carried a high risk of imprisonment. Now, more than a million Arabs came under Israeli rule. Palestinian writer and citizen of Israel, Emile Habibi, likened Palestinians in Israel to 'people in prison who awoke one day to find that the rest of their family, from whom they had been separated for twenty years, had suddenly been incarcerated with them'.[8] People on the two sides began to connect; they longed to meet and talk.

The state moved to stifle this contact. It issued prohibition orders to all Palestinians on its 'lists' from entering the newly occupied territories. Hundreds of people were placed under house arrest and many were forbidden to leave their towns or villages without permits.[9] In Jerusalem, the authorities forbade Palestinian students of the Hebrew University from going into the old city. Students of Israeli colleges that were moved into the old city after the war were forced to follow prescribed routes so as not to interact with Palestinians.[10]

Israel was swept up on a wave of victory and might, a conviction of having the strongest army in the Middle East. All voices of protest and reason, even among Jews, were snuffed out. The Zionist project expanded with the assertion that 'never again should Eretz Yisrael, the Land of Israel, be divided'. Ignoring international calls to return to armistice lines of 1949, Israel annexed East Jerusalem and placed the West Bank and Gaza under military occupation. Bulldozers moved in, tearing down historic realities to make way for Jewish settlements.

The state eased its policies against its Palestinian citizens (within the 1949 borders) and moved these measures to Palestinians in the newly occupied territory of 1967. Some felt that it did not want to instill the sense of a shared predicament among the two groups, lest they come closer and establish a united front. Palestinians in Israel, though, were experiencing a new awakening. Before the war, isolated and cut off from the Arab world, they had had no possibility of armed struggle. Sabri also recalled their futile attempts at political work. Now, he felt there was no route but armed resistance. *Nothing works with these people, except guns!* he thought. Many others felt the same. Young Palestinians had not forgotten al-Ard. After the war, many began to support guerrilla action against Israel, for there was no justice or democracy for them in the state.

Thus, Sabri was ready when, one afternoon, he heard a knock at his door. He opened it to see an unfamiliar face. 'Mr. Sabri?' the man enquired. 'May I speak to you?'

He invited him in and made to close the door. 'No, leave it open,' the visitor said. 'If anyone comes, we can see.'

As they sat down, he got to the point. 'I'm from Fatah. We've heard about you, and we want you to join us.'

Sabri paused. Then, he asked: 'How can you approach me like this? What if I turn you in?'

'You won't. We know you. You'll either say yes or turn me away, but you won't turn anyone in.'

'How can I believe you?'

'Give me a signal,' his guest replied, 'and we'll broadcast it from the Voice of Fatah in Cairo.'

They agreed on a famous line of poetry. Three days later, it was broadcast from Cairo during Fatah's forty-five-minute segment. Sabri never saw the man again. For thirty years, he would ask about him in the PLO, but he disappeared without a trace.

When the next visitor came, Sabri told him he was ready.

'What do you need?' the man asked.

'As a first step, three things. We need you to train people that we select, and we need help in supplies and logistics.'

'Done,' the man said. 'You'll go to the YMCA in Jerusalem, to see someone from the West Bank. He's a blond man who will be holding a newspaper and drinking coffee.'

The man was Mustafa Issa, a leading Fatah member who would, three decades later, become the first governor of Ramallah under the Palestinian Authority. He looked like a European Jew and seemed to move around Jerusalem without attracting attention. He took Sabri in his car to Shu'fat, a neighborhood in the eastern part of the city. They met several men, including Subhi Ghosheh, a physician and one of the founders of the first armed group in Jerusalem. Not all were in Fatah, but they were members of smaller factions that worked together. They welcomed him warmly and wanted his guidance on Israel. They asked questions about political parties, the military, the economy. Then they told him what they wanted to do, and that someone would be in touch with him. Again, they disappeared.

Fatah's operations had expanded the previous year, and Nasser had shown open support for the organization. The 1967 defeat and Nasser's resignation had struck Arafat 'like a thunderstorm'.[11] After the war and the Arab discord over how to respond to the new occupation, he and other Fatah leaders decided to shift their operations to the West Bank and Gaza. On 28 June 1967, Arafat secretly made his way from Jordan to the West Bank to establish Fatah's underground headquarters and infrastructure. Some Arab states pledged financial aid.

Less than a month after the war, Sabri joined the resistance. He recruited a friend, Nimer Shaqqour, into his new cell. Their first task was transporting half a ton of arms from the Lebanese border to the West Bank. They worked for three months. Palestinian guerrillas crossed the border from South Lebanon, carrying the Chinese-made arms in 40-kilogram packages, and deposited them in the Galilean forests. Those on the other side went to pick them up and take them to the West Bank, a very dangerous undertaking. After his YMCA meeting, Sabri was introduced to the Fatah leaders in the West Bank. In time, all of them would be expelled from the country.

To organize their operations, instructions came through encrypted messages from the Voice of Fatah in Cairo, using very simple means. After the evening news segment, there would be fifteen minutes of messages and announcements. Strings of numbers would be broadcast. Each party had a copy of a book, and the first number in the message would be that of the page; the second, the line; and the third, the word. The Israeli intelligence could not crack this method, as it was so primitive and depended on a random book. The books were frequently changed.

Geris had finished school the year before, and he turned to his brother. Sabri connected him to Nimer, then drew back. The brothers did not want to know any details of each other's work, so that they would not inadvertently expose each other if caught. Nimer made the connection with someone in Nablus, and Geris found his way to another cell in Fatah.

The cell was organized in small groups of three or four people, who used code names to communicate. Geris was 'al-Mulatham', the masked one. Their task was also to transport arms and ammunition from Lebanon to the West Bank. He worked with a warehouse assistant, a young man from Sakhnin, in the Galilee, and they connected with fishermen in Acre, who brought the supplies from Lebanon on their boats. Sometimes, they dropped them in the sea for fishing boats from Gaza to pick them up.

At the time, Geris' 'day job' was distributing newspapers. Sabri, too, continued working with Naqqara in Haifa. After the war, the Communist Party opened a small legal office in Jerusalem to help detainees and their families, and Sabri worked there, too, with Ali Rafa and Felicia Langer, an Israeli lawyer and human rights activist. If Sabri or Ali were caught traveling from Haifa without permits, they would be arrested and fined by a military court. After ten 'breaches', they would be imprisoned for several weeks. Sabri was fed up. He broke the restrictions tens of times.

Even when Ali married, he was not given a permit to visit the house of his in-laws in East Jerusalem. He could not go to his bride's family to ask for her hand. The marriage had to be conducted at the legal office on Jaffa Street.

IV

With Hanneh's persistence, she had received her family's blessing for her marriage to Sabri. The couple were engaged in September 1967. She transferred to Haifa University. 'I'll finish the year here, after we get married,' she told Sabri. 'And, Mother is complaining that you don't visit.'

'What?'

'She said: "Where is this fiancé? We never see him!"' Hanneh smiled.

'Well, we're never in the village together, between your breaks from university and my visits ...' he trailed off. But she was right.

A few days later, on his next visit to Fassouta, he knocked on Um Nour's door.

'Welcome!' She invited him in. Nida and Najwa looked at him bashfully. They were threading tobacco leaves that they had just picked, to hang them up in bunches to dry. Most homes in the village had small metal hooks spaced out across the ceiling, for tobacco season. Sabri sat down and asked for a needle and thread. 'No!' Um Nour protested.

'What, are you going to treat me like some fancy guest?' he asked.

He worked with them as the girls stole furtive looks at him and giggled. Um Nour brought fruit, sweets, and coffee. 'It's very important for me to tell you something ...' she smiled.

'Yes?' He hoped this was not an interrogation about his work. It would be difficult to be evasive with the woman who would become family.

'It's about Hanneh. I'll put it to you straight. She can't fry an egg.'

'What?'

'She can't cook at all, and I need you to know that, so you don't say, after marriage, that we tricked you! She's been busy with schools and books all her life and I've never been able to teach her.' Um Nour sighed, relieved to get the topic off her chest.

Sabri began to laugh. 'Thank you, dear Mother-in-law. I'm sure we'll manage!'

He walked back to his parents' house, saying hello to a few passersby. Some only gave cursory nods or kept their greetings hurried. He and Geris were black sheep in the village. Though nothing was known about their work, people knew they resisted the authorities, somehow, and many avoided them. Most of the village had been coerced into cooperation with the state. Ignorance and fear played a large part. Some seeds of hope had sprouted with the coming of the Popular Front, though its reach was limited. But the few who joined it, or who did political work not approved of by the authorities, were feared or reported on by the others.

As his mother set the table for lunch, Sabri hoped to eat in peace, this time. The door of the house was ajar to let in a breeze. A neighbor stopped outside. 'Hello, Sabri!'

The man lived close by and belonged to one of the larger village clans. Sabri invited him in. 'No, no ...' the guest protested.

'I insist. Mother, one more plate!'

'So, where are you working these days?' the neighbor asked, as they ate together.

'Still with Naqqara,' Sabri answered.

'And ... with the *fellows*?' the man winked.

'Oh, I'm very busy with the law work, you know ...' Sabri said, as though he had not heard. A couple of glasses of arak mellowed his guest, and, finally, the man got up to leave.

'Thank you, Um Sabri, lovely food!' he said.

'You're welcome ...' she replied, pursing her lips as he closed the door behind him.

Sabri turned to her. 'Mother, where's my bag?'

'Why?'

'I'll be leaving soon.'

'But you just got here!'

'Trust me ...' he sighed. 'They'll be here soon.'

In a few minutes, the police car stopped outside. Sabri knew the routine. He had broken his house arrest in Haifa. Looking at his mother, he said: 'Our dear neighbor called them, before he came here.'

V

As the year drew to an end, the occupation of the new territory was finalised. Armed resistance grew. Nasser met with Fatah leaders in Cairo and began supplying them with arms and facilities. Fatah carried out hundreds of military operations in Israel, many through guerrillas crossing over from Jordan. Israel moved to crush the resistance in the West Bank and raided civilian targets in neighboring Arab countries, shelling villages and refugee camps.

At the same time, the PLO's armed struggle was launched from its bases in Syria and Jordan. In its first years, the organization's effect had been limited. PLO fighters were integrated into the armies of the Arab states, and the guerrilla organizations within it had little impact on its policy.

The 1967 war changed all that. Palestinians sought greater autonomy and political independence. Nasser supported Fatah and declared Arafat 'leader of the Palestinians'. In December, Ahmed Shuqairi resigned his post as PLO chairman in favor of Yahya Hammuda, who invited Arafat to join the organization—an offer he would take the following year.

Fatah had emerged as a major Palestinian force. In 1968, it stood its ground against an Israeli attack on the Karameh refugee camp in Jordan. On 21 March, the Israeli army launched an intense raid on the camp with armored troops and fighter jets. Fatah resisted, surprising the Israeli military, which lost about thirty soldiers.[12] The Jordanian army got involved, forcing Israel to withdraw in order to avoid more casualties and a war.

Despite its heavy death toll, Fatah clinched a moral victory, especially in the wake of the Arab defeat the year before. The name of the battle, Karameh (Dignity), also elevated its symbolism. Fatah's numbers swelled as many young Arabs, including hundreds of non-Palestinians, joined its ranks. It received military and financial support from Arab and other countries, and its operations grew.

VI

The wedding was set for 28 April 1968. All week, friends and neighbors gathered at Elias' house. Twenty goats were slaughtered. Sabri's cousins played music as people danced the dabke.* The day before the marriage, per custom, Sabri had a shaving ceremony at the neighbors' house. The next day, a long procession of his friends and relatives led him to the bride's home. After Hanneh's goodbye to her family, the couple was escorted by the villagers, singing and clapping on either side of them, to the church. A shower of rice and flowers rained down. They were pronounced man and wife as the sound of happy trilling filled the air.

After the ceremony, the young men insisted on taking the long route, through the middle of the village, to escort the newlyweds home. Elias' house, with its two floors, was filled with tables, and a sumptuous lunch was laid out.

---

* *Dabke* (Arabic): a popular circle dance of the Middle East, performed by holding hands and moving in identical steps.

Even for his honeymoon, Sabri needed permission to travel. He and Hanneh left to the nearby seaside town of Nahariya with a permit in his pocket: *'Purpose: Honeymoon'*.

The couple then moved to Sabri's apartment in Haifa. They hoped to settle down into their married life, but Sabri was frequently detained and put under house arrest. The authorities suspected him of 'subversive action'. His phone was tapped, his movements watched, but they could not find proof.

Hanneh graduated, but she did not work for the first couple of years. Her aunt, Farha, lived close by. She checked up on her niece and taught her to cook. One day, Sabri came home to find a simmering casserole of kafta, a meatloaf. After Hanneh's less successful attempts with other dishes, she was thrilled that he liked this one—so much so that he lamented, a few weeks later: 'Please stop! I can't eat kafta every other day!'

His sisters, Najibeh and Na'ima, visited often. They understood that Hanneh knew about his work, but she did not say anything and they did not talk about it. Sabri did not want her to be locked up with him. When there were good movies on and he was under house arrest, he told his sisters to take her to the cinema. He was not even allowed to visit his next-door neighbor. Each day, at 4:00 pm, he had to report to the police.

One evening, when Hanneh and his sisters came home, she discovered that she had forgotten her key. They knocked on the door and waited. There was no answer. They knocked, again. As the minutes went by, they began to panic. 'Do you think something's happened?' Hanneh asked. 'Maybe they've arrested him! Or someone's kidnapped him!'

'No! I'm sure it's fine,' Najibeh said, but worry had gripped all three of them. They knocked more urgently. Suddenly, the door opened and Sabri emerged, laughing. 'Don't pull pranks like that again!' Najibeh cried.

Despite the hardship of his confinement, Sabri was better off than many others. Saleh Baransi, his friend from al-Ard, was arrested on charges of connection to Fatah and plotting to set up an armed cell. Sabri defended him at his military trial, but Saleh was convicted and sentenced to nine years in prison.

Habib Qahwaji and his wife spent one and a half years in administrative detention with no trial and no proof against them. Sabri knew they could be kept much longer, and he negotiated with the authorities to let them leave the country. The couple had to sign a statement that they were leaving 'of their own, free will'. They went to Cyprus, then to Syria, and Habib eventually moved to France. He would only visit Israel fifty years later, as a French citizen.

One day, when Sabri was home, a man came to see him. He explained that he was the owner of the building where Sabri and Hanneh lived. He had been driven away in 1948 and the state had seized his property and sold it to others, which is how Elias came to buy the apartment. Sabri looked at the man as he told him his story. There was nothing he could do in the face of his bitter pain.

They were all living in the Nakba's aftermath. When Palestinian fedayeen sneaked in from Jordan or Lebanon and they were caught, Sabri found himself defending them in Israeli court. The court gave a minimum sentence of ten years to anyone charged with 'joining an illegal organization'. Those fedayeen were not Israeli citizens, but Palestinian refugees from neighboring countries. The state had to appoint lawyers for them, and the director of the bar association in Haifa called Sabri. 'No Jewish lawyers will take them,' he said, 'and these are your friends!'

Presumably, he meant that Sabri sympathized with their work, not that he actually worked with them. But, for three years, Sabri continued to practice law and work with the resistance at the same time. He made contact with Khalil al-Wazir (Abu Jihad), the commander of al-Asifa, Fatah's military wing. Abu Jihad was in charge of Fatah's Western Sector and was in contact with all the fedayeen groups. Sabri joined this sector, which operated in Israel and the occupied territory.

In 1968, at the fourth meeting of the Palestinian National Council, the legislative body of the PLO, in Cairo, Fatah joined the PLO. The following year, Yahya Hammuda stepped down as PLO chairman and Arafat was elected in his place. Other guerrilla factions then joined the PLO, but Fatah was the largest and best funded.

Arafat worked in a grim reality, trying to restore the name of his scattered people in a web of Arab dictatorships. Arab leaders, subservient to the West, neglected the Palestinians and used their cause to serve their own agendas. Inevitably, clashes erupted between

Palestinians and the countries they had been ousted to, which had no desire for confrontation with Israel.

VII

In June 1969, Israel destroyed the neighborhood of al-Zawiya al-Fakhriya, or Abu al-So'ud Corner, near al-Aqsa Mosque in Jerusalem, including the childhood home of Arafat. Two months later, Michael Rohan, an Australian Christian extremist, set fire to the mosque, causing significant destruction and reducing one of the pulpits to ashes. Palestinians rushed to put out the fire and protests erupted in the city.[13]

Hanneh was visiting her mother and helping her thread tobacco when a neighbor dropped in. His son worked in the Israeli police. A small number of Palestinians had made their way to the state apparatus, lured by the power and benefits. But they were not allowed to progress beyond the lowest ranks.

'My son hasn't come home yet. He's still in Jerusalem. They've been on alert since the event,' the neighbor said.

'Aren't you ashamed of yourself?' Hanneh turned on him.

He looked at her, startled. 'Oh, I see. If your husband works against them, it doesn't mean everyone else has to—'

'I can see that!' she interjected.

'Um Nour ...' he got up, 'I wish you a good day.'

'Why did you do that, Hanneh?' her mother turned to her. 'For shame!'

'They should be ashamed, Mother!'

Sabri had been detained for most of the year. A new bride, Hanneh had found herself dashing about between police stations and prisons. She did not show anyone that she was scared, kept her head high when people pointed in scorn: 'You didn't find anyone except him to marry?' But the cracks began to show. She would lie awake at night, anxious and frightened. And, when she came to the village, her patience was very thin.

'You're too stressed, dearest,' her mother's voice cut into her thoughts. 'Tell me, are you alright? Have you seen a doctor?'

She was trying to change subject, Hanneh knew, but it was to a more difficult one. 'I did, Mother. He said nothing is preventing it.'

It was the fear, she knew, though she would not worry her mother and tell her. It kept her from having children, though she really wanted a baby, and her family was beginning to ask questions. She had asked Najibeh, too, who had comforted her and given her and Sabri some supplements.

Najibeh had, at Sabri's advice, finished her nursing studies and was working at the hospital in Nahariya. On her way home in a service taxi, a man from the village stole a sidelong glance at her. 'How's your brother?' he leered.

She looked away and did not answer. But he persisted. 'It will end badly, what he's doing. This is all your father's fault!'

'Listen!' she lashed out. 'You're not fit to clean my brother's shoes!'

'Can you drop it, both of you?' the taxi driver intervened.

Najibeh's face flushed with anger. It was not the first time she had been taunted. She did not trust anyone anymore, not those who pretended to be Sabri's friends, nor those who came to the house to ask after him or to request some legal work. They were all secret agents. Everyone became suspect to her. Fassouta was sliding deeper into submission every day, and open collaboration. Most were cowardly, due to the minority status they felt as Christians, which the state had worked hard to perpetuate. The few who sympathized with Sabri and his friends kept quiet.

Elias was nervous for his sons. Though they never told him, outright, what they were doing, he knew they were at odds with the authorities. But he was angry with the villagers. 'They lean on the wall of might!' he spat. 'Change the wall, and they'll lean on the new one!'

VIII

Sabri continued to work with Fatah. He began to have a wider awareness of the Palestinians outside Israel, whom he had known little about before the 1967 war. Two years earlier, the Arab League office in Jerusalem had issued an Arabic translation of *The Arabs in Israel*. The work had become a seminal text on Palestinians under military rule. After his reading on Zionism, Sabri wanted to write a reference book for his people. He began working on his second book, *A History of Zionism*, in Arabic, using the notes he had made in Safad.

George, his youngest brother, had turned fourteen and finished school in the village. In September 1969, he came to study at the Arab Orthodox College in Haifa and stayed at boarding school, to give his newlywed brother and his wife privacy at their home. Subhi, the remaining brother, who was four years older than George, was not interested in higher education. On the morning of his eighteenth birthday, he was at Sabri's apartment in Haifa, asking for help to get a driving license. He began to drive a delivery van that doubled up as a taxi.

The younger generation carried the weight of defeat, the blows of two major wars. They had grown up in an atmosphere of fear and repression and, like their older brothers, the ethos of military rule was heavily imprinted on their lives. They were not allowed to express their identity, speak of Palestine, nor raise a Palestinian flag.

In Haifa, the staff of the Arab Orthodox College were exceptional both in their academic standard and in their attempts to defy these controls. The teachers could not directly refer to the Nakba, for fear of the authorities, but they spoke to their students about the wars and the occupation, as much as they could. Encouraged by the nationalist atmosphere, George began to read, trying to make sense of the injustice he felt. His small outbursts were somewhat misguided. To begin with, he refused to study Hebrew.

'You need this language!' his teacher said.

'I don't,' he replied, defiantly.

'How do you plan to survive without it?'

'They're the strangers here. Why should I study Hebrew? They should learn Arabic!'

The teacher sighed. 'Son, you won't be able to continue your education, nor find a job,' he said.

But George was too angry. Every week, his journey to Haifa was an exhausting ordeal because of the stops and searches. At his young age, he was enraged at the humiliation. One day, an old man, Nichola, got on the bus with him from Fassouta. They stopped at a checkpoint in Ma'alot, the Jewish town, and a soldier got on board to search the passengers. 'Get off the bus!' he said to Nichola, as soon as he saw his headdress.

George looked at the soldier in disbelief. Nichola, holding the back of the chair in front of him for support, slowly hoisted himself up. He was very old and could barely carry his thin frame. Slowly, he made his way off the bus, where the soldiers stood him in the sun and frisked him. They snapped at him in Hebrew, which he did not understand. He looked at them, bewildered, as they raised their voices.

George, watching from the window, was livid. The soldier on the bus asked for his identification. 'No! I won't show it to you!' he answered. 'How can you do this? He's an old man! And you're a soldier, not the police. How can you ask me for ID?'

'Really?' the soldier replied. 'I'll get you the police, no problem!'

Unexpectedly, the voices of the other passengers broke out. 'He's a kid! What are you doing?'

The bus driver turned in his seat. 'Leave the man alone, he's an old man, people know him …' he said to the soldiers.

Finally, the soldier turned away from George and climbed down from the bus, and Nichola was allowed back on. In Nahariya, George had to change buses to Haifa. Again, he went through the same search, and then again when they got to the Krayot district outside the city. They had abolished military rule by name, but most of its practices remained. Tension between Palestinians and Jews ran high. The civil laws of the country were crafted to ensure Jewish control, and it was very difficult for Palestinians to get professional jobs or benefits. National insurance laws were skewed, and Palestinians were not eligible for health insurance unless they were in the Histadrut, the trade union federation, which allowed few of them to join—and only after proven allegiance to the ruling party.

By that time, the most active political parties among Palestinians in Israel were the Communist Party and Mapam, the United Workers Party. The latter's efforts were geared towards labor rights and equality between Arab and Jew, but both parties evaded the Palestinian national issue and grievances. Mapam was part of the Zionist movement, and several of its kibbutzim, or agricultural settlements, were built on Palestinian land.[14]

George was much younger than Sabri and did not talk about these issues with his brother. Each week, he visited Sabri and Hanneh and had a good meal before returning to school. Sabri had, with the crushing of al-Ard and the 1967 war, lost interest in trying to work through the Israeli political system. But his young brother was still feeling his way forward, confused by all he saw. He did not know what his older brothers were doing.

Geris was immersed in his underground work. His Fatah cell worked tightly and carefully, yet, after one of its operations, it was exposed. Some of its members were arrested, but they did not know the others, so the police could not catch them all. Their work was filled with moments of tragedy. One of their funders was a man from Nablus, who hid his work by posing as a figure of the governing authority that Israel had put in place. He was wealthy and gave the group large sums of money. Eventually, the authorities found out and arrested him. In prison, the Palestinian detainees thought that he was a spy planted amongst them, and killed him. Geris mourned his loss for a long time.

Geris' group was exposed, again. It was caught receiving arms through the sea in Acre, and the fisherman was arrested. The sea became too dangerous. 'I could open a new path,' Geris said, 'through Lebanon.' He knew the area north of Fassouta like the back of his hand. Unknown to him, it was the same route that Sabri's cell had used. It was less visible than the sea, quieter.

It seemed like a good plan. Until things went horribly wrong.

IX

On 5 February 1970, Geris and Nabil, another member of his cell, walked stealthily through the night, breathing heavily as they carried the guns to the car. A radio signal from al-Asifa had told them the delivery was ready. They had parked as close as they could to the forest and walked about 4 miles to get to the hiding place. The way back was more difficult. The road curved upwards between Netu'a and Elqosh, the nearby Jewish settlements, and the two men carried a load of about 70 pounds each. Darkness fell, but they knew the route. They walked steadily on, keeping their eyes peeled.

Finally, they reached the car and loaded the guns into its trunk, before leaning against it to catch their breath. 'Let's go,' Geris whispered. It was close to midnight when they finally drove back south.

'Take it easy,' he said. He did not want them to be stopped for speeding.

Nabil pressed his foot lightly on the brake. They drove on in silence, smoking anxiously. It was a three-hour drive, but they knew the routes to avoid the checkpoints, and it was quiet at that time of night.

They did not expect a sudden roadblock near Suhmata, twenty minutes later. 'Damn!' Nabil said, panicking.

Geris' heart began hammering painfully. 'Don't stop!'

'What?' Nabil gasped.

'Don't stop!' Geris repeated, frantically. 'Just keep going!' A search of the trunk would put them both away for life.

It all took place in a few seconds. Nabil accelerated. As he picked up speed and drove through the roadblock, the police shot at the car from behind, hitting one of its tires. It swerved and hit an olive tree. The two men leapt from it, grabbed two guns, and ran for the forest. The shooting continued behind them. They kept running until they felt their chests would explode, until the shooting stopped. Finally, they came to a halt in the thick of the trees, gasping painfully, their senses on terrifying alert. A few minutes passed of heavy silence.

'To Rmeish,' Geris whispered. Nabil nodded. They had to get out to Lebanon. The police would comb the area, and, even if they did not find them, the abandoned car was registered to Nabil's wife.

They continued north from Suhmata. The moon lit their path as they quickened their pace, drenched in sweat. It was about 2 miles later that Geris began to feel a warmth on his left leg. He stooped down to look. He had been hit by a bullet, and blood was seeping from the wound. But they could not stop. Nor could they take the visible roads. Trekking through the forests, they walked up to Elqosh, where Deir el-Qasi had once stood, and beyond it to the northern border. Dawn was breaking as they crossed over into South Lebanon. It was a good 9 miles to Rmeish, on top of the nine they had walked earlier. When they arrived, their legs could not carry them any longer. They stopped at the first house, full of relief at having reached Arab land.

A man opened the door. His eyes widened and he took a step back.

'My friend is hurt,' Nabil panted. 'Can you help us?'

The man looked at their guns and motioned them in. 'Who are you?' he asked, his face pale. His wife stopped her baking and stood up.

'Don't be afraid. We're fedayeen,' Nabil explained. 'Please take us to the army or to the police.' Those were their instructions if they had to escape to Lebanon. Palestinian resistance was strong in the country and had influence over the Lebanese authorities. They would hand them over to Fatah.

'We can't do anything for you—please leave!' the man said.

'Fine!' Nabil said, in agitation. 'But this man is bleeding! Give me something to clean his wound!'

'And water, please ...' Geris said, weakly. His throat was parched dry. He felt like he had been hit by a hundred bullets, not one.

The man gave them water and arak to clean the wound. 'The police station is in the middle of the village, near the big pond,' he said, closing the door hurriedly behind them as they left.

In the small station, two policemen sat huddled around a small heater. They looked up in surprise as Nabil and Geris hobbled in. 'We can't deal with this,' one policeman said, after hearing their story. 'We need to call the army. They'll find your people.'

Geris' leg had begun to swell and he collapsed on a chair. The bullet had penetrated a muscle. 'I need to go to hospital,' he told the soldiers who arrived.

To his shock, they blindfolded him and Nabil, hauled them into a car, and drove away. Geris had never imagined that, on reaching an Arab country, they would face this. But he was glad that they were no longer exposed. He could hear the whirr of helicopters overhead, probably looking for them. Finally, the car stopped and their blindfolds were removed. They were in a hospital in the middle of a forest.

The facility was run by nuns. 'What's your name?' one of them asked Geris as she cleaned his wound.

Thinking quickly, he told her a fake name.

'How did this happen?'

When he explained, she frowned. 'Why are you working with the Muslims?' she chided. 'Why get yourself into this trouble?'

'Are you finished here?' a soldier asked. They had orders to take them to the army barracks in Sidon.

'You have Israeli ID?' they asked them there. 'Sign this.'

Geris and Nabil refused to sign any papers that would prove their presence. The soldiers threw them into a cell. Geris began to shout. His leg was very swollen and they took him to the clinic in the barracks. He needed treatment and he desperately needed sleep. He collapsed in exhaustion. But, every couple of hours, the guards changed and woke him up, wanting to hear his story. They had heard he was a fedayi, and such people were legends. He asked for food and begged them to let him sleep. They brought him some stale leftovers that looked like they had come from the garbage. 'Can I just have some bread?' he asked.

From the cell, Nabil insisted: 'Tell Fatah about us! We want to get to them!'

The soldiers ignored him. But, in a miraculous sweep of luck, another Palestinian fighter was held with him, who had also been captured after an operation. 'They will return me to Fatah tomorrow morning,' he told him.

'Please, tell them we're here!' Nabil beseeched him. The man agreed.

X

Najibeh had an afternoon shift at Nahariya Hospital. She had been working there for a year, since finishing her studies, and was about to be made a permanent employee. At noon, she was at home in Fassouta, getting ready. There was no bus at that hour, so she would stand on the main road outside her parents' house and hitch a ride.

She was about to lock up when a car stopped outside and two men disembarked. She recognized one of them, Nimer Shaqqour. He had come to their house, once, in Haifa. When she had asked Sabri, he had told her that he was a client who had divorced his wife, and he was handling his case.

'Is Geris here?' he asked.

'No, he's not ... I'll try to find him. Please, come in!' she answered. But they saw that she was alone and they politely waited in the car. She called her youngest sister, Huda, who was in the goat pen. 'Go look for Geris in the coffee shop or in Nimer Ghattas' house. These people are asking for him. I have to go to work!'

She told the two men to wait and they nodded their thanks. As she stood on the road to wait for a ride, they looked at her oddly. Najibeh felt uneasy. She finished her shift that night and headed to Haifa, as she did when it was late and there was no traffic back to the village.

Sabri was under house arrest. 'Where's Geris?' she asked him. He did not know. She told him of Nimer's visit.

'He probably wanted to see him about something or other ...' Sabri brushed it off. But Najibeh could not shake her worry.

XI

Geris and Nabil were terrified that, because they were Israeli citizens, the Lebanese army would hand them over to Israel. But the man in the cell was true to his word. The next day, a car pulled up outside the barracks and two Fatah members climbed out. 'We understand you have two of our men here,' one of them grunted.

A Lebanese soldier denied it.

'We also understand they haven't signed any papers,' the Fatah man continued, as though he had not heard him. 'Which means,' his voice dropped, 'you can pretend you haven't seen them, right?'

'We have no one here,' the soldier repeated.

'Listen,' the man leaned over, impatiently. 'We know they're here. You give them to us, quietly, or we blow this place up and take them?'

They were released. 'Please send a signal to my brother!' Geris urged them. A radio signal was dispatched to Sabri using their code names: 'Saqr Quraysh and al-Mulatham are fine.'

Geris was taken to al-Naqaha Hospital, a rehabilitation center for Fatah fighters in Beirut. He received a hero's welcome. Visitors poured in to see him, this young revolutionary who was working in Israel. Finally, he met Abu Jihad, with whom he and Sabri had exchanged numerous signals. The meeting had a great effect on Geris, who felt a deep respect and admiration for the leader.

A few days later, Geris was sent to the Fatah headquarters in Amman. Nabil stayed in Lebanon. With the car used for their mission registered to his wife, he could not return to Israel. But Geris thought that, because his name was not connected to Nabil's, he could, eventually, go back. They had not been acquainted before the operation. If the Israelis had not found out about him, he hoped to return when his leg healed.

In Amman, trouble was brewing between the Palestinians and the Jordanian authorities. Since 1967, King Hussein had allowed Palestinian guerrillas to assemble on the east bank of the Jordan River and carry out resistance operations, as a way to pressure Israel to return the West Bank to Jordan. After the Battle of Karameh in 1968, Fatah's popularity had soared in Jordan, and it carried out hundreds of such operations from across the river. But the harsh Israeli retaliation now alarmed the king, who felt that Fatah and its parent organization, the PLO, were beginning to threaten his power and endanger his peace with Israel. Geris arrived in Amman to witness the first clashes between the Jordanian army and the Palestinian guerrillas.

After the blow of his reception in South Lebanon, it was another shock to see Arab fighting Arab. With limited knowledge of how to use weapons, he took part in the defense with the guerrillas. Luckily, the skirmishes were limited. He returned to Beirut to see if he could go home.

But, shortly after he and Nabil had left, the Israelis had found out who was in the car. Someone from the hospital had told them, Geris thought, or from the Lebanese army. He suspected it was the nun who had treated him. News flew very fast around those small localities, and the Catholic archbishop of the area had found out. He was known to collaborate with the Israeli authorities, and he had told them, after telling Geris' father, whom he also knew. Elias would curse him for the rest of his days.

At twenty-two years old, Geris found himself a fugitive, far from his family, home or country, not knowing where to turn.

XII

In Fassouta, all hell broke loose. Policemen charged into Elias and Wardeh's house. They rummaged through cupboards and flung everything on the floor, tore through pillows and mattresses, broke plant pots. They sat on the roof, watching the surrounding area. They thumped around at night and shone strobe lights through the fireplace at those sleeping below, then dragged them out, half asleep, for questioning.

Within a week, Najibeh was fired from her job. 'I'm so glad they didn't catch him!' she told Sabri, tearfully. 'They would have destroyed our whole family!'

Ten days later, they arrested her, Sabri, Subhi, and several of their cousins. George was at school in Haifa and was spared. They rounded up Geris' classmates and friends: Nimer Ghattas, and Ibrahim and Baheej Shaheen, Hanneh's brothers. But no one knew anything. The police could not find anyone connected to the case. They knew of a third person who had helped the escapees, but he had managed to follow Geris and Nabil to Lebanon.

Najibeh was held at the Jalameh prison, in Haifa. Despite her fear, she was calm, because she knew nothing. She was repeatedly interrogated. 'I have nothing to do with it,' she kept saying. 'All I know is that Sabri is a lawyer, and he works in Haifa.'

'What about Geris?' Three men towered over her, one on either side and one above her head. 'Who is the young man who came to see you in Fassouta, on the day he left?'

'I only saw him once before. But I don't know who he is.' She would not tell them she knew Nimer Shaqqour, or any of Geris' friends.

'We'll find out. And if you don't tell us, we'll bring your sister, Na'ima, to keep you company! How about that?'

Na'ima had visited earlier to bring her fresh clothes, but the guards would not let her see Najibeh or take anything in. All Najibeh got was a small bar of soap from the prison, and she had to wash the clothes she was wearing and wait for them to dry. She was held with about twenty other women from the Galilee. For three weeks, she saw no one from her family and had no idea what was going on. The warden, an Iraqi Jew, spoke Arabic and told her about the wife of Habib Qahwaji, Sabri's friend from al-Ard. 'She was here for one and a half years, before they were kicked out of the country!' she snapped. She assigned Najibeh to clean the toilets and cells. Two weeks later, Najibeh began to scratch her scalp. To her horror, she found lice.

Her uncle, Khalil, was watching TV and was shocked to see his niece on the news, being labeled a 'suspect'. He immediately got up and dashed to see a man from a large clan in the village, who was a known collaborator, to see if he could help. 'I've never heard of a girl being imprisoned!' Khalil said, angrily.

Every day, Wardeh opened the cupboard in the corner of the room where she and Elias slept. Her hands shook as she took out one of Geris' shirts and sniffed it, choking on her tears. She had hoped there was some mistake, that they had mixed him up with someone else, that her boy was safe and sound in Haifa and would soon come home. But weeks had gone by, and her world had fallen to pieces.

He was in Lebanon, they said. She sobbed into the shirt. She could not talk to him. There were no phone lines to that country, so close, yet so far away.

Sabri, Subhi, and Najibeh were in prison. The family was cornered. Elias had to place all his livestock as guarantee to get them released. Weeks later, they were all let go, except for Sabri. He was held in administrative detention, again, at the Damon prison in Haifa. 'You're a very dangerous man!' the interrogator snapped. 'Every troublemaker has a line that connects to you, a long line that twists and turns, then cuts short just before reaching you! You're staying until you talk!'

Since the war, Israel had been using administrative detention at a new level. When Sabri was held, in 1970, some eighty people had already been detained for more than two years without charge or trial; this had not happened in the first twenty years of the state. Any talk of repealing or even modifying the Defence (Emergency) Regulations had disappeared. Instead, the Israeli authorities extended administrative detention, house arrest, curfews, and closed areas to Palestinians in the newly occupied territory.

Sabri rubbed his temples, wearily. Hanneh had come to see him earlier, asking when he would be released. Na'ima was with her. She would go to Haifa to stay with Hanneh whenever Sabri was detained.

His administrative detention order was issued for one month at a time, by the northern district army commander, and renewed at the end of each month. At other times, it would be issued for three

145

or six months, or even for a year, and it could be renewed indefinitely. There were no charges against Sabri, other than that he was a 'security risk'.

On 31 March 1970, he and seventeen others announced a hunger strike. They were among the first Palestinian detainees to make this move. The strike continued for three days and attracted wide attention. Newspapers publicized it, and hundreds of Palestinians protested in Haifa and Tel Aviv. Lawyers from Nazareth sent letters condemning the military government to the prime minister, the defense minister, the minister of police, and the newspapers. Demonstrations by Palestinians and Jews were held in front of the Knesset and the Damon prison, and statements of support came from Jewish voices. A petition was signed by numerous Jewish cultural figures and published in the Israeli *Haaretz* newspaper:

> The Arab poet, Fouzi el-Asmar, and Advocate Sabri Jiryis are now on a hunger strike at the Damon Jail [in Haifa]. Both of them, together with scores of Arab Israeli citizens, have been under arrest for nearly a year without a trial. All they request is the basic right to be brought before a court of justice and that the charges against them be made known. Since their requests have so far been turned down, and considering that their arrest is periodically renewed by administrative military ordinance, they do not see any alternative to arousing public opinion by a hunger strike. We call upon the public and the government to remove this stain from Israeli democracy, to cease using the notorious British Defense (Emergency) Regulations, and to bring these citizens before a court of justice or release them. Let us not have two types of law for two types of citizens![15]

A second strike, on 29 April, spread to 600 prisoners throughout Israeli jails, including detainees from the occupied territory. Public protests increased in Israel and abroad. Weeks later, most of the prisoners were released, including Sabri. But he was kept under house arrest. This time, however, things took a serious turn. Since the beginning of the year, Fatah had been exchanging information with the Russian intelligence services. One of the first things the KGB agent had relayed is that Sabri's name had come up frequently on the Israeli authorities' list of people being watched. 'It seems they're planning to put him away, for a long time,' the tip said. On

Sabri's release, Abu Jihad immediately sent word to him, advising him to get out of the country.

Sabri did not want to leave. For several weeks, he battled with the decision. But Abu Jihad was persistent. He asked him to direct the Hebrew radio segment of Fatah in Cairo. Sabri and Hanneh knew there would be no turning back. Returning to Israel would be impossible. The move would cut them off from their families for who knew how long.

But, despite themselves, they both knew it was the only option. 'It's either that, or they put you away for life,' Hanneh said, as they thought painfully. They sold their apartment in Haifa and moved to a nuns' guest house for a few months. Sabri was working on a large case involving the seizure of land belonging to the Qahwaji family in Fassouta, and he returned the file to them to give to another lawyer. He also assembled the notes for his book, *A History of Zionism*, to take with him.

Suddenly, it all looked very real.

XIII

Geris was back in Amman. Within a few months, he had gained the trust of Abu Jihad, who had given him an open check book to finance resistance operations and a document to travel between Syria and Lebanon. Geris returned to work, organizing arms transport to Israel. He changed his name several times to protect his identity and begged his colleagues not to carry out any operations near the borders, wanting them to stay open so that people and ammunition could be smuggled through. But shocks unfolded for him in rapid succession. Ignorance was rampant, effectiveness was low, moral and nationalist values were mixed up in the rhetoric. Tired fighters sat around idly, waiting for their salaries. Geris began to question himself. Was this the revolution he had dreamed of? He would not even allow himself to go to the cinema, such was his dedication to his cause. But it was clear that his idealism had no place in the setup in which he found himself.

In June, fighting broke out again with the Jordanian army. The inability of his superiors to think in basic strategic terms appalled him. For months, he battled with feelings of letdown and frustration. Even at his young age, he quickly lost hope in the revolution and those who stood behind it. Another pain settled on his chest like a boulder: the way the Arab nations had failed his people, and the flimsiness of the notion of Arab unity, no more concrete now than it had been in Nasser's dreams.

In July 1970, Nasser and King Hussein of Jordan agreed with Israel to end the war of attrition, which had been waged on the borders between their countries since 1967. William Rogers, US secretary of state during the Nixon administration, drew up plans for an Israeli-Arab settlement and the declaration of Jordan as a Jordanian-Palestinian state.

The Palestinians rejected the plan, seeing it as a regional conspiracy to override their cause. Some called to overthrow the monarchy in Jordan. Huge demonstrations broke out against Nasser and he closed the PLO and Fatah offices in Cairo. Left-wing Palestinian groups resorted to desperate tactics and hijacked airplanes to attract attention and to stop Arab and Western countries from signing off on their fate.

Geris returned to Beirut. He was haunted by the dream of going home.

XIV

Sabri and Hanneh were saying their goodbyes. Their families were in shock.

'No! Leaving where?' Nour burst out. 'Are you crazy?'

Um Nour looked at her daughter, aghast.

'What am I going to do, wait until they lock him up for good?' Hanneh cried.

It took weeks for the family to absorb the news. Sabri gave his mother-in-law a document. 'Um Nour, you need to keep this, carefully,' he said. Hanneh had relinquished her share in the inheritance of her father's land. Sabri knew, from his work with Naqqara, that she had to do that in order to bypass the Absentee Property Law. Otherwise, the state would classify her as an 'absentee' after she left and seize her property.

Um Nour nodded, folding the paper in her lap. 'Where are you going?' she asked, panic-stricken.

'To Greece.' He and Hanneh had decided not to share their final destination. Their families were sure to be questioned.

But Sabri took his father aside and told him the truth. He tried to soften the blow. 'Don't sell the land,' he said. 'I need a piece to build a house on when I return.'

'Sell the land?' Elias gasped. 'Would I ever do that?'

'Listen to me, carefully. You need to make a will, in which you split the land between George and Subhi.'

'Why?'

'So the state doesn't come and claim that Geris and I aren't here, and seize our part of it,' Sabri explained.

A heavy silence fell. Elias broke it. 'Are you going to your brother?'

Sabri nodded. 'We'll let you know what happens with us, Father. Don't worry.' He urged Elias not to tell anyone, and he knew he would keep it to himself.

His father complied with the request. 'You heard, they're going to Europe ...' he said, when his other children pressed him.

Hanneh gave some of their furniture to her aunt in Haifa and the remainder to Sabri's sister, Mariam.

Even to leave, Sabri needed a permit. In his life in Israel, from high school in Nazareth, in 1953, through his university years in Jerusalem and his work in Haifa, until 1970, he had never been a free man.

'Where are you going?' the policeman asked.

'I'm emigrating. You're oppressing me and I don't want to live with you anymore.'

'We know where you're going,' the man nodded. 'To join your friends. But you won't be able to live with them, trust me. It's better here!'

'I'm going to Europe,' Sabri said. The policeman was not inclined to pursue the matter. He pushed the permit across at him. Of the four leaders of al-Ard, Sabri and Habib had been voluntarily expelled, Saleh was in prison, and Mansour continued to face hassle.

On 9 September 1970, Sabri and Hanneh boarded a plane to Athens, taking one last look at their homeland before it disappeared from view.

6

EXILE

I'm afraid to look into their eyes, for I am ashamed. They, that dust of humanity, are the only people in the world I cannot look straight in the eye. I'm not ashamed of fighting them in the battlefield, I'm not ashamed of being their enemy, or of defending against them; I'm not ashamed to be an adversary or a fugitive or beggar, or anything ... But a thief—a thief in the night I do not want to be.

Ezriel Carlebach
'Cry, the Beloved Country'[1]

They spent two weeks in Greece. They could not enter Lebanon with Israeli passports, so Geris flew to Athens to meet them with Syrian ones. The passports were supplied by the Syrian government which was then backing the PLO.

It was Geris' first time on a plane. He did not know whether to be happy because he would be reunited with his brother, or sad because of their parents' heartbreak.

Geris had little choice; his new life was catching up with him. 'Beirut is under my control,' he joked to Sabri, trying to lighten the surreal situation in which they found themselves. He helped his brother and Hanneh to rent a furnished apartment in Ain al-Mraiseh along the coastal Corniche, near downtown Beirut.

Barely a week later, the skirmishes in Jordan escalated into a war between the Jordanian army and the Palestinians. Between 21 and 27 September 1970, Nasser led the first emergency Arab League Summit in Cairo. A ceasefire was agreed upon, but it did not hold. The PLO was defeated and the Jordanian army killed thousands of Palestinian refugees. Most Palestinian guerrillas were disarmed and forced north from Amman to Jerash.

The events became known as Black September. Nasser, who had failed to stop the massacre, died of a heart attack on 28 September. Millions came out in mourning across the Arab world. Sabri and Geris felt deeply sad. Despite the 1967 defeat and his concessions since, Nasser had been the only Arab leader that most Palestinians trusted, and his pan-Arab dream had been a guiding light. Numerous Palestinian villages in Israel held symbolic funerals for him. The authorities arrested many of those who organized them and took part.

In Beirut, Sabri was taken to the regional office of Fatah, where he sat for a few hours and met various people. Telex messages kept coming in from Palestinians all over the world: the Arab countries, Africa, Europe, and South America. Many wanted to ask about relatives in Jordan, members of the Fatah guerrillas. As Sabri sat there, he began, for the first time, to grasp the true dimensions of Palestinian dispersion.

The terrible events in Jordan were matched by a grim reality in Lebanon. Twenty years after the Nakba, the country was teeming with Palestinian refugee camps, sordid dwellings of misery and humiliation. The tents had become huts and corrugated iron shacks that spread over slum districts. The Lebanese government refused to give the refugees resident status or citizenship, regardless of how long they lived in Lebanon. Its purported reason was for them not to 'lose their cause' by becoming naturalized, but the real motive was the fear of a change in traditional power structures. The country stood in precarious sectarian balance between Christians, Shia Muslims, and Sunni Muslims, in which a Christian minority ruled. Palestinians, most of whom were Muslims, were seen as a threat. They were kept out of society and could not claim the same rights as other foreigners living and working in the country. They were barred from social benefits and from practicing tens of professions, a situation that would persist for decades, even when their numbers grew to an estimated 10 per cent of the population.[2] Instead, they were turned over to UNRWA, the United Nations agency for Palestinian refugees, which took over health and education services in the camps. But it could not provide beyond the basic necessities.

It was not much better elsewhere. Refugee identification cards and travel permits issued by Arab countries were labeled by Palestinians as 'documents of suffering'. They marked their holders as stateless aliens, making it very difficult to travel or work. It took years for their circumstances to improve, and, eventually, they were better assimilated in Syria and Jordan. But, in Lebanon, they continued to struggle, living in cramped spaces where food was scarce, water was polluted, sewage flooded the streets, few toilets were in use by hundreds of people, and disease was widespread. For years, they lined up for rations, their dignity and former life a shadow of the past. Work was difficult to find, and most of them worked for low wages in difficult conditions. Some opened small shops or services in the camps, naming many of them after their towns and villages in Palestine. They lived in shocked denial, never able to absorb what had happened to them. The elderly held on pitifully to the keys to their homes, keys that now opened nothing. The young turned to armed resistance. Driven from Jordan and suffocated in Syria, the PLO intensified its presence in Lebanon and carried out attacks against Israel, which countered with raids, mostly into the south. As had happened in Jordan, the Lebanese government tried to restrict the Palestinian guerrillas, and sporadic fighting broke out with the Lebanese army.

Sabri and Hanneh began to absorb the terrible mosaic that was Lebanon.

II

In Fassouta, Hanneh's mother, Um Nour, was sick. Her brother, Faheem, hastened to her house. 'Where is she?'

'Inside. She's had a fever and bodyache and she can't get up,' said Nida, his youngest niece, who opened the door.

Faheem made his way to the room where the family slept. His sister looked at him feebly and propped herself up on her pillow.

'What's going on?' He approached her and sat on the chair opposite. But he knew. 'Um Nour, she had to go with her husband; how many times are we going to say that?'

Tears gathered in her eyes. They were puffy and he knew she had been crying.

'Sister,' he sighed. 'She couldn't let him go alone, could she?'

'She left so young,' Um Nour replied, tears coursing down her withered cheeks. 'Why did she have to take this road? University and I don't know what! She could have stayed here, with me, with her brothers and sisters. I never saw her properly. I never did!'

Faheem shook his head. 'All this talk, it's for nothing now. She's married, she can't leave her husband alone, can she?' he repeated. 'Pray that they'll be alright. And stop crying. It's a bad omen!'

She wiped her eyes, blew her nose. 'Make some coffee for your uncle,' she said, weakly, to Najwa, who was hovering in the corner of the room. Then she turned back to Faheem. 'Two men were here earlier, saying they were from the government.'

'What?'

Only ten days after Sabri and Hanneh's departure, agents of the Custodian of Absentee Property had come to Um Nour's house, said they were surveying the land, and asked for the ownership documents. She had told them that Sabri had left a paper with her. One of the men had winced. 'Sabri left a paper?'

'Yes. I'll get it for you.'

'Don't bother ...' the man had said. They had left shortly afterwards.

'They wanted to take the land!' Faheem exclaimed. 'It's good Sabri sorted that out.'

They sat awhile, talking about other things. 'I'm not leaving till you get up and wash your face. You're not going to let these two take care of the house, are you?' He attempted a laugh, pointing at his young nieces. 'They'll ruin it!'

Um Nour quietened down, holding it all inside. But, each day, she took out Hanneh's photograph and gazed at it, wiping away the tears that fell on the pretty face.

III

'The police are outside!' Sabri's youngest sister, Huda, burst through the door of her parents' home.

'What?' Najibeh, who was living at home after losing her job, leapt up. 'Where's Muna?'

'She's still in the yard!' Huda began to cry. The two children were cleaning out the yard when they found themselves facing the barrel of a gun. Huda was terrified and ran back to the house, while Muna stood there, frozen in fear.

'Shhh!' Najibeh said. 'I'll go get her.' She opened the door and stepped out. Jeeps had surrounded the house. A dog growled from one of them. She stared in alarm. None of her brothers were home. They had arrested Subhi, again.

A policeman stopped her on the steps. 'Where are you going?'

'To get my sister. She's a child. She's in the yard! What do you want?'

'Stay indoors. Where are your brothers?' he asked.

'I don't know! They're not here! My father isn't here, either!' Her mother and Na'ima were in the kitchen. They heard the exchange and came running. 'I have to get my sister. She'll be scared!' Najibeh pressed.

Just then, she saw her father heading home with the goats. He hurried up to her, trying to keep the animals in tow. 'What's going on?'

'Where were you?' the policeman turned to him.

'With the goats!' Elias had seen the police follow him to the fields. They had stopped him and asked him if he was meeting his sons, if they were sneaking in from the Lebanese border.

'Did you see your sons?' the policeman asked, again.

'What? I told you, I was grazing the goats!' Elias made to open the pen to take the animals in, which were beginning to scatter about on the road.

'Stop!' the policeman said. 'Get in here!'

'Effendi,'* Elias panicked, 'I need to take the goats in. They'll run away!'

But the policeman grabbed him and threw him in the back of the jeep with the dog. 'What are you doing?' Najibeh screamed.

'Move aside,' he ordered, roughly, slamming the door.

'Let him out!' Najibeh cried, as the dog began to bark. Elias huddled in terror, shielding his face. Wardeh screamed and ran to find Elias' brother, Khalil. The police charged into the house. Na'ima scrambled after them. They flung the cupboards open and began rummaging through. In the kitchen, they moved jars aside roughly, toppling them over. She stared, aghast, as oil and flour poured onto the counter and down on the floor. Then, they went back to the rooms. The sisters had been cleaning that day and had just finished washing and stitching back together the woolen quilts. The police threw everything on the floor and trampled it. They ran up the stairs to the second floor. 'Open the door!' they shouted.

Na'ima obliged, hands shaking. The top floor was locked. It had Sabri's books. She watched in horror as they tore through them, then she dashed back down. 'Where's Mother? Where's Uncle Khalil?' she screamed at Najibeh, who was fighting with the police outside to release Elias.

Wardeh had given up on her brother-in-law, who could not be found, and had run to one of the families who were known to work with the authorities. They had turned her away. She stumbled home in tears. Finally, the police finished their search and left, shoving Elias out of the jeep and driving away in a cloud of dust.

---

* *Effendi* (Arabic, Turkish, Persian): a title of courtesy used in the Levant, including in Palestine during Ottoman rule and the British Mandate.

Najibeh helped her father into the house. He was vomiting. 'Go, get the doctor!' she said to her sisters. Muna, sobbing, dragged Huda with her and they scampered off. Wardeh's wails could be heard from inside.

IV

The doctor surveyed the scene in the house as he examined Elias. 'He's had stomach pain for a while,' Najibeh said. 'It keeps coming back. And they pushed him into a jeep with a dog just now. And he won't say anything! Father!' She turned to him in anguish.

Elias, face white as a sheet, remained silent. Sweat glistened on his brow. His hands and body shook. 'He's in shock,' the doctor said. 'I'll give him an injection to help him sleep and something to stop the vomiting. But bring him to the clinic to do some tests.'

It was only then that Khalil showed up. 'This is all your brothers' fault!' he yelled at Najibeh. 'They didn't think of their parents? Their sisters?'

'I don't need this now!' she cried. 'We don't need you here! The police are gone already!'

'Some manners ... Who's going to marry you?!' Khalil snapped, storming out again and slamming the door.

Najibeh turned to her mother. 'Why did you have to get him? Why? He never comes to help us. He waits until they're gone!'

The doctor shook his head and injected Elias, who remained silent. Wardeh collapsed on a nearby chair. After the doctor left, Najibeh turned to her. 'Mother, who else did you call? I keep telling you: I'm here, I can take care of you. These people will never do anything for us! Don't ask any of them again!'

She called Na'ima and rushed out with her to gather the goats. When they returned, Elias had drifted off into a weary sleep. Wardeh cried herself to sleep, too. Muna and Huda huddled next to Najibeh. She told them to wash and get changed, and she managed to light a fire and give them something to eat. Na'ima was back in the kitchen, cleaning up the mess.

The family had never felt so alone. People whose sons and brothers were Sabri's friends now badmouthed him to curry favor with the authorities. Najibeh recalled, bitterly, how they used to come to the house when he visited from university, how they asked his opinions on politics, pretending to admire him and be best buddies. After he left, these same people tore him and his family to pieces. Many were co-opted to watch the family's every move. And many were afraid, too afraid to mix with them.

A young man, one of Sabri's friends, had been interested in Najibeh. She had heard from her aunt that he was asking about her. But weeks of silence followed, and her aunt finally told her that his brother-in-law had lashed out at him: 'If you even think of her, I'll shoot you! Plenty of girls to marry! And she's just out of prison, too!'

Najibeh sighed. They would not take her back to her job at Nahariya. 'Your brothers are terrorists!' they spat. She had spent months looking for work.

Her sisters began nodding off, and she put her arms around them. Muna was thirteen; Huda, eleven, too young for all of this. Najibeh wondered where her brothers were, what they were doing. She missed them, terribly.

V

It took four months for Sabri to see Abu Jihad. 'Welcome!' he shook Sabri's hand and smiled. After three years of working together, it was their first meeting, but it was as if they had known each other a long time.

The offer of directing the Hebrew radio segment of Fatah in Cairo was gone. Nasser had closed down the station before his untimely death. Abu Jihad asked Sabri what he wanted to do. 'I'm going to research,' he answered, 'but I'll still be with you.'

In February 1971, King Hussein ordered his forces to oust all the remaining Palestinian guerrillas from northern Jordan. Arafat was going back and forth to Syria to navigate his next steps. Sabri went, with a friend from Fatah, to meet him. When he was introduced to him, Arafat smiled. 'I know about you. Abu Jihad always hides the good things from me and keeps them to himself! Welcome!'

His words rose above the horrors of the previous months. Browbeaten and displaced after the Jordan war, with thousands of his people killed, Arafat had another problem in Syria. His relations were sour with President Hafez al-Assad, who had ousted his pre-decessor, Salah Jadid, and come to power. Assad wanted to control Lebanon and the Palestinians and emerge as the negotiating power in the region. Arafat was unlikely to stay in Damascus.

When Sabri went out on the balcony to smoke, he was intro-duced to Mahmoud Abbas (Abu Mazen), the finance officer of Fatah. As they chatted, Abbas asked him about any Israeli peace groups it was possible to negotiate with. At the time, this was a very tentative idea which few Palestinians dared to express.

On his return to Beirut, Sabri began working at the Institute for Palestine Studies, an independent Arab organization for research and publication. Hanneh joined him. He asked for a secretary who knew Hebrew, and Soad Hayek was appointed. She was from Nazareth and had married her cousin, Suheil, a refugee who had somehow managed to acquire Lebanese citizenship. The couple had three daughters. Soad and Hanneh quickly became friends.

Hanneh began to miss her family. She had no idea when, or if, she and Sabri could ever return. Their village was just an hour away, yet they were completely disconnected. The borders were closed, there was no post or phone. When Father Kareem, the priest of Fassouta, walked into their apartment in Beirut one day, her eyes filled with tears.

'Relax, my dear … It's alright,' he said. He pointed to the reli-gious habit he was wearing. 'I can go and come, easily. They don't hassle me.'

'Can you …'

'Yes, I can. Write a letter to your parents.'

VI

Father Kareem knew he would be in grave trouble if he was found out. But he also knew the authorities did not bother religious clergy, having co-opted many of them and assumed the rest were in line. A week later, he knocked on Elias' door. Na'ima answered it. The priest was a good friend of her father's and visited them often. 'Where's Abu Sabri?' he asked.

'Out,' she replied. 'Come in, Father.'

Najibeh coaxed her mother out of bed. 'Mother, the priest is here. Get up!'

Wardeh had taken to sleep. A lot of sleep. She was not eating much. 'Welcome, Father,' she said, sinking into a chair and rubbing her eyes.

'Wardeh, you're not looking so well. What's the matter?'

'She loves Hanneh like she loves us ...' Na'ima muttered, sadly. 'She's been like this since they left.'

'I have something for you,' Kareem replied, his voice dropping to a whisper. They all looked at him. He took a piece of paper out of his pocket and passed it to Na'ima.

'From Sabri and Hanneh!' she breathed. Wardeh began to cry.

Najibeh snatched the paper from her. 'Let me read it!'

'What are they saying?' Wardeh sobbed.

'They're fine, Um Sabri, they're fine!' Kareem urged. 'Where's Elias?' he asked, again.

As though on cue, the door creaked open and his friend walked in. 'I was waiting for you,' the priest smiled.

'Father, welcome! Have they given you coffee?' Elias shook the hay from his clothes and sat down. 'Why is this fire dying out? What's this?'

'It's a letter from Sabri and Hanneh!' Najibeh chirped. 'They say they're doing fine, and they send us all their best, and say not to worry about them.'

'From Sabri? Give it to me!' Elias' hands shook as he held the paper and stared at it. At that moment, he wished more than anything that he could read. Kareem felt a painful lump in his throat.

'How are they?' Elias turned to him, still clutching the paper. 'Did you see them?'

The priest nodded. 'They're fine! Now stop this commotion before any of the neighbors hear us!'

Elias sniffed. He gave the letter back to Najibeh, who hid it. As she peeled an orange for their guest and Na'ima warmed the coffee, Kareem made a small, almost imperceptible signal to Elias. After they had eaten the fruit, Elias got up. He went into the kitchen and came out with a small tin of cheese. 'I'm going out with Father,' he announced. 'I won't be long.'

Outside, the two hurried along to the priest's house. Elias' heart raced painfully. He was not religious, but he had been praying, in his heart, every day since they had left.

STRANGER IN MY OWN LAND

The priest unlocked his front door. 'Welcome, Abu Sabri,' he said, loudly. 'Thank you for the cheese! Come in.'

As soon as they were inside, he closed the door and went around, closing the windows and shutters. Then he turned to his friend. 'Sabri is in a conference in France. He's going to call now.'

Elias nodded, breathlessly. Kareem made more coffee and they sat and waited. At the time, it was very difficult to install a phone in the village. The process took years. Kareem was one of three people to have a phone at his home.

The minutes dragged. 'You're sure?' Elias finally asked. The shrill ring made them jump. Kareem rushed to it.

'Yes, yes. He's here. Here you go!' He handed the receiver to Elias, who grabbed it, hands shaking.

Kareem sat outside, sipping his coffee. A weak sun peeked out, but he did not mind the cold. He wrapped a woolen scarf around his habit and waited. The villagers passed by and greeted him, and he answered them in his easy manner. Little did they know that he was keeping watch.

Elias finally made his way home, trying to keep his tears in check. 'All of you sitting there like idiots and none of you got it!' he said, gleefully. 'I just spoke to Sabri!'

VII

Um Nour trudged slowly up the road, pausing for breath as a cousin passed her and said hello. Was she imagining it, or did everyone look at her in pity? Her cousin did not ask about Hanneh. People were too scared. Um Nour was scared, too. Reaching Elias' house, she knocked and waited.

'Come in!' a voice called.

She brightened up when she saw Na'ima, who was the closest to her and always gave her news. 'How are they?' she asked her, fervently.

'They're fine!' Na'ima smiled. 'I have something for you!'

When she produced the letter Hanneh had written to her mother, Um Nour, too, dissolved into tears. Na'ima tried to soothe her. 'It's alright! Sabri called, as well. Father spoke to him two days ago!'

'What? Why didn't you tell me?' Um Nour gasped.

'It all happened on the spot. Sabri was alone,' said Na'ima, her heart breaking for the woman, who seemed to have aged twenty years since her daughter had left. 'He said she'll be with him, next time, and you can talk to her!'

Um Nour sat down. 'Can you read me the letter?' she said, handing the paper back to Na'ima. Wardeh came to sit with them. Sabri had joked to his mother, when he had gotten married, that there were now two roses* in his life. As Na'ima read the letter, both of them listened, their tears falling. Afterwards, they just stared into space.

Eventually, Na'ima made coffee and drew them into a small chat. It was surreal, she thought, how they found other things to talk about, how they somehow pretended their loved ones were just away on a trip. Beneath the comfort they tried to give each other, both families fought the feeling that they may not see their children for a very long time.

VIII

'Najibeh's here,' Na'ima told the two other women, seeing her sister through the window. She was getting off the bus, which stopped just in front of the house.

'George has been arrested!' said Najibeh, stumbling in.

'What?'

'They found a gun in his things!'

His mother looked like she was about to faint.

'A gun?' Um Nour cried out in alarm. 'Dear God, why are they doing this to us?'

George had, indeed, been following in his brothers' footsteps. But he was not careful enough. 'What's this?' A policeman had brandished a pistol he had found in the wardrobe of George's room in Haifa. 'Fancy yourself a little revolutionary, hey?'

George had been itching to take part in the resistance. His brothers' leaving and the backlash the family had endured had

---

* *Wardeh* (Arabic): rose.

sealed the deal. He was recruited by Mousa Assi, from Geris' group. Mousa had been arrested four days earlier. Had he told on him? George wondered.

The policemen shoved him into the car and took him to the station. It turned out that Mousa had tried to recruit someone else, who was exposed and had told on him. They had seized Mousa and tortured him until he had given information about the others. At sixteen, George faced the charge of belonging to Fatah, an illegal organization. The hearing was held at a military court in Lydda, near Tel Aviv. 'You're lucky, being a minor,' the judge frowned. 'I could have given you a much longer term, and you would have deserved it!' He was sentenced to one and a half years in prison.

IX

In Beirut, Geris heard, from Sabri, what was happening back home. The rest, he guessed. He was tormented by pangs of guilt, especially for his parents. Why did they have to endure this suffering? It confused him, made him question if he had done the right thing. He was also desperately homesick. He and Sabri had each other, but they were both aliens in an alien land. Their grandfather, Jiryis, passed away in Fassouta, at the incredible age of 104. They were very sad that they could not see him. They thought of their conversations with him, of the love that the old man had shown them.

Sabri had to forge ahead. He immersed himself in politics and research. The picture became larger than Israel or Fassouta. He missed his family, but he began to feel that his location was less relevant as long as he was working for his cause. He stayed in Fatah but moved out of the organizational work and into the Western Sector's Advisory Council.

At the Institute for Palestine Studies, his task was to conduct research on Israeli affairs and direct others in doing the same. But, there, and in Fatah, he saw people's debilitating lack of knowledge. Few Palestinians had come from Israel to join the PLO; most were 1948 refugees who had grown up in neighboring countries. 'Before you came,' Abu Jihad admitted, 'I, personally, did not know there was a difference between the head of state and the prime minister in Israel.'

In July 1971, the remaining Palestinian fighters were driven out of Jordan. Arafat and about 2,000 of his troops came to set up their new headquarters in Lebanon, beginning another chapter of the PLO's history.

The same month, Sabri and Mahmoud Darwish were elected to the Palestinian National Council during its ninth session in Cairo. They were the first Palestinian citizens of Israel to become members. Mahmoud had left the country in 1970, like Sabri, and decided not to return. He had gone to Moscow to study and, a year later, had dropped out and moved to Cairo, where he worked at *al-Ahram* newspaper. A small number of voluntary exiles from Israel, such as Imad Shaqqour, Elias Shoufani, and others, also joined the PLO. But, when Sabri was asked to establish an Israeli studies department at the Institute for Palestine Studies, he had no idea where to start.

His first suggestion was to compile a daily bulletin of Israel's news. Those with knowledge of Hebrew followed the news and commentary in Israeli newspapers, translated the most useful into Arabic, and distributed a bulletin to subscribers. Sabri also wrote numerous articles and studies. Hanneh worked with him in research.

They moved out of the furnished apartment to an empty one on Corniche el-Mazra'a, in West Beirut, and bought their own furniture. To their delight, they met a few others from Fassouta.

Nour Shammas had left to study for the priesthood at the Jesuit College in Lebanon, but had not finished his education. He found work at the Jesuit printer and married a Palestinian refugee from Haifa.

Wajiha Khoury, Um Saleem, was also from Fassouta and her relatives still lived there. She was married to Toufiq Mitri, a refugee from Pequi'a, near Fassouta. The couple had four children. Um Saleem was very kind to Hanneh, who found in her a new mother.

Toufiq also introduced them to Ratiba Sima'an, a refugee from Suhmata who worked as a housekeeper for the French ambassador to Lebanon.

Hanneh was grateful to have this circle. The only contact with her family was through the letters with the priest or with friends who traveled to Europe, so they could mail them to Israel. The unsigned letters were addressed to Um Nour and Na'ima, without a return address. Each time Sabri travelled abroad for meetings or conferences, he would phone his father. Hanneh had accompanied him on one trip to Paris and had spoken to her mother. But it was hardly enough. She longed to see her, to see them all.

X

George began to feel lost. He was in Grade 11, but there was no way to continue school in prison. With his weak Hebrew, he could also not follow the radio, nor read the newspapers that were allowed in. Suddenly, he remembered his teacher's warning. Leafing through the paper, George found a Hebrew study page in each issue for Jewish immigrants. He began to improve his language. Each day, he listened to the news, tried to find the corresponding item in the newspaper, and used a dictionary to decipher it.

All inmates were assigned some work. George worked in a small printing press at the prison. Then, the warden placed him in charge of the library and teaching the younger children. About fifteen were held with him, some for petty crimes, others for trying to escape to Lebanon to join the resistance. Six months later, he was transferred out of the juvenile facility and to the Damon prison in Haifa, where Sabri had been held. There, he found older political detainees, among them a man named Atta, from Jerusalem.

When he heard George's charge, Atta shook his head and spoke in soft tones. 'I understand your motives, and I'm with you. But this is futile.'

George looked at him. Was he a spy, he wondered, planted among them? He said nothing.

Sensing his hesitation, Atta smiled. 'I'm like you,' he continued, 'but the problem is we're not like the others, the ones fighting from outside. We're not even like our brothers in the West Bank and Gaza. We're stuck here, with the Israelis, in the midst of them. Taking up arms only has this result,' he gestured around him. 'And we're not much use to anyone, locked up.'

George nodded. He had heard that Mousa Assi was in very bad shape. Mousa had been tortured and had exposed Geris' cell, as well, which had continued to work for two years after Geris had left. All of its members were caught. George was thankful, in this instance, that his brother had left the country.

XI

'It's your fault! You raised them this way!' Elias' shouts rang out as Najibeh opened the door.

'What's going on?' she gasped, rushing into the house. Na'ima followed quickly behind her.

'When they were fine, they were your sons!' Wardeh retorted, as though she had not seen them. Her brief spells of wakefulness were spent fighting with Elias.

'Mother, stop!' Najibeh's head was throbbing. 'We saw George. He's fine. They wouldn't let him keep the blanket, though.' She put down the bag she was holding.

'When is he coming out?' Elias asked, a sudden quiver in his voice.

'Next month.' Najibeh took her shoes off, wearily.

'See? This is all your doing! Big heads, all of them!' Elias turned to Wardeh again. 'They wouldn't be content with our life, oh no!'

She did not answer this time, simply burst into tears and left the room. The girls knew better than to argue with him. They followed her to the kitchen. She sat on a stool and sobbed into her apron. 'The neighbor, this morning ...' she cried. 'You know what she said to me? "Some sons you had! They'll never come back!"'

Wardeh struggled on all fronts: with her own pain, with the village, and with Elias, who was taking his wrath out on her. 'Damn the hour I saw you!' they heard him yell from inside.

Najibeh stormed back into the living room. 'Enough!' she snapped. 'Go! Check on the goats! Or do something—just get out of the house!'

It had taken her two years to find a job, this time with Leumit, a national healthcare provider. She worked at their clinic in Hurfeish, a village nearby. Najibeh was thankful both for having found work and for being so close, to intervene in her parents' quarrels. Her father was intimidated by her, she knew. Sometimes, she could stop him in his tracks.

Elias wandered off to al-Bayyad, an area east of the village. It was known for its rocky land, and he had bought a piece there that was planted with olive trees. It was the land he had set aside for Sabri and Geris to build on.

But, as he approached it, he was shocked to see a bulldozer tearing down the trees and clearing space. 'What are you doing?' He rushed up to the mukhtar, who was surveying the work.

'Opening a road here. So people can get to this place without shrubs and thorns.'

'But this is my land!' Elias gasped.

'And we have permission. We told you that, already, Abu Sabri.'

'I did not give permission!'

'It's a government project; landowners have to give space for the roads,' the mukhtar replied, impatiently. 'We sent you the papers!'

'I don't care about any papers!' Elias raised his walking stick in fury as the bulldozer knocked down an olive tree. 'Stop it!' he cried, frantically.

The mukhtar snapped. 'What are you kicking up a fuss about? You think they'll ever come back?'

Elias stood, frozen to the spot. Blinking through a mist of tears, he turned around and stumbled home.

XII

In Hurfeish, Najibeh became popular and able to talk to the women who visited the health center. But politics had to be carefully avoided. Her family was still being watched.

She and Na'ima had taken a rare tourist trip by bus with some other people from Fassouta. Afterwards, the police had questioned those who were with them, asking where they had gone and what photographs the sisters had taken. 'They're all like hens, squawking at the first chance they get!' Na'ima fumed. They were shocked at the lies that people could make up.

One afternoon, when Elias' family had eaten their lunch and laid down for a rest, two police cars stopped outside. 'We have a search warrant,' a policeman said. He charged in with three others. 'Who's this?' he poked his gun roughly at Elias, who was napping on his mattress, still wearing his headdress.

'It's my father!' Najibeh said. 'Searching for what? Haven't you searched already?'

Elias, who had woken up in bewilderment, sat on the mattress pitifully as they repeated the ordeal. Wardeh and the girls stared at them as they turned the house upside down. Najibeh was close to tears, this time. The fedayeen had carried out a resistance operation in Pequi'a. Each time anything happened, everyone pointed fingers at Elias and his family. *'It must be Abu Sabri's children!'*

'This house is coming down,' the policeman barked. 'Outside, all of you!'

'What?' they cried.

'Outside, I said!' he yelled. They were horrified to see a bulldozer standing by the house. The policeman pushed Elias, who fell onto its blade.

Two other policemen scrambled up from the goat pen below, covered in mud and hay. 'Nothing here,' they told the officer. He nodded, lips pursed.

Na'ima managed to escape and run to the neighbor's house, the one who had told on Sabri so many times. He was sitting with his relative and two men in civilian clothes. She immediately guessed that they were undercover police officers or secret agents. 'What does my father have to do with it?' she asked them, angrily. 'He's an old man and you know he has no hand in this!'

The men looked up, slyly, and mumbled to each other. The neighbor turned to her and frowned. 'Go home; we'll take care of it. Your problems never end!'

Na'ima walked away, bitterly. She hated asking for their help. But it was only because of them that the house was spared.

XIII

In October 1972, George was released from prison. His school would not take him back because he was over eighteen, so he decided to sit his final exams on his own, in order to obtain his high school certificate. He went around to his friends and asked for their notes, and he found work for a few days each month to cover his expenses.

His biggest shock came when, one day, his father needed help with the goats. Elias was getting older and more tired. George took a break from his books and followed him to the fields. As he approached, he heard loud sobbing. He rushed up and found Elias alone, rocking back and forth. 'Damn all schools and education!' he cried.

George's heart broke. He had never seen him like this. 'Don't worry, Father,' he knelt next to him. 'A day will come when you'll see Sabri and Geris again, I promise.'

After passing his exams, he went to Haifa to look for work. He began to distribute *al-Ittihad* newspaper, then he found a clerical job in accounting. After his prison experience and his brothers' exile, he began to see the fight of the Palestinians in Israel as one of identity, to preserve their existence. As his fellow detainee had said, there was no room for military conflict in their situation. George joined the Communist Party and worked to raise votes for it in the village.

At the time, the party sent many of its young members abroad to study, and he was offered a scholarship in medicine in the Soviet Union. He knew that, if he had mentioned university to his father, the old man may have blown a fuse. But Elias eventually asked him what he wanted to do.

George told him about the scholarship. 'But I don't want to leave you and Mother. And I don't want to do medicine, anyway.'

Elias nodded. He seemed at a loss for words. 'You know what's best,' he finally said.

'I don't want anything,' George said, patting his father's knee. 'You take care of yourself and Mother. I'm working and supporting myself, and if I want to continue studying, I can. Don't worry.' He was planning to enroll in accounting at a college in Haifa.

'The land,' Elias mumbled. 'I want to give it to you and Subhi.'

'What?'

'Sabri told me to make a will, so the government doesn't take the land. I'm going to leave it to you and Subhi. When your brothers return, you can divide it properly among you.'

George nodded. 'They will return, I promise,' he added, for the second time. He did not know how he knew. Perhaps it was just strong, wishful thinking. But George simply knew.

At Christmas, he tried to cheer his father up. Holidays were particularly difficult. The gap left by the missing children seemed to fill the house. 'Look, Father! Aren't we enough? Look at all this family around you!' he said.

But Elias choked on his response. 'If you had a hundred sheep and lost one of them, wouldn't you leave them all and go after that one to find it?'[3]

XIV

'You're looking photogenic!' Arafat chuckled when Sabri walked into his office, dressed in a new suit and tie.

'It's Christmas, Abu Ammar. Hanneh wants to go to a party,' Sabri smiled. He was hoping that he would not be kept for a long discussion, as frequently happened. He had become Arafat's advisor on Israeli affairs. Their talks went on for hours and, often, Arafat insisted that he stay and eat with him and his staff.

But that evening, he waved him off, handing him a Christmas card before he left. 'I can talk to you later,' he said. 'Merry Christmas!'

Hanneh wanted to celebrate, for a small miracle had occurred. After five years of marriage, she and Sabri were having a baby.

'We need one more room,' she declared, after the New Year. 'I'm not squeezing the baby in with us!' For the third time, they moved, this time to Ein el-Rummaneh, in East Beirut.

Their circle was growing. Mahmoud Darwish had moved from Cairo and begun working at the PLO Palestine Research Center, editing its new journal, *Palestine Affairs*. The friends were reunited and he visited Sabri and Hanneh often, especially when Hanneh made the delicious kubbeh that so reminded him of home. They felt the air of the Galilee when they were together. It was like the old times, so recent, yet so far away.

Hanneh's cooking repertoire had grown, and she made many dishes that delighted Sabri and their visitors alike. When he invited Arafat and Abu Jihad for dinner, though, she balked. 'What will I cook?'

They settled on catered food, readily available among the many conveniences of Beirut. During the meal, Hanneh made an innocent slip. 'Abu Ammar, would you like a drink?' she asked, holding up a bottle of whisky. Arafat smiled, graciously, and declined. He asked for juice instead.

Sabri smiled, too. He knew that Arafat did not drink. When he went to visit the Soviets, he told Sabri, they would pour alcohol for themselves and juice for him. He kept whisky and arak at his office, and, when foreigners visited him, he often asked Sabri to drink with them. Though Arafat was conservative, he was not religiously strict. In his hectic life, he did not have time for the five daily prayers required of Muslims. Sometimes, when he was angry, he would curse religion, as was customary in Arabic slang. Then, he would stop for a second and mutter: 'I seek the forgiveness of God, the Mighty!'

Yet, though there were happy times, there was no safety around them. A few months before, on 8 July 1972, Ghassan Kanafani, a writer, had been assassinated in Beirut. A bomb went off in his car as he started it, killing him and his seventeen-year-old niece, Lamees Najim. Kanafani, thirty-six, was one of the most prolific Palestinian writers, with a rich collection of stories and novels, as well as political essays. He left behind a wife and two young children.

On 16 October 1972, the Mossad killed Wael Zu'aiter, the PLO representative in Rome. He was shot dead on his doorstep.

And on 10 April 1973, three Palestinian leaders: Kamal Udwan, Mohammed Yousef al-Najjar, and Kamal Butros Nasser were killed in an Israeli raid in Beirut. Udwan was a politician and PLO leader; al-Najjar, a commander of Fatah's military wing; and Nasser a writer, poet, and official spokesman of the PLO. The latter had not taken part in any military activity. An Israeli commando unit led by Ehud Barak, later to become Israel's defense minister and prime minister, stormed their apartments in West Beirut and gunned them down, killing Nasser in front of his family and killing al-Najjar's wife, as well, as she tried to defend her husband. Several other PLO members, Lebanese security men, and civilians were also killed.

Most of the assassinations were carried out by the Israeli intelligence, the Mossad. They would continue for decades, killing scores of Palestinian leaders and intellectuals.

XV

In 1972, Geris was in China. Under Mao Tse-Tung, the country gave tremendous support to the Palestinians. He spent a year there, with thirty other young men, for training. He saw what, to his young mind, was a near-perfect manifestation of popular struggle. It was a life-changing experience. When he returned to Beirut, full of fire and enthusiasm, he continued his military work within the PLO. But, again, he was shocked at the shortcomings. Chaos, nepotism, sectarianism, and ineffectiveness plagued him at every turn. Many who returned from China with him felt the same. Several were killed in operations, and many left the ranks, feeling they had not made use of their qualifications and zeal. Geris had long, sometimes fiery, discussions with Sabri, which marked their relationship for many years.

Their grandmother, Rahjeh, passed away a few months after her husband. She had lived to a ripe old age of ninety-nine. It was a reminder of the loved ones they would lose, the joys and sorrows they would experience alone, far away.

XVI

On 8 June 1973, Hanneh went into labor at the Khalidi Hospital in Beirut. After nine hours, I came into the world, at midnight. Sabri stared at the baby girl, his daughter, who lay with her eyes closed and mouth open. 'She's hungry!' the nurse laughed. 'We'll feed her, not to worry!'

He and Hanneh had an agreement. They would have two children. She would name the first baby; he, the second. She chose 'Fida', after a friend of hers from boarding school in Nazareth.

When he went to register the birth, the clerk asked: 'The ninth of June, yes?'

'She was born on the eighth, at exactly ten minutes to midnight,' Sabri noted, meticulous with detail, as always. The clerk laughed as he issued the birth certificate, and the family came home. They hired Um Mustafa, an elderly caregiver, to help. Hanneh wished her mother were nearby. At that moment, she missed her more than ever.

Friends gathered around to congratulate them. The baby became Hanneh's world. She doted on their little daughter, and Sabri took too many photographs. Each chance they had, they sent them, with letters, to Fassouta.

XVII

Only four months later, another war broke out. Since its 1967 defeat of the Arabs, Israel had been in a state of narcissism and arrogance, belittling any notion of a peace proposal. It was all-confident in its uncontested power, certain that the Arabs would need years to rebuild their shattered defenses. But Egypt was ready to fight with new, Soviet arms. The sand periodically extracted from the Suez Canal to facilitate the movement of ships was piled on its banks and formed a barrier, which hid Egypt's military preparations west of the Canal. On 6 October 1973, a raid by more than 200 Egyptian planes blasted the Bar-Lev defensive line, a chain of fortifications built by Israel along the eastern bank of the Canal after it had occupied the Sinai Peninsula during the 1967 war. A large Egyptian force, with tanks and armored vehicles, crossed the Canal on floating bridges. Within hours, the Bar-Lev Line was destroyed and Egyptian forces were advancing into the Sinai. At the same time, hundreds of Syrian tanks pushed through the Golan Heights, also occupied by Israel in 1967. The chosen day was Yom Kippur, the holiest day of the Jewish year and a national holiday in Israel. The Israeli army was caught off guard and sustained heavy losses.

The Arabs, more than anyone else, were dumbstruck. Euphoria mixed with disbelief. Sabri hastened to Arafat's office. But the leader seemed depressed. 'They're saying the whole war is a fiasco, just an act!' he said. 'So Israel can give Egypt a victory and they can negotiate a peace deal to sidestep us!'

'The Israelis are not in good shape,' Sabri replied. 'Let me make a quick trip to my office.' Half an hour later, he returned, carrying a stack of Israeli newspapers. 'Look here, Abu Ammar.' Tens of obituaries of soldiers were splayed across the pages.

'Oh, my God, it's true!' Arafat said.

'It's a real war,' Sabri replied. 'Its goals and planning, we don't know, but it's definitely real.' It was clear that this was the start of a new historic path, although they did not know where it would lead. The intense debate within the PLO was centered on one thing: if Egypt were to reach a settlement with Israel, and Syria followed, what would become of the Palestinians? Would a deal be made behind their backs, as had happened in 1948, when the Arab states signed truce agreements with Israel? 'We should not allow them to sidestep us, again!' Sabri insisted.

That night, he wrote a hasty article, in Arabic: 'Israel Facing the Danger of Peace', and sent it to *an-Nahar*, a Lebanese newspaper. Usually, it took an-Nahar three or four days to publish material. This time, he was surprised to see his article in their pages the following day. In it, he stated that the Palestinians and Arabs should not worry about any concessions they would have to make to Israel in negotiations with it towards a peace settlement. From his study of Zionism and knowledge of Israel's inner workings, he believed that the state wanted neither peace nor negotiations to achieve it. Decades later, his belief would turn out to be almost prophetic, after the breakdown of the Oslo Accords and other peace initiatives.

The United States intervened and delivered a massive airlift of arms to Israel, which forced the Egyptians and Syrians back, but there were heavy losses on all sides. Israel sustained about 2,700 deaths and significant damage to equipment. In the last days of the war, the Israeli arsenal was about to run out, and the United States set up an air bridge to supply Israel with new ammunition. The Israeli army continued to advance, encircling 20,000 Egyptian soldiers on the east bank of the Suez Canal.

Through American and Soviet pressure, a ceasefire was reached. Israel withdrew several miles inward, losing Egyptian territory that it had occupied in 1967. Fighting with Syria continued until a ceasefire was reached the following year, and, again, Israel returned a narrow strip of land, occupied in 1967, to Syria.

Even before its end, the war had become political, with Egyptian President Anwar Sadat calling for a peace conference, which the United States moved to dominate. Thus began the long chapter of unequivocal American support for Israel.

After the war, Geris' frustration boiled over. His disillusionment began to push him away from military work, but he kept hoping that things would change. The final straw came when he was assigned a new unit leader who had come from Gaza. Geris went straight to Abu Jihad. 'The man has no knowledge of the Galilee or South Lebanon!' he fumed. 'How is he supposed to oversee operations there? He's giving us commands that will cause a disaster!'

Abu Jihad explained that he had been compelled to bring the recruit in because he was related to someone. 'Listen, I'll assign you to Syria, instead,' he said.

Geris had worse problems there. Before long, he was back in Abu Jihad's office. He liked and admired the leader and understood the pressure he was under, but he could not cope with what was going on. Finally, Abu Jihad suggested: 'I'll send you for security training; how about that?'

Geris hated all police and security personnel from his time in Israel, and told him as much. Then, he added: 'You already sent us on training. If we applied what we learned in it, we would be light-years ahead by now!'

Abu Jihad shook his head and said he would sort it out. Geris remained in Syria, waiting for a decision, but none came. The Jordan front had been cut off since Black September, in 1970. He returned to Beirut. 'I'll help you for free, if you need anything from me,' he told Abu Jihad, and decided to part with military work.

At this point, Geris seriously considered returning to Israel, as risky as it was. He began to plan it with his friend from the resistance, Nimer Shaqqour, who had also escaped to Beirut. They met someone who told them he would be able to smuggle them across. But, at the last minute, they got cold feet. It was just as well, for they found out he was a spy for the Israelis, who had laid a trap for them.

Finally, Geris began to work for the PLO's Palestine Research Center. At first, he translated Hebrew news. Then, he began to produce a bulletin on Israeli affairs, like what Sabri was doing. He covered topics that were in high demand, such as Jewish settlement, the Israeli army, and military strategy. The bulletin was distributed to the media and to writers and researchers. He felt he was doing more of a service in this work.

Sabri, on the other hand, was on his way out of the Institute for Palestine Studies. After his article in *an-Nahar*, the director of the institute called him in. He greatly enthused about what Sabri had written, but was upset that he had published it at another venue. Sabri explained that it would have taken the institute weeks to publish it because of their review process, and it was urgent to get the article out, as political developments would not wait. The director insisted that he should reserve his writing for them, and Sabri resisted. Finally, he said: 'You're pushing me into a corner. I may leave you and work for the PLO!'

The director said nothing. Upset, Sabri left his office and called Abu Jihad. 'This is intellectual tyranny!' he fumed.

'What? Doesn't he know we're doing him a favor by letting you work there?' Abu Jihad joked. 'Go see Abu Ammar. And you're very welcome to do this work with us, at the Western Sector.'

When Sabri explained the situation, Arafat smiled. 'Do you want to work in my office?'

Sabri knew the hours were grueling, from afternoon until early morning. He also wanted to stay in writing and research. He had another offer, and he took it. In November 1973, he joined Geris at the Palestine Research Center as a researcher in the Israeli Studies department. Hanneh finished her maternity leave and joined in the same capacity, working part-time so she could care for the baby.

The Palestine Research Center was established in 1965 as the PLO's first civil institution and the cultural arm of its mission in Beirut. Its objective was to study the Palestinian-Israeli conflict. Eighty-two employees worked at the Center, which was housed in two buildings on Colombani Street, in Ras Beirut. At the time, the Palestinian revolution had burst forth and attracted thousands of followers from the Arab world. The revolution brought with it a growth in the political, cultural, and intellectual spheres, in which the Center played a vital part. Beirut was the capital of Arab culture at the time.

The Center studied Israeli affairs in depth and was probably the only institution that was allowed to bypass the rules of the Arab boycott and import books and newspapers from Israel. It was also independent in its work and often critical of the Palestinian leadership. But Fatah and the PLO never interfered; a strong revolutionary atmosphere prevailed that forbade intellectual oppression. Quickly, the Center became a leading hub of research and publication, producing books, periodicals, translations of Hebrew news, a twice-daily Israeli press bulletin, and the monthly *Shu'un Filastiniyya* (Palestine Affairs), an Arabic journal. At its height, the journal's circulation was about 30,000 copies per month, a staggering number for sociopolitical or economic magazines at the time.

The Center's library was the largest archive on Palestine outside the country. It was open to the public and was painstakingly compiled. Anis Sayegh, director of the Center since 1966, visited most Palestinian communities in Lebanon, Syria, and Egypt. Many donated books and documents. He also visited British libraries and archives, especially the records of the Colonial Office. On a trip with his wife to London, he chanced upon an old bookstore opposite the British Museum. The basement store was small and covered in dust, but it had a precious collection of books on Zionism. Anis struck up a conversation with the shop owner and posed as a Jew.

He wanted to buy the whole lot, but did so slowly on each trip he took, while his wife stayed in the street each time, keeping watch.[4]

His fear was well-founded. As the Center grew, it became a target for attacks by pro-Israel agents or those who resented the Palestinian presence in Lebanon. In 1969, explosives were thrown at its entrance from a speeding car, shattering the glass. In mid-1971, a pack of dynamite was detonated in front of the Center in the early morning hours, breaking the windows and doors. Following this, Sayegh asked for official help, and a Lebanese policeman was stationed outside. But, in July 1972, Sayegh was sent a letter bomb that nearly took his life, disfiguring his face and causing the loss of three fingers and most of his hearing and eyesight. Despite his injuries, he remained in his post for five years.[5]

In 1973, the Israeli Studies department was in nascent form, and Sabri's job was to develop it. At the same time, he was gearing up for a political struggle which would lead to much resistance within the PLO. He wrote about the results of the Sinai war, that the shake-up of Israel's military superiority should be used to coerce it into negotiations with the Palestinians. He was one of the first to suggest a peaceful two-state solution, as he had done in al-Ard. But the notion of a negotiated peace with Israel was still an emerging concept among Palestinians. The rejectionists in the PLO, who opposed any dialogue with Israel, attacked him heavily. He was even labeled 'the Israeli' in some circles. Hanneh was dismayed.

'You don't want to upset your friends, right?' he guessed. Some of her friends' husbands were in the Popular or Democratic Fronts, within the rejectionist camp. 'For the sake of so-and-so, I have to give up on one of our most important fights!' Sabri exclaimed.

'Well, you could just ... tone it down a bit,' she suggested.

'You know what?' he winked. 'When they ask you, deny it. Say it's not your husband, but someone else!'

Hanneh smiled. Then, she said, thoughtfully: 'As a matter of fact, I agree with what you're writing ...'

XVIII

In June 1974, the Palestinian National Council held its twelfth meeting in Cairo and adopted the 'Ten-Point Program', calling for the establishment of a Palestinian national authority 'over every part of Palestinian territory that is liberated'. This was the beginning of the PLO's shift towards a two-state solution, due to pragmatic considerations and international pressure. Many Palestinians saw it as a massive departure from the PLO's founding aims, and several factions opposed it, forming the rejectionist front within the PLO.

During the meeting, Sabri was nominated for membership of the PLO Executive Committee. Against the fierce refusal of the rejectionists, the Council sessions had to be extended for one day to deliberate. Finally, his membership was dropped and he was replaced by another candidate, a Christian clergyman.

On break from the Council's sessions, Sabri visited a nearby shopping area and went into a baby clothes shop. It was his daughter's birthday. He asked the assistant for help in choosing something for a one-year-old and settled on a frilly white dress.

Back in Beirut, he opened his suitcase and took it out. As Hanneh held the baby, he came near, held the dress up and smiled. The baby suddenly leapt forward. '*Baba!*' she cried, and he laughed, taking her into his arms.

'Unbelievable!' Hanneh looked at her daughter, who was clutching the dress. 'I've been looking after you day and night, and you still haven't said *"Mama!"*'

Sabri had only just begun to hold the baby. When she was younger, he was wary of picking her up, afraid he would 'break something'. Hanneh had laughed, telling him to stay in his books and leave it to her.

In fact, between the Center, his writing, political developments, and his work with the PLO, his hands were full. And for the Arab League Summit in October, he had been given a particular task.

'I only have ten minutes to speak,' Arafat told him, 'and many topics to tackle.' Sabri held back a smile. Arafat liked to think of himself as a chieftain. He had a finger in every pie and planned to use most of his speech to try to resolve conflicts between other member states, although his own people were most in need of help. 'So, I only have one and a half minutes to cover Palestine,' he continued, 'and I need to talk about Israel's designs. We need to get the Arab League to recognize us, so we can move on.' Arafat had begun to seek the world's acceptance of the PLO.

'We can bring up the Allon Plan,' Sabri replied. Drafted by Israeli minister of labor Yigal Allon after the 1967 war, the plan was to divide the West Bank between Israel and Jordan, such that the Palestinians would lose any claim to what was left of their land.

Arafat said: 'I need you to write it out and bring it to me. You, personally, to bring it—not send it by courier.'

When Sabri handed him the drafted speech, Arafat quickly leafed through without reading it. He saw that it was tidy and said, satisfied, 'I'll read it there.'

At the summit, he spoke about the need for Arab recognition of the PLO. Then he read the paper and finished with: 'Our experts on Israeli affairs are of the opinion that the policy espoused by the Allon Plan has not changed.' When Sabri heard this, he smiled. The Research Center had acquired a glowing reputation, leading people to think that its bulletins were the secret work of high intelligence.

Through pressure and persistence, Arafat's wish was granted. The Arab heads of state recognized the PLO as the sole legitimate representative of the Palestinian people and admitted it to full membership of the Arab League.

Two weeks later, on 13 November, Arafat addressed the United Nations General Assembly in New York. He was the first leader to represent a national liberation movement, not a member state. In a dramatic appearance, he held an olive branch and wore a gun holster on his belt. In his speech, he explained:

> It pains our people greatly to witness the propagation of the myth that its homeland was a desert until it was made to bloom by the toil of foreign settlers, that it was a land without a people, and that the colonialist entity caused no harm to any human being ... Palestine was the cradle of the most ancient cultures and civilizations. Its Arab people were engaged in farming and building, spreading culture throughout the land for thousands of years, setting an example in the practice of freedom of worship, acting as faithful guardians of the holy places of all religions.

Arafat wanted to be clear on the context of the PLO. He continued:

> The difference between the revolutionary and the terrorist lies in the reason for which each fights. Whoever stands by a just cause and

fights for liberation from invaders and colonialists cannot be called terrorist. Those who wage war to occupy, colonize, and oppress other people are the terrorists ... The Palestinian people had to resort to armed struggle when they lost faith in the international community, which ignored their rights, and when it became clear that not one inch of Palestine could be regained through exclusively political means ...

The PLO dreams and hopes for one democratic state where Christian, Jew, and Muslim live in justice, equality, fraternity and progress ... I have come bearing an olive branch and a freedom fighter's gun. Do not let the olive branch fall from my hand.

Arafat received a standing ovation. More than his words, the appearance of a Palestinian guerrilla leader among statesmen in the halls of the United Nations was a turning point. His speech raised international recognition of the PLO and sympathy with the Palestinians. On 22 November 1974, the United Nations adopted Resolution 3236, affirming the inalienable rights of the Palestinian people in Palestine, and Resolution 3237, giving the PLO observer status at the General Assembly.

Israel and the United States saw this as one of their greatest diplomatic defeats. On 10 December—international Human Rights Day—a missile was thrown at the Research Center in Beirut, hitting the library and ruining dozens of books.

It was a tiny peek into a disastrous chain of events to follow.

XIX

Lebanon's political and social turmoil predated both the PLO and Israel. In 1920, at the start of the French Mandate, Christians were a slight majority in Lebanon and they ruled the country. When it gained its independence in 1945, a national pact was made where Maronite Christians were given the presidency; Sunni Muslims, the premiership; and Shia Muslims, the position of speaker of parliament. But Christians were still politically and economically dominant. By the early 1970s, the Maronites were only a third of the population and the Shia were the largest bloc. Muslim resentment grew at their inferior status, and many pan-Arabist and left-wing groups opposed the pro-Western government.

The arrival of Palestinian refugees raised the number of Muslims in the country, which irked the dominant Christians, especially with the Palestinians' revolutionary mindset. The PLO's military, social, and cultural institutions were growing in Lebanon, and Israel also wanted to destroy the organization. Israel and the Christian forces colluded in 1975, when Lebanon slid into civil war. On 13 April, gunmen fired on a church in Ein el-Rummaneh, on the outskirts of Beirut, killing four people, including two Maronites. Hours later, Christian militias, the Phalangists, killed thirty Palestinians on a bus in the same area. Clashes erupted around Beirut, with heavy exchanges of fire.

On 23 May, Sabri was kidnapped. The Tigers, a Christian militia, laid siege to the building where he and Hanneh lived. A sniper from the Lebanese National Movement, which opposed the militia, began shooting at them from inside. The militiamen made their way into the building and up to the fourth floor, where they knocked on the door and grabbed Sabri. In vain, he tried to explain that he was not involved. But they realized he was a Palestinian and took him to their headquarters, an apartment a short distance away. He told them that he was a Christian, which seemed to placate them, somewhat. They questioned him on what he did. He explained and asked them to bring *an-Nahar* newspaper, where he showed them his articles. The men seemed bewildered and did not know what to do. They held him for four hours. Finally, a saving phone call came through from their boss, who told them to let him go. Were it not for Arafat, who intervened with their leader to release him, he may have been killed.

It was too dangerous to stay in Ein el-Rummaneh, which was under Maronite control. Soad Hayek, who had moved to the Research Center with Sabri as his secretary, found a speedy solution. An apartment was vacant in the building where she lived, in Corniche el-Mazra'a, the neighborhood of West Beirut where Sabri and Hanneh had lived before. They moved back without delay. The area was mostly inhabited by Muslims and the Lebanese National Movement, and was under the control of Fatah.

Geris, who saw the disaster to come, became all the more aware of the shortcomings in his life and the extent to which he had sacrificed because of his militant path. He had met a Syrian student,

Deema, and wanted to marry her. But he had no real passport, no money, and an unstable life. Many Palestinians were still on refugee documents. Geris and Sabri now held Sudanese passports, given as a gesture of support by the Sudanese government. But these were merely travel documents, issued as exceptions, and did not grant citizenship.

Geris was doing excellent work at the Center, but he could not progress or get a raise without a degree. In these circumstances, he could not get married, and he told Deema he had to leave. In September 1975, he flew to the United States on a tourist visa, found a scholarship, and began studying political science and history at the University of New Britain in Connecticut.

As soon as he arrived, he sent a letter and photographs of himself to his parents. He was sorry he had not contacted them before, but he knew they had been watched after he had left, and it was too dangerous to disclose his whereabouts.

Meanwhile, he hoped Deema would wait.

XX

In Beirut, events escalated into a terrible war. Quickly, the conflict revealed itself as a sectarian one. The killing of four other Phalangists in December led their militias to set up roadblocks in the city where they inspected people's identification. Many Palestinians or Lebanese Muslims were killed on the spot. Hundreds of people were kidnapped.

Initially, the PLO decided not to interfere in a local war that would drain it and distract it from its struggle against Israel. However, as Palestinian refugees were targeted, it was dragged in. Palestinians, most of whom were Sunni Muslims, were allied with Lebanese opposition groups, mainly the Lebanese National Movement, while Israel moved in to arm the Christian militias. Syria had its interests in Lebanon, as well, and sided first with the Palestinians, then with the Christian militias. Downtown Beirut was completely destroyed, and a demarcation line was drawn between the east and west of the city. The PLO and Muslim militias controlled the predominantly Muslim West Beirut, as well as South Lebanon, while the Christian militias controlled East Beirut, which was mostly Christian, and the Christian part of Mount Lebanon. The government soon lost control: the army was weak and split among the two camps, and tens of rival militias and thugs exploited the situation.

Palestinian refugees bore the brunt of a cruel, sectarian war. In November 1975, the United Nations passed Resolution 3379, which determined that 'Zionism is a form of racism'. To the refugees, who faced terror, starvation, and death, it meant little. On 4 January 1976, Christian militias began a siege of the Palestinian refugee camps and slums in East Beirut. The Karantina slum was inhabited by Lebanese Shia, Palestinians, Armenians, and Kurdish refugees. Two weeks later, the militias moved in and massacred about 1,500 people. Palestinian and Lebanese Muslim militias retaliated with a strike on Damour, a Maronite Christian town south of Beirut, leaving hundreds dead and causing the remainder to flee. In the panic that overtook the city, large numbers of Muslims and Christians fled their homes to areas under control of their own sects.

Sabri and Hanneh tried to navigate through the chaos. To return to Israel was impossible. To emigrate again was a difficult option, especially as they were committed to their cause. But the mounting hysteria in Lebanon was frightening. Law and order had broken down, and guns ruled the streets.

XXI

In Fassouta, Wardeh held the photographs she had just received from Geris and wept. She would have to hide them very carefully. The police were still hounding the family. The same week that Subhi had gotten married, they had turned up to search the house.

Muna's sudden entrance startled her. 'Why are you back?' Wardeh asked. Muna, at nineteen, had finished school and was working at a textile factory that employed women from the village. It was only her second week.

'They sent me home and told me not to come back.'

'What?'

'They said: "You're Sabri's sister, aren't you? Go home!"'

Muna found another job, and another. She worked for a month here, two months there, before the same thing happened and she was dismissed.

That year, the uneasy calm among Palestinians in Israel was shattered. When the government announced its plan to confiscate thousands of dunums of land in the villages of Arrabeh, Sakhnin and Deir Hanna in the Galilee, Palestinians called for a general strike on 30 March 1976, declaring it 'Land Day'.[6] The night before the planned protests, the government sent the police and imposed a curfew on several villages. The curfew failed, the strike went ahead, and demonstrations broke out. During the violent police response, six Palestinians were killed, about a hundred wounded, and hundreds more arrested or dismissed from their jobs.

It was the largest protest by Palestinians in Israel since 1948. Land Day became a symbol of their struggle. This community, suffering alone for so long, was finally attracting attention in the Arab and Western world. That year, Sabri's book, *The Arabs in Israel*, had been translated into several languages, and he was surprised at the international interest. The Research Center published the book in Arabic and French, and the Institute for Palestine Studies published it in English. An abridged French version later appeared in Paris and was translated into German, Swedish, and Italian. But none of these translations were complete, because of the material removed by the Israeli military censorship. Sabri added this back into the book and updated it with developments since its publication ten years earlier. This fuller English edition was published in the United States in 1976, the same year as the first Land Day.[7]

Meanwhile, he was facing a new reality that was getting uglier and messier.

XXII

For seven months, the Christian militias and their allies in Beirut laid siege to Tel al-Zaatar and Jisr al-Basha camps, inhabited by thousands of Palestinian refugees. Food, water, and medicine deliveries were blocked, and electricity was cut off. Many victims, including children, starved or died of dehydration. On 22 June 1976, the militias began a military assault on the camps with fierce bombardment and armored tanks. Jisr al-Basha fell within a week, but Tel al-Zaatar held out for fifty-three days before falling on 12 August 1976. Several thousand refugees were killed, scores of bodies were mutilated, and many women were raped. As thousands of people were evacuated from the camp, some survivors were marched into West Beirut, lined up and machine-gunned by the militias. Others were killed with knives and grenades. The camp was then completely obliterated.[8]

In Beirut, the fighting raged on. There were tens of thousands of casualities. Refugees from other camps were expelled and massacred. To the PLO, it was clear that armed resistance, in the midst of the onslaught against it, would not bring back Palestine. The need for a political solution became ever more urgent, but Israel refused any negotiation or settlement.

Arafat and Mahmoud Abbas began making connections with Israeli leftist and peace factions. The small groups that were ready to meet were marginal and made up of intellectuals. In Israel, they were accused of talking to 'terrorists'. In the mid-1970s, Sabri, Issam Sartawi, and other moderate PLO members held meetings in Paris with the Israel-Palestine Peace Council, including General Matti Peled, Uri Avnery, and Aryeh Eliav. In October 1976, Arafat sent Sabri and Sartawi to Washington to open a PLO representative office. However, the United States refused to deal with the PLO until the organization accepted the State of Israel and the United Nations Security Council resolutions calling for a negotiated solution to the conflict. Sabri and Sartawi were denied meetings with any American officials. They met, however, with prominent Jewish groups in New York and Washington, including Rabbi Max Ticktin and Rabbi Arthur Waskow. On 18 November, Sabri formally registered the PLO office with the Justice Department.[9] He and Sartawi were within a few hours of holding a press conference to make the announcement when Secretary of State Henry Kissinger, working with Israeli prime minister Yitzhak Rabin, halted it. Sabri and Sartawi were informed that their visas were canceled and they had to leave.

Geris' American visa was also a problem. He applied to change his status from tourist to student and was told that he would have to leave the United States and apply for a student visa from abroad. His Sudanese passport was close to expiry and he was afraid that it would not be renewed, and he would not be able to return if he left. He made repeated appeals to explain and change his status but was rejected. He began a race against time, trying to defer his deportation until he could finish his degree.

7

HAPPY TIMES

What if the fugitive bird
remembered home?
If it gathered the trickle of springs
and the soft scent of jasmine
And made
of its wounds
a song of waiting?

Jamal Qa'war
'Hanneh'[1]

I

My earliest memories are from when I was about four. Mum and Dad took me to the Raoucheh seaside promenade in Beirut with my little red tricycle. They strolled along, talking and laughing, and I pedaled ahead, turning back to make sure they were watching me. The sea was the largest thing I had ever seen, and noisy seagulls flapped their wings above. Mum was pregnant and told me I would soon have a little brother.

We lived at the apartment on Corniche el-Mazra'a, on the sixth floor. One of my favorite hobbies was to fling Dad's keys from our balcony onto the street below. Minutes later, someone would ring the doorbell and Dad would thank them, bashfully, as they handed them back to him.

Soad Hayek and her family lived on the second floor. Her daughters, Rima, Randa, and May, were my playmates. On 23 October 1977, I was with them when their mother called me to the phone. 'Fida, sweetheart, your father wants to speak to you!'

'You have a brother!' Dad's voice came through, excitedly.

'What?'

'A little brother,' Dad repeated. 'He was just born!'

'OK.' I was not sure what to do with this information.

Dad was very happy. 'I'll see you soon, sweetheart. Let me talk to Aunty Soad again!'

I returned the receiver and ran off with the girls. It was only two days later, when a little bundle was brought home, that I understood that something had changed.

The baby's name had been decided on long before his birth. Due to my father's study of Jewish affairs and Zionism, his friends had nicknamed him 'Abu Mousa', father of Moses, and the name had stuck. When Mum complained, he reminded her of their agreement that he would name the second baby. Then he said: 'It's bad luck to change the name; it was meant for him!'

Soad had always wanted a son, and she congratulated my parents and said to Dad, longingly: 'It's good to have a mix ...' She was thrilled by the arrival, as was Mum. Naturally, I did not take this very well.

'I don't know what's wrong with this boy!' Mum exclaimed, one day. Mousa would be lying happily in his cot, and suddenly he would let out a scream and start crying. This happened several times. She checked the mattress and the room; there was nothing that could be biting him. He was fed and washed. He did not seem to be in pain or to have any sign of illness. But the screams continued. 'What shall I do?' she asked, exasperated.

'Leave it to me,' my father said. He waited until things were quiet, tiptoed to the room I shared with the baby, and stood behind the door. A few minutes later, he saw me checking to see that the coast was clear, sneaking up to Mousa's cot, pinching him, and darting back to my toys. Suddenly, my parents materialized, as though out of thin air. 'Your brother!' Mum cried. I jumped, caught like a deer in headlights.

Um Mustafa, the kindly old lady who helped my mother at home, left us when her husband wanted her to stop working. My parents found Um Assaf, who was equally kind and helped care for us children. Mum was fussy about the baby and gave her detailed instructions on what to feed him. But, when he was seven months old, Um Assaf took matters into her own hands. My mother was at work, and the baby would not stop whimpering. Milk and puréed fruit did not quieten him down. Um Assaf had cooked mjaddara, a lentil dish, that day, and she fixed Mousa on her lap and fed him several spoonfuls as I watched in fascination. When my mother returned from work, she threw a fit. But Um Assaf was undeterred. 'He needs solid food! He's done with all that baby stuff!'

I was alarmed, because I did not want them to stop making Cerelac. I loved the instant baby cereal and circled around Mum whenever she was feeding it to him. She would give me an occasional spoonful before taking one herself. 'It's good, isn't it?' she would grin, as I nodded happily.

Mahmoud Darwish came to visit and congratulate my parents. He worked with my father on the same floor of the Research Center, two offices apart. He presented Dad with his latest poetry collection, dedicated *'To the little one, Mousa'*. Mahmoud knew that my father read no poetry and virtually no literature. As they sat down, he teased: 'You know what, Sabri? Take it with you to the bathroom; you might find some entertainment in it!'

Afterwards, my father decided to give him a surprise. When his friend held an exhibition of his complete works in Beirut, Dad went along. It was one of very few literary events he had ever attended, and Mahmoud grinned from ear to ear when he saw him. 'What a great honor! Sabri himself at my exhibition!' he laughed.

My parents had a wide circle of friends in Beirut. Mum was lively and sociable, and our apartment frequently filled up with guests. In addition to Soad, we were close to Katrine el-Far, secretary of the Center, and Sirine Khairy, an editor of the daily Arabic bulletin. They were Palestinian refugees from Lydda and Ramle. Shadia el-Mutasem, an assistant librarian, also visited us. Her family were refugees from Tarshiha. She was studying library science and was doing a course on child psychology, and she came to read a few stories to Mousa as part of her coursework. I loved these women, whose laughter often filled our apartment.

It was a big year for my father, not just for the birth of his second child, but for the completion of his second book. Part I of *A History of Zionism*[2] was published by the Research Center, in Arabic.

In truth, everyone was trying to muster as much normality as they could amidst a horrible reality. The first two years of Lebanon's civil war had killed about 60,000 people and maimed thousands. Beirut was torn apart, with areas controlled by factions. It was dangerous to be in the wrong place at the wrong time, and killings or kidnappings for ethnic or religious reasons were common. Alliances shifted quickly and unpredictably, and people scrambled to adapt.

Regionally, Palestinian misgivings in the wake of the 1973 war grew. The war had brought about a major shift of power as Israel lost its military superiority, and Israel and the United States sought to remove Egypt from the equation. Egyptian president Anwar Sadat succumbed to the pressure. On 19 November 1977, he visited Israel, marking the first official trip by an Arab statesman. The next day, he addressed the Knesset, speaking of peace and reconciliation. It was a devastating shock to the Arab world and a clear message to the Palestinians that their cause was being sidelined. They were expected to join the tide of 'pragmatism', which meant surrendering their historic rights. My father responded to the unfolding events in an article:

The Palestinians may, in certain circumstances, be ready to seek a settlement in the area to which Israel is a party. But they are not prepared to conclude an agreement recognizing the legitimacy of Zionism; no Palestinian Arab can ever accept as legitimate, a doctrine that he should be excluded from most parts of his homeland, because he is a Muslim Arab or a Christian Arab, while anyone of the Jewish faith from anywhere in the world is entitled to settle there. Realism may require recognition of the existence of a Jewish state in Palestine and that this fact be taken into account in seeking a settlement. But this can never mean approving the expansionist and exclusivist tendencies of Zionism.[3]

II

My uncle, Geris, returned to Beirut from the United States in January 1978. He had finished his Bachelor's in a record two years and four months and had managed to get a voluntary deportation order, allowing him to go back in future. He had made good friends and could have found a way to stay, but he felt like a fish out of water, away from everything that mattered to him.

His trip back was surreal. With his expired passport, he had a one-time travel document from the Sudanese Embassy in New York. The Beirut airport was closed, except for limited travel, so he had to fly to Amman. When he landed, he checked into a small hotel until he could figure out how to return to Lebanon.

His roommate in the United States had given him the number of his uncle, a doctor in Amman, but the man ignored Geris' calls. At the hotel, the phone operator was Palestinian. When he heard Geris' story, he wanted to help. My uncle also had the number of a friend of Deema's in Syria, and the operator put the call through for him. Geris told her that he was unable to call through to Beirut and asked her to ring a contact of his in the Palestinian factions, so they could pick him up from the airport. It was too dangerous to go on his own. She made the call immediately and called him back four hours later. 'Go to the airport tomorrow,' she said. 'Abu Jihad has an entry order for you.'

There was one more hurdle to cross. When he went to book his ticket with Jordanian Airlines, the clerk refused. 'Your travel document is to Khartoum. You have no papers to enter Lebanon.'

Geris convinced him that he was going back to Sudan, but to book the flight via Beirut. Seeing the clerk's resistance, he slipped him 300 US dollars, a huge sum at the time. It was a tenth of the money he had brought back from his work on the side during his studies in the United States.

The next day, he boarded the plane to Beirut. As soon as it landed, a Lebanese police officer climbed on board and called his name. Geris panicked. He would be arrested, he thought. The officer escorted him off the plane and into the airport. But the official at the desk stamped his entry document and wrote it was by request from Abu Jihad. The Palestinian resistance was a major force to be reckoned with in Lebanon, so much so that the Lebanese authorities had reduced powers. The officer gave the document to Geris and told him he was free to go. When he finally came out of the airport, he looked behind him, not believing he had made it.

My uncle stayed with us for two weeks, then found a place with some friends. He returned to the organizational work of Fatah, but, after his recent experience, he did not want his life to be in anyone's hands anymore. He also suffered a shock: Deema had gotten married. She had given up waiting for him and had married a friend of his. He felt betrayed by them both.

Eight years after leaving Palestine, he was still haunted by homesickness. One night, he dreamt that he had returned to Fassouta and built a house there. He knew his father's land and saw the exact piece in al-Bayyad, saw himself in a house on it. The dream was so vivid it shook him awake. But he knew it was impossible; he would be imprisoned if he went back. He had not even been able to call his parents from the United States because he knew it would get them in trouble. A couple of times, he had called the priest, Kareem, to relay his news to the family. After his return to Lebanon, my uncle wondered where the insanity of the country would take him.

III

The PLO was heavily present in the south and used guerrilla tactics to fight Israel. In March 1978, after a Fatah operation in Haifa, Israel invaded South Lebanon and occupied most of the area up to the Litani River, killing about 2,000 Lebanese and Palestinians and displacing hundreds of thousands. PLO forces were driven out and forced north into Beirut. The United Nations called for an immediate Israeli withdrawal and deployed the United Nations Interim Force in Lebanon (UNIFIL) to establish peace. Israel withdrew later that year but kept control of South Lebanon through a wide security zone along the border, and continued its raids and bombardment of the PLO and Lebanese National Movement.

The arrival of thousands of members of the PLO forces in Beirut exacerbated the civil war. We lived in West Beirut, and all our movements—my parents' work, my school, even our brief outings—were within this area. But the Phalangists were only a stone's throw away, in the east of the city. With two young children to care for, my mother was very strained. She wanted to leave work on time each day to be with us, and also to relieve Um Assaf, so she could return to her family. But, sometimes, as my mother waited for my father to come home with her, he had last-minute work and kept her waiting. She got upset and argued with him, but his responsibilities had grown. After five years at the Research Center, he was one of its deputy directors.

Anis Sayegh had resigned as director the previous year and Mahmoud Darwish had been appointed in his place. But Mahmoud began to struggle. He did not want the position and disliked being tied to management work. He would come in late and not stay on top of what was going on at the Center, to the bemusement of the employees, who loved his poetry but were lost in his administration. My father and the other deputy directors headed the various departments and planned the general strategy of the Center. A year after starting in the job, Mahmoud resigned and convinced Arafat that my father was the best fit for the post. In July 1978, Sabri was appointed director, as well as editor of the monthly *Palestine Affairs*.

From the start of the civil war, the staff were anxious for the Center's library. The books could be replaced, but the main worry was the original archive documents. In his time as director, Sayegh had given directions to copy them, and, after my father assumed the position, this work was completed. As the Center suffered intermittent attacks and the war intensified, he made a decision to keep a copy of the entire archive outside Lebanon. An agreement was reached with the Israeli Studies Center in Baghdad and the documents were safeguarded there. They included the record of land ownership deeds (Tabo) in Palestine, which the British Mandate authorities had prepared for the United Nations in January 1946.[4]

In his new post, my father reported directly to Arafat, as the Research Center was administered by his office. Arafat approved staff appointments and budgets before they were presented to the Palestine National Fund, which managed the PLO finances. But he did not interfere in the publication work of the Center and left all decisions to its editorial team.

My father was careful to maintain this independence. Though he was a member of Fatah, he shied away from official positions in the party, such as in the Fatah Revolutionary Council, even to the point of leaving council sessions while elections were being held. He wanted to write freely. As director of the Research Center, he was at liberty to publish his opinions, which Arafat and others respected.

My father sometimes saw Arafat several times a day, and, often, very late at night. As he grew closer to Arafat, he was awed by the leader. The man seemed a patriot, gangster, dreamer, genius, con artist, fighter, and man of peace, all in one. Arafat had one overriding mission: Palestine. And he used any and all means at his disposal to achieve his aims. He had two tools, money and guns, and his management style was catastrophic: he bribed, cajoled, threatened, bred internal conflict to remain in control, and refused to delegate. He could flatter, be evasive, and slip mercurially between people, situations, and crises. His strategy was to never cut ties with anyone. 'You know, Sabri,' he told him, 'I went on the Hajj pilgrimage to Mecca, and, as per custom, they gave me seven stones to throw at Satan. I threw five and kept two in my pocket. One never knows when I might need to talk to Satan, so I didn't want to cut all ties, you know what I mean?'

My father was dumbfounded. 'If Machiavelli were reborn,' he said to a friend, 'he could learn from this man!'

Arafat not only had to seek the world's sympathy with his people, but to act as leader to those people, scattered across geographical and political divides. He had a remarkable ability to rally Palestinians around him; he went to their streets and camps, mixed with young and old, listened to their stories, was a father and guardian. Many felt his charisma and traits to be the most important factors in keeping the Palestinian cause alive, despite his many mistakes.

Yet, the Palestinian situation grew more precarious. As the civil war intensified in Lebanon, the PLO factions slid into internal chaos. Their leaders struggled to keep order and often lost control. The alienation of the Palestinians from the Arab states also intensified. Undeterred by the Israeli invasion of Lebanon that spring, Egyptian president Anwar Sadat was moving ahead on his peace plans. In September 1978, he signed the Camp David Accords with Israeli prime minister Menachem Begin. In March 1979, the Egypt-Israel Peace Treaty was signed, and Israel withdrew from the Sinai Peninsula, which it had occupied in 1967. But Israel did not agree to the establishment of a Palestinian state, nor was the PLO involved in the negotiations.

It was the final blow for Palestinians. Everything that Nasserism had stood for was gone. The treaty disregarded not just the Palestinian cause, but the bravery and sacrifices of thousands of Egyptian soldiers who had fought several wars against Israel. Egypt's peacemaking was seen as a surrender to American pressure, and Egypt's standing crumbled in Arab eyes.

IV

My uncle was as disappointed as everyone else and sank deeper into disillusionment. He wanted to find some semblance of normality and he returned to his research and writing, this time at the Institute for Palestine Studies. He also did freelance work for the Research Center, translating Hebrew news from Israeli radio stations into Arabic for their daily bulletin, and enrolled for a Master's in political science at the American University of Beirut.

Ammo,* my uncle, was the only family we had in Lebanon, and he visited us often. He was a fascinating character to us children. I was almost seven years old; Mousa was going on three. Ammo told us stories that kept us spellbound for hours. The protagonists were good rabbits, evil foxes, and brave lions; he weaved together a long chain of events as we listened, wide-eyed, barely breathing. He had an incredible gift and narrated the stories in episodes, breaking off

---

* *Ammo* (Arabic): colloquial address for uncle or other older man; used by both uncles and nephews/younger people to address each other.

at the most exciting points and leaving us waiting impatiently for the next day. Sometimes, it was too much to bear, and we nagged him to continue for a few minutes, especially when the hero was in a real fix. One day, in a vexing scene, the rabbit was stuck in a hole, the fox was waiting for him outside, and a pack of wolves was circling the area. In addition, the poor rabbit had injured his leg, so he was unable to escape. At that precise moment, Ammo took a sudden breath and said: 'That's it; we continue tomorrow!'

'No!' Mousa cried. 'You have to sort it out before you go home!'

My uncle laughed and kept going for a while longer. But Mousa was agitated and kept interrupting, and Ammo got cross and told him to leave the room. 'Only Fida will hear the rest!' There was no point in arguing, so Mousa left, holding back his tears.

The next day, my uncle returned and we jumped up to see him, begging him to continue. 'Where were we?' he asked, as we settled down around him.

'The fox went away, but the rabbit was still stuck in the hole,' said Mousa, in a small voice.

'What?' Ammo blinked. 'How do you know this?' He turned to me: 'Fida, did you tell him?'

I shook my head. But Mousa continued, sheepishly: 'I hid behind the suitcase.'

My father had just returned from travel and a suitcase was propped up at the other end of the room. Ammo laughed and drew us to him. He was very involved in our lives. It was he who noticed my first adult tooth growing behind another and made me open my mouth for a careful inspection. He cajoled me into eating meat, onions, and garlic, all of which I would not go near. 'These will make you grow and be strong!' he told me. He brought Mousa the little toy cars he loved so much and watched him arrange them on the floor and make a 'traffic jam', so characteristic of Beirut in those days. He listened to me revise for my tests while I sat cross-legged on the carpet in front of him and rocked back and forth. 'Turn the page, Ammo!' I said, sometimes, at which he laughed and returned the book to me.

My mother continued to work at the Research Center as a researcher and analyst of Israeli affairs. She was an idealist, highly educated and knowledgeable, yet simple and humble. Her colleagues loved her sweet, easygoing disposition and were impressed by the depth of her writing. Mum had her own room at the Center, in which everyone was always welcome. She had a radiant smile that put people at ease, and she often laughed till tears came to her eyes, so she would have to remove her glasses and wipe them. Her colleagues came to her for personal as well as work issues. She was deeply loyal to my father, in work and in life, and her friendships with her co-workers made her shift uncomfortably in meetings where he had to give warnings or directives.

But her first priority was her family. Mum was calm, organized, and meticulous. At home, everything was in order. Occasionally, Dad complained, only half-jokingly, that she focused on us and forgot about him. She constantly sought the best of everything: food, clothes, schooling, and even toys for us. I went to St. Mary's Orthodox School in Ras Beirut. Mum oversaw my progress carefully and continued to send letters and photographs to our grandparents as often as she could. They were relayed by Father Kareem, until he was eventually harassed and interrogated in Israel.

When I was seven, she wrote to her mother, Um Nour:

> Fida has started to read and speak some English, as well as Arabic. I always teach her myself, Mother, because I want her to be outstanding, always.

Little Mousa had just turned three.

> I wish you could see him, even if only for a moment, how beautiful he is. He reminds me of my brother, Baheej, when he was young. Like him, his smile doesn't leave his face, and his talk is so sweet, and he loves to eat, just like Baheej!

Mousa was upset that he was left at home while I went off with my schoolbag each morning. When he turned four, he started kindergarten at the same school. On the first day, Mum accompanied him as the teachers had asked the parents to do. At recess, I went to his class to see them and heard a cacophony of crying. Children clung to their mothers and I felt very grown-up, wondering what all the fuss was about. Mum was smiling and playing with Mousa, showing him the toys and colored pens. He got used to it quickly, for he really wanted to come to school with me.

Each morning, I took his little hand and we went down to wait for the bus. The schoolbags were heavy; we did not keep anything at school and brought in all our books each day. When the bus arrived, I hauled him up onto its steps, passed him his bag, hauled myself up with my bag, and tried to find a seat. It was not always easy. One of our first hints that we were 'different' came one day on the way home. An older boy, Fuad, was lying on two seats, his legs stretched out on the other two across the aisle. He was very tall and intimidating, but I gestured to him to let Mousa and I sit. He pushed me back, roughly, hissing: 'You *Palestinian!*'

I was too young to understand. I thought he was just a bully. I left Mousa with the bags and scrambled back down to the canteen to get ice cream before the bus left. Mum gave us pocket money, and this was my daily habit, if we had not spent it earlier in recess. Back on the bus, I gave Mousa his ice cream and we enjoyed it on the way home, although we remained standing and tried to ignore Fuad, who glared at us.

In art class, the teacher asked us to draw the flag of our country. Ghada, my friend who sat near me, and I drew the flag of Palestine as the other children were busy drawing the cedar tree of Lebanon. The teacher walked around the desks, surveying progress. When she saw what we had drawn, she frowned. 'The flag of our country, I said!' she snapped and snatched away our papers.

But they were small incidents that I did not pay much attention to. I loved school and did very well. In her letters to my grand-parents, Mum proudly wrote that I was always first in class and sent them copies of my report cards. Reading was my favorite subject. Each year, as soon as I got my new schoolbooks, I pounced on the Arabic comprehension book and read all the stories from start to finish. Mum and I often read together. I loved snuggling up to her as she flipped through the pages. She taught me to tell the time and bought me a colored watch, which I proudly showed off to my friends.

She also encouraged me to write, and I joined her in composing letters to my grandmothers. I sat at the dining table where I did my homework, often by candlelight because of the power cuts during the war. Mum and I drafted the letters together as I wrote in my childish script, trying to be neat and stay straight on the lines in order to impress each teta.*

Yet, Palestine was far away, a place only in my imagination. In a cassette tape recording of Mousa and me, we had a Lebanese accent from school even though our parents spoke the Palestinian dialect at home. My mother missed her family, terribly. Her letters were heart-rending and filled with longing, as there was no end in sight to their separation. In one letter, she poured forth her anguish and hope:

> You cannot imagine how much I miss you all, especially you, dear Mother. You don't leave my mind, and my heart is always with you, though I may be far. I always tell my children about you and about their father's family, to the point where my daughter now recognizes you all in the photographs, and always asks me when she'll see her grandma. I miss you, Mother, and can't even imagine that I may not see you for several years. I don't know anything about you at all, like I'm in another world.

> How I wish peace would prevail and I could see you. I have never lost hope that I shall see you all, especially you, dear Mother. I want you to meet my children. You'll be proud of them. They're smart grandchildren. I so long to see the children of my brothers, too. God willing, a day will come when we shall meet.

Our families in Fassouta held on to the same hope. The villagers did not believe them and some felt sorry for them, but my grandparents, aunts, and uncles never lost faith that we would return. On her bedside cabinet in Beirut, Mum kept a baby photograph of her first nephew, Raji. He was the son of Nour, her eldest brother, and had been named after Nour and Hanneh's father, who had died when they were young.

In Beirut, Mum tried to create a little haven for us. When there was a lull in the fighting, she took us to see children's shows at the theater, or we went to play with friends. At our nagging, she brought us a cat, a stray given to her by a friend. Though she was female, we named her Kojak, after a police detective in a TV series of the same name, starring Telly Savalas. The cat's name was then shortened to

---

* *Teta* (Arabic): colloquial address for grandmother.

Koji, and her many talents included leaping up onto the door handle of our room and opening the door so she could come in and sleep next to us. We were small children, with no idea of the turmoil around us and the difficulties facing our parents. The highlights of our young lives were our birthday parties. Mousa and I could not contain our excitement, milling and chattering around Mum as she prepared cake, Jell-O, and juice. When the singing began, we clapped our hands in glee, waiting to cut the cake. They were the happiest times of our childhood.

Sometimes, when Um Assaf was off or Mum had to pick us up from school early, she took us with her to the Center. She gave us papers and colored pens to draw, and her colleagues were very kind to us. We knew many of them from their visits to us at home. We saw a lot of Soad, too, for we were always at each other's apartments. She was then heading the administrative department of the Center.

My father was busy with his tasks during the day and often had to bring his writing home. But Mum usually finished during her working hours so she could devote the rest of her time to us. Mousa and I usually returned from school to find Um Assaf waiting, the smell of lunch filling the apartment. Shortly afterwards, my parents would arrive from work. Sometimes, Um Assaf stayed to help with the dishes, but Mum often took it from there. She set the table and we ate together. Then, she and Dad napped while I did my homework as quickly as possible so I could play with Mousa, trying not to make noise.

When Mum awoke, she would make coffee and sit with me to go over my homework. Then it was time for dinner and cartoons. Mousa and I had a perching position next to each other on the carpet, backs against the couch. Our favorites were Zeina, the bee, and Grendizer, the robot. We were packed off to bed at the early hour of 7:30 pm. I remember lying there, sometimes while it was still light outside, staring at the horizontal slivers of light peeking through the curtains. But Mum was adamant. Each time Children's World came on television at 7:30, it was a fight to let us watch it. We sometimes resorted to Dad. Once, on a weekend, I tearfully refused to go to bed, telling her I was older and did not want to sleep like a little kid. Dad smiled and told her to let me be, and that I would sit next to him in the living room 'like a big girl' as he worked. I was thrilled, but, half an hour later, I fell asleep on the couch.

Dad spent much of his time writing. He wrote everywhere, in the living room and in his study, filling reams of paper with his tiny handwriting. The study was out of bounds, but I frequently broke that rule; it had an irresistible pull, this strange world that Dad inhabited, alone. Sometimes, I snuck in as he bent over his papers, and, if I kept quiet, he would not object. I took a blank, white piece of paper from the little pile on his desk and pored over it with my coloring pens, pretending to be hard at work, like him. On one occasion, I traced the watermark on the paper with a black pen, and he showed it to Mum. 'See how smart this kid is?' he smiled in delight.

Mum very occasionally brought work home. She wrote in the evenings, usually in the dining room. There was a mechanical typewriter that I sometimes played with, hitting the heavy keys with my little fingers and watching them fly on the ribbon, imprinting the letters on the page. I turned the lever and heard its distinct sound as the page jumped down a line. When Mum made a mistake, she had to take the piece of paper out, put correction fluid on it, wait for it to dry, then reinsert the paper and position it exactly, so she could type the correct letter in place.

During periods of relative quiet, they took us on outings and gave us treats. A large delicatessen shop, La Gondole, was our favorite. To us children, the place was huge, with long refrigerators featuring rows of cakes and sweets and another section for cheese and deli. Mum would buy a few things and allow us to pick something, which we agonized over, given the overwhelming choice. On Sunday mornings, Mousa and I would be up like roosters, waiting for our parents to have their coffee so we could set off to the bakery. We would bring mana'eesh—savory pies covered with cheese and thyme—and knafeh, its cheese simmering in delicious syrup.

My parents tried to give us the best they could and shield us from the war. We fared so much better than thousands of others, who lost their loved ones in the fighting and massacres, were displaced time and again, endured crushing fear and poverty, or who were missing, not known to be alive or dead.

But our illusory sense of safety could not last. After the Egypt-Israel Peace Treaty, Arafat and senior members of the PLO began to talk about recognition of Israel in return for partition of the country and the establishment of a Palestinian state. But Israel, after pushing Egypt out of the Israeli–Arab conflict, set its sights on destroying the PLO. On 17 July 1981, Israeli warplanes bombed buildings in the Fakhani area of Beirut, mistaking them for PLO headquarters and aiming to kill Arafat. But he had left the area. The attack killed dozens of civilians. On 8 October, Majid Abu Sharar, a Palestinian writer and journalist, was killed by a detonating device planted in his hotel room at a conference in Rome. At the same time, Israeli defense minister Ariel Sharon began drawing up plans to attack the PLO in West Beirut, where we lived.

8

THE DARK HOUR

The images of bloated bodies, the grotesque scenes of mutilated children and of people slaughtered in the most barbaric ways are now a permanent part of history. Most who remember believe that justice has not been served. The survivors live with both physical pain and psychological scars. Their losses, their memories of what happened in those hours have remained with them, have become part of their daily consciousness. Most remain in the camps in Beirut, where they know they are never safe. All of them still live in fear.

Ellen Siegel
Jewish American nurse[1]

I

'Quick!' I said to my brother, panting as we spread the ribbons around. It was Mother's Day, 21 March 1982. We were preparing a surprise for Mum, who had popped out. We found the ribbons in the drawer where we knew she kept them for our birthdays. Then, we blew some balloons and spread them around the living room. I cut out several sheets of paper from my big coloring book and, using lots of crayons, wrote: 'Happy Mother's Day!', 'We love you, Mum!', and spread them on the chairs. I then found a cassette tape she had gotten us, with children's songs. One was famous for Mother's Day: 'Your day, Mum, is the most beautiful. Children around the world celebrate!' I loved the song, which we listened to all the time. I put it on and raised the volume. My heart was thudding. Mousa was fiddling with the balloons, and, like me, barely keeping still as we waited for the key to turn in the lock.

Suddenly, she was there. Coming into the room, she looked around and broke into a smile, then into happy laughter. 'My darlings!' she exclaimed, scooping us into her arms. The music played, we sang, and I wanted the moment to go on forever.

Soon, we were preparing for Easter. Mum took us to Hamra Street, a busy shopping district, and we walked excitedly as she held our hands, maneuvering us through the crowds. I got a new dress, Mousa got a smart little suit, and we got new shoes, too. We wore our new outfits to church on Palm Sunday, carrying the large candles that Mum had decorated with flowers and olive branches for the procession. She sent photographs of us to our grandmother, with her usual letter:

> I thought of you so much this Easter, Mother, especially as I was making the cookies and colored eggs. I remembered how you used to make them for us and how happy we were.

It was the last stretch of calm we felt.

II

On 6 June 1982, Israel began its invasion of Lebanon. With unprecedented force, the Israeli army bombarded the Palestinian refugee camps in the south while 40,000 troops drove into the country. Israel called the operation 'Peace of the Galilee'. Its stated aims were to oust the PLO fighters from the south and form a 30-mile security belt along the border, but Israeli troops also occupied the southern cities of Sidon and Tyre and kept pushing north. With the backing of the Christian Phalangists, they reached East Beirut, occupied the presidential palace, and laid siege to the west, where the PLO and Lebanese National Movement were based.

The same day, the United Nations Security Council passed Resolution 509, demanding that Israel withdraw. But the Israeli army cut off food, water, medicine, and electricity from West Beirut as it bombarded it by land, sea, and air. Explosions erupted all around us. The places we lived, studied, and my parents worked—Corniche el-Mazra'a, Hamra, and Ras Beirut—were all under fire.

The PLO and Lebanese National Movement fought back. They rushed to erect sand barricades and plant land mines at the entrances to the besieged city. In a hopelessly unequal war, they aimed desperate fire at planes roaring above. The smell of gunpowder and burning tires filled the air. It was completely incomprehensible to us children; we saw the panic-stricken faces of the adults and watched normality evaporate.

There were no emergency shelters. The best we could do was to crowd into the basement of our building. Entire buildings were falling, but there was nowhere else to go. Without warning, the shelling would intensify and we would find ourselves running downstairs in terror, neighbors jostling over each other. Families ran to basements, schools, cinema theatres—anywhere they could get to. But the raids came from all directions. There were constant clashes at the entrances to the city, as well as the main junctions and the beach. Israel was intent on destroying the PLO even if it meant annihilating everyone. For weeks, thousands of buildings in West Beirut were targeted, with more than half a million rockets and shells.[2] Palestinian and Lebanese fighters and civilians fell by the hundreds.[3]

Taxi journeys out of the city cost exorbitant sums of money, both for the danger and the shortage of petrol during the siege. Families who tried to escape to their villages in the south saw the horror: flattened buildings, destroyed factories, people living on the rubble of their homes, zinc huts and shacks with roofs blown off. The southern cities were ruins, with signs of the Israeli invasion everywhere. Refugee camps were destroyed. The Israelis had spread rumors that they would not arrest any unarmed civilians and had given people movement permits to make them feel safe. When the bombing of the south subsided, the refugees slowly returned to their homes. The Israeli army then moved in. With the help of its Lebanese collaborators, it rounded up thousands from the villages and camps, including wounded men from hospitals and random people off the streets. Only the women, young children, and elderly were left, with no money, shelter, or breadwinners. They slept in fields, deserted buildings, or on the remains of homes and shacks, and some escaped to Beirut or further north. Lost children walked alone.

The men taken captive were left for days on the ground, in the sun. Their hands and feet were bound. Every day, a piece of bread was thrown to each of them. There were no toilets. Soldiers spat in their faces, swore at them, and made them carry stones in the heat. Eventually, they were blindfolded, hauled onto trucks, and taken to Israel. A journalist who was captive with them described the cries and screams as they were beaten on the way.[4] Many fainted on the journey without water or food. The soldiers also searched them and took all their money, watches, rings, and cigarettes. When they crossed the border, Israeli civilians from the north came to look at them, hitting the prisoners and throwing water and hot drinks in their faces.[5]

In Israel, the captive men were shoved into a large hole, surrounded by barbed wire and high sand barricades. There were two open buckets to defecate in. Each prisoner was given a number and a card with his name. They were photographed and any of their remaining belongings were taken. Then they were ordered to take their clothes off and sprayed with disinfectant, before being dragged off for interrogation at one end of the hole.

For days, hundreds of shackled men remained there under the sun. They were then taken to other camps in the north of Israel. Each morning and evening, the guards came to count them, and they had to keep their heads down and feet crossed for more than two hours. In each tent, which held tens of people, it was forbidden to talk or stand, with the threat of standing in the sun for long hours as punishment. The prisoners spent days with very little food, amidst a stream of verbal abuse by the guards. It was forbidden to move their bodies during sleep, and they were beaten if they did.

In these camps, toilets were holes in the ground, which ten people used at a time. There was no soap or medical care despite the high number of fainting and injured prisoners. When they asked for treatment, the Israeli commanders replied: 'Let them die.' They were tortured with extreme cruelty, stripped and thrown into cold water, then beaten with pickaxe sticks or whipped until their skin tore.

Other prisoners were held in cells, including young children and old men. In South Lebanon, the Israeli army used a convent school in Sidon as a prison. Hundreds of people were blindfolded, shackled, had cloth bags tied around their heads, and sat on the ground in the school's playground, the hot tar burning their skin. This went on for days, without food or water, and they had to defecate in their clothes, as the soldiers kicked them and beat them with sticks and water pipes. They were tortured by pulling their nails, putting cigarettes out on their bodies, having acid thrown at them, and being attacked by dogs. Many were given morphine injections to make them numb to the pain, only for the torture to continue, killing dozens.

In Beirut, the Israeli siege and shelling intensified, with extreme violence in the heart of populated areas. As the desperate resistance continued, people came together. Bakeries rushed to make more bread, electricity generators were installed in neighborhoods, and small excavators dug into the ground, looking for water. During any brief respite, people rushed out to buy food. We had to bring it up the six flights of stairs to our apartment. The power was out, and, even if it was not, no one took the elevator, for there could be a raid any minute. We spent long nights in darkness, lighting candles and fumbling our way around, until someone brought an electricity generator for our building. But petrol was in short supply and the generator was only run for a few hours at a time.

We could not store anything in the refrigerator and had to rely on cans, dried food, and powdered milk. Food was scarce and prices

sky-high; finding bread became a rite of suffering, with people queu-
ing up before dawn to try to get one pack. Garbage collection
stopped, and the stench filled the city, made worse by the summer
heat. As the piles grew, people had to resort to burning it. Even in
adulthood, decades after we had left Beirut, the smell of burning
garbage or tires would instantly take me back there.

The water supply was cut for more than a month, and we had to
buy bottles. Then, water trucks drove around the city. My father
managed to buy six canisters and struggled up the stairs with them
to our apartment. He stopped, panting heavily, then carried two of
them up to the roof, where he lifted and emptied them into the tank
so we could have running water. He came downstairs, drenched in
sweat, and asked Mum if he should take up any more. 'No!' she
said. She economized on every drop. After days of no showers, she
placed a little water in Mousa's baby bath and sat us both in it,
shampooed our hair, and used one bucket of water to rinse us both.

As children, we laughed and squealed at this sudden change, and,
at the start, we found hiding in the underground basement to be like
a little adventure. But the terror caught up with us very soon. We
huddled in fright at the roaring of planes, the whizzing of shells, and
the sudden explosions that shook the ground. One night, we were
fast asleep when there was a raid. Mum ran into our room and did
not have time to wake us. She yanked us from our beds and dragged
us out. I woke up, bewildered, feeling the painful clutch of her hand
on my arm as we bounced down the stairs.

The basement was filled with amenities as we spent more and
more time there. Families took down mattresses, blankets, gasoline
cookers, food, and other supplies to last them through the raids. But
soon it became too dangerous to stay in our building, even underground. We emerged from the damp of the shelter and blinked in
the sudden light. Mum rushed us upstairs to grab a few clothes and
go to friends' homes in one of the quieter areas. Any safe spot could
change in a matter of hours. Dad was constantly on the go, nervous
about staying in one place for fear of being found by Israeli soldiers
or their Lebanese agents. When there was a lull, he went back to
check on our apartment and bring us clothes or things we needed.
Mum asked him to bring some of our toys and books. He asked us
what else we wanted, and we both cried: 'Feed Kojak!'

He looked at Mum and they smiled in exhaustion, faces drawn from their sleepless nights. It was difficult to explain to a nine- and five-year-old what was going on. Warm coffee mornings with the neighbors were gone. School, shopping, happy visits, playing on the staircase of our building with friends—all were gone. We were not allowed out on the street or even on the balcony. The adults were snappy and impatient. Time stood still as I moved from couch to couch at friends' homes. I read so much that, for the first time, I got tired of books.

My uncle was also on the run. When the invasion began, he hid at the American University of Beirut campus, where he was study-ing. One of his friends, a journalist, could move around with her press card, and she smuggled food, blankets, and a radio to him. The Israelis were combing neighborhoods, bringing people out of their homes to inspect their identification. My uncle saw the sol-diers through the window, in the outer courtyard of the university. For a moment, he thought that was it; he was finished. But the president of the university somehow stopped them from entering, due to its academic immunity as an American institution. For days, my uncle continued to hide while his friend sneaked in whatever she could. As soon as the soldiers left the area, he made his way out. He had finished his Master's the year before, but he still had his student card, so he could use it as identification when moving around. He had lost count of the number of coincidences that had kept him alive.

He came to my father and told him we had to leave. There was no point in staying just to die. In July 1982, a booby-trapped car exploded near the Research Center, breaking its doors, wrecking some of its contents, and injuring one of the guards. A similar attack followed weeks later. The cars could not get close enough because of the guards, and only the glass and outer walls were damaged. 'They will suffocate you even more; you can do your work any-where!' my uncle beseeched. But, to my father, the Center was important to the struggle. He could not simply pack up and leave.

In mid-July, the Israeli army erected a large detention camp near Ansar, a village in South Lebanon. The camp served as a holding ground for thousands of prisoners, mainly Lebanese and Palestinians. Most were civilians. There were dozens of sick, mentally ill, disabled, or blind people, as well as amputees, the elderly, children, and clergy. Whole families and neighborhoods were incarcerated. Some had been brought in their pajamas.

The horror continued at Ansar. The guards got drunk and tortured the prisoners, killing many men and children. Tiny rations of food were provided, and there was no soap or sanitation and no medical care. Prisoners suffered from diarrhea and were forbidden to use the toilet at night. Disease was rampant and many died due to lack of treatment. The guards also taunted the prisoners by telling them to get ready for their release and lying to them; many suffered nervous breakdowns. Israeli student groups came to see them from time to time, like animals in a zoo. The International Red Cross only arrived after two months of their incarceration and did little for them except take letters to their families.[6]

Beirut turned into a hellhole. Thousands died or were never seen again. People were traumatised and many became numb, as though death was but a matter of time. 'No one knew what a lucky coincidence it was to be alive except those who were stuck in that tiny square of West Beirut,' wrote my father's colleague, Faisal Hourani.[7] 'Like gamblers who had lost everything, they didn't seem to care anymore.' They engaged in little acts of defiance. Some women wore makeup. Children ran out to get hot loaves of bread, like small miracles, from the bakeries that kept going. A sense that life could end at any moment made people want to grab every drop of it. And all throughout was an overwhelming terror that nothing could shake away. The scenes of war became uglier. Corpses were everywhere, buried under the rubble. Medical teams could not get to them because of the shelling. Hospitals suffered from severe shortages and were also bombed. Entire neighborhoods were destroyed, holes gaping out of buildings like silent screams. Moving around was a nightmare. On one of our runs, Mum pleaded with a taxi driver to take us to another area, but he stopped short and dropped us off helplessly, telling her he could not go further. We scrambled from the car, she held our hands tightly and we ran in terror as gunfire whizzed above our heads. And all we saw paled amidst the horrors witnessed by others, the starvation in the refugee camps that pushed people to eat cat and dog meat.

III

The resistance held out, in a near-suicidal mission. With RPG-7 grenade launchers, basic artillery, and Kalashnikov rifles, the fighters faced off an army of about 100,000 Israelis equipped with the most advanced military technology and complete air and naval control. There was no Arab help. The Palestinian and Lebanese resistance used guerrilla tactics and crept up behind Israeli bases, destroyed tanks, and caused hundreds of deaths and injuries. For two months, they managed to stop the Israeli army from entering West Beirut, for fear of greater losses among its soldiers. The United States vetoed all United Nations resolutions and sent its envoy, Philip Habib, to push for Israel's conditions: the surrender of the PLO and evacuation of its fighters by the International Red Cross.

On 6 August 1982, Beirut fell under eighteen continuous hours of bombardment, destroying large parts of the city. The Israeli army began Sharon's plan of gradually penetrating the west. The PLO was left with no alternative but to withdraw to spare the city from complete destruction. More than 17,000 people had been killed and 30,000 wounded in the Israeli invasion.[8] The United States brokered an agreement with Israel and the Lebanese Christian militias guaranteeing the safe exit of the PLO. Before agreeing, the PLO insisted on strong assurances from the international community, Israel, and its Lebanese allies that no harm would come to Palestinian civilians and institutions remaining in Lebanon.

Arafat had been moving around constantly during the siege as the Israelis made many attempts to kill him. By the end, he was staying in deserted, dilapidated buildings with no phones or wireless communication. Only a handful of people knew where he was, and no one could visit him except those he personally asked for. They would be taken to see him on a motorcycle driven by one of his aides. Before leaving Beirut, Arafat asked for my father, who was taken to see him in this way. The driver dropped him off at some distance from the place of 'al-khitiar', the old man, as Arafat was known, and explained how to get to him.

Arafat and my father discussed the fate of the Research Center and decided to keep it in Beirut after the PLO left. As the sole remaining institution, the Center would support the families of the leaving fighters as well as other Palestinians who remained in the country. At the end of the meeting, Arafat asked my father to leave through another door, not the one he had come through. My father went out to find himself in a maze of side streets and walked for half an hour, with a heavy heart, to where he was staying.

At the end of August, guarded by a multinational force, the PLO guerrillas left Beirut by land and sea. Thirteen thousand were evacuated by ship to countries around the Middle East. Each fighter was only allowed to carry one gun and a small satchel. They could not take any personal belongings. The expelled also included many who had not fought, or who were writers or activists.

Arafat left Beirut with the last group of guerrillas on 30 August. The Beirut Arab University neighborhood, where many of them had lived and worked, was ransacked. Their offices and apartments were looted; what the looters did not want, they threw on the floor or out on the streets. Samih Shbib, my father's colleague, walked around the area a few days later. He picked a large ledger up off the ground. In it were the names of members of a small Palestinian faction, with the position of each and his salary. Such was the tragic end of an era in Beirut.

IV

Israel wanted its allies to come to power in Lebanon, and it put pressure on the Lebanese National Assembly to elect the leader of the Christian Phalangists, Bashir Gemayel, as president of the country. Ariel Sharon had met him before the invasion and told him of Israel's plans. On 1 September 1982, Gemayel met Israeli prime minister Menachem Begin, who asked him to sign a peace treaty with Israel as soon as he took office.

On 11 September, the international forces that had supervised the departure of the PLO fighters left Lebanon. They had promised to protect the remaining Palestinian civilians, and the United States had given written guarantees that defenseless Muslims in West Beirut would be safe. Arafat demanded that the international troops return. 'I ask Italy, France, and the United States: What of your promise to protect the inhabitants of Beirut?'[9] he decried.

My parents were nervous and we were still on the run. School was supposed to start, but it did not. At first, with childlike glee, I was happy to not have to go, but I was soon so bored and restless that I began to miss it. 'When are we going home?' we kept asking Mum, but all we got were more hurried moves.

On 12 September, Gemayel met with Sharon and told him that the Lebanese Army would enter the Palestinian camps to disarm any remaining fighters. Sharon promised the support of the Israeli army. But the camps were devoid of fighters. Only their families remained. A Phalangist was quoted telling an Israeli official: '[T]he question we are putting to ourselves is—how to begin, by raping or killing?'[10]

Two days later, on 14 September, Gemayel was assassinated by a car bomb with twenty-six other Phalangist leaders at their head-quarters in Ashrafieh. Habib Shartouni, a Lebanese Christian, was arrested and later confessed. Nevertheless, revenge was wreaked against the Palestinians. The next day, Israeli tanks rolled into West Beirut.

The assurances given to the PLO before its departure included the Research Center staying on. The staff had just returned, after being unable to work for two months. With no electricity during the siege, they had gone to the building from time to time only to see each other and chat. Now, they were busy preparing for the Center's new responsibilities. But they soon heard that the Israeli army was advancing towards Corniche el-Mazra'a and Ras Beirut. In panic, they began to remove the Center's contents, starting with those that would hurt any employees if they fell into Israeli hands. They emptied out all the personal and financial records, the con-tents of the safe in my father's office, and whatever else could fit into his car. When they heard that the army had arrived in Raoucheh, nearby, instructions were given to the employees to leave alone or in small groups to any place where they could hide, so they would not be captured. Two hours later, Israeli soldiers stormed the Center.

At home, I stood on the balcony as Dad took several trips up and down to the dumpster in the street, where he burned many files and documents. I watched the black smoke rising from the sheafs of paper and did not understand, but there was no time to ask. Mum was throwing things in a bag and rushing us out. Dad had more things to sort through and could not leave. He told her he would catch up with us. A short while after we left, he noticed a strange car on the street below, and three men climbed out of it. Summoning his nerves, he placed a newspaper under his arm and went casually down the stairs as they were coming up to find him. He would wonder, for a long time, how they did not identify him or have a photograph. One of the men rubbed shoulders with him briefly on the stairs, but they did not stop him and kept climbing, allowing him to make a narrow escape. The Israelis also went to the homes of other senior employees of the Center and continued to hound them until the Israeli army left Beirut.

On Thursday, 16 September, Israeli forces surrounded the Sabra neighborhood and Shatila refugee camp and bombarded them heavily. Sharon then allowed his Christian Phalangist allies to enter the defenseless camps. About 1,500 Lebanese militiamen assembled at Beirut Airport, which was occupied by Israel. Under the command of Elie Hobeika, they began moving towards the camps in Israeli army jeeps, with Israeli guidance on how to enter.[11]

The camps were mostly inhabited by Palestinians and Lebanese Shia, as well as poor people of other nationalities. The Phalangists went in and began to slaughter, rape, and mutilate the residents while the Israelis blocked the exits and illuminated the area with flares. An Israeli commander, who was standing watch on the roof of a nearby building with Hobeika, later testified that he had heard a radio conversation between him and one of the Phalangists in the camp. The man was asking Hobeika what to do with fifty women and children who had been taken prisoners. Hobeika answered: 'This is the last time you're going to ask me such a question. You know exactly what to do.' Others on the roof burst out laughing.[12]

Residents who ran from the camps saw the Lebanese militias drinking alcohol and injecting each other with needles. Israeli soldiers were with them. The Phalangists drove people away in jeeps and killed them. They dug holes and pushed victims into them before shooting them. Those who survived lay motionless among the corpses and pretended to be dead, waiting for hours until the militias left. Bulldozers went through the camps, destroying homes. Each time the militias heard movement, they shot in its direction.

The hospitals were flooded with the dead and injured. The Phalangists went into Acre Hospital, murdered patients, and took other patients and doctors away. They raided Gaza Hospital, called everyone out on loudspeakers, and drove the patients and doctors to Sabra, where they shot them all. Some who fainted woke up hours later to find themselves in a mass of corpses.[13]

It went on for two days. While the Israelis kept guard outside the camps, about 350[14] Palestinians and Lebanese were butchered with knives or gunned down as they pleaded for their lives and for their loved ones. Those who managed to escape went back later to find the corpses of their families. Some were deliberately left alive to suffer the horror after their entire families were killed.

We were taking shelter at a friend's house. The news had begun to leak out. My parents were sitting on stools in a bare room, listening silently to a small radio on the floor between them. Their friend stood near them, listening, too. They all had terrible expressions, but I was used to this by now, and to not asking questions. Mousa and I took the opportunity to run around the large room and play chase, squealing at each other. My father, straining to hear the news, suddenly screamed at us: *'QUIET!'* We froze in our tracks, staring at the ashen faces of the adults, feeling that something terrible was amiss.

The first foreign journalists were allowed into the camps at 9:00 a.m. on Saturday, 18 September, one hour after the Phalangists had pulled out. Retching from the overpowering stench, witnesses saw bloodcurdling scenes of genocide. Hundreds of dead bodies filled the houses and streets. Groups of young men, hands and feet bound, had been lined up or tied with chains and machine-gunned.[15] Many corpses were severely mutilated. Young men had been castrated, scalped, or had the Christian cross carved into their bodies.[16] American journalist Janet Lee Stevens, who was to die seven months later, in April 1983, in a bombing of the American Embassy in Beirut, described what she witnessed in the camps at the time:

> I saw dead women in their houses with their skirts up to their waists and their legs spread apart; dozens of young men shot after being lined up against an alley wall; children with their throats slit, a pregnant woman with her stomach chopped open, her eyes still wide open, her blackened face silently screaming in horror; countless babies and toddlers who had been stabbed or ripped apart and who had been thrown into garbage piles.[17]

Robert Fisk, a British journalist, also recounted the horrific scenes in Sabra and Shatila:

There were babies—blackened because they had been slaughtered more than 24 hours earlier and their small bodies were already in a state of decomposition—tossed into rubbish heaps alongside discarded US army ration tins, Israeli army equipment and empty bottles of whiskey.[18]

The attackers had smoked copious amounts of cocaine before entering the camps. One boasted that he wanted to test the range of his Magnum pistol, so he and his friend lined up three small children on a table in one of the homes in Shatila. One infant slid down, but the attacker pushed the other two together and shot sideways through the head of one of them, noting with satisfaction that he killed both. He did not see the blood, he said, for 'the bright Israeli floodlights blinded everything'. As he left the house, he saw, out of the corner of his eye, the child who had fallen. He turned back to give another shot. The small movement stopped.[19]

V

During the same days, the Israeli army was seizing the contents of the Research Center. Some were brought down on wooden crates with ropes, others were flung down the stairs or from the windows and loaded onto trucks. What the soldiers deemed unimportant, they left in the street. Each day, a convoy of laden trucks took off to Israel.

Thousands of valuable documents were seized, including rare books, films, photographs, documents and press releases of PLO departments and Palestinian factions, unpublished memoirs, and taped testimonies of key Palestinian figures. The historical archives included documents of the land authority under the British Mandate, maps of Palestine, records of destroyed villages, newspapers and magazines of the Mandate era, and the correspondence of Palestinian leaders from the start of the century. The Center had published more than 400 books and manuscripts. All were seized, as well as cassettes and microfiche tapes, reader machines, recording equipment, printers, copiers, radios and televisions, phones, telex machines, electric equipment, fire extinguishers, and all the furniture that was in good condition, including chairs and carpets. The soldiers emptied out cupboards and drawers and took everything, even personal belongings.

They stayed in Ras Beirut for a week. Working in broad daylight, they emptied out four floors of the Center and loaded thirty-five trucks. At that point, international pressure on Israel mounted due to the massacres, and it had to withdraw. Before leaving, the soldiers either destroyed or defaced whatever they could not take. They broke the remaining furniture and equipment, tore documents, left profane language on the walls, and defecated on the floors. Piles of garbage littered the rooms. Even plant pots were turned over. In the library, the rows of bookshelves stood empty.

Two of the six floors survived. Ironically, one of them held the Hebrew newspapers collected by the Center since its establishment, while the other was where the Israeli press bulletin was prepared.

In the last week of September, a multinational peacekeeping force was deployed in Lebanon. The Israeli invasion had killed about 20,000 people, mostly civilians. It was difficult to ascertain the number due to the colossal destruction and the haste with which people had to be buried in mass graves. The refugee camps and most of West Beirut had been destroyed.

A month later, we finally came home. We found a large hole in the living room where a shell had ripped into the wall. Kojak had somehow survived, through Dad's visits. On the balcony of a nearby apartment, a child's bedsheets hung on the clothesline, the faded cartoons on them fluttering in the breeze. They had been hanging before we left. We did not know if the family ever returned.

VI

Mum set about to try and restore some normalcy. The priest managed to visit us with news from the family, and she wrote to my grandmother with an urgent request.

> I think of you in the day and dream of you at night, Mother. I'm back home, I've cleaned and tidied it, and I'm getting the children's clothes and books ready for school, which will open soon. It was very late this year, for reasons you know. They're very happy to

come back to their home and school, after the very tough circumstances we went through. I'm trying to do all I can to return them to their normal life. We just celebrated Mousa's fifth birthday, and he was so happy.

I write to you with a request, Mother, and I pray that you won't turn me down, no matter what. I have decided to see you this year, for we have spent twelve years apart, and, if we continue, you may not see me, ever. Please, Mother, don't be afraid of anything; no one can blame you for seeing your daughter and her children. Many others in a similar situation have met their relatives without any ills befalling them. Please, Mother, I want to see you at any cost, and I ask you urgently to get a passport. I'll take care of everything.

The rain began, washing the war-torn country. We went back to school. My parents began to go to and from work in separate cars, in case anything happened. The staff of the Center returned to the destroyed building to try and resume their work. With the material that had been in their homes and survived, they put together an issue of *Palestine Affairs* covering the months of August–October. Due to the circumstances, it was the first time that such a 'bumper' issue was released.

Much of the work had to be done in secrecy, and much of it centered on documenting the terrible events of the period, gathering testimonies from Palestinian leaders of the resistance, survivors of the Ansar detention camp, and dozens of testimonies of the Sabra and Shatila massacre.

Over the next months, the staff managed to rebuild about half of the Center's library by printing out microfilm copies of books and through donations from private collections. They also produced three more issues of *Palestine Affairs*. But, despite the motivation and commitment, the overriding feeling was that another attack was coming. The Center was the only PLO institution that remained in Lebanon. As the cultural arm of the PLO, it had diplomatic immunity, and was formally allowed to continue its work pending negotiations between the Lebanese authorities and the PLO over the ultimate fate of Palestinian organizations in the country. But the agreement between the Lebanese government and Israel was to oust all the remaining Palestinian institutions. Several threats had been made against the Center and against my father. Two Lebanese Army soldiers stood guard outside, and the situation was extremely tense.

In the south, the refugees returned to their miserable dwellings. Their homes were unfit to live in. Thousands of relatives of people in the camps were dead or missing. The survivors were in shock. The attitude of the Lebanese towards them, which had ranged between apathy and hatred, had turned into intense hostility. They blamed the Palestinians for all the disasters that had befallen them, and had no interest or desire to help. In Beirut and the south, Palestinians faced the worst repression, especially in the camps. Many slept outside the camps for fear of Christian militias kidnapping them or carrying out more massacres.[20]

At Christmas, Mum decided to put up the tree. 'For the children,' she told my father. We helped her decorate it. In a tradition she carried every year, she planted chickpea and wheat seeds in cotton wool underneath it and watered them. We watched as the little shoots sprouted, growing as we approached Christmas. To her, it must have symbolized some tiny blooming life going on after the carnage. She waited for my grandmother's response to her letter, for their meeting. But her wish was never fulfilled.

VII

On Saturday, 5 February 1983, at 2:00 pm, my mother was leaving work with a group of other employees. They held the elevator and she asked my father if he was coming. He told her to go ahead and that he would leave later.

No one anticipated the force of the attack that took place. As the employees were coming out, a car carrying explosives equivalent to 550 pounds of dynamite exploded outside, setting the building on fire and blowing the windows out of nearby apartments. The explosion's force covered a 500-yard circle; it tore the facades off the stores along the street and shook buildings throughout the heart of West Beirut. Pedestrians and drivers nearby were engulfed by the blast.

The employees on the upper floors heard no sound. All they saw was a bright blue light, flying glass and falling walls. It took them several minutes to realize that there had been an explosion and that they had to find their way out. They were surrounded by raging fires. As dense black smoke billowed from the Center, they gathered by windows and balconies, screaming for help. Women waved their scarves frantically on the balconies to attract attention. A few people slid down a drainpipe onto the shoulders of Lebanese Army soldiers, and some jumped into a nearby tree in desperation. Others held on until the fire engines arrived, twenty-five minutes later, with ladders and rope. The smoke was suffocating, and by the time survivors jumped to the bottom floors, the scene was a horrific one of blood, bodies, water hoses, and ambulances carrying charred corpses. Amidst this, my father stood, holding himself together and giving short instructions. In his office, all the doors had caved in, landing in front of him and around him, but none had hit him. He got out covered in dust and soot.

Soad Hayek, our neighbor, lost one of her legs, whimpering pitifully in the midst of the terrible destruction. The horror around her made the ambulance teams feel her case could wait. Relatives of the dead and missing rushed to the street, wailing and wrestling with policemen to get into the wrecked buildings. Horribly disfigured bodies were pried from the debris. Several people were trapped inside an elevator in the Center and died of smoke inhalation. Dozens of people were wounded. Survivors, blood dripping down their faces, staggered about in shock.

French paratroopers serving with the multinational force helped the Lebanese police try to bring order to the scene, which was horrifying even in war-torn Beirut.[21] Bloodstained glass and clothing covered the streets. Fragments of charred papers from the Center were blown into the air and fluttered back down to the street for an hour after the blast.

My father went to the American University Hospital, where the ambulances had taken the dead. When he walked into the lobby, he saw my mother, lying on a stretcher.

She had lost her life.

VIII

After leaving the building, my mother had stopped at a grocery shop down the street to buy sweets for us. She died with her friend, Sabah, in the blast.

Six other employees lost their lives: Sana Odeh, Muna Khattab, Subhi Eleiwan, Saleem el-Esaawy, Mohammed Azzam, and Bahaeddine Mansour. Two soldiers from the Lebanese army, Tony Sheet and Diab Habaqa, who were guarding the Center, were also killed, as were eighteen visitors and passersby, of whom could be identified Lina el-Ouf, Mustafa Bisani, Wafa Khaled, Ghinwa Deeb, Eid Jurdaq, and Carol Khoury.

The March–April edition of *Palestine Affairs* carried a three-page commemoration of those who lost their lives, entitled 'Martyrs of the Research Center' (see Figs 50–1):

Hanneh Shaheen Jiryis (Fassouta, Palestine, 1946), wife of general director, Sabri Jiryis, and mother of two. Researcher who enriched the Arabic library with many studies on Israeli affairs, published in *Palestine Affairs* since 1974. Completed a book on 'Sectarianism in Israel' to be published by the Center. Quiet, humble, and a good friend to all her colleagues.

Sabah Kurdieh (Al-Bireh, Palestine, 1955), young activist, mother of three. Studied Hebrew, worked as a translator in the Israeli Studies department at the Center and was training to be a researcher. Completed her first—and last—report one hour before she was killed.

Sana Odeh (Jdeideh Marjeyoun, Lebanon, 1963), member of Lebanese Democratic Youth Union and keen worker in the Archives department of the Center. Killed at the start of her journey, while preparing to celebrate her engagement one week later.

Muna Khattab (Ashrafiyyeh, Beirut, Lebanon, 1960), like Sana, killed at the start of her journey.

Subhi Eleiwan (Sinjil, Ramallah, Palestine, 1918), receptionist at the Center. Father of two martyrs and grandfather of several activists. His smile welcomed employees and visitors daily.

Saleem el-Esaawy (Tarshiha, Palestine, 1926), head of the Center's guards and member of the Palestine Liberation Army. Dedicated himself to the Palestinian revolution and was known for his humility and vigilance, finally giving his life in his watchful care for others' safety.

Mohammed Azzam (about forty-five years old), friend of Esaawy, colleague in guarding the Center and long-time activist.

Bahaeddine Mansour (nom de guerre), (Zahleh, Lebanon, 1961), a Maronite who joined the ranks of the Palestinian revolution. Since working at the Center, he was ever-present with his silent story that few people knew.

May they and all martyrs rest in peace.[22]

Eighteen employees and dozens of others were wounded. The attack was planned to bring down the building and kill everyone, and, primarily, my father. It only failed to achieve its full purpose because the car was not allowed into the underground parking lot. In the weeks prior to the attack, a young woman had regularly parked the car on the street near the Center and had managed to befriend the guards. On the day of the bombing, she asked one of them if she could use the Center's basement parking, but he turned her down. She parked the car very near the entrance and told him that she had to run a quick errand. When he objected, she gave him her identification card and the car keys, saying she would only be gone for a few minutes. To assuage him further, she left an infant in the back seat, claiming it was her son. He was blown up with the car.

A few months later, Hezbollah[23] would send my father a report on the cell that had perpetrated the bombing, after a similar attack was waged against a senior Hezbollah cleric. The attack on the Research Center was carried out under instructions from Elias Beitar, the security advisor of Lebanese president Amine Gemayel, of the Christian Phalangist party, who had succeeded his assassinated brother. The bombing of the Center was planned with an Israeli officer named Maoz who lived in Bechamoun, in Mount Lebanon.[24] Three years later, thirteen of the sixteen perpetrators would be caught and executed, after their confessions were videotaped.

IX

On that Saturday, Mousa and I were playing at home. Um Assaf was with us. She began to look at her watch and mutter nervously. 'Your parents are late ...'

I only felt fleeting worry. Mousa and I continued to play. But the minutes dragged, and Um Assaf became very agitated. I stopped playing, suddenly worried, too. It was unlike them to be so late. We could not reach them by phone, and I sat with her, waiting.

Two hours later, the door finally opened and my father walked in. He was covered in soot. His face was black, his hair a smoky mess. He looked exhausted, disheveled. We knew immediately that something was very wrong. He collapsed wearily on a chair and drew us to him.

'Where's Mum?' we both asked.

He explained that there had been an accident, Mum was injured, and she was in hospital.

'Can we go see her?'

He told us that we would, as soon as she felt better, and held us in his lap.

My uncle had been with him after it happened, and they had scrambled around in shock, going through the arrangements for her burial. My father had broken down and could not bring himself to tell us. My uncle agreed to break the news to us slowly. There was no one to take care of us and explain. I was nine; Mousa was five. Dad told us Mum's situation was difficult and she may not live, and sent us to stay with friends. He could not eat anything for three days, only managing water. Mousa and I did not attend her funeral.

Father Kareem, the priest, found out immediately. He was in Fassouta and went to see Um Nour's brothers in the evening. Together, they made their way to her house. When they came near, they called Nida, my aunt, who was married and had three young children. 'I'm bathing the kids,' she said to her uncle, as she was throwing out the bath water. There was a light rain, and she did not want to take them out in the cold. But her uncle Najeeb insisted: 'Leave it and follow me to your mother's house, Nida. I need you there.'

They asked for Hanneh's brothers, as well, and broke the news. Her mother lost her senses, sobbing and screaming. It was a nightmare, too horrific to comprehend. They rang the church bell in mourning and held a funeral for her the next day. The family went through the rites, received people at their home, and held a third-day service for her. But no one could believe it. Her mother needed sedatives to get through and was in and out of consciousness.

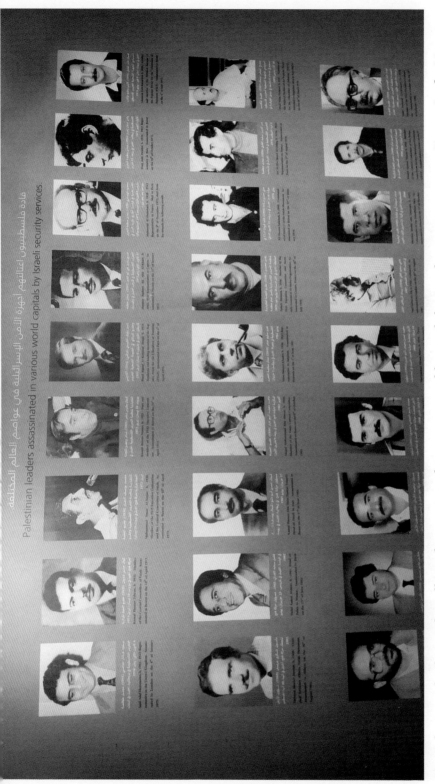

20. Palestinian leaders and intellectuals assassinated in various world capitals by Israeli security services, Yasser Arafat Museum, Ramallah, Palestine, 2019.

21. Ghassan Faez Kanafani, born 1936. Novelist and member of the Political Bureau of the Popular Front for the Liberation of Palestine (PFLP). Assassinated in Beirut on 8 July 1972.

22. Wael Adel Zwaiter, born 1934. PLO representative in Italy. Assassinated in Rome on 16 October 1972.

23. Mahmoud Al-Hamshari, born 1938. PLO representative in France. Shot in Paris on 8 December 1972; died from his wounds the following month.

24. Hussein Ali Abu Al-Khair, born 1943. PLO representative in Cyprus. Assassinated in Nicosia on 25 January 1973.

25. Basel Raouf Al-Kubaissi (Iraqi), born 1934. Academic and leading member of the Popular Front for the Liberation of Palestine (PFLP). Assassinated in Paris on 6 April 1973.

26. Kamal Butros Nasser, born 1925. Poet and member of the PLO Executive Committee. Assassinated in Beirut on 10 April 1973.

27. Muhammad Yusuf Al-Najjar, born 1930. Member of the PLO Executive Committee and the Central Committee of Fatah. Assassinated in Beirut on 10 April 1973.

28. Kamal Hassan Edwan, born 1935. Member of the Central Committee of Fatah. Assassinated in Beirut on 10 April 1973.

29. Said Adel Hammami, born 1941. PLO representative in the United Kingdom. Assassinated in London on 4 January 1978.

30. Wadi' Elias Haddad, born 1927. Member of the Political Bureau of the Popular Front for the Liberation of Palestine (PFLP). Poisoned in Baghdad; died in East Berlin on 28 March 1978.

31. Izz Al-Din Saeed Al-Qalaq, born 1936. PLO representative in France. Assassinated in Paris on 2 August 1978.

32. Ali Hassan Salameh, born 1940. Commander of Force 17 of the Fatah Movement. Assassinated in Beirut on 22 January 1979.

33. Zuheir Mohsen, born 1936. Member of the PLO Executive Committee and Secretary-General of Al-Saiqa Organization. Assassinated in Cannes, France on 26 July 1979.

34. Naim Saleem Khader, born 1939. PLO representative in Belgium. Assassinated in Brussels on 1 June 1981.

35. Majed Mohammad Abu Sharar, born 1936. Member of the Fatah Central Committee. Assassinated in Rome on 9 October 1981.

36. Kamal Hassan Abu Dalu (Kamal Yousef). Head of Fatah in Italy. Assassinated in Rome on 17 June 1982.

37. Fadel Saeed Aldani, born 1945. Head of Fatah in France. Assassinated in Paris on 23 June 1982.

38. Ma'mun Shukri Marish, born 1948. Occupied Territory Affairs, Fatah Movement. Assassinated in Athens on 20 August 1983.

39. Fahd Dawoud Al-Qawasmi, born 1939. Member of the PLO Executive Committee. Assassinated in Amman on 29 December 1984.

40. Khalid Ahmad Nazzal, born 1948. Member of the Central Committee of the Democratic Front for the Liberation of Palestine (DFLP). Assassinated in Athens on 9 June 1986.

41. Munther Jawdat Abu Ghazaleh, born 1933. Commander of the Palestinian Navy. Assassinated in Athens on 21 October 1986.

42. Naji Salim Al-Ali, born 1938. Cartoonist. Assassinated in London on 29 August 1987.

43. Muhammad Hasan Bheis, born 1945. Occupied Territory Affairs, Fatah Movement. Assassinated in Limassol on 14 February 1988.

44. Mohammad Bassem Altamimi (Hamdi), born 1951. Occupied Territory Affairs, Fatah Movement. Assassinated in Limassol on 14 February 1988.

45. Marwan Ibrahim Kayali, born 1951. Occupied Territory Affairs, Fatah Movement. Assassinated in Limassol on 14 February 1988.

46. Atef Fa'ek Bseiso, born 1948. Senior Officer in the Unified Security, Fatah Movement. Assassinated in Paris on 8 June 1992.

47. Fathi Ibrahim Shiqaqi, born 1951. Co-founder and Secretary-General of the Islamic Jihad Movement. Assassinated in Valletta on 26 October 1995.

48. PLO Research Center building, Colombani Street, Beirut, 2010.

"All the News That's Fit to Print"

The New York Times

Late Edition

Weather: Overcast skies, cold with snow developing by evening today; snow continuing tonight, ending early tomorrow. Temperatures: today 30-35, tonight 25-29; yesterday 21-32. Details on page 37.

VOL.CXXXII.... No. 45,581 — NEW YORK, SUNDAY, FEBRUARY 6, 1983 — ONE DOLLAR

$1.25 beyond 50-mile zone from New York City.

18 DIE IN BOMBING AT P.L.O.'S CENTER IN WESTERN BEIRUT

LIBYAN OFFICES WRECKED

Blast Strikes Research Bureau, Palestinians' Last Formal Institution in the City

By THOMAS L. FRIEDMAN

Special to The New York Times

BEIRUT, Lebanon, Feb. 5 — At least 18 people were killed and 115 wounded today when a car packed with explosives blew up in front of the Palestine Liberation Organization Research Center, setting the building on fire.

The blast also destroyed an apartment building across the street housing Jana, the Libyan press agency, and the temporary quarters of the Libyan Embassy.

Other Violent Incidents

It was the latest of several violent incidents in the Lebanese capital in the last few days. On Friday Druse militiamen shelled residential neighborhoods of East Beirut, killing 5 people and wounding 45, in their continuing battle with Christian militiamen. On Thursday a bomb shattered the offices of the Syrian press agency in West Beirut.

Lebanese Phalangists are reportedly terrorizing Palestinians in Sidon in an effort to expel them. Page 19.

The force of today's explosion blew the license plates off a nearby car and the shutters and windows out of many apartments in the neighborhood. The streets were left choked with blood-stained glass and clothing. Fragments of charred papers and documents from the center were blown into the air and fluttered to the street for an hour after the blast.

P.L.O. Blames Israelis

A shadowy group calling itself the Front for the Liberation of Lebanon from Foreigners, which has taken responsibility for several attacks on Syrian and Palestinian institutions, said it was responsible for the bombing. The assertion was made in calls to local news agencies, but there was no reliable way to determine its validity.

The P.L.O.'s diplomatic representative in Beirut, Shafik al-Hout, called the bombing another crime by the Israelis against the Palestinian people and urged the multinational peace force to protect West Beirut from "further Israeli atrocities." He offered no evidence that Israel was involved in the bombing.

The P.L.O.'s research center was established in 1965 as the cultural arm of the organization's official diplomatic mission in Beirut. After the withdrawal of the Palestinian guerrillas from the

Continued on Page 18, Column 1

United Press International; Associated Press

Residents of Beirut running for cover shortly after bomb exploded yesterday, and, below, a rescue worker helping a woman wounded in the blast.

3d-World Group Appears to Ease Radical Stance

A Draft Paper Criticizes Both U.S. and Soviet

By BERNARD D. NOSSITER

Special to The New York Times

UNITED NATIONS, N.Y., Feb. 5 — In a shift reflecting a move from radical to more moderate leadership, the nations grouped as nonaligned are considering a declaration that implicitly blames the Soviet Union as well as the United States for most of the world's tensions.

The paper, which was prepared for a meeting of nonaligned nations in New Delhi in March, is regarded as a triumph for such countries as Egypt, Yugoslavia and India. It appears to represent a successful effort by them to recapture the leadership of the movement from radicals like Cuba.

At the last gathering of its leaders, held in 1979 at Havana, the movement repeatedly condemned the United States by name in a similar summary of the state of the world.

Soviet Moves Cited

An African delegate close to the drafting attributed the more evenhanded treatment of the superpowers to the Soviet intervention in Afghanistan and the takeover of Cambodia by Vietnam, a Soviet ally. The latest draft, 35 pages long, is restrained on both issues. It calls only for the withdrawal of foreign forces from both countries.

When the leaders meet in New Delhi March 7-11, the pro-Soviet nations are expected to make a determined effort to toughen the text against the United States. Even the current document, although more evenhanded, does make more unfavorable, if indirect, references to the United States than to the Soviet Union.

In the one instance in which the United States is mentioned by name, it is urged to adopt a "constructive position" and negotiate with Nicaragua, a nation described as the victim of attempts to "harass and destabilize" the country.

Paper Drafted by India

The paper was drafted by India, which is replacing Cuba as the movement's chairman for the next three years.

Among passages critical of both superpowers is one saying "the inflexible positions adopted by the most powerful nuclear weapons states" were responsible for the failure to achieve agreement on disarmament at the special General Assembly session last June. The document urges a freeze on the production, development, stockpiling and deployment of nuclear weapons as a prelude to complete disarmament.

The text strongly condemns Israel, accusing it of "systematic onslaughts against Palestinian camps in Beirut which assumed genocidal proportions."

But the paper contains an implicit

Continued on Page 15, Column 1

PREMIER OF CHINA WILL MEET REAGAN IN U.S. THIS YEAR

TRIP ARRANGED BY SHULTZ

Zhao Accepts Invitation and Is Expected to Make the Visit in June or September

By BERNARD WEINRAUB

Special to The New York Times

WASHINGTON, Feb. 5 — The White House announced today that President Reagan and Prime Minister Zhao Ziyang of China would hold a meeting in the United States this year.

Administration officials said Mr. Zhao's visit to the United States would probably take place in June or September. They said today's announcement had been timed to coincide with Secretary of State George P. Shultz's visit to Peking.

In Peking, Mr. Shultz said at the end of his four days of talks with Chinese leaders that his visit had established a new atmosphere of mutual trust and had "set the stage for renewed advances" in relations. [Page 9.]

Officials here view Mr. Shultz's meetings in Peking as aimed at signaling that after a period of considerable difficulties, relations between the two nations are back on track.

White House officials said tonight there was a possibility that President Reagan would visit China, perhaps even this year. "Nothing is ruled out, including a visit this year," one official said.

Invitation Disclosed by Zhao

Mr. Zhao said Friday that he had accepted Mr. Reagan's invitation to visit the United States but made the plan sound somewhat tentative by adding that he hoped the trip would take place even though "the obstacles in our relations cannot be removed." He said the Taiwan problem remained the main obstacle to better relations.

Administration officials conceded that there were "various problems" in the United States-Chinese relationship and said the planned visit was intended, in effect, to permit continued efforts to improve the ties between the two nations despite some strains. In the last two years, the key difficulty has been caused by American military sales to the Chinese Nationalist regime on Taiwan.

One Administration official said that despite "difficulties" in the relationship, the planned visit was intended to underscore the "steadiness" in the two countries' ties. The official noted that ranking Administration officials, including Vice President George Bush, Treasury Secretary Donald T. Regan and Mr. Shultz had visited China, and Defense Secretary Caspar W. Weinber-

Continued on Page 8, Column 1

EX-SPY CONVICTED IN EXPLOSIVES PLOT

Wilson Guilty on All 4 Counts Tied to Libyan Terrorists

By WAYNE KING

Special to The New York Times

HOUSTON, Feb. 5 — Edwin P. Wilson, a former agent of the Central Intelligence Agency, was found guilty today of four counts of illegally transporting 20 tons of plastic explosives to Libya in 1977.

A Federal jury of six men and six women deliberated six and a half hours to reach its decision, which rejected an assertion by the defense that Mr. Wilson had continued to act with the authority of the C.I.A.

Shortly after the verdict, the prosecution filed a motion asking Federal District Judge Ross Sterling to declare Mr. Wilson "a dangerous special offender" because of a purported attempt to pay an assassin $1 million to kill two prosecutors, five witnesses in the case, and two others.

Could Lengthen Sentence

That move could add eight years to Mr. Wilson's possible sentence of 17 years in prison and a $145,000 fine. He also faces a 15-year sentence and a $200,000 fine resulting from his conviction in November of smuggling firearms to Libya.

Mr. Wilson, 54 years old, was found guilty of four counts growing out of an elaborate plot that, according to the Government's case, resulted in the shipment of 42,300 pounds of strategically sensitive C-4 plastic explosives for use by Libyan terrorists.

The former agent was found guilty of conspiracy to transport explosives ille-

Continued on Page 31, Column 1

2 More Held in $11 Million Theft

By SELWYN RAAB

In predawn arrests in Miami and on Staten Island, the Federal Bureau of Investigation seized two more men yesterday in the theft of $11 million at a Bronx armored car company.

The men were described as cousins, one a convicted narcotics trafficker who officials said was probably the "main motivator" and the other the owner of a Queens travel agency where part of the planning was believed to have been done.

But officials said they still had not recovered "one penny" of the missing $11 million from the largest cash robbery in the country's history.

"If I knew were it was," said Lee F. Laster, head of the F.B.I. bureau in New York City, "I'd be out there with a shovel looking for it." He said he believed it was hidden somewhere in the New York area.

The arrests were the third and fourth in connection with the theft at the Sentry Armored Car Courier Company on Dec. 12. The authorities said one of the suspects arrested earlier last week was "cooperating," and had implicated the three others arrested and at least two other suspects being sought.

A detailed account of the seven-week investigation and the trail that led to the four arrests began to emerge yesterday. Investigators were helped early on

Continued on Page 37, Column 1

Poll Shows Lessening of Fear That U.S. Military Is Lagging

By WILLIAM E. SCHMIDT

A recent sampling of national public opinion suggests a growing number of Americans no longer fear that the United States is lagging behind the Soviet Union in military prowess and feel the Reagan Administration is spending too much money on sophisticated new weapons systems.

In his proposed budget for the 1984 fiscal year, presented last week, President Reagan asked Congress for a 14 percent increase in military spending, and at the same time sought a freeze on spending for domestic programs. The Reagan Administration says the increase is necessary to counter a Soviet advantage in military power.

But according to interviews conducted with a wide variety of political and community leaders across the nation, and supported by data in a recent New York Times/CBS News Poll, the weight of public opinion favors less rather than more spending on military programs.

In large part, the tendency appears to reflect heightened public concern over the state of the national economy, including ballooning Federal budget deficits and the highest levels of unemployment since World War II.

"We have to have a strong defense," said Donald J. Canney, the Mayor of Cedar Rapids, Iowa, and a veteran of the Korean War. "But given the economic mess we're in, the defense system has to suffer its cuts along with everything else."

In the public-opinion poll, taken last month, 48 percent of those surveyed said they believed the United States was spending too much on new weapons, compared with 25 percent who said spending levels were about right. Only 11 percent said more money should be spent on new weapons systems.

The Reagan Administration has begun a costly program to build more Trident submarines. Page 17.

At the same time, there appears to be a growing belief that the military standing of the United States, versus the Soviet Union, has improved. When asked whether the United States was militarily superior, equal in strength or not as strong as the Soviet Union, 32 percent of those surveyed said they felt the United States trailed the Soviet Union, as against 44 percent of those asked the same question a year ago.

Nearly half of those surveyed last month said they thought the United States and the Soviet Union were roughly equal in military strength, despite Mr. Reagan's contention that the United States is still trailing.

"In 1980, the guy who used to stand up

Continued on Page 12, Column 3

INSIDE

Nazi Is Returned to France

Klaus Barbie, a former Gestapo official accused in the deaths of thousands, was taken to Lyons after being expelled from Bolivia. Page 3.

City Faulted on Homeless

New York City has failed to provide enough decent emergency shelter and permanent housing for homeless families, a study concludes. Page 34.

Today's Sections

Section	1 (2 Parts)	News
Section	2	Arts and Leisure
Section	2A*	The Guide
Section	3	Business
Section	4	The Week in Review
Section	5	Sports
Section	6	Magazine
Section	7	Book Review
Section	8 (2 Parts)*	Real Estate
Section	9*	Employment Advertising
Section	10	Travel
Section	11†	Regional Weeklies

*Included in all copies distributed in New York City and the suburban areas.
†Included in all copies distributed in Long Island, Westchester, New Jersey and Connecticut.

Index to Subjects

	Section	Page
Amusements	1	49-55,58
Around the Nation	1	22
Art	2	1,29
Bridge	2	32
Chess	2	34
Dance	2	18
Editorials	4	16
Fashion	6	56
Film	2	15
Food	6	50
Gardens	2	30
Letters	4	16
Music	2	1,19
News Summary & Index	1	2
Obituaries	1	36
Op-Ed	4	17
Photography	2	31x
Puzzles	6	60
Recordings	2	21
Ship Movements	1	44
Society	1	58-62
Sound	2	21
Stamps/Coins	2	33
Style	1	56
Television	2	25
Theater	2	1,3-4
TV (Late Listings)	1	37

United Press International

Secretary of State George P. Shultz and Foreign Minister Wu Xueqian during a toast at farewell dinner in Peking.

Evangelicals Strengthening Bonds With Jews

By RICHARD BERNSTEIN

After years of mutual alienation and distrust, evangelical Christians have been meeting with Jewish leaders in New York and elsewhere to offer support for Israel and to forge a new relationship with Jewish groups.

Jewish leaders are talking of a surge of support from a wide range of conservative Christians, including fundamentalists.

Jewish leaders who want to build ties with evangelicals also point to pro-Israel editorials in evangelical magazines and to theological pronouncements by Christian preachers saying they will not proselytize among Jews. There have been rallies and newspaper advertisements supporting Israel, participation of evangelicals in synagogue services and the creation of pro-Israeli organizations among Christians.

But while many Jewish leaders have openly welcomed the evangelicals' eagerness to build ties, others say they are uneasy. They say they harbor deep doubts about the wisdom of alliances with conservative Christian groups that, they feel, want ultimately to convert the Jews and, on many political issues, often hold profoundly different, more conservative points of view.

"The evangelical community," said Rabbi Marc H. Tanenbaum, national interreligious affairs director of the American Jewish Committee in New York, "is the largest and fastest growing block of pro-Israeli, pro-Jewish sentiment in this country.

"Since the 1967 war," he said, "the Jewish community has felt abandoned by Protestants, by the groups clustered around the National Council of Churches, which, because of sympathy with third world causes, gave an impression of support for the P.L.O. There was a vacuum in public support for Israel that began to be filled by the fundamentalist and evangelical Christians.

"For myself, as a result now of knowing thousands of evangelicals, I came to the conviction that Jews had to change the basic image of them as Bible

Continued on Page 42, Column 1

49. *The New York Times* front page, 6 February 1983, reporting the bombing of the PLO Research Center building. (Photographs omitted to avoid copyright infringement).

شهداء مركز الأبحاث

فقد مركز الأبحاث، نتيجة الاعتداء الأخير، ثمانية من العاملين فيه:

● حنة شاهين جريس (قسومة، الجليل، ١٩٤٦)، زوجة المدير العام للمركز صبري جريس ورفيقة دربه النضالي والعلمي، باحثة اغنت المكتبة العربية بالعديد من دراساتها في الشؤون الاسرائيلية التي تنشرها مجلة شؤون فلسطينية منذ العام ١٩٧٤. وستبقيها اكثر بالكتاب الذي انجزته قبل استشهادها بايام وموضوعه «الطائفية» في اسرائيل، والذي سيصدره المركز قريبا. هادئة ومتواضعة ورفيقة انيسة لكل زملائها.

● صباح كردية (البيرة، ١٩٥٥)، المناضلة الشابة، التي كان لشخصيتها الحلوة عند زملائها وقع الندى في ايام الجفاف. أم لثلاثة اطفال، بادرت لتعلم اللغة العبرية، وعملت مترجمة في قسم الدراسات الاسرائيلية في المركز. ثم لم تتوقف عند هذا، بل راحت تتدرب لتصبح باحثة في القسم، وانجزت اول تقاريرها — وآخرها للاسف — قبل ساعة واحدة من استشهادها (التقرير منشور في هذا العدد).

● سناء عودة (جديدة مرجعيون، لبنان، ١٩٦٣)، عضو اتحاد الشبيبة الديمقراطي اللبناني، موظفة مثابرة في قسم التوثيق. استشهدت وهي في بداية رحلة العطاء فيما كانت تستعد للاحتفال بخطوبتها في الاسبوع التالي لاستشهادها.

● سليم العيساوي (ترشيحا، ١٩٢٦)، رئيس حرس المركز، عرفته حلقات المجاهدين الفلسطينيين قبل عام ١٩٤٨، ومع تجدد الوعي واعادة بناء الكيان الوطني كان بين اوائل الملتحقين بصفوف جيش التحرير الفلسطيني. اعطى العيساوي في صفوف الثورة خيرة وضرب المثل في التواضع واليقظة، وفي حرب الشهور الثلاثة لم يشاهد الا في مواقع الخطر، واخيرا بذل حياته ثمنا ليقظته وحرصه الدائم على سلامة الآخرين.

● محمد عبد الله عزام رفيق العيساوي وزميله في السهر على سلامة المؤسسة الفلسطينية، مناضل في كل ساحات الخطر.

● بهاء الدين منصور (اسم تنظيمي) (زحلة، ١٩٦١)، ماروني، التحق بصفوف الثورة الفلسطينية، ومنذ التحق بالعمل في المركز وهو حاضر في كل لحظة ما صنت وقصته التي لا يعرفها الا القليلون.

فلهم، ولكل الشهداء، المجد الخالد.

● منى خطاب (الاشرفية، بيروت، ١٩٦٠)، مثلها مثل سناء، استشهدت وهي في بداية رحلة العطاء.

● صبحي عليوان (سنجل، رام الله، ١٩١٨)، موظف الاستقبال في المركز، تموجت حياته، شأن ابناء جيله، مع تقلبات الصراع العربي — الصهيوني فشهد مراراتها بحلواتها. أب للشهيدين، وجد لعدد من المناضلين. ومنذ استقر في عمله في المركز وبابتسامته تستقبل العاملين والزوار وتودعهم كل يوم.

شهادات

ياسر عرفات يتحدث عن الحرب:
معركة بيروت شهدت الولادة الفعلية
للقوات العسكرية الفلسطينية

اعداد: سلوى العمد

لا ادلي هنا بشهادة. فالشهادة تقتضي ان اقول كل شيء، وانا لا اريد ان اقول كل شيء في الوقت الحاضر.

توقعنا: اسوأ الممكن باستمرار

منذ اللحظة الاولى لعودتي من مؤتمر فاس الاول، دعوت الى استنفار عسكري شامل في صفوف، جماهيرنا وكوادرنا. استنفار في القوات العسكرية، والطلاب، والعاملين في الأجهزة الثقافية كالاعلام والابحاث والتخطيط، والعاملين في الأجهزة الاجتماعية والمنظمات الشعبية كافة. دعوت لاستنفار كامل سواء في صفوف المقاومة الفلسطينية او في صفوف الحركة الوطنية اللبنانية. لكن، للاسف، لم يدرك الكثيرون مدى خطورة الأوضاع التي بدأت تنبيء وتغلف المنطقة كلها بعد فاس الأول. لكنني واصلت التحذير رغم ذلك كله وفي اكثر من مناسبة. فعلى سبيل المثال، قلت في احتفالنا بذكرى مولد الشهيد كمال جنبلاط، ان الغارون يخططون للنزول في الدامور، فاهلا وسهلا به، نحن بانتظارهم.

اكثر من مرة تحدثت عن النفق المظلم الذي يمر نمر به، وللاسف، ظن البعض انني اكثر. فعلا، تحدثت كثيرا عن حرب «الأكورديون» حيث تطبق القوات المعادية على القوات اللبنانية، من كل جانب. لم يدرك احد معنى حرب «الأكورديون» الا بعدما حدث. في زيارة للهند والباكستان، قبل اندلاع الحرب بأيام، قلت في خطابين اثنين، في كل من نيودلهي واسلام آباد، ربما لا تكون اقوى الجيوش في المنطقة وما اكثرها ولكنها، ولكننا القوات التي لديها الاستعداد الكامل لان تقاتل وتستشهد في سبيل قضيتها وفلسطينها. وحدثت اكثر من مرة من اننا نقترب من ساعة الصفر، خاصة وقد بعثت برسائل الى كل الأصدقاء والاشقاء ابلغهم فيها ان هنالك حشودا عسكرية اسرائيلية تقدر بثلاث فرق. فلاسف، ضحك بعض العسكريين العرب وقال، «ثلاث فرق»؟! هل سيحتل هؤلاء لبنان بثلاث فرق؟! ثم باكثر من ثماني فرق تقدم لاحتلال لبنان. واذا بدأت الحرب، واذا باكثر من ثماني فرق تقدم لاحتلال لبنان.

50–1. Commemoration of employees killed in the attack on the Research Center on 5 February 1983. *Palestine Affairs* journal, March–April 1983.

52. A man overlooks a tent that serves as a school in a Palestinian refugee camp, following the Nakba.

53. The bodies of Palestinian and Lebanese civilians lie between the wreckage of the Sabra and Shatila refugee camp massacre on 18 September 1982, the third day after the killings.

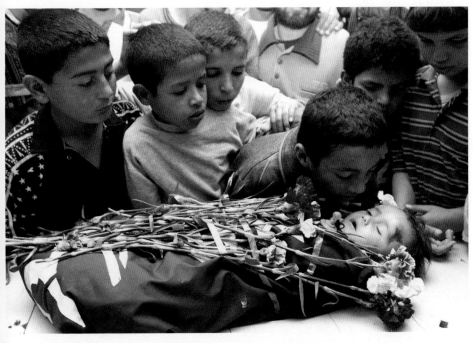

54. Palestinian boys take a last look at eleven-month-old Hoda Shalof, killed after an Israeli tank shelled her home in Rafah refugee camp in the south Gaza Strip, 1 May 2002.

55. Israeli soldiers patrol the streets of the Dheisheh refugee camp, near Bethlehem, 5 July 2002, during a curfew. Israeli curfews and closures have exacted untold damage on the Palestinian economy.

56. A Palestinian woman holds a girl's hand as they walk near the Israeli Separation Wall at the Qalandiya checkpoint, near Ramallah, 19 May 2009.

57. A Palestinian youth is detained by Israeli border police during clashes in the Shu'fat refugee camp near Jerusalem, on 9 February 2010.

58. The Israeli Separation Wall is seen north of Jerusalem, encircling the Shu'fat refugee camp, on 23 November 2013.

59. A Palestinian boy throws stones at an armored wheel loader of the Israeli army during clashes following a protest against the nearby Jewish settlement of Qadomem, in the West Bank village of Kofr Qadom, near Nablus, 17 October 2014.

One of my father's friends who helped to organize the funeral was interrogated by the Israeli police, as were many people who attended. Friends and people who had known my parents flocked from all over the country to pay their respects. Mansour Kardosh, my father's friend from al-Ard, and Jamal Qa'war, a poet, wrote eulogies for her in the newspapers. 'Peace be to Hanneh's family, who walk the path of pain,' Mansour wrote. 'She lives for us and in us all.'

In Beirut, my father had still not told us. I had been preparing for First Communion and the nuns had taught us to pray. I knelt in bed every night and prayed for my mother to get better. When we came home a few days later, I wrote to my grandmother.

Dad, Mousa and I are OK, and Mum is in hospital. We came home today at noon, and we'll stay here now. I hope my mum recovers soon.

We were at the house of Mum's friend, Um Saleem, and we slept there a week, because Dad had to leave the house sometimes, and my little brother was with me. But today all of us returned to stay here together.

It took several days for my father to be able to tell us. When he finally broke the news, in his and Mum's room, we stared at him in silence. Mousa's little voice broke it. 'What does that mean?'

'It means she's gone and we'll take care of each other,' Dad said, his face contorted in pain.

'We won't see her?' Mousa persisted. Dad's voice was coming from somewhere very far away.

'No, we won't, sweetheart. But I'll stay with you, always. We'll take care of each other,' he repeated.

I ran to the room I shared with my brother, crawled into bed, pulled the covers over my head, and cried for a long time.

X

For many nights, we slept on either side of Dad, in their bed. 'After your mother's death,' he told me, years later, 'I lost the will to live. I had a gun at home; everyone did. I was ready to end my life. But I looked at the two of you and thought, what would become of you?'

He took us to her forty-day memorial, and we stood next to him at the Catholic Church in Hamra. People came to shake his hand and leaned down to kiss us, many of them in tears.

In Beirut, everyone expected to die. My mother had asked my father to take care of us if anything happened to her. He was true to her wish. Slowly, we tried to go on. He sat with me to go over homework, and I helped my little brother. We managed to come first in class in our mid-term exams; Mum had gone over all our studies with us. Dad bought us toys and took us out each weekend to visit friends. As children, we could not process what had happened, and no one talked to us about it. We stuck to our routine, trying to pretend that all was normal. But a gaping hole filled our lives. I continued writing letters to Fassouta. At Easter, Dad decorated the candles for us and took us to a Palm Sunday service, as he and Mum had done, and we sent photographs to my grandmother. I consoled her, in words that he taught me. We missed our mother terribly but did not know how to express it.

It was time for my First Communion, and the nuns told us to wear white shoes. Dad did not understand and sent me in my white sneakers. On the day, I looked at the other girls, wearing fancy shoes with the long white habits, their hair all done up, while I stood there in my sneakers, having combed my hair alone and put two clips in it. I felt so alone and out of place, and missed Mum, suddenly feeling how cold and empty the world was without her.

The remaining employees of the Center, after this crushing blow, managed to produce the next issue of *Palestine Affairs* for March–April 1983. The basement and distribution floor that the Center had occupied in another building on the same road had survived, and the employees worked from there.

My father wrote a foreword: 'On the explosion of the Research Center: A word to the attackers.' The attack, he said, was part of the Israeli plan to exterminate the Palestinian national movement. Yet, Israel's crimes would not deter the Palestinians from the path to realize their rights.

The issue had the last articles by my mother and Sabah. My mother's piece was about Israeli revenge killings of Palestinians in the 1950s, describing the ideology of Ariel Sharon, who had formed and trained Unit 101 of the Israeli army to kill Palestinians and destroy their localities. She had recounted some of the major operations of this unit, which had killed tens of innocent civilians:

> Unit 101 was a professional gang of terrorists, a private army for Sharon, who later became one of Israel's most notorious leaders, known for their military and political extremism in light of their intense enmity to Arabs. The unit was tasked with carrying out revenge operations against civilian areas in neighboring countries, with the aim of killing the greatest number of Arabs. The criminal methods employed by Unit 101 were the basis on which the Israeli army founded its system of terrorist warfare, as seen in Israel's repeated wars against the Arabs, and especially the Palestinians. Its intense bombardment by land, sea and air that destroyed the Palestinian refugee camps in the south and killed and displaced thousands of their residents, then the constant bombing of Beirut while locking its civilian population under a heavy siege, are no surprise from an army that came from Sharon's terrorist school.[25]

Thirty years later, Sharon had led the invasion of Lebanon. On 8 February 1983, three days after my mother was killed, the Kahan Commission, set up by the Israeli government to investigate the Sabra and Shatila massacre, published its findings that Sharon was personally responsible for the massacre and should resign.[26] He remained in government as a minister without portfolio, but went on to assume several ministerial posts and eventually became prime minister of Israel.

Sabah's article was on the reaction of the Palestinians in Israel to its war on Lebanon and to the massacres. Israel's Palestinian population had come out in massive demonstrations of anger and grief.

Sabah's three sons were sent to Jordan. Her mother was to raise them, but she died in pain over her daughter twenty days later and was buried next to her. Their paternal grandmother had also lost two sons to Israel. She lived in Nablus, in the West Bank, but the children could not go there because their father had been a political prisoner in Israel, expelled and forbidden to return. Finally, they were placed in an orphanage, then sent to boarding school in Syria before rejoining their father in Amman. I missed them, for we had often played together on the stairwell of our building.

Thousands of children lost mothers or fathers, like we did. My father was trying to help us and himself to cope. My mother's friends, too, came to see us often. They all tried to be there for us but they were severely traumatized, and many had injuries that took years to treat. Um Assaf left because her husband felt it was too dangerous for her to stay. But in June, Dad insisted on celebrating my tenth birthday. 'We'll invite your friends on Saturday,' he said, 'because you have school on Wednesday. How about that?'

Mum's friends brought the cakes and sweets that she used to get. My classmates gathered around and sang happy birthday.

Then, Dad disappeared.

XI

My uncle took us to his house for a few days. Then he took us back to Um Saleem. We kept asking where Dad was. They told us he had to work and would be back soon.

Um Saleem and her husband were very kind to us. They were like the grandparents we missed, and we called them teta and jiddo.* Their children were all abroad and I never met them, but I knew they were older. Fadia, their daughter, had many dolls in her room, and I played with them and tried to practice with her exercise hoop.

Abu Saleem always ate standing up. His wife urged him to sit down, but he grinned at us and said, in his booming voice: 'This way, the food goes straight down, *whoosh!*' We giggled, and Mousa stood up, too, to eat like jiddo. Their warmth made us feel at home and helped us when we missed our parents.

Dad did not return. My uncle moved us to the home of Hussein Abu el-Namel and his wife, other friends of my parents. Hussein was a 1948 refugee from Arab al-Aramsheh, a Bedouin community near Fassouta. He was quite a character: tall, broad-shouldered, and, to us, rather like a friendly giant. He pulled pranks all the time, running after my brother and making us laugh. His wife, Doria, was Egyptian and his polar opposite, petite and soft-spoken. She was very loving and gave us many hugs and kisses.

---

* *Jiddo* (Arabic): colloquial address for grandfather.

It was strange to be at those homes without Mum. Sometimes, I caught the adults with a tear in their eye, which they tried to hold back under cheerful faces. They were also hiding my father's whereabouts. He had been arrested by the Lebanese authorities. The new government had signed a peace deal with Israel, and the campaign of revenge and terror against the Palestinians had intensified. All who remained in Lebanon were targets, even if they were not in armed resistance. Many left their homes to seek safety. Employees of the Research Center, members of civil society organizations and international NGOs, as well as artists, writers, radio hosts, and anyone suspected of helping Palestinians, could be arrested or killed. My father and uncle lost many of their friends. Even liaison officers between the Palestinians and the Lebanese authorities were arrested.

As the director of the Research Center, which had diplomatic status in Lebanon, my father had immunity. Despite this, the Lebanese authorities imprisoned him and made accusations against him. No lawyer dared to approach his case. My uncle, in desperation, finally found Salim Othman, a brother of the head of internal security forces in Lebanon. He demanded a fee of 8,000 dollars, an exorbitant amount at the time, and told my uncle they would likely take my father to military court. 'Please, just get them to let him leave the country,' my uncle asked him. A deal was made. Other employees of the Center were also arrested. Faisal Hourani, editor-in-chief of *Palestine Affairs*, was deported to Syria. Ahmed Shaheen, a Syrian dissident, was deported to Cyprus, while Samih Shbib fled to Syria. The Research Center was finished in Beirut, and we were among the last Palestinians to leave.

XII

Shadia el-Mutasem, who had worked at the Center, came to our house with my uncle. Before the explosion, she had been in the library on the second floor and had left her desk to give some papers to her colleague. Suddenly, she was flung to the floor and momentarily blinded. She did not know what had happened, but groped her way along the corridor and up the stairs to the landing, where she found the cleaning lady, who shouted at her not to go outside because she would be engulfed in the fire. As she regained blurry vision, Shadia made her way out through a bathroom window that led onto a plank adjoining two floors of the building, then jumped down. She saw the horrific scene, with mutilated bodies in front of her. Scrambling away, she climbed over the neighbors' fence into their garden. She had serious injuries to her face and along the right side of her body, but was lucky to be among the first victims to be taken to the American University Hospital.

She was lucky, again, when a good plastic surgeon walked in and took her case. He operated on her face and sent her home. It took a long time to heal her injuries. When she came to our house with my uncle, two months later, her teeth and eyes were still being treated.

Um Assaf came with them. In five suitcases, they packed as much as they could of our clothes and toys. 'What about Kojak?' I pleaded.

My uncle said he would take her to a kind man, Hajj Yahya, a caretaker at a nearby building who kept many cats in the basement. 'He'll take care of her with them!' he assured me. He packed the cat in a box and left with it. I did not know if my uncle had just made this man up, but I wanted to believe him.

He then took us with the suitcases to my father. We walked into a dark office where a man wearing army uniform sat behind a desk. He had a stone-cold expression and did not smile or try to talk to us as other adults did. I wanted to rush over to Dad, but I felt the tension as my uncle looked at me and motioned for Mousa and me to sit next to him. There was a lot of talk I did not understand. Next thing I knew, we were being taken on a plane.

Oblivious to what was going on, we sat with Dad in excitement and he buckled our seatbelts. We had flown with him and Mum before, but I was too young to remember much. I loved the smoked salmon that came with the meal, and he smiled and gave me his. Hours later, we landed in Tunis. Mousa and I found ourselves on the lap of a kind, bubbly man with a wild beard, who kissed and tickled us. He had a huge smile, and we grinned back shyly as he asked my father: 'Only two, Sabri? You should have more!'

Dad smiled, ruefully. 'I'll try to raise these two, Abu Ammar ...'

Arafat looked at him and nodded. 'May she rest in peace,' he said, quietly. Then, he motioned to one of his men, who took us by the hand and led us out. Dad nodded to us to go, as they kept talking.

Outside, the man, who seemed to be a guard, took us to a toy store. It was huge, and Mousa and I walked along in bewilderment. 'Choose anything you like, Ammo,' he said, ruffling our hair and smiling. We were shy and picked one toy each, but he bought us several before Dad caught up with us in protest.

It was decided that the political arm of the PLO would stay in Tunisia, the only Arab country which would not meddle in its affairs. The cultural institutions needed to be closer to the Middle East. The PLO made many attempts to convince the authorities of other Arab countries to allow it to reestablish the Research Center there. But they all failed. Out of the blue, our destination became the Mediterranean island of Cyprus.

9

SAFER SHORES

I tell the world ... I tell it
about a house
with the lantern
they shattered
About an axe
that killed a lily
And a fire
that burned a braid
I tell about
an ewe that was never milked
a mother's dough that was never baked
A thatched, grassy mud roof
I tell the world ... I tell it.

Samih al-Qasim
Smoke of the Volcanoes[1]

The taxi sped along a two-lane highway, dotted with shrubs and low hills on either side. The simplicity of the place was its starkest feature. There were no crowds of buildings or bustle of people as in Beirut.

We stayed at a small hotel in Nicosia while my father worked on the logistics. A friend of his, Walid Khadduri, came to meet us. He was an oil expert who worked for OPEC and had also lived in Beirut. His wife, Maha, had been my mother's friend and had worked with her at the Institute for Palestine Studies. Our schooling was my father's first concern, and Maha told him: 'Enroll them at the Falcon, Sabri. It's a great school and our kids go there.'

We walked into the headmaster's office in early July. Mr. Ierides, an elderly man with thinning grey hair, welcomed us and exchanged a few words with my father. Then he gave me an English test. When I finished, he looked at the sheet and said: 'I'm not sure she'll make it in Grade 6.' But Dad insisted that I go on as I had left Beirut. The headmaster nodded. 'We'll try. By the end of the first term, if she can't cope, we'll have her repeat Grade 5.' Mousa was going into Grade 1.

At the hotel, I burst into tears. 'I can't go to an English school!' I wailed. 'How will I understand?' I only knew some basic words from school in Lebanon. All my lessons had been in Arabic.

'You'll be fine,' Dad assured me. 'I'll help you!' He bought us a collection of Ladybird books, *Peter and Jane*, and asked me to help Mousa, too. I calmed down and began to practice. We treated ourselves to ice cream in the hotel lobby each time we finished a book. Life was empty and scary otherwise, in this new world that we found ourselves in.

We moved to the second floor of a house in Engomi, a sleepy suburb of Nicosia. The apartment was large and empty. Dad bought some basic furniture and our school uniforms, and asked about the nearest supermarket. We traversed the aisles, picking up some things to eat. All of us were lost. I fell into a surrogate mother role for my little brother, caring for him as best as I could, when I desperately needed someone to care for me. My father did his best but was grossly inept at housework and childcare. Mum had completely taken that role and left him to his work. Now, he had no idea what to do. He toiled through making meals, giving us showers, and sorting through our books and uniforms. I was too young to be of much help, or to comfort him or understand his grief. It was obvious we needed a solution, and fast.

'How about writing to Teta?' he suggested. From Cyprus, he could call our families in Fassouta. He found out that my uncle, Baheej, had just had a third daughter and named her Hanneh. My world was mixed up; I began by telling my grandmother that we had moved to Cyprus, then I told her about my recent birthday party in Beirut, and congratulated my uncle on the baby. Then, at Dad's urging, I told her the same things my late mother had said a few months before. 'I miss you very much, Teta; please get a passport and come see us!'

It did not take long. Within a few weeks, we went to the airport. I did not know what to expect. This person I had envisioned, whom Mum had told me so much about, was finally coming to visit. As she walked out into Arrivals, we rushed up to her with Dad. But, instead of the smiles I expected, she clutched Mousa and me, crying uncontrollably. People stared, but I was lost in the arms of this old lady, with deep lines in her face and a scarf over her hair. We walked to the car. She sank into the back seat, between Mousa and me, and continued to hold us. She would not stop crying. The meeting that Mum had been trying to arrange was supposed to take place here, in Cyprus.

Teta stayed with us for two weeks. One day, as I was playing in the kitchen, I heard my father talking to her. He was asking about my mother's younger sister, Najwa, who was single. 'I need someone to help take care of the children,' he said, 'and I don't want to bring them a strange stepmother.' He wanted to marry her.

My grandmother was not in favor. She worried that their temperaments were different, that they did not know each other. She and Dad talked about other solutions, and I heard the strain in their voices. When my grandmother flew back, the matter was still unresolved.

We were struggling. The first day at school was a blur. Dad dressed me in the uniform the wrong way, putting on the summer

dress above the shirt and skirt, as we had done in Beirut. A kind
teacher corrected it for me and took off my dress. Someone managed
to put me in the right class, and there, I just copied what everyone
else was doing, not understanding a word of what the teacher was
saying. For weeks, I just sat there, listening desperately and trying to
absorb the foreign language. I copied furiously from the board into
my exercise books, as we had done in Beirut. It was not the custom
to do that at this school; the students simply listened and followed
along in their books. But Miss Morrison, our young, gentle British
teacher, did not say anything. She was very kind and kept smiling at
me as I began to make out a few words of what she was saying. I felt
so alienated that I burst into tears on a bench in the playground. A
classmate saw me and rushed up to me. 'Fida! What's wrong?'

'I don't have friends!' I stuttered in the little English I knew. I
had never felt so alone, so scared.

'I'm your friend!' she said, and put her arm around me, in a
gesture I have never forgotten.

Things were very strained at home. We ate so many boiled potatoes and eggs that we got sick of them; Dad had no idea how to
cook. He bought vegetables and other ingredients, but we ended
up throwing them away and getting takeout instead. Our showers
were hectic, and he was frustrated at having to give us some kind
of routine, help us with our homework, and keep up with everything. He kept calling my grandmother, urging her to accept his
marriage proposal to my aunt. He felt she would be kind to her
sister's children.

And she was. As soon as we saw her at the airport, with her
striking resemblance to Mum, we were drawn to her. She was smily
and cheerful, and she instantly took us under her wing. In October
1983, she and my father were quietly married in Nicosia. Ironically,
the ceremony took place at the Lebanese Maronite church, the only
Arab church on the island.

My father's younger sister, Muna, came with her and was her
maid of honor. My uncle, Geris, also arrived from Beirut. Mousa
and I sat with him in the front pew as the old priest conducted the
ceremony. We were the only people in attendance. Najwa wore a
simple cream-colored suit, out of respect for her sister. Dad looked
drained and weary, but he felt he had done the right thing.

We moved out of the apartment into a house in Ayios Dhometios, another suburb of Nicosia. The house had a beautiful garden that we played in, and there was a football field nearby where Mousa would go and kick a ball around. Mr. Nicos, the house owner, lived on the second floor with his wife. They were both retired teachers, and he had been a headmaster. Their children had married and moved out. Mr. Nicos would see me playing and smile, his teeth gleaming in his wrinkled face, and teach me the Greek names of the nearby geography and the flowers in the garden. He held my hand and pointed it towards the Kyrenia Mountains. 'See?' he leaned down and whispered in his soft English, spreading his hand near mine, in silhouette against their peaks. 'They look like five fingers. This is why we call them Pentadaktylos. *Pente* is five, and *daktylos* is finger!'

He straightened and beamed at me, satisfied with the little lesson, and I beamed back. I loved Mr. Nicos. Sometimes, we went upstairs to visit him and Mrs. Nina, who gave us tasty treats.

Things quickly fell into a routine. Our aunt was very kind to us. Each morning, she helped us dress, combed our hair, and prepared breakfast and our sandwiches. When we came home from school, she had made lunch, and she hovered over us like a kind hen as we did our homework. A motherly atmosphere warmed the house again. Two weeks later, she came into my room to put some laundry away, and I stood next to her. 'Aunty, can I ask you something?' I asked, shyly.

'Of course you can, sweetheart!' she smiled.

I hesitated. She looked at me and I blurted out: 'Can I call you Mama?'

Sudden tears came to her eyes. She put the clothes down and held me close. 'You can call me anything you like, darling,' she whispered into my hair.

II

My uncle, Geris, had packed what was left of the Research Center and shipped it to my father in Cyprus. Finally, the library seized by Israel was also returned to the PLO. In September 1982, during the invasion of Beirut, eight Israeli soldiers had been captured by the Palestinians. A year later, through the intervention of the International

Red Cross, six of them were released in exchange for 4,500 Palestinian and Lebanese prisoners in the Ansar camp and Israeli jails, as well as the library of the Research Center.[2] The materials were delivered to Algeria.

My uncle had stayed on in Beirut after we had left. Despite the danger, he did not want to leave. He felt he would be going to his death in one of the Arab deserts, where he would have nothing to do. But, as he lost many of his friends to the terror campaign that unfolded, nothing remained for him in the ravaged country. At the end of the year, he joined us in Cyprus. He wanted to marry Shadia, my parents' friend and colleague from the Research Center, and he asked her to catch up with him. But she had to renew her refugee document in Lebanon to be able to travel. She made many trips back and forth to the authorities, who hounded her with questions. Who did she know, what was she doing at the Center, what kind of contacts did they have? Where were the remaining employees? Were any of them still in Lebanon? Her parents' house in Bourj el-Barajneh camp was searched several times. Shadia told them it was just a job and she did not know anything. When they kept pressing her on why she had worked at the Center, she told them: 'You don't let us work elsewhere, and I took this job!' It took months for them to renew her travel document and let her leave.

In January 1984, she and my uncle married in Cyprus. It was also a quiet affair. We were all bearing our scars, trying to adjust as life went on. Cyprus was a safe haven and gave respite from the horrors we had seen. The Research Center was reopened in Nicosia on a smaller scale. Again, it had diplomatic status as a cultural arm of the PLO. The *Palestine Affairs* journal resumed, as did some of the Center's other research and publications. My uncle worked with my father for a while, then launched *al-Malaf*, a political and economic journal, with partial funding from the PLO. At the time, Cyprus was the best destination for PLO publications, and *Filistin al-Thawra*, *Balsam*, *al-Carmel*, *al-Hadaf*, and other magazines of the Palestinian factions had also moved there from Beirut. Cyprus offered them the freedom to work and was close to Palestine and Lebanon. The Cypriot authorities did not censor or even look at any printed materials, and it was easy to ship them to the Arab world.

In Cyprus, too, the rest of our family could finally visit. Our grandfather, Elias, was the next to come. People in Fassouta were

afraid and told him it could be dangerous. But he had waited forever, and, after Um Nour's visit, nothing could stop him. 'What
will they do, put me in prison?' he scoffed. At seventy-four years of
age, he got on a plane and came to see us. Mousa and I were smitten
with sido, who wore traditional dress: wide black pants, a white
shirt, and a white headdress. It was springtime, and my parents took
him around to see the olive groves, fruit orchards, and churches of
Cyprus. He saw flocks of sheep everywhere and was happy, feeling
the country's resemblance to Palestine. Mum asked him to do a
barbeque for us and took him with her to buy the meat.

We had a large fireplace at home, and he sat in front of it, with
Mousa and me on either side. A small piece of burning coal rolled
out. Sido casually flicked it back with his hand. We leapt up madly
and ran to tell Dad. My grandfather looked up, startled, and asked
him what the matter was. Laughing, Dad answered: 'They're telling
me that sido is holding fire!'

My grandfather nodded and, a minute after we had returned and
sat next to him, gave a sudden poke to the heaped coals with the
iron rod, causing one of them to roll out again. He nonchalantly
held it and flicked it back, smiling at our squeals of glee. Then, he
began to barbeque the food and, sitting next to him, we ate all the
meat, such that Mum had to go out and buy more. 'You have good
kids, son!' he beamed to my father. 'Not like Subhi's, who don't
eat anything!'

Things got better at school. At the end of the year, I managed to
pass. Being so young, Mousa and I picked up the new language
quickly. Dad was happy with our progress and took us out on weekends to explore the island. On summer nights, we went to the luna
park and to get ice cream.

The pain of my mother's loss waned at times, flared up at others.
Our new environment was, perhaps, the best we could have asked
for to help us cope with her loss. As a child, I blocked it out and did
not think about it, but it remained, a flame that flickered in our soul.
Our aunt did not try to erase our mother's memory. She loved her
sister and was just as heartbroken as we were. Through the years,
she kept Mama Hanneh alive in our home, mentioning her, lighting
candles, and taking us to a memorial service for her every year. At
the same time, my aunt treated us like we were her own.

242

In July 1984, my uncle, George, got married and brought his bride to spend their honeymoon with us. It was the first time that we met any of our parents' brothers or sisters, other than my uncle, Geris, and, of course, Mum. We clambered onto Uncle George's lap and ran our hands through his big, black beard. He laughed and pointed to two small moles on his cheeks. 'See these?' he whispered to Mousa. 'At night, before I sleep, I press them to take off my beard, then I put it back on in the morning!'

Mousa, seven years old, stared at him, eyes wide as saucers. 'Really, Ammo?'

My uncle nodded. Nothing would convince Mousa to go to sleep before he saw him 'taking off his beard'. It took much laughter and a stern word from Mum to get him to bed.

The following year, when I was twelve, I composed my first piece of writing. It was grandly titled *The Culture Magazine*. On several sheets from my exercise book, I wrote snippets of news and trivia, illustrated them, and forced my parents to 'subscribe' at one Cypriot pound each. Mousa did not have the money, for our school allowance was half a pound. I only drafted one more issue before I abandoned the project, but my father kept the first issue for many years.

We nagged Dad to move closer to school, as we were on the other side of town and had an hour's bus ride each way. He found an apartment in Strovolos, only a few minutes away. Like the previous place, the owners lived on one floor and rented the other. We missed Mr. Nicos and Mrs. Nina, but, to our joy, the new house had children we could play with. Two daughters and a younger son stole furtive glances at us. They were our ages. Their parents, Krista and Andreas, were very welcoming. Krista's parents also lived with them. Her father had been a headmaster of a school in Alexandria and still knew some Arabic.

When the children took us to the garden to play, I had a lovely surprise. Several cats wandered around, and I asked the girls if they were theirs. 'We keep them, yes,' they told me, smiling shyly. 'Do you like cats?'

I nodded and told them about Kojak.

'What happened to him?' they asked.

'It was a "her", but we called her Kojak,' I explained. 'My uncle took her to someone to take care of her when we left.'

243

I had missed Kojak but suddenly there were four cats in her place. The girls had given them Greek names. Soon, I was sneaking food down to the garden and playing with them.

In our new house, Dad bought us a red bicycle. I spent many happy hours skidding around our neighborhood. Cyprus was very quiet and very safe.

Though they were afraid of trouble in Israel, more of our relatives visited us. My grandmother, Um Sabri, came to our new house. It had been fourteen years since she had seen my father and uncle. Two years earlier, someone had told her that they had both been killed during the Israeli siege of Beirut, and she developed organic paralysis. She was cured when she saw them. It helped to lift some of her depression, too, which had plagued her since my mother's death. She adored us and seemed content to simply sit near us, kiss us, and listen to our chatter and play. My two youngest aunts, Muna and Huda, came with her. After that, a stream of aunts and uncles followed. They all had suitcases full of goodies, and all showered us with love.

Dad needed his car to go to work every day, so Mum had to use taxis. He encouraged her to get a driving license and promised her a car of her own. More importantly, he wanted her to be able to take us out so she could relieve him of our nagging. Mousa and I sat with her to help her learn the traffic signs. She had picked up some English on the island, but her understanding was still very poor. 'You'll never figure this out!' we groaned. But she laughed, as she always did, and told us not to worry. For two days, she walked around the house with her head buried in the booklet. We never knew how she managed to pass the theory test, first time around. The practical took a little longer, but she passed it on the third attempt.

When it was time to buy her a car, Mousa and I argued fiercely about the color. Finally, Dad bought her a maroon Mazda. She started taking us on trips and visits to friends. 'Out of my hair!' Dad grinned. 'Leaving me to work in peace!'

Mum loved life and loved to go out, and she found, in us, eager companions. We spent our summers on the island's beaches. Every weekend, she filled a large icebox with sandwiches and fruit and we set off. In the winters, we drove to the mountains, dotted with picturesque villages and quaint coffee shops, and stopped to buy delicious sweets and preserves. In Nicosia, she found the farmers' market and made a trip each Saturday for fruits and vegetables. Cyprus was generous in its food, produce, and the warmth of its people. They were simple and open-hearted, with culture and traditions very similar to ours. My father joked that they were Arabs who spoke Greek.

They were also very welcoming and sympathetic to the Palestinians, who they felt had suffered a similar tragedy to theirs. In 1974, Cyprus had been ravaged by a war between its Turkish and Greek communities, and Turkey occupied the northern part of the island. Greek Cypriots and Turkish Cypriots were thrown out of their villages, lost all their properties, and had to resettle in refugee communities. The war had long since ended, but hundreds of their loved ones were missing and presumed dead. Cypriots related to the plight of the Palestinians, and we found, on the island, a home away from home.

III

By the end of our second year, we were doing really well with our studies. The Falcon School provided an excellent education and had an incredibly diverse student body, with children of foreigners working on the island as well as Cypriots. We had friends of many nationalities.

Our friendship with the neighbors also grew very close. We became a family, growing up with their children, celebrating birthdays and holidays together, and going up and down to each other with food and sweets. Each day, my mum had afternoon coffee with Mrs. Krista and her parents, and we met her cousins and friends. Across the street, another neighbor, Mrs. Maroulla, and her family were also close to us. We played with the children, riding our bicycles and kicking footballs around. Dad was surprisingly tolerant of the noise, especially as our 'football field'—an empty plot of land—was next to the house, and the basketball hoop was installed beneath the window to his office.

The cats had given birth multiple times and were now a tribe. I began to give some of them Arabic names, but, with the girls, we used the Greek ones. I wrote the names and family tree in a little file on my father's computer, which was new. Unknown to me, Dad saved this file and showed it to me some thirty years later. The cats roamed the garden and often came up to our apartment. One day, Glikoulli, a grey, white, and orange cat whose name meant 'little sweet one', climbed up the tree to my room, jumped down onto the balcony, made her way into my wardrobe, which was half-open, and gave birth among my shoes. Mum was appalled. 'Get her out!' she screeched.

'I can't!' I pleaded. That night, we had a serious problem. At 11:00 pm, I went to Dad, who was still working in his study.

'Yes, sweetie?' he raised his brow. 'Why are you still up?'

'I need you to go get a syringe for me!' I told him. The cat had disappeared, leaving four tiny newborns screaming in her wake. 'I need to feed them!'

I was expecting a rebuff, but Dad got up, patiently, got dressed, and went to the hospital. There were no pharmacies open. Half an hour later, he was back with four syringes. He had told the nurse he had a child who needed insulin, for he was too embarrassed to tell her they were for the cats. I filled a syringe with milk and fed the poor blind creatures, one drop at a time.

Half an hour later, Glikoulli sauntered back in. I jumped up and pounced on her, tying her paw to the foot of my bed with the belt of my robe. 'You stay right here!' I fumed. She sat with her kittens. In the morning, I fed her and let her go, thinking she would not return. But I came back from school to find her with them.

Soon, we had a dog and two chickens, too. Mum and Dad kept us busy in our new world. I began to take piano lessons. Once, I came home from one of them with a heavy heart, and found myself in tears, in my room, for a reason I could not comprehend.

Then it dawned on me. Mrs. Danae, my teacher, reminded me of Mama Hanneh.

IV

In 1986, my father published the second part of his book, *A History of Zionism*, in Arabic. Each day, we heard various news broadcasts from the radio in his study. One was from the Voice of Israel in Hebrew. The language drifted about the house, and I grew familiar with it in the background, yet it remained foreign, abrasive. I knew enough to know that Israel was the enemy, that it had brought all the pain in our lives. We were close to my father's colleagues at the Center and their families, visiting them and going out together. A few had shared some of their stories with Mum, which I had overheard.

In my third year at school, someone pointed out two Palestinian children, a brother and sister. I had seen them before; they were in other classes. The first thing that anyone noticed was a haunted look on their faces, a seemingly deep sorrow that did not shift. Even when they smiled, their eyes only lit up for a second before the sadness returned. They had survived the Sabra and Shatila massacres three years before. The little boy had hidden in the bathroom and covered his younger sister's eyes while their family was being slaughtered. Somehow, the attackers did not see them. The children stayed there for hours until the massacre was over and the first journalists were allowed in. A British photographer chanced upon them, crying and shaking, still holding each other in the bathroom. He decided to adopt them. He brought them to Cyprus and enrolled them at our school, and I saw him, sometimes, coming to coach the football club, saw the warmth of their relationship with him. I never approached these children or talked to them; the scars ran too deep, for all of us.

My father did not want our identity to dissolve. At home, we were raised on our culture and language. He continued to teach us Arabic for a while, then he found a private teacher, Mr. Abdallah, a short, Egyptian man with a big smile. He came to our house twice a week, carrying his books and assortment of colored pens. Mousa dreaded his visits and tried to do everything he could to evade them. He had not studied any Arabic, as he had started school in Cyprus, and he found it a heavy chore and wanted to go out and play instead. I was more comfortable, having learned the language in Beirut, and I enjoyed the lessons, particularly when I could distract the teacher and get him to chit-chat. Somehow, Mousa and I both managed to pass our British O-Level Arabic exams with the help of Mr. Abdallah, though we had no curriculum and he seemed to pick the lesson content at random. His face always lit up at two things: the moment we understood something, and when Mum served him tea and homemade sweets.

In my teenage years, I became an avid listener of Arabic music, especially the romantic songs of Abdul Halim Hafez. An Egyptian shop in Nicosia sold books and cassettes, and Mum took us there often. When Dad traveled to the Arab countries, usually to attend the sessions of the Palestinian National Council, he also brought back books and movies. I read Egyptian and Palestinian writers. Ghassan Kanafani drew me in with his short stories, often narrated through the eyes of children. I listened to Marcel Khalife sing about homeland, resistance, and longing. When I was fourteen, I went to see an Arabic play in Nicosia, al-Mutasha'el (The Pessoptimist), based on a novel by Emile Habibi. The protagonist was a Palestinian living in Israel during the years of military rule. Mohammed Bakri, an actor from the Galilee, played the part with striking drama. I stared at the man from home, from that place that was engraved in us, yet was so far away, and absorbed each move he made and syllable he uttered. The message was the same. The stories were the same. A loss of a homeland, a grave injustice, the pain of exile, a longing for our roots. I wore a kufiyyeh and drew our flag on my schoolbooks. The feeling was growing stronger in my heart that we belonged elsewhere, that our life abroad was temporary until we could go home.

In 1987, my maternal uncles and their wives went to Egypt on a tour, and we flew with Mum to see them. It was the first time that Mousa and I met them, and the emotion was overwhelming. We came out of the hotel elevator to find them waiting. They broke down, crying and hugging us as the staff looked on in confusion, trying to move us to the side. We finally sat, eyes fixed on each other, as they wiped their tears. I did not know what to say. Mama Hanneh had told me about them all through my childhood, and I missed her painfully as I looked at the faces that so resembled hers.

We returned to Cyprus, shaken by the experience. I began writing letters to my cousins. In the summer, my father sent me on a computer training camp in Cairo, where I met other Palestinians from Israel for the first time. I spent three weeks with children my age from Haifa, Nazareth, and the Triangle, sharing meals and singing around campfires at night. I also met a young man from Fassouta. We were too shy to exchange more than a few words, but it was another moment of awe that I was seeing people from the village, which was becoming real to me. That world had just materialized, and, with it, the painful realization that we could not go there.

V

The antenna on our roof enabled us to view Syrian TV channels, which were the closest that we could pick up. In December 1987, we began to see images of the intifada, the uprising that erupted in the West Bank and Gaza. Within days, the occupied territory was overtaken by fury. Tens of thousands took to the streets. Shopkeepers closed their businesses and went on strike, and laborers refused to work in Israel or in Jewish settlements. People boycotted the Israeli civil administration and refused to pay taxes.

Israel responded with great violence. Images of soldiers bashing teenagers with clubs leaked out. The army used plastic-coated bullets, killing hundreds of people, including dozens of children. But the momentum only grew. The youth, faces covered with kufiyyehs to protect their identity, pelted the soldiers with stones or used slingshots. Those who perfected the slingshot threw marbles to break the windows of hovering Israeli helicopters. They laid blankets down on roads so the chains of Israeli tanks would get entangled in them.[3] The Israeli authorities turned to collective punishment. They arrested hundreds, demolished homes, and imposed heavy fines on the families of stone-throwers. Soldiers beat up handcuffed youth and hurled tear gas canisters into schools, hospitals, and homes. Palestinian refusal to pay taxes was met with confiscation of property, termination of business licenses, and imposition of new taxes. The army enforced thousands of curfews; closed schools and universities; cut off water, electricity, and fuel; uprooted trees on Palestinian farms; and blocked produce from being sold.

In response, Palestinians moved to organize networks of home schooling, medical care, and food aid. People grew what they could in their little patches of garden and shared it with others. Families hid runaway stone-throwers at their homes, pretending they were their children when Israeli soldiers charged in. There was an unbreakable community spirit and a unity of purpose, a determination to resist peacefully, even in the face of the growing Israeli repression.

But the Israeli response grew harsher. In January 1988, Defense Minister Yitzhak Rabin implemented his 'Iron Fist' policy to 'break the bones' of Palestinians. On 16 April, Abu Jihad, who was the visionary of the uprising, was assassinated by an Israeli hit squad in Tunis. About twenty Israeli agents were ferried to the Port of Carthage. They went to his home, killed his guards, and emptied several rounds of gunfire into him in front of his family. He died with seventy bullets in his body.

My father and uncle were devastated. Abu Jihad was a pure, forward-thinking man with unshakeable ideals and who was willing to make heavy sacrifices. He was Arafat's top aide and one of the founders of Fatah. He had fought in the Battle of Karameh, Black September, and the siege of Beirut before becoming 'the engineer' of the intifada. On the night he was killed, he was writing a letter to its leaders in the occupied territory. *'No voice rises above that of the intifada'* were his last words, and they became the movement's slogan.

Yet, the uprising raged on, putting pressure on Arab states, as well. For the first time, Palestinians were moving towards self-determination. The PLO moderated its demands, wanting to use the momentum of the intifada to realize a Palestinian state alongside the State of Israel. At a meeting of the Palestinian National Council in Algiers, in November 1988, the PLO recognized United Nations Resolutions 242 and 338 (which it had previously rejected), affirming Israel's right to exist and calling for its withdrawal from the occupied territory. On 15 November, during the Council meeting, and in an intensely emotional moment, Arafat declared, from exile, the State of Palestine in the West Bank and Gaza, with East Jerusalem as its capital.

The declaration of independence was written by Mahmoud Darwish. My father sat in the back row of the meeting. Tears clouded his eyes as everyone rose to their feet, clapping wildly as the declaration was read out. The Palestinian state was declared on the territory occupied in 1967, a mere 22 per cent of historic Palestine. But the leadership felt it was the only realistic option.

Yet, it was not enough for the West. To enter into dialogue with the PLO, the United States pressured it to renounce 'terrorism', by which it included Palestinian resistance. My father and others were distraught at Arafat's acquiescence to this demand. At the meeting, my father voted against this move. Nevertheless, in December, Arafat addressed the United Nations General Assembly, recognized the right of Israel to exist and renounced 'all forms of terrorism'.

Though I was busy with school, my ears were with the adults. I heard them talking about the intifada. It was in the news, in pictures, in the Palestinian journals published in Nicosia. For a multicultural event at school, Laila, the daughter of my father's colleague, Faisal Hourani, led a group of us in a dabke dance. I wore a traditional Palestinian dress and felt proud.

The United Nations and 104 member states recognized the State of Palestine. The United States began talks with the PLO, for the first time, and pressured Israel to do the same. But the new path was not without its dark side. Many Palestinians saw the negotiations as a capitulation and as relinquishing their historic rights. After Abu Jihad's assassination, Israel continued killing Palestinian leaders who expressed this conviction. Hamas, the Islamic Resistance Movement, was founded during the intifada. It opposed the change in PLO policy and kept a hardline stance against Israel, which began to arrest and deport its leaders.

As the PLO faced immense pressure, regional events dealt it another blow. In August 1990, Iraqi forces invaded Kuwait and annexed the tiny oil-rich state. Arab leaders hastened to condemn the invasion, and the PLO found itself in a difficult position. Iraq was one of its core supporters, financially and politically. While Arafat did not condone the invasion, he supported Iraqi president Saddam Hussein's stance that the conflict should be solved regionally, without external interference.

Hussein also linked his withdrawal from Kuwait with Israel's withdrawal from the occupied Palestinian territory, a position that the PLO had to support. But most Arab regimes sided with the United States and some joined its war coalition against Iraq. Arab Gulf countries, especially Saudi Arabia, retaliated against the PLO by cutting off financial support and expelling thousands of Palestinian workers from the Gulf.

In January 1991, the United States–led coalition launched the First Gulf War, codenamed 'Operation Desert Shield', on Iraq and Iraqi forces in Kuwait. A month later, Hussein's forces were ousted and Kuwait was liberated. Many Palestinians were then killed in Kuwait in acts of revenge, and most of the Palestinian population of 400,000 fled the country.[4]

In this climate of Arab hostility, the PLO was politically sidelined and found itself without its major funders. In the summer, I finished school and was accepted to study computer science at Lancaster University, in England. Though financial worries were looming, my father managed to secure my tuition fees, which were given as PLO scholarships to the children of martyrs. Meanwhile, he worried, as other Palestinians did, about what was next.

VI

In September 1991, my parents took me to the airport, where I boarded my first flight to Britain. I was a shy, nervous eighteen-year-old. When I stepped out into the arrivals lounge at Manchester, my head began to spin. I saw a group of young people standing together. They were speaking Greek. I walked up to them and asked where they were going. 'Lancaster!' a girl said. 'Do you want to share a taxi?'

I was so relieved. They were from Cyprus, and it was their first year, too.

An hour later, the taxi wound up the road leading to the university, through lush fields. It was outside the town, in a beautiful expanse of countryside. The arrival was hectic. We reported to student services and I was assigned my accommodation. I unlocked the door to the small room and saw a small bed, table, chair, wardrobe, and tiny sink. The kitchen and bathrooms were shared. I put my bags down and wandered down the hall, where I met my first dormmate.

'I'm Julie!' a tall, broad girl with red curls extended her hand to me. She had a thick accent which I would learn to recognize in the area. We were herded down to the Great Hall, where the president delivered his welcome. From there, it was a scramble of timetables, unpacking, figuring out where to buy food and how to take the bus into town, and, finally, sitting in my first lecture.

There was one phone in the dormitory, on the landing of the second floor. Dad told me he would ring every Sunday at 5:00 pm, so I could wait nearby. Mum wondered how I was doing for food, and I had to ask her how to cook some basic things, as I had barely entered the kitchen in Cyprus. My first pasta was a disaster, and my attempt at rice yielded a coagulated mush. I stocked up on baked beans and chocolate biscuits.

In my first week, I was walking down the busy throughway of the university when I saw a woman wearing a black and white kufiyyeh.

I stopped short in front of her. 'Excuse me, are you Palestinian?' I smiled, shyly.

'Yes!' she grinned. 'Do you speak Arabic?'

I nodded. Her name was Raja. She was from Ramallah and was doing her Master's. 'Come, let's go to the cafeteria!' she laughed and linked her arm through mine. 'There are a few other Palestinians here. Not many, but I'll introduce you to them!'

Soon, I made friends from many nationalities, as well as the locals. But, within a few weeks, I began to spend most of my time with the Palestinians. Sawsan, who was my age, was also from Ramallah and was studying at a nearby college. The two of us sometimes looked after Abboud, Raja's infant son, who was with her. A fourth friend, Rima, was from Bethlehem. It was funny, I mused, how I had never lived in Palestine, yet they were the group I stuck with. From them, I heard about the intifada firsthand, how they threw stones, distributed leaflets, and went to demonstrations behind their parents' backs. 'They were worried about us,' said Raja, lighting her cigarette, the only luxury she allowed herself on her student budget. 'They fought with me when they found out. But we couldn't stay away. Everyone was on the streets! It was damn hard.'

I found out much about life in Ramallah, and my pain grew deeper that I could not even visit. Raja took care of Sawsan and me and cooked warm meals for us. We were all very different, yet our friendship grew stronger in that gloomy British winter. She lived in a house in Lancaster and we spent the night there, sometimes, when it was late and there was no bus back to our dorms. But she was only there for a year, and, in June, she finished her Master's.

She came to my room to say goodbye. I was dreading the moment. We both knew that the chances of seeing each other again were slim. I could not visit her, and, as a Palestinian, it was difficult for her to get a visa to travel elsewhere. We held each other, and, before we knew it, we broke into heavy sobs. It was much more than the sorrow of parting. I felt we were crying for Palestine, for a scattered people, for a terrible situation we could not change.

There was a knock at the door, and one of my dormmates asked if we were alright. 'Yes,' I thanked her, wiping my tear-streaked face.

Back in Cyprus over the summer of 1992, I told my father about my new friends and how much I longed to visit Palestine. 'Perhaps it will happen, one day,' he nodded. He was anxious and distracted. The PLO was almost bankrupt and could no longer make salary payments to its thousands of employees. We had to cut down on our spending, and arguments broke out between him and Mum. The employees were beginning to leave the Research Center as they could not afford to remain in Cyprus without pay. In September, I returned to university in the UK with worries looming over my family.

Arafat felt not just the financial strain, but the political one. The PLO was diplomatically isolated and faced pressure from Hamas and Islamic groups in the occupied territory. For several months, tentative PLO–Israeli talks had begun regarding a Palestinian state within the 1967 borders in return for the PLO's recognition of Israel. Arafat was forced to make concessions. In Israel, too, the left-wing bloc had a narrow majority in government and needed a political breakthrough.

My father was privy to these communications and was skeptical. Since his involvement in the peace talks in the early 1970s, he had not had great hope for their fruition. When word began to spread about the Oslo peace process, he thought it impossible. 'Either the Israelis have gone mad, or the Palestinians have!' he exclaimed. Joking about the so-called return, he told his friends who always felt cold that they would be sent to Jericho, where it was warm. For those who hated the summer heat and suffered in Cyprus, he teased: 'We'll send you to Gaza. You'll see what heat is like!' Those he loved the most, he would bring to the Galilee, for that was the highest honor, he told them. To him, the whole thing was a fantasy, for he knew the Israelis and felt that a leap to recognizing the Palestinians was, as yet, very remote.

Yet, though his intuition was almost always accurate, it failed him on this count. Under tremendous pressure, Palestinians took the first step in renouncing 'terrorism' and recognizing the State of Israel. Israel did not recognize the State of Palestine, but only the PLO as the representative of the Palestinian people. Back in Cyprus after my second year of studies, I was in for a shock. On 13 September 1993, my family and I sat glued to the TV in our living room in Nicosia, watching the Oslo Accord signing ceremony between Arafat and Rabin, now the prime minister of Israel, with

US President Clinton presiding. The historic handshake on the White House lawn was meant to signal a new era of peace and reconciliation. It was agreed that an interim Palestinian Authority would be established in the West Bank and Gaza Strip for a period of five years, while negotiations continued to reach a final solution to the conflict.

As the cameras flashed and applause broke out, I turned to my father incredulously. 'What does this mean? Can we go home?'

'Eventually, yes,' he smiled.

10

A MIRACLE OF SORTS

There was no such thing as Palestinians ... It was not as though there was a Palestinian people in Palestine considering itself as a Palestinian people and we came and threw them out and took their country from them. They did not exist.

Golda Meir
Israeli prime minister[1]

Such lofty ambitions, however, needed time to materialize, and, meanwhile, I flew to England for my final year of studies.

Despite the signing of the new agreement, the situation in the Palestinian territory remained very tense. On 25 February 1994, Baruch Goldstein, a Jewish settler, opened fire inside the Cave of the Patriarchs (Ibrahimi Mosque) in Hebron, killing twenty-nine worshippers and wounding more than a hundred before he was overcome and beaten to death. Goldstein was an American-Israeli army physician and religious extremist who lived in the illegal settlement of Kiryat Arba, overlooking eastern Hebron. He belonged to a militant Jewish organization founded by Meir Kahane, leader of the far-right Kach Party.[2]

In the protests that followed the massacre, the Israeli army killed a further twenty-five Palestinians and imposed a two-week curfew on the 120,000 residents of Hebron, leaving its 400 Jewish settlers free. Goldstein's tomb was erected at Kahane Park in Kiryat Arba. Right-wing Jews visited the site and revered him as a hero.

On the fortieth day after the massacre, the end of the mourning period, Hamas carried out a suicide bombing in a Jewish settlement, the first of many such attacks. Nevertheless, the Oslo Accords went ahead. The second agreement was signed in May 1994, as I was sitting my final exams. It concluded Israel's transfer of power in most of Gaza and Jericho to an interim Palestinian Authority. On 20 May, while still in Tunisia, Yasser Arafat formed the first government of the authority in preparation for his return.

My father was apprehensive. The PLO was relocating and he waited to see what would happen. After one and a half years of no salaries, most employees had left the Research Center. Only he and the secretary were left, and they had to move to the PLO building in Nicosia to save on rent. Eventually, the secretary had to be dismissed.

My uncle could not hold out any longer. He had lost the PLO funding for his magazine and all the subscriptions from the Gulf states after the Gulf War. His wife, who worked for the Palestinian

Embassy in Nicosia, also spent months without pay. After the Oslo Accords, the Sudanese government refused to renew his passport. Completely stuck, he applied for political asylum in Britain.

In June, when I graduated and returned to Cyprus, he brought his wife and children to our house to say goodbye. I could not believe they were leaving. They were the only family we had had throughout the years. I held my little cousins tight, not knowing when we would be reunited.

We were staying put until the situation became clearer with Dad's work. Leafing through the newspaper, I saw a job advertisement for a software developer in Nicosia and applied. In three weeks, I got an offer. The company was a software startup with about thirty people. It was my first job and I felt nervous, but I shared an office with a Sudanese programmer, Salwa, and we became friends. We loved Egyptian plays and quoted lines and laughed together. Talking to her helped me adjust to the daunting, eight-hour workday. I was not used to sitting in one place for so long. Salwa was a petite girl and did not eat much. At lunchtimes, she was glad to pass me most of the food her mother had given her, despite my protests.

When I got my first paycheck, my joy was mixed with worry for Dad. I gave him my salary so he could pay the rent. His face bore a pained expression. 'I'll give this back to you, sweetie, when the situation improves ...'

On 1 July 1994, Arafat finally returned to Gaza, to the jubilant welcome of hundreds of thousands of Palestinians. They gathered to hear his triumphant speech from the balcony of the former headquarters of an Israeli military commander. The next day, members of the new Palestinian Authority took an oath of office before him as its first president. A tide of hope and optimism swept over Palestinians—except those who opposed the Oslo process. Samih Shbib, my father's colleague, was part of the first group that returned. Sitting next to his friend on the bus to Gaza, he looked at the crowds lining the streets and remarked, sourly: 'See these people cheering and throwing sweets in the air? Soon, they'll be spitting at us!'

It was a hint of the crises to come, although no one had any inkling at the time. Over the next months, about 4,000 PLO personnel and their families arrived in the West Bank and Gaza.

They included members of the Palestine Liberation Army and Fatah, who formed the core of the new security forces. In the murky background, they began to crack down on Hamas, Islamic Jihad, and other opponents of the Oslo process.

From Cyprus, my father called my uncle in London. Ammo was struggling. His family was given subsidized housing and could just about survive on the meager state allowance. He had found work in a couple of Arab media networks, but was hemmed in by their politics and agendas. 'I'm not doing anything of value!' he told my father. 'I can't find my place here.'

'I want to go back,' said Dad.

There was a breathless silence. 'Back?'

'Yes. I'm going to the Israeli Consulate to apply.'

'But, why not with the PLO?' my uncle asked, not quite believing what he was hearing. He had not wanted to harbor any hope for fear of having it shattered.

'I'm going back as part of the PLO agreement, but I want to apply as an individual, so I can go to Fassouta. I don't want to be stuck in the West Bank or Gaza; I want to go home. All the accusations against me have been dropped, as per the Accords,' Dad said.

The agreements allowed a very small number of PLO members to return to their towns and villages in Israel, on a case-by-case basis. My uncle did not believe it would happen. He waited, torn between possibility and doubt. It was an incredible dream—beyond a dream, too scary to even hope for.

The next day, my father went to the Israeli Consulate in Nicosia. He drove his car with diplomatic plates registered to the PLO mission in Cyprus. The guard let him in. 'Yes, sir?'

'I'm an Arab from Israel,' he said, in Hebrew.

'Welcome,' the guard said.

'I work for the PLO office,' Dad continued.

'Welcome!' the man repeated.

They've given them instructions to be polite to us, Dad thought. 'I've come to apply for my passport so I can go back home,' he told him.

The man seemed to get excited and ushered him in. My father presented his Israeli identification card, tattered but still distinct. It had survived Beirut and twenty-four years of exile.

The consul knew who he was. 'We don't have specific instructions yet,' he told him. 'You want a passport? Fill out an application, I'll send it in, and we'll let you know.'

One month later, Dad received a phone call asking him to come to the Consulate, where he was given a one-time entry permit to Israel. The response to the passport request was not clear, although they had written his ID number on the application. 'I'll sort them out when I get there!' he told a stunned Ammo. 'This means I'm still in the system.'

'You're really going to do this?' my uncle asked.

'Yes.'

II

He booked the ticket for 29 November 1994 to Ben Gurion Airport in Tel Aviv. When he left, Mum and I began feverishly pacing at home. What if they were waiting for him? He had scoffed at our fear before he left, telling us solemnly: 'International agreements have been signed. This is no joke!'

It did not make it easier, though. Time seemed to stand still as we looked at the clock in the hall. Its loud ticking had always annoyed me, but, now, it was deafening. 'He should have landed,' Mum said. We shifted our stare to the phone, willing it to ring. But it maintained a frosty silence. My chest was tight, and a feeling of nausea kept washing over me.

On his arrival, four agents had asked to see his papers. He presented his PLO and Fatah membership cards, his diploma from the Hebrew University, and the Israeli lawyer's license. 'Sir, who are you?' one of the agents asked, confused.

'All of these,' Dad answered, and explained.

'Alright. If you had told us at the beginning, we would have treated you better.'

'You've treated me just fine.'

'Well, we're done, but they want to question you further. Please wait here,' one of them finally said.

He waited for one and a half hours before another man came in. 'Sabri, how are you?'

'Fine,' he replied. 'And you are?'

'The head of the Shabak in Acre.'

You're still as stupid as I thought, my father said to himself. During his years in Israel, he had lived in Fassouta, Nazareth, Jerusalem, and Haifa. He had never brushed with the intelligence services in Acre. Presumably, they had sent them because Fassouta was in the Acre district.

'Well, where were you all this time?' the man asked.

'You know where I was.'

'You know we don't know everything …'

'You know enough, that I was working with Arafat.'

The man launched into politics, wanting to find out my father's views. They spoke until after midnight. Finally, he let him go, warning him about Hamas. 'You'll have a problem with them.'

'We'll take care of it,' Dad said, drily.

We were still pacing up and down in Nicosia. It took four hours for the phone to ring. Mum grabbed the receiver, almost dropping it in her haste. 'I'm alright!' came his voice, buoyant, confident as always. My uncle, Subhi, was waiting for him outside the airport. They were calling us from his mobile. The technology was still new and resembled a walkie-talkie, with a large receiver installed in Subhi's car. Dad asked him not to tell the family in Fassouta that he had arrived. He needed a few days in Gaza. My uncle obliged, drove him to Gaza, then left.

Arafat was delighted to see him. He gave him a big welcome and kept him for five days, not letting him leave. He took his arrival as a sign of support, for my father was the first PLO member of his circle to come. Arafat had returned alone, and none of the others had yet joined him. He offered my father a promotion from general director of the Research Center to a ministerial post.

Dad thanked him and said: 'No, Abu Ammar. You have many refugees, and I don't want to be another one. I want to go home.'

Tears glistened in Arafat's eyes. 'You can go back. I can't,' he said, hoarsely. 'But, if you want to do that, I'm 100 per cent with you.'

'We've been fighting for the right of Palestinians to return, and if I can fulfill that right and go back to where I came from, why would I stay elsewhere?' Dad answered.

Arafat nodded. 'But you will come to me, work with me,' he said. 'You will find me by your side.'

III

The next day, my father called his parents' home in Fassouta. It was late in the evening and they were asleep. He let the phone ring, and, finally, my aunt, Muna, answered.

'It's Sabri,' he told her.

'Huh?' she said, sleep still in her voice.

'It's Sabri. I'm in Gaza.'

'Huh?' Her heart leapt. Suddenly, she was wide awake. She wondered if she was dreaming.

'I'm in Gaza and I'm coming to you tomorrow. Put Mother on the line.'

My aunt did not believe him. She thought someone was pulling a prank. My grandmother, though, recognized his voice. 'It's him!'

He also spoke to his father. After they hung up, they all sat there in a daze. None of them could believe it. 'Don't tell anyone, yet,' Sabri had said. *The village would be thunderstruck*, my aunt thought.

My grandmother's sudden exclamation startled her. 'We have to cook!'

'What?'

'Your brother is coming! He needs to eat!'

'Mother, it's one in the morning!'

But my grandmother was already in the kitchen. She turned the lights on and began making freekeh soup, a broth of coarse wheat grains with meat stock to ward off the cold. My aunt stared at her in stupefaction. Her mother had been in a deep depression, sleeping through days at a time, refusing food, and not speaking to anyone. After that call, she sprang up like a coil. She stayed up all night and cooked three more stews. My grandfather shuffled about the house restlessly. In the early morning, my aunt coaxed them back to bed and tried to get a little more sleep. But none of them could. They got up and went into a flurry of activity, as much to allay their racing nerves as to prepare. They lit the fire, cleaned the house again though it was spotless, aired blankets, and roasted coffee beans. My grandmother showered, changed out of her dark clothes, and tied a fresh scarf around her hair. A worry was gnawing at my aunt that it may not happen. She desperately hoped that it would, for her mother's sake. In those short hours, Wardeh was transformed.

My uncle drove to Gaza, again, to get my father. At 3:00 pm, they arrived at their parents' house in Fassouta. Dad made his way in.

Twenty-four years later.

His parents broke down in heavy sobs. He sat on the sofa between them as my aunts crowded around him, weeping uncontrollably. My uncle, George, burst into tears and had to step outside. When my father found his voice, he asked them not to tell anyone else yet, not to bring sweets, or cause any commotion. But many people had heard and started to come. The family went to my uncle Subhi's house, which was bigger and further from the center of the village. A helicopter whirred overhead, and they felt they were being watched. The women had cooked more food, but no one could eat. They stared at my father. My aunts kept wiping away tears, only to cry again.

By morning, the news had spread in the village and crowds of people flocked to my grandfather's house. My father barely had time to wash his face before he was swamped. His sisters began to make coffee in large saucepans to keep up, and his brothers bought huge trays of sweets to go around. Outside, a large group of men formed a sahjeh, a dance done at weddings. The house was crammed, and people kept crowding in until my aunt was afraid that the cement floor, held by concrete poles above the goat pen below, would collapse. Half the village was gathered outside. It was like someone had landed from outer space.

My father greeted the stream of visitors. Some he remembered, others took a while to register or had to tell him who they were. It went on for three days as people came from near and far. My aunts made countless pots of coffee, collected the cups, and washed them for the next rounds. The family was exhausted; they could barely get a few hours' sleep. But the guests continued to flock to the house. Relatives, neighbors, and friends all came, as well as younger people who had only heard of Sabri and wanted to see him.

On the fourth day, he woke up, washed, and went out. For three hours, he walked around the village. It had grown in ways he barely recognized. New roads and houses had sprung up in places that he remembered as fields. On his way, he bumped into people who knew him. They rushed to greet him and invite him in, but he continued walking, taking stock of everything.

He was finally home.

IV

At the branch of the Interior Ministry in Haifa, he presented his identification card and asked for renewal. The clerk turned it over in her hand, eyebrows arched. 'What's this?'

'I've been away for many years and didn't have the chance to renew it.'

'I can see that!' Tapping her keyboard, she looked at the screen for a few moments.

'I also need a new passport,' my father added.

'OK, take a seat and wait for your number, please.'

'Just like that?' my uncle, Subhi, asked him in shock. He had driven him to Haifa and was standing next to him, agape.

'They have nothing against me. I was never tried or convicted of any crime in Israel,' my father answered, coolly. In fact, he was shocked to discover that, in all his time away, his name was still on the electoral register. He could, technically, have delegated someone to vote on his behalf!

His number was called, and the clerk gave him his newly printed card in a blue cover. 'Your passport will be ready in two weeks,' she said.

'The children?' Everyone posed the question. We, too, were on tenterhooks in Cyprus, asking him each time he called. He arranged for entry permits for us, the same way he had come, and we booked our flight.

V

We boarded the plane from Larnaca. The trip was very short, at fifty minutes. It was incredible how a place that was so close had been so far. 'Welcome to Tel Aviv,' a voice announced over the intercom. We made our way down and stood on the asphalt.

At twenty-two years old, I set foot in my country for the first time.

Mum was herding us to the terminal. Inside, our gaze flew to the wall opposite. A huge Israeli flag hung on it. An involuntary shiver ran down my spine. I looked around, trying to absorb where we were. We stood in line amidst the crowds. I saw unfamiliar dress, heard a foreign language. *The radio language*, I thought. I wondered where the Arabic was, where the Palestinians were.

Mousa seemed to read my thoughts. He leaned over and whispered: 'It's full of Jews here!'

I would only laugh at this comment years later, for it showed how lost we were, how little we knew what to expect. We had come from our comfort zone in Cyprus, and neither of us had any clue of what this country was like. My parents had not prepared us. The only things they had told us about were Fassouta and our family, and we had nursed the romantic vision of Palestine that we had grown up with.

At the counter, the clerk looked at our documents and drew back, pressing a button. Five security people materialized, as though out of thin air. I became nervous. This was not something we had ever experienced in Cyprus.

It was not every day that three Sudanese nationals entered the State of Israel. Questions and answers went back and forth as Mum explained. But the visas were fine, and they stamped everything and waved us through. Mum relaxed. She had only left the country twelve years before, at the age of thirty, so she quickly got her bearings. It was Mousa and I who were in a daze.

Outside, my father was waiting for us with Uncle Subhi. We laughed happily as they hugged us and led us to his minibus. Dad sat in front and we sat in the back with Mum. She chattered with them as Mousa and I fell silent. My uncle drove out of the airport and onto a highway, the scenery rushing by as he picked up speed. We stared at tall buildings and city lights in the distance. It was one of the most surreal moments of my life.

It was a long journey. I kept piping up to ask where we were. Two hours into the drive, the landscape changed. We began climbing a narrow, winding road, plunged into darkness. It was close to midnight. I felt we had driven so long that a little question popped into my mind: had we reached Lebanon? Again, I asked Dad where we were. He turned to me and said: 'In ten minutes, we'll be in Fassouta.'

Unexpectedly, tears began streaming down my face.

VI

The whole world seemed to be waiting for us. We were stunned to see the number of people at my uncle's house. Eleven aunts and uncles were there, with their spouses and children. I recognized some of them, but the rest were too many to place. We were swamped by hugs and kisses, helpless in the tide of emotion. They had never expected to see us among them, even less than we had expected it ourselves. It took a good half hour for it to subside. My uncle Subhi's wife pleaded with everyone to sit down as she dabbed her eyes.

It hit me then. I was in Fassouta. I half expected to wake from a dream. Everyone looked at each other, unsure what to do. We were all wiping our tears and trying to regain some calm. My uncle's wife invited us to eat. The table was laden with a huge meal, which we looked at in confusion; it was now past one in the morning, hardly time for kebab and stuffed vine leaves. We only managed a few mouthfuls before my uncle told everyone to go home and let us rest.

I opened my eyes in the morning and, momentarily, tried to remember where I was. We had coffee and delicious date cookies, which my uncle's wife had made for Christmas. Then we went out to walk around the village, taking in the narrow roads, the houses, the few grocery shops, and the breathtaking scenery. A bright sun shone to welcome us, despite the cold. Our first stop was my grandparents' house. As soon as they saw us, they took us in their arms, crying and holding us tight. My aunt, Muna, seemed to be crying nonstop. Mousa and I knew them from when they had visited in Cyprus, but this was different. They were too happy to speak. They kept bringing us food, juice, sweets. 'Enough! I'll bring them back,' Dad finally said. 'I need to take them to Um Nour.'

It was equally emotional at my other grandmother's house. On seeing us coming down the steps, she began to weep. 'Hanneh is back!' she cried, and my aunts and uncles, standing around, burst into fresh tears as she held Mousa and me in a tight embrace.

'Sitti ...' I whispered, and she cried harder. Her little house was bursting with everyone. She made us a feast of stuffed chicken, spicy rice, and delicious salads, followed by more date cookies, almond sweets and chocolates, until we could eat no more.

I decided to stay with her and sleep over that night. Two of my cousins, Rima and Rania, joined us. They were the daughters of my uncles, Nour and Ibrahim, and were exactly my age: we had been born one month apart. Grandma prepared a modest dinner of labaneh and eggs, which I was glad for, as I was still full from lunch. But the temptation was too strong. When she brought the steaming toasted bread and cups of sweet tea, I dived in with my cousins. 'This sage is from the mountains, sitti picks it herself!' Rima told me, smiling. It tasted so good. We called our grandparents sitti and sidi, here, rather than teta and jiddo as we had done in Lebanon.

My cousins and I sat, getting to know each other, giggling and warming ourselves at my grandmother's small electric heater. Her house was simple, with a cement floor and old wooden shutters. The windows creaked as we closed them to block out the biting cold air. We chatted late into the night, captivated by each other. They wanted to know about me, and I wanted to gobble up this new world. But, finally, eyes droopy with food and warmth, we spread out on the rickety sofas to sleep. I snuggled below a thick woolen blanket, staring into the darkness. A dim light peeked from the window, and I looked through the crack in the curtain at the moon, glowing through the cloudy night. Hundreds of stars twinkled above, lighting up the Galilean sky. I shifted my gaze to the ceiling, spotting small, iron hooks at equal spaces along it. I had noticed the same hooks at my other grandparents' house. They were used for hanging bunches of tobacco to dry, my grandmother told me, in the days when people lived on agriculture. As my eyes got accustomed to the dark, I turned over and looked at the quaint cupboard with a full-length mirror on one of its doors, still there from sitti's wedding. It was half a century old, she had said.

It was the same cupboard as when Mama Hanneh was here, I realized. There was a sudden lump in my throat, and it took me a long time to sleep.

VII

In the morning, I drew the curtains and was speechless. Thick forests covered the mountains, and a shy winter sun reflected off the dew, dancing in thousands of little sparkles. I loved the mountain villages in Cyprus, where Mum often took us, and, here, the village was so similar, nestled between deep slopes of green as far as the eye could see.

'Where are my darlings?' a cry rose outside, and I smiled. I recognized my mother's youngest sister, Nida. She was petite, but with an extraordinarily loud voice. She had visited us in Cyprus, and Mousa and I had loved her.

'They're here,' my grandmother said, shuffling to open the door. 'Stop making such a racket!'

But my aunt charged in, grinning from ear to ear. 'Good morning!' she boomed, smothering my cousins and me with kisses. She could not contain her happiness. She sat next to me, stroking my hair and smiling, and held me to her, again. 'Have you made them breakfast?' she turned on my grandmother.

'They just got up!' Sitti replied. But she was already busy at work in her little kitchen. 'Come help me, instead of yakking and giving us a headache!'

My cousins, still drowsy, rubbed their eyes and giggled. I grinned, seeing the fiery interactions between my aunt and grandmother for the first time.

The wooden door creaked open and Randa and Rasha, Nida's daughters, shyly walked in. They were younger and blushed furiously as they looked at me. Randa, too, had visited us in Cyprus. 'You slept here?' she asked, in a somewhat envious tone. I welcomed them. We did not want them to feel like we were a 'big girls' club', and we sat them next to us. I had never felt so cozy; five of us crowded Sitti's small space, to her delight, while ten dishes appeared for breakfast.

When we finished and went for a walk, en masse, through the streets of the village, Mama Hanneh was very present with me. *She grew up here*, I kept thinking. She walked those roads and sat in those houses, saw the mountains and smelled that air. I felt connected to her, again, felt her almost by my side, holding my hand and walking me through. Fresh tears glistened in my eyes and I tried to blink them away.

My grandmother threw a party for us that evening. All my aunts and uncles, along with their children, squeezed into her house. A sumptuous meal was again laid out. As everyone bustled around trying to help, my uncle, Ibrahim, jokingly called to my aunt: 'Nida, I can hear you, but I can't see you!' Laughter broke out as she playfully punched him. Two of my father's cousins were invited who had a small band that performed at weddings. They played the oud and darbuka³ and we sang and danced into the night.

My father asked my grandmother if he could use the telephone. He called my uncle in London. 'Can you hear us?' he asked him. 'I'm here with Najwa and the children, and Um Nour is having a party for us. Your cousins, Nimer and Nasser, are playing the music.'

Ammo could not believe it. 'Here, one minute,' Dad said. He called my grandmother and put her on the line.

'Everything is good, son!' Um Nour said, joy spilling from her voice. 'We hope to see you here, too!'

Two weeks flew by in a blur. We visited aunts and uncles, family elders and a hundred cousins. Curious neighbors popped in to see us. We slept at various homes and were introduced to so many people that we could barely keep up. It was very humbling to be received with such a tide of love. Half the time, I was in another world, processing that I was in Palestine, in Fassouta, and the thousand things I felt.

We managed a few outings, too, to see some of the country. It was a paradise found for me. We went to Haifa, drove up to Stella Maris Monastery on Mount Carmel and saw the city's breathtaking bay. Dad took us to the apartment where he and Mama Hanneh had lived for two years before leaving, and to his school, the Terra Sancta College, in Nazareth. We visited the churches and the old city of Jerusalem, ate fish in Acre and walked the old walls, swam in the Banias springs of the Golan Heights, and went up to Ras el-Naqoura, on the Mediterranean border with Lebanon, to see the grottos. It was staggering to feel that we were now on the other side of that frontier.

On Christmas Eve, we attended mass at Fassouta's church. Small and humble, the stone structure was a century old, with thick pillars and arches, mosaic windows, and Catholic icons. Families crowded together, dressed in new clothes, and children scampered outside with fireworks. Flowers and candles adorned the church and a huge Christmas tree glowed by the entrance. I squeezed onto a pew and felt, for the first time in my life, a true homecoming. The choir burst into hymns as my soul soared. My heart lurched painfully as I wished, again, that Mama Hanneh was with us. Our return would have made her so happy.

271

VIII

Before our flight back to Larnaca, I stopped at a bookstore in the airport. There were no Arabic titles and very few English ones. Near the checkout, I came across a Hebrew language study pack. I picked it up and turned it over. On a whim, I bought it.

In Cyprus, I had diarrhea and kept vomiting. Mum took me to hospital. I explained the recent trip to the doctor and he nodded in understanding. Cypriots shared our Mediterranean diet and love of food. 'You had too much to eat! Mix up!' he said, in a thick accent. 'You rest now, don't eat anything! We give you only fluids, eh?'

He laughed before patting my head and leaving. I did not find it so funny; my stomach felt like a boiling cauldron and I could not keep anything down. Three weeks of erratic and excessive feeding had taken their toll. Everyone had invited us, and they had gone to so much trouble that we could not let them down. We had had four or five meals a day of rich, fatty foods, even aside from the non-stop sweets.

It took several days to recover, during which I lay in bed and thought about the recent experience. I was sure that I wanted to return to Palestine. The twelve years in Cyprus seemed to fade as memories of my mother came vividly to the surface. I wanted to retrace her steps, to have a sense of continuity of my family's history. I wanted a country and belonging, not to feel like a foreigner anymore. This was a dream coming true! The years of statelessness were behind us.

I was not thinking practically of what it meant to move and start a new life. I was on cloud nine: young, infused with love for Palestine, and completely oblivious to its reality, which a short visit, in my awestruck frame of mind, was certainly not enough to reveal.

I began nagging my parents. In any event, it was happening of its own accord. After the establishment of the Palestinian Authority, the PLO was moving its institutions, including the Research Center, to Gaza.

Dad had returned to Cyprus with his new Israeli passport. He photocopied it, together with his ID, and sent them to my uncle in London. Ammo was on tenterhooks to return, but he was worried because of the way he had left. 'There's no charge against you, nothing at all,' Dad reassured him. 'And, according to the agreements, they can't bring you to trial. Don't worry!'

My uncle decided to take his chances. He went to the Israeli Embassy in London and applied for an entry permit, the same way my father had.

In Nicosia, my father took Mousa and me to the Israeli Consulate and applied for passports for us, by virtue of his citizenship. He gave the clerk our birth certificates from the Khalidi Hospital in Beirut. This, definitely, did not happen every day.

The Israeli consul came to greet us. Seeing my eagerness, he decided to pull a little prank. 'We'll only give the boy a passport, not the girl,' he said, winking at my father.

'What?' I exclaimed, as they laughed. All of it seemed inconceivable to me, this atmosphere of light cordiality. The passports would be ready in a few weeks, the clerk told us.

Meanwhile, I had gotten off to a great start in Cyprus. I was doing very well at my job and really liked my colleagues. The company had a system for new recruits; we spent the first year rotating between the various departments before deciding the best fit. I finished three months in software development and moved to quality assurance, a new department with only one member, Michael. Together, we set up a formal testing process. The company was growing fast in the lucrative software industry that was sweeping the world at the time.

Mike was a Cypriot who had grown up in Britain and recently returned to Cyprus with his wife and children. He was kind and down to earth. We laughed when we found out that we lived on the same street; he gave me a ride home each day and we became good friends. My parents met his family and I sometimes babysat his young sons.

A few weeks later, I was at the office when the secretary stuck her head around the door and told me my father was outside. Puzzled, I followed her to the hallway, where Dad stood, beaming. 'I have something for you!'

It was my new Israeli passport. I flicked through it in disbelief. 'Did Mousa get one?'

He nodded and showed it to me. It was now real.

I introduced him to my colleague, Salwa, who almost fell off her chair. 'Israeli passports?' she stuttered. She knew we had held

Sudanese ones until then. 'You're a disgrace to Sudan!' she added, laughing. Salwa would never quite absorb this development, even after we had left Cyprus and I had returned to visit.

A few weeks later, the CEO called me to a meeting. He was a British Iraqi, a jovial, larger-than-life character with an imposing presence. The employees were nervous when he was around, and so was I. 'Well, how are you doing?' he smiled.

He was offering me a promotion. 'I hear you're doing fantastic work, and I'd like you to be assistant manager to Michael. This is the first time the company is giving such a position to someone so young!' he added, his smile growing wider.

'I ... Thanks,' I mumbled. I was delighted, but my heart fell. 'There's something I wanted to tell you.'

'Yes?' he raised his eyebrows.

'We ... My family and I are returning to Palestine.'

'You've leaving?' he asked, incredulously. I had only been with them for nine months.

'Yes, I'm so sorry. But the Accords, you know ... We're going home!'

He looked at me then, taking this in. Something seemed to pass in his eyes, but, after a pause, he seemed to think better of it. 'Well,' he drew a breath. 'I'm very sorry to hear this! We would have loved for you to stay with us. But I wish you the best of luck!'

I returned, crestfallen, to the office I shared with Mike, where I broke the news. My friend was shocked. 'What? You're leaving?'

He knew about my recent visit. I explained, with a catch in my throat. 'It's beyond a dream, Mike ... We never expected to go home.'

'I know ...' he nodded. 'I felt that way when I returned to Cyprus. I wanted to come home. But we'll really miss you!' He looked at me in distress. 'This is all so sudden!'

I thanked him and turned back to my screen, my mind whirling. I swallowed, painfully, as I thought of what I had just turned down, but, more so, as I suddenly realized what I was leaving in Cyprus: a life, home, friends, memories, familiarity, job prospects.

My colleagues gave me a farewell lunch. I left the building with a heavy heart. Our neighbors, too, were very sad, and the goodbyes were heartwrenching. But our return to Palestine was too much of a miracle not to take the opportunity. Mrs. Maroulla, who was a refugee from the north of Cyprus, understood. Tearfully, she told us she wished she could return to her home, just as we were about to do. In July 1995, we sold our furniture, shipped our belongings, and boarded the plane.

I looked out of the window at the receding island, soft waves lapping its shores, and wondered, for the first time, what lay ahead.

11

THE RETURN

If American Jews were excluded from 'all-Christian cities' or lands owned and administered by a quasi-official 'Christian National Fund', or deprived of development funds, electricity, water, etc., for reason of religious origin, no one would hesitate to denounce these racist practices. The reaction would be no different if the United States government ... were to institute a program of 'making New York White', modeled on [Israel's program of] 'Judaization of the Galilee'.

Noam Chomsky
Foreword, *The Arabs in Israel*[1]

I

Practical matters quickly took over. The first step was to visit the Interior Ministry in Acre for our new identification cards. Although our passports had been sent to Cyprus, we had to get our IDs here.

At the entrance, we were surprised to see a revolving metal gate and a security guard. People stood in line, emptied their pockets, and handed over their bags for inspection. We had never seen anything like this in Cyprus, except at the airport.

Once we were through, we took a number and waited among dozens of people. 'Everyone comes here for IDs, passports, birth registrations, everything ...' Dad explained. 'This branch serves all the area and villages near Fassouta.'

I thought, suddenly, of the millions of Palestinians who should have the right to come home like we did, but are denied it.

Quickly, our return went from dreamlike to very concrete. My father rented a house belonging to his sister, Mariam. She had built it for her eldest son to marry in. As there was no bride, yet, we could stay in it until we figured things out. The house was empty, and Dad left Mum to choose the furniture and handle the logistics while he rushed off to Gaza.

When we moved into the new place, it was strange and alien, nothing at all like a home should feel. It was all new, I told myself; it would soon become the norm. The first adjustment for Mousa and I was having to share a room, as there were only two bedrooms. He was going to university in England, in September, and Mum told us to bear with it for the two months. But it was awkward, at our ages. The kitchen had no cupboards. My aunt was yet to install them, so we put up plastic shelves in the meantime. The dining table was placed against a wall and became Dad's makeshift office. He was not around much. Every week or two, he went to Gaza.

Arafat pressured him, again, to take a post with the Authority. But my father did not want a bureaucratic position and felt it would hold him back after his years of independent research and writing. He helped out at the PLO Planning Center and remained in an advisory capacity to Arafat, seeing him at his office, in hotels, or with friends. The Research Center was reestablished, but only on paper; it would take a while for a political decision to be made about where to base it.

My father was also trying to find his bearings in Israel, which had changed so drastically in his years away. The apparatus of military rule had been moved to the West Bank and Gaza. Palestinians in Israel were free of the hassle that he had endured before he left, although they had a more blanketed system of discrimination to deal with. It took him a while to adjust. 'I can go and come as I want; no one stops me, no one comes to the house or asks me anything!' he told my uncle in London, who tried to visualize this unfamiliar picture. Ammo was desperate to catch up with us. After waiting for three months with no answer from the Israeli Embassy, he went to a lawyer in London and asked for help.

A few weeks after we arrived, Dad took us on a drive, nearby. We did not go far, just over a mile, and found ourselves entering a small village. 'This is the site of Deir el-Qasi,' he said. The sign read: 'Elqosh'.

We drove through quiet roads, dotted with houses and willowy trees. There were a few chicken coops. Dad stopped the car and we got out. 'See this?' he pointed to an old, stone structure. 'This is one of the original homes of the village.'

I stared at it as the sinking reality hit me. All my life, I had read and heard of the tragedy of Palestine. Now, I was looking at it.

'They didn't tear down all the houses,' Dad was saying. 'They kept a few, because the newcomers were from Yemen and they liked the Arab homes. There's another one ...'

I followed his gaze and saw a couple more structures, visibly older than the others. Three Jewish communities, Netu'a, Mattat, and Abirim, had also sprung up on the site of Deir el-Qasi. The Jewish Yemeni newcomers were replaced by Jews from Kurdistan.

'Your grandfather,' Dad was reminiscing, 'had many friends here. They bred livestock and traded together.'

'What happened to them?' I asked, knowing the answer.

'They're in Lebanon. Do you remember Fouzi?'

Fouzi Younes was a young man who had worked with my father at the Research Center in Cyprus. His parents were refugees from 1948 and he was born in Ein el-Hilweh refugee camp in Lebanon. In

1982, he and his young wife fled to Cyprus after the Israeli invasion. Fouzi was a humble man with a permanent sadness in his eyes. In Nicosia, his two daughters were born. We often visited his family.

Fouzi had spent hours with Dad, typesetting the Center's journal, *Palestine Affairs*. When finances became tight after the Gulf War, he struggled, like everyone else. Before we had left Cyprus, he had insisted on inviting us for dinner at his home. We were very embarrassed, especially because he had moved to a poorer suburb, yet had splurged on a big meal for us. Tears had glistened in his eyes as he said to Dad: 'Say hello to the Deir ...'

Fouzi could not return, like we did. He went back to Lebanon. Ours was a tiny, special case. Although the Accords allowed for the return of several thousand PLO personnel to the Palestinian territory, only a very small number were allowed to return to their towns or villages in Israel, and only if they had held Israeli citizenship before they had left. Their files were given to my father to follow up on. There were forty-seven names, the total number of Palestinians who had left as Israeli citizens and joined the PLO. However, not all of them were as lucky as my family. As tension resumed between the PLO and Israel, only about ten were able to return, and few brought their families with them.

We had no frame of reference to compare ourselves to, no one to talk to who had gone through our experience. My father's colleagues from the Center were scattered. Those who found political asylum went to Europe; others had to make their way back to the Arab countries. Only one, Samih Shbib, found his way to Ramallah, and another, Imad Shaqqour, returned to Israel and eventually settled in the same city.

II

Mousa and I had a steep learning curve: we had to adjust to the new surroundings, figure out the system of the country, and get to know our extended family. We spent our first weeks at their homes. Something delicious was always cooking, or one of my aunts was baking. Before long, I was helping them fold the thin bread as it came off the stove, drinking coffee on their balconies, and joining in a little bit of gossip. Everyone gave us a lot of love and helped us in any way they could. We began finding our way around the village, the few shops, the post office and bank, and we were picking up the local accent. People smiled when they saw us and complete strangers stopped to kiss us. It was unnerving to feel that everyone knew who we were, but we barely knew anyone. I got lost a few times and they showed me the way. 'How can you get lost in Fassouta?' they laughed.

Young women were beautifully dressed and perfectly groomed. Cyprus was simpler and far less worldly when we left it, and I felt like a plain duck in their midst. My cousin, Rania, showed me how to apply mascara, foundation, and products that I did not know existed. Next was hair. Babbling excitedly, my cousins offered many suggestions, and a bottle of mousse was thrust into my hand. Clothes took a little longer. My aunt frowned and asked why I dressed in this flowing, hippie style. I squirmed in embarrassment, and she decided to give me a makeover. We trooped off to the mall and I stared at myself in a new outfit: a jacket and a short, snug skirt with high-heeled boots. I had never bought anything so daring, though, to them, it was all standard fare.

On the bottom floor of my aunt's house, on a small hill overlooking my grandmother's home and the beautiful mountains, I asked my cousins, the boys this time, to teach me dabke. Our traditional dance was done in a circle, holding hands. My young cousins took me through the steps as my aunt and the girls looked on, laughing. I was able to join the dance at a wedding that I was invited to with my parents. A friend of my father's told him, in astonishment: 'I was wondering who this girl was, that I didn't know. I had no idea it was your daughter. I thought she was a local!'

Weddings were the big thing, the main social activity of the summer, generating a flurry of excitement and tons of gossip. They were a microcosm of the village, reflecting its family ties and clans, and were the best way to get to know all the faces. They were also a hotspot for singles to meet. My cousin, Rima, was married soon after our arrival, and she asked me to be her bridesmaid. My first experience of these celebrations was overwhelming. They began one week before the marriage. Each night, people gathered at the homes of the bride and groom, singing, dancing, and eating special foods prepared by throngs of women. The bride threw a party, akin to a hen night, with her family and friends. Another party was thrown for the groom: a '*hlaqa*' (shaving), or '*zyaneh*' in other areas of Palestine. In the past, this took place on the wedding day. The groom would be washed and shaved by his friends, with singing and dancing outside, then clad in his wedding clothes. In recent times, the ceremony was held a few nights before the wedding. The groom would be raised on a platform and his face lathered with shaving soap as everyone took photographs with him and a huge party unfolded.

On the wedding day, the bride's parents would host a lunch at home. This moment, when the young woman was about to leave her family and embark on her new life, was emotional for everyone, especially the bride and her mother, and there were many tears as I looked on in bewilderment during Rima's ceremony.

Meanwhile, the groom would be dressed by his friends at his parents' house or at the house of a friend or neighbor who had invited him. While the family sang and danced outside, the groom's friends would pull pranks on him. His shoes would go missing, he might be given a resounding slap or two, or a scrub with the toilet brush. When the noise got out of hand, someone would call out to them to finish and leave him in one piece. He would finally emerge, with his best man, in their matching suits, and the party would set off to the bride's house, where the men of the family would formally ask for her hand and receive the blessing of her parents. The couple would then walk through the village to church, with two long lines of people doing the sahjeh dance, moving slowly and clapping on either side, and women throwing rice and sweets. The procession would pause from time to time as someone passed around a glass of whisky or arak.

After the ceremony, congratulations would be given outside the church, then the party would be held at night—the last of the celebrations. This would usually be in the village schoolyard or at banquet halls in nearby towns. Family and friends would line the rows of tables, savoring a feast as loud music and dancing filled the night. I was overcome by shyness, feeling the stir my family caused wherever we went, people smiling as they recognized us or were told who we were.

It was not for the faint of heart. The process took months of preparation and a week of dressing up, being photographed, singing, dancing, and eating. At the end, everyone collapsed in exhaustion, including the new couple. But such was tradition, and no one was bold enough to cut any of the rituals out, for fear of losing face.

III

After all the excitement and novelty, Mousa and I were beginning to feel estranged and to miss Cyprus. We were trying to make friends in the village, but it was difficult. It was easy to get on with people when we were just visiting; we enjoyed our differences and found them curious and appealing. But now it was becoming a struggle to understand a new culture and adjust to its expectations. Our cousins were the first circle, but we could not talk about many things with them; we had different histories and experiences. They were very sweet, trying to absorb us into their world, but I often saw blank looks on their faces, as though they wondered which planet we had dropped from. We were also uneasy at not knowing the local customs, and we made many blunders. My father became even stricter than he had been in Cyprus, to the point where my aunt, Mariam, exclaimed: 'He still thinks the village is as he left it twenty-four years ago, but it's changed since then!'

Yet, it was a conservative culture. Parents were strict with their daughters and did not let them go out freely; most 'outings' were to weddings or home visits with relatives. The topic of relationships was taboo unless it was formalized in marriage, and my two or three cousins whom I became close to entrusted me with their secret loves, hoping they would end in that path. Boys had it easier, but, for both Mousa and me, it took a long time to understand the nuances of this culture and create friendships.

At home, things were very tense. Our financial situation, so dire for several years, remained difficult. In September 1995, the PLO and Israel signed the Oslo II Accord to extend Palestinian self-rule beyond Gaza and Jericho to other parts of the West Bank. After twenty-seven years of exile, Arafat traveled to cities in the West Bank as Israeli occupation forces transferred them to the Palestinian Authority. But the new Authority was struggling to establish itself and pay the thousands of public service employees it had taken on. My father was under a lot of pressure. The move had cost a lot, and he and Mum worked furiously to put everything together on a tight budget. She needed his help with the logistics, and he was spread thin between Fassouta and Gaza, spending hours driving back and forth. Tension was at a peak and tempers flew. Mousa and I spent a lot of time outside the house. A few weeks later, he left for university in England, and I missed him and felt very alone.

One afternoon, I took a walk to my uncle Nour's house. My cousin, Raji, was sitting on the balcony in shorts and a flannel vest, sweating in the summer heat. I asked him if his parents were home.

'No one's here,' he said. 'But, here, sit down. What's wrong?'

It seemed we were both down. As I began to tell him, he suddenly interrupted. 'Do you want to go to Nahariya?'

I nodded. It would be great to get out of the village, I thought. He disappeared inside the house, got changed, and drove us to the beach in my uncle's work van. I told him how overwhelmed I felt and about my life before coming here. He told me about his troubles with his father, who was a construction contractor and was stuck in a difficult company partnership with his cousin. Their financial situation was also very strained.

It was easy talking to Raji. He was kind and humble, and I felt like I had known him a long time. I told him that his baby photo had been on my late mother's bedside cabinet in Beirut. He nodded, sadly. 'I never got to meet Aunt Hanneh ...' he murmured. 'But I heard so much about her from my parents.'

I was shocked when, as we got in the car to drive back, he turned to me and said: 'I want to come to your parents and ask for your hand.'

I was very quiet. Was this the way things happened here? I wondered. From the little I had gathered, it seemed that it was. Marriage between cousins was also customary in Arab society, though it had become less common in modern times.

He was waiting. I nodded and smiled. He drove me home, and I made sure to get out of the car before we approached our street. I had come to expect the nosy stares of everyone.

In my room, I paced about nervously, feeling a mixture of shock and giddiness. Had I just accepted a marriage proposal?

IV

We began to talk, and he visited us more often. Mum did not think anything of it; my cousins were in and out of our house all the time.

But it was tricky to meet elsewhere. I did not tell anyone until we got to know each other a little better.

Meanwhile, I had to find work. My father's younger brother, George, worked for the Yellow Pages and lived in Haifa. He found a job for me with one of his clients, a Palestinian firm that sold educational software. The salary was too low but I had to start somewhere, and they did not need knowledge of Hebrew. Haifa was one and a half hours away and I could not afford to buy a car. I had to move there, and I found a room in an apartment with first-year university students from Fassouta.

The place was old and dingy, but it was all we could afford on our budgets. I shared a room with one of the girls, and the other two shared the other. It was difficult to have any privacy, and I was the odd one out, as they were cousins and seemed unsure how to relate to me. On our first evening there, I helped them clean the apartment and we had dinner. I could not sleep till late, tossing and turning, and I was not sure if my roommate slept, either. But I felt awkward trying to talk to her.

The next morning, we barely managed some toast before leaving. Our nerves were racing: it was their first day at university and mine at work. I had no idea how to get around, but they read the bus signs and helped me. Their stop was before mine, and they got off and turned around to smile and wave. I waved back weakly, fighting a sense of panic. They were lucky to be together, I thought. They told me the bus would eventually get to the port area, where I worked. Once there, I hoped I would recognize the place where I had done my interview two weeks earlier.

I looked to the front again and saw two soldiers getting on. My eyes bulged. They were carrying guns. They walked down the aisle and sat down on the empty seats in front of me. I stared at the rifles slung over their shoulders. It was the first time I had seen the cold metal so close. I swallowed, hard. No one had carried guns in Cyprus! Why were there guns on the streets? Was this normal? What if one of them went off?

I wanted to change seats. My eyes darted around, but they were all taken. There was one seat at the far back, but there were more soldiers there. Everyone was chatting normally as the bus continued on its route. I was the only one who was breaking into a cold sweat.

I also seemed to be the only Palestinian. I told myself to be calm. It was probably not long to my stop now.

Try as I might, though, I could not stop the terrified thought racing through my mind: *I'm on a bus with Israeli soldiers!*

Ten minutes later, I recognized the area, rang the bell hastily and scrambled off. In the street, I took a deep breath and made my way to the building. I had a jarred, surreal feeling, almost like I was in a bad dream.

The owner of the small firm welcomed me and showed me around. I wanted to ask him about the soldiers, but I worried it may be inappropriate.

The first day at work was, as always, awkward. I was alone in a small, windowless attic with a low ceiling, where I was assigned to test software. The secretary, Dina, seemed to be my age and said a quick hello. At lunch time, I went down and explored the street. It was shabby and dirty, but my hunger led me to a falafel shop. I bought a sandwich and juice and made my way back up to my room, where I ate, with a somewhat heavy heart. It was a great relief when it was 5:00 pm and time to leave, but another knot of fear clenched my stomach. I hoped I would find my way home! I had not thought of that in the morning. I had to ask Dina. She told me to simply stand on the opposite side of the road and wait for the same bus, and I thanked her, feeling foolish.

On the bus, I gazed outside the window as we inched forward in rush hour. The billboards and street signs were all in Hebrew. There were only a few Arabic names of some restaurants. The conversations around me were in Hebrew. More soldiers got on, jostling for space on the crowded bus. It was at that moment that a cold feeling gripped my heart. I was not in the Palestine of my dreams.

At the apartment, I found a small housewarming do. The girls had brought pizza and cake. I ate with them and joined in their talk as much as I could, trying to get to know them. When we finished, I thanked them and paid my share. Then I went to my room, sat on my bed, and let a few tears slide down my cheeks.

V

Things fell into a routine, of course. Sundays to Thursdays, I went to work and the girls to university. The weekend was Friday and

Saturday, which took some getting used to. On Thursday after-noons, we made our weekly trip to Fassouta, returning on Sunday mornings. I did my laundry at home and Mum gave me Tupperware containers filled with food to reheat. One look at the kitchen in Haifa, with its worn, greasy surfaces and yellowed counters, and I gave up on any thought of cooking there.

I thought about moving to a better place but could barely afford the rent on this one, and most other apartments in Haifa were the same: decrepit, box-like structures with tiny spaces and no balco-nies. Except for the upscale areas on Mount Carmel or the outer neighborhoods by the sea, both of which cost a fortune to live in, the city was rather rundown. We lived in a congested, commercial area, the Hadar, a low-income neighborhood with dirty alleyways, cheap shops, and junk food. Row after row of ugly rectangular buildings, like army barracks, lined its narrow streets. They had been built to house the waves of Jewish immigrants to Palestine before and after the Nakba.

I worked in the even worse port area, on Ha'Atsmaut Road, named after the declaration of independence of Israel. This fact sat on my chest like a boulder every morning as I got off the bus. The area was a squalid part of town riddled with drugs, mafias, and prostitution. I had to leave promptly at 5:00 pm when I finished work, and, even then, it was scary in the winter months when it was already dark. I came across beggars, peddlers, dodgy-looking men with scarred faces, and women who looked like they had been bat-tered a lifetime. Fluorescent lights, trinket stalls and a stale smell of frying pervaded the area, with its Hebrew and Russian signs, and I could not wait to leave.

At the apartment, there was no relief. I hated the place, with its run-down interior and peeling paint. I tried to make my room look better, but there was little I could do with cheap furniture and a tiny space. Worse, I did not fit in with my flatmates. They were nice to me, and I to them, and we tried to forge some kind of friendship, but we could not. They lived as a herd, going to class, eating, and studying together, and they were overwhelmed as it was, even without trying to accommodate a stranger in their midst. I tried to break their rigid routine and get them to go out or do something, but they frowned in disapproval, true to village tradition. From such young people, I found this stifling and soon gave up.

My job, too, was mundane and clerical, hardly the glowing start I had made in Cyprus. The salary barely covered my expenses. As my confidence waned and stress and boredom overcame me, I began to wonder if I was the same person that, a few months earlier, had been offered a position of assistant department manager at an international software company. Cyprus, so recent, seemed a thousand miles away.

Thankfully, my cousin, Rania, lived in Haifa, studying at college and working part-time. She often called me to meet up. Rania rented a room at the home of a woman in Wadi Nisnas, a crowded, downtrodden neighborhood inhabited by Palestinians. The old lady, Um Habib, lived alone, and she loved my cousin like one of her daughters. Sometimes, Rania and I went out, walking around the Hadar and buying cheap clothes or cosmetics on our shoestring budget. The city was weighing down on me. After the Nakba, only 3,000 of Haifa's 70,000 Palestinians had remained in it. They were forced into certain neighborhoods, where they lived in grueling conditions. The Israeli government set about completely changing the character of the city, destroying many Palestinian properties, taking over others for Jewish use, replacing Arab street names with Hebrew ones, and obliterating Palestinian cultural heritage, so rich and vibrant in Haifa before its ruin. Everywhere we walked, surviving homes peeked out at me, ghosts from another era.

My only respite was when we went to the malls, as they were disconnected from the outside reality. But, even there, everything was in Hebrew. There were no Arabic signs at all, though it was the second official language of the state and many of the customers were Palestinians. Arabic road signs in the country were full of glaring spelling mistakes, and the Hebrew names of towns were transcribed into Arabic instead of using the original Arab names.

At the entrance of every mall, government office, or public building, guards and metal detectors were standard. If a bag was left on a bus or at a train station, or if someone left their luggage for a minute and went to get something, it became an emergency. People looked around frantically and if the owner was not found, things could quickly escalate. At the central station, I witnessed the scene as warning sirens sounded, the site was evacuated and a bomb squad was brought in to dismantle the suspicious object, which turned out to be someone's clothes! The sense of constant alarm was palpable, yet it was treated as something normal.

I sought comfort in the village. But home was like a pressure cooker. The new Authority did not have funds for scholarships and my father had to take care of Mousa's university expenses. Mum was trying to reintegrate into her surroundings. After twelve years away, this was not easy. Bored housewives gossiped, pulling everyone apart. Jealous relatives belittled her experience abroad and refused to understand it, but she loved them and let things pass. I was distant from her at this time, wrapped up in my own problems. I also had to find ways to see Raji, which was tricky, but it was too early to tell my parents. Our sense of unity, the small, cozy family we had been in Cyprus, was severely hit, and we grew apart in that year.

Each Saturday night, as I packed my things, I dreaded having to go to Haifa the next day. I woke at dawn to catch one of the two taxis out of the village. It took every ounce of willpower to drag myself out of bed, especially in the biting cold of the winter months, and the two-hour journey finished me off. The day was a total loss.

The only good thing about moving to Haifa was that it was easier to see Raji, though it was a long trip for him, on top of his long commute to work. As our relationship was not yet public, he brought his best friend along, a cousin of two of the girls. They came to see us at the apartment and the girls welcomed them, though I could sense that they were wondering what was going on. Soon, he gave up on that and began to visit me on his own. We went out for coffee or dinner, but I could not stay long in order not to raise suspicion at the apartment, and he had to get back to the village early, to leave for work at dawn with his father. It was messy and people began to talk, so I decided to tell Dad.

I did not expect his reaction. 'Don't you think you're rushing into this?' he asked. 'We've barely been here a few months.'

I explained that he was a good man and that he loved me. But my father rubbed his temple. 'I'm sure he's good, but you're very different from each other. I don't want a day to come when you tell me you want a divorce!'

I did not realise how accurate his premonition was. With the stubbornness of youth, I insisted on it. He let the matter be, but his brooding silence bothered me. I decided to take a breather, a short trip to Cyprus. He encouraged it, perhaps hoping I would think things over.

Later that week, on 4 November 1995, my parents and I were visiting my aunt when breaking news came through on TV. Israeli prime minister Yitzhak Rabin had been shot and killed during a rally in support of the Oslo Accords in Tel Aviv. The assassin was a Jewish Israeli ultranationalist who opposed the Accords and Rabin's peace initiative.

It was, as many Palestinians feared, a blow to the peace process. My father was anxious, wondering how things would pan out.

I booked my ticket to Cyprus.

VI

It was cheaper to go by ship, leaving Haifa in the evening and arriving in Limassol the next morning. I checked in at the port and the security agent scrutinized me. I held an Israeli passport and was born in Lebanon, and I did not speak Hebrew. She pounded me with questions. I explained that I had returned after the recent Accords. She asked who my father was, what he did, where we lived, what I did, why I was going to Cyprus, who I would see, what I would do, how long I planned to stay. I was stunned. I tried to answer as best as I could. Her tone was terse, and she scowled as she asked more and more questions. I began to feel really stressed and like a criminal under investigation. Then she leaned over and delivered the punch line:

'You're not going to Cyprus to see your friends. You're going to meet terrorists from Lebanon!'

I was dumbfounded. I gaped at her, then I answered: 'I'm sorry, but I'm going on holiday as I told you. I have no connection with anyone in Lebanon. We left there when I was a child.'

Scowling, she returned my passport, put a yellow sticker on my bag and sent me to be searched. Next to me were a Palestinian couple, looking just as agitated as I felt. They had answered the same questions; I heard the woman say she was from Acre. A female agent led her into a nearby cubicle for a body search, while a male led her husband to another. They drew the curtains. I waited.

Suddenly, I heard a resounding *Whack!* I sat up, startled, as the woman yelled: *'Don't touch me!'*

The Israeli agent burst out of the cubicle in tears, running towards the check-in counters at the other end. It was obvious that the woman being searched had slapped her. In a second, five or six other agents materialized and everyone was screaming as the furious woman emerged from the cubicle. We did not know what had happened in there, but she kept yelling at the top of her voice, telling them not to touch her. Her husband was beside her, shaking at the insults hurled at them. As the scene spiraled, they were both taken away.

I sank into my chair. It was my turn. The agents asked me to unzip my bag. They flung it open and yanked the contents out. I swallowed my own anger as my clothes and belongings were strewn around. The bag had already been scanned by X-ray; what was the point of this? I wondered. I squirmed as they took out my underwear and placed it on the side in mechanical movements. My jeans, blouses, and pajamas followed. They unwrapped the presents I had bought for my friends and took them to scan. They took each and every bottle and sanitary item. I was standing there, powerless and fuming, when another agent came up and asked me to accompany her to the search cubicle.

Inside, she drew the curtain and asked me to take my sweater off, unzip my jeans and take them down. I obliged, anger rising like bile in my throat. I felt like I was being admitted to prison, not travelling. I was going on holiday, for God's sake!

She ran a metal detector over my jeans, bra, and shoes. Then, she ran her fingers through my hair. Finally, she told me I could get dressed. When I came out, they told me to repack and close my bag. I could not speak or look at any of them. I was consumed with anger. Finally, I took my bag and boarded the ship, hours after I had arrived at the port.

There was a sense of relief among the passengers. I gathered they had all been through the same ordeal. To my surprise, the couple from Acre were there. We exchanged a smile and I said: 'You made it!'

'We did!' they chuckled, munching on a pack of chips between them. They sat there, an ordinary couple with ordinary lives, trying to regain a sense of their dignity. I did the same. But I was still shaken when I arrived in Cyprus. As I told my friends about the last few months, I realized how bizarre it all sounded. I was staying with Salwa. Like millions of Arabs, she had grown up hearing of Israel and its violence. To her, it was unthinkable that I now actually *lived there*.

I showed her a photograph of Raji, and she seemed as surprised as Dad was. 'So soon?' she teased. I felt a nagging discomfort at her reaction, as well as my own muddled feelings. My friend sensed it.

'Fida, is that really where you want to be?' she asked, softly. 'Why don't you come back to Cyprus? You could return to work tomorrow. They'd love to have you back!'

I thought about it. It was even more tempting when I visited the office and one of my colleagues said the same. Somehow, I felt, too, that Dad would not mind. I could rent an apartment and be back to my old life in a jiffy.

But it did not feel right anymore. Sadly, Cyprus already felt so far away. So much had happened that this life now seemed very distant, though it had only been a few months. I needed to tough it out in my own country, now.

VII

At Christmas, Raji and I had a humble engagement. My father still looked uneasy, but he seemed to have reached a grudging acceptance.

A week later, he went to welcome Arafat, who finally arrived in Ramallah. From the roof of al-Muqata'a, the previous Israeli military headquarters, Arafat shouted a victorious message to a cheering crowd of thousands. The Palestinian Authority was now in control of large areas of the West Bank, although Israeli forces could still intervene.

At the welcoming procession, one of the guests saw my father and exclaimed: 'What are you doing here?'

They looked at each other, shock and recognition on their faces. The man was Mustafa Issa, Abu Firas, who had met my father in Jerusalem in 1967 and introduced him to the resistance. Abu Firas had been imprisoned and deported by Israel. He had ended up in

Lebanon, where he had worked in the military arm of Fatah's Western Sector. My father had seen him from time to time. After the siege of Beirut, Abu Firas had left for Tunis.[2]

Now, they broke into laugher. 'You're the last person who should ask me that question!' Dad joked. 'You brought me here!'

Abu Firas shook his hand, warmly. 'Yes, and I'll always be proud!'

'What are you doing?' my father asked.

'I'm the new governor of Ramallah,' Abu Firas smiled. Celebrations filled the streets. After twenty-eight years of occupation, Palestinians in the West Bank and Gaza were getting their first taste of self-rule. Their new police force moved into buildings that had housed the Israeli occupation. Palestinian flags, once outlawed, fluttered everywhere. Previous Israeli army compounds were opened to the public, and thousands of Palestinians streamed through them. Many saw the prisons where they had been incarcerated.

There was a sense of euphoria, mixed with disbelief. Future prospects looked bright. The international community was lending every support to the new Authority, and Palestinian expatriates were returning to invest in the new economy.

On 20 January 1996, Palestinians held their first free and democratic elections in the West Bank, Gaza Strip, and East Jerusalem. Arafat was elected president of the Palestinian Authority, and Fatah won the majority of seats in the legislative council.

Hamas continued to oppose the peace process. The same month, shortly before the final status talks of the Oslo Accords were set to commence, Israel assassinated Hamas leader Yahya Ayyash in Gaza, the mastermind behind the first suicide attacks in Israel after the massacre in the Cave of the Patriarchs (Ibrahimi Mosque) in Hebron. Hamas continued its suicide bombings in Israel, which pressured the Palestinian Authority to crack down on the Islamic movement. The rift was growing deeper, and Hamas did not take part in the elections.

VIII

As Palestinian returnees attempted to rebuild their lives in the West Bank and Gaza, I had the equally daunting task of trying to find my place in Israel. So far, I had had almost no interaction with Israelis. I did not speak Hebrew; I lived between my village and an apartment with Palestinian girls in Haifa; and I worked in a Palestinian company. When I went down to the street to buy lunch, all the falafel and shawarma shops were owned by Palestinians. When I got on the bus or bought something at the supermarket, and it was an Israeli driver or cashier, I just fished out my money and handed it over, not understanding the amount they were saying but looking at the cash register to see it. They gave me the change and it ended there. Hearing the language made me cringe. I saw Israelis everywhere but had a completely separate and parallel existence to them, and I was hit by a painful feeling, one which has never left me, since. I was a stranger in my own country.

'Go to an ulpan,' Dina suggested.

This, I found out, was a Hebrew course given to Jewish immigrants. I enrolled for a class and took the subway up Mount Carmel. At the Carmel Center, an upscale hotel and shopping area at the top, I asked for directions and walked down the posh avenue, gazing at the fancy boutiques, feeling liberated from the poverty and grime of the lower city. It was warm, even on a winter day, and a bright sun shone as I looked down at the panoramic sea view and beautiful bay below. This was a part of Haifa I had not seen.

The language center was in a quaint building surrounded by lawns and trees. I was early, so I sat outside on a bench to wait. I smiled, transported to my university years in England. If someone had told me, I mused, when I was scuttling through the rain to my classes at Lancaster, that I would be in Palestine in two years' time and be sitting on a bench at a Hebrew language school, I would have laughed at them.

Yet, though I tried to relax and enjoy the scenery, I walked into class with a sense of trepidation. The group of students was comprised of eight Russians, three Ethiopians, and myself. At the time, the collapse of the Soviet Union had brought large waves of Russian Jews to Israel. Any Jew, anywhere in the world, only had to prove that he or she had Jewish roots to qualify for instant Israeli citizenship, while Palestinians who were driven from their homes in 1948 had no right to return. I gathered I was probably the only Palestinian ever to have taken this class. Those who were born in Israel studied Hebrew at school.

The teacher spelled out the first letters of the alphabet. I got this in about a minute, as Hebrew and Arabic had the same Semitic root. I ground my teeth as the others practiced, sounding terrible. Two hours later, we had barely covered a few letters. I went back for one more class, which was a repeat of the first, then I stopped. I did not have the patience to sit in a hundred classes, at this rate.

At the apartment, I often sat alone, lost in thought. My relationship with Raji did not feel right; I felt I had rushed into it. Three times, over that summer, I tried to end it. Each time, he told me it was just the alienation I felt, having just come into the culture, and that things would get better once we were married. I wanted to believe him, and he was the only one who stood by my side through my confusion and turmoil in those overwhelming months.

Things were worsening with my flatmates. By now, we spoke very little. I left them to their world and they seemed to leave me to mine. One weekend, they went to Fassouta, while I stayed behind. Raji came over to the apartment to visit. Somehow, they found out, and, when they returned, they faced me with stony expressions and began lecturing me on tradition and proper behavior. I had a very short fuse, and a huge fight broke out. I burst into tears, packed my things, and went to my uncle, George.

I stayed with him and his family, sleeping on the couch in their tiny apartment. He gave me a lot of love and support, but I was crowding their space, and I was weary of the job, the commute, Haifa. Two weeks later, I resigned and went home.

IX

My dejection was softened with good news. My uncle, Geris, had finally returned to Gaza. After more than a year of waiting, his entry permit had been issued. Unlike my father, he made sure to come back through Gaza to be covered by the Oslo Accords, for fear of being tried in Israel. Then, he made his way to Fassouta.

My grandparents' happiness was complete. Twenty-six years had passed since Geris had left the country. With both her sons finally near her, my grandmother seemed born again, cured of most of her illness. She did not stop cooking. 'Your brothers have to eat!' she repeated to my aunt, Muna, who gawked at the number of dishes that filled the kitchen. My grandmother covered my father and uncle with blankets when they took naps at her house, doting on them like children. '*The boys!* That's what she still calls them!' my aunt laughed to her sisters.

'I'm so glad our parents were alive to see you return,' my uncle, George, told his brothers in a choked voice. 'They waited a very long time.'

Arafat asked my uncle to direct the PLO Planning Center. But Ammo had the same reservations as my father, and he wanted to live in Fassouta. I asked him what he was going to do.

'It's a new beginning, a new horizon ...' he said, his eyes shining. 'A chance to come back and start our lives at home!' He was still employed by the PLO, but he only helped out with small projects while he figured out his next steps. He had waited for this all his life. He wanted to build a house and bring his children to the village.

Hearing his words strengthened my resolve to try harder. Uncle George came to the rescue, again. He introduced me to another client of his who had a small software company in Yarka, a village about an hour away. I was hired as a programmer and was very happy to live at home. Transport was an issue, though. There was no bus to get there. While there was ample public transport in Jewish communities, it was severely lacking in our villages. If people did not have cars, they were really stuck. Three buses came to Fassouta daily, at 7:00 am, 2:00 pm, and 4:00 pm, and two taxis left at 6:30 am. Otherwise, people had to stand on the road for hours to try and hitch rides. For mothers with young children, there was no day care center in the village. Our local council did not receive a sufficient budget from the government to have one. It seemed to explain why so many women stayed home. A very small number of Palestinian women were working.

I had to go with one of the taxis leaving the village each morning, which dropped me off at the Kafr Yasif junction, then hitch a ride for the remaining twenty minutes. It took one and a half hours each way for a forty-minute trip, and I was up at dawn every day. I was exhausted, but I stuck it out. We were a young team of three programmers, an accountant, and a secretary. We had lunch together every day, chattering and laughing, and I began to feel a sense of belonging to a workplace, again.

Yarka was a Druze village. Before going there, I had not heard of this religion. I was too young when we left Lebanon, and, now, I began to find out about this minority, which inhabited several countries of the Levant. In Israel, the state had worked hard to segregate them, marking them as a separate ethno-religious group from Palestinians, falsifying their history, and creating a separate education system for them.[3] Most Druze in the country dissociated themselves from their Arab identity and supported Israel, fighting in its wars and serving its oppression of the Palestinians. There were voices of opposition in the community, but they were silenced.

Yet, the Druze did not gain much from their allegiance to Israel. The state did not treat non-Jews with equality, even if they served in its army. The majority of Druze lands were confiscated for Jewish use, and the state demolished homes in Druze villages where building permits were denied—just like it did in other Palestinian communities. Their neighborhoods were congested, underfunded ghettos, like those of Christians and Muslims. Most Druze men ended up as security guards, low-ranking policemen, or prison wardens, and most of their women stayed home. Their community was heavily militarized and was ostracized by other Palestinians.

I was starting to see the military ethos and deep religious divides that marked Israeli society. Yarka felt like a ghetto, albeit a very rich one. Many Druze who served in the army had a history of smuggling and crime in Lebanon and the Palestinian territory during Israel's wars there. I remembered my friends from Ramallah telling me that Druze soldiers were particularly brutal during Israeli incursions: 'It's like they have something to prove, that they're just as good, just as loyal to the state as the Jews.'

It was difficult for me to grasp this, in what had been a Palestinian Arab community. I got on with work, trying to allay the shock and dismay I felt. In mid-May, I experienced my first Israeli Independence Day. Israelis were out flag-waving and having parties and barbeques on what was Palestinian land. The country was plastered with flags for weeks before and weeks after, even more so than usual; I noticed that Israel had an obsession with hanging its flag everywhere. Did we really need one at the swimming pool in Nahariya; at a small, grimy coffee shop near the bus station; at the bus station, itself; and again every few yards on the beachfront?

On that day, I was so depressed I simply elected to stay home.

X

A month later, my aunt invited me to go with her family to the beach. Desperate for any happy reminder of earlier summers, I grabbed my swimsuit and towel and joined them on a Saturday morning as they honked their car horn outside. 'Where are we going?' I asked, settling into the back seat with my cousins.

'Al-Zeeb,' Randa said. 'It's really nice, there's green grass on the beach and space to have a barbeque.'

Splashing in the sea with them, my spirits were lifted. I had missed our beach trips with Mum in Cyprus. She still didn't have a car here, and Mousa was away in England. I relaxed, swimming lazily and looking around. Soon, the smoke from my uncle's barbeque beckoned us.

'What's that?' I asked, pointing to a building in the distance. It was a little higher up on the beach, with a dome and a large, decorative arch on the front. It seemed to evoke something, like a place of worship, and was strangely at odds with the picnic site around it.

'That's al-Zeeb, the village,' my uncle said. 'It's where it used to be. Those buildings are the remains. That used to be the mosque, but now it's a tourist place. And that,' he pointed to a relatively large structure, 'used to be the mukhtar's house. They made it into a museum.'

I put my plate down. 'You mean this was a village before 1948?'

'Yes. It was a big fishing village, and they also grew a lot of fruit ... Bananas, oranges, figs ... Olives, too. But all of it was destroyed.'

In fact, on 14 May 1948, just one day before the end of the British Mandate, al-Zeeb was captured by the Haganah's Carmeli Brigade, which expelled its 2,000 people and razed the village to the ground. The Jewish kibbutzim of Sa'ar and Gesher HaZiv were built on its lands.

As we watched, people milled about in swimsuits, and tourists visited the 'archaeological' site. Smoke arose from many barbeques, carrying a delicious aroma as families sat together, enjoying the view. But my food was suddenly tasteless. 'Where are its people?' I asked.

'In Lebanon, mostly,' said my uncle. 'And some of them are in Mazra'a, not far from here.'

We went to Mazra'a once a week to buy fruit and vegetables from its large market. Even the most mundane places here seemed to be part of a haunting story.

I looked back at the dome, standing sadly in the middle of the site. My cousins were playing ball as my aunt and uncle watched, eating sunflower seeds and drinking coffee. My aunt turned to me with a smile. 'So, how are the wedding preparations coming along?'

XI

Things had been busy, so hectic I had not had time to deal with my rising feeling of doubt. I pushed it aside among the discussions on the hall, the band, the list of guests, the fittings for my dress, and Raji's ongoing project to fix up a couple of rooms underneath the house of his parents. We planned to live there for a while, until we built our own. Everything was zooming towards September, and, before I knew it, it was the night before my wedding, and I was in tears.

Rania was my bridesmaid. She held me to her and teared up, too, thinking it was about my late mother. She did not know what to say, and I could not explain the huge knot of fear in my stomach. For a fleeting moment, I wondered why I was doing this, if I could still pull out. But it would be crazy, I knew, and would put both families to shame. In the morning, Rania and I went to the salon, put on our beautiful dresses, and went back to my parents' house, waiting for Raji and his family. The occasion was heavy with emotion; his mother, who was also my father's cousin, cried when they came to take me to church, and all the women cried with her. I had asked the salon to do my hair in a simple lift, with small white flowers, and only later did I realize that Mama Hanneh had done the same at her wedding. She was present with me, tugging at my heart like never before.

After the service, we had a huge party in the schoolyard. Hundreds of people came; almost the entire village was there. My family's return was nothing short of a miracle, and the wedding felt more like a carnival. The sky darkened ominously and we were worried, but it held on until the last guests had left. Raji and I got into the car to leave, and large, heavy raindrops began to pelt the windshield.

I seemed to be replaying history. We went to Nahariya for our honeymoon, just like my parents had done. Then, we drove south to East Jerusalem and stayed at a hotel near the old city walls. An old waiter delivered breakfast to our room, and we suddenly found ourselves embarrassed, for he seemed to be my grandfather's age. Though it was his job, it felt wrong, somehow, for him to bring us a tray of food up the stairs. We chatted with him, and Raji felt even more awkward when he gave him a tip. 'Poor people …' he muttered, after the man had told us a bit about life in the city.

After Israel illegally annexed East Jerusalem in 1967, the city's Palestinians were not given Israeli citizenship, but residence permits. These could be revoked if people spent more than seven years outside the city.[4] The government relentlessly seized their land for Jewish settlement and to make Jerusalem the de facto capital of Israel, in contravention of its international status. Building permits were not granted to Palestinians in East Jerusalem, causing severe crowding and forcing people to build illegally. Families were then forced to demolish their own homes or pay for the municipality to do so; otherwise, the homeowners could go to prison or be given huge fines.

We opted not to go to West Jerusalem, the Jewish part, despite the lure of the shopping arcades and restaurants. Instead, we stayed east and walked to the old city walls, near Damascus Gate, seeing shopkeepers and old peasants selling their produce. Many wore traditional dress. It was my first experience of an Arab environment since my visit to Egypt as a teenager, and I felt like my father had done when he saw East Jerusalem for the first time, after the 1967 occupation. I stared at everything, feeling the Palestinian atmosphere that I so yearned for. We had a traditional lunch of msakhan, a delicious dish of chicken, olive oil, and sumac, served on thick flatbread. In the basement restaurant, strangely named 'Philadelphia', we struck up a conversation with the waiter and heard more about the situation in the city. Then we bought a few souvenirs and set off to Eilat, in the south of Israel.

Even in a five-star hotel on the Red Sea, I could not relax. This was Israeli luxury at its height, but I felt uneasy and out of place. It was fake and uncomfortable, more so when Raji's father and brother turned up to say hello. They were working in Eilat on a construction project and they came to see us, in their work clothes. I squirmed, somehow ashamed to be enjoying myself at that fancy place while they toiled in the scorching heat.

That afternoon, I stood on the balcony of our room and felt, for the first time, the full weight of my fears. I knew, then, that I had walked into the marriage simply to feel the belonging that I was so desperate for after we had returned. Raji was a great man, but we were worlds apart. I had tried to ignore that realization, but now that we were together and the bustle of wedding preparations had ended, it settled heavily on my heart. I wondered if I should get a divorce. But the terrified thought only lasted a second before I pushed it away and embarked, firmly, on my married life.

XII

We bought some cheap furniture and tried to make our apartment as homey as we could. It was a small space, but we knew it was going to be temporary, though I was not thinking ahead too far. Raji's parents—my uncle, Nour, and his wife—lived on the floor above us, and our grandmother, Um Nour, lived on the other side, with a shared wall between us. Each day, she grasped her cane, climbed the few steps from her house, walked around my uncle's house, then descended our stairs to visit me for coffee. She was delighted when I asked her for recipes, and kept urging me to come over and eat at her house.

My uncle's family quickly became a second one to me. His wife loved me and we had none of the problems that often emerge between in-laws. After the rains of October, I accompanied them to my first olive harvest on my uncle's land. We spread large tarpaulins on the ground and picked the silver-green fruit by hand, letting it fall and gathering it at the end. Standing under a tree, my feet planted in the slightly damp earth, a scarf tied around my head against the bright sun as I reached up and picked the olives, I felt like I had been there a lifetime. There was an infinite serenity to working in an olive grove. A thin film of sweat moistened my forehead as birds and crickets chirped. The air was so clean, and I gulped lungfuls of it. My hands became a little rough from clearing branches and twigs and lightly tainted with a layer of soil. I paused to rest, gazing at the mountains around me.

When we stopped for breaks, we sat, cross-legged, on the warm ground and delved into fresh pita, boiled eggs, labaneh, tomatoes, and olives from the last season. Afterwards, my uncle's wife passed around coffee from a large thermos, with some wafers or cookies. The simple food felt like a feast, a cool breeze blowing softly around us, the sun peeking through the branches from a brilliant blue sky.

We worked until late afternoon, gathering the day's harvest into sacks. I could only help out at weekends because of work, but the family continued on the other days. Two weeks later, my uncle took the olives to the nearby press in Hurfeish and we waited to hear how many gallons of oil they had made.

At the office, as I typed, I noticed the little scratches on my arms and smiled to myself. In other circumstances, I might have happily taken up farming. But olives did not make a living, not from fifty trees, at any rate.

Raji continued to work with my uncle at construction sites. Thankfully, they had taken a new project in Haifa, so he did not have to sleep in Eilat or Tel Aviv, as they had done before. But it was exhausting. They were up at dawn, and, by the time they made it back to the village in the late afternoon, he could barely manage to shower and have dinner before flopping on the couch. The pay was minimum wage. I was dismayed to see that many men in the village had similar jobs. There was no work in Fassouta other than at the school and local council, where competition for positions was fierce.

Most of the state's budget for infrastructure and economic development went to Jewish communities. We had no business initiatives, and no industry or factories. Many of our local councils were insolvent, and most had to raise their own funds to install basic infrastructure such as water and sewage systems.

More than half of Palestinians in Israel lived below the poverty line. In my village, most families made about half the earnings of an average Jewish family, and some breadwinners supported five or six people on the equivalent of 800 dollars a month, barely enough for one. Our communities had a lower life expectancy and a higher number of people suffering from stress-related diseases such as diabetes and hypertension.[5]

To add insult to injury, the Hebrew term 'avoda aravit', Arab work, was commonly used to denote work of poor or slapdash quality—despite the sad irony that most of the State of Israel was built by Palestinian hands.

Our neighbor was another construction worker with five children, who had been out of work for almost a year. He had to resort to social benefits, which were meager, and to scraping a few days of casual work here and there, whenever someone needed him. His wife was trying to find a job. The clothing factory where she worked had closed and moved to Jordan, where the cost of labor was lower. She was always in the fields, picking herbs or vegetables, and she raised a few chickens in her backyard, as she struggled to put food on the table.

It was not easier for the educated. Young people whose parents managed to put them through university often left the village to try and find work in the cities. Yet, it was very difficult to find jobs in their fields. Raji had an engineering diploma and had applied to many offices to find work, but he was not even called for an interview. Several of my cousins had university degrees and they were always applying, but no one called them. 'They ask for your army number ...' they explained. Upon finishing school, every young Israeli had to complete military service. Doors were then open for study loans, jobs, and generous mortgages. Palestinians in Israel, apart from the Druze, were exempt from service, and very few of them enlisted. But the completion of army service was a requirement for many jobs and social benefits. 'They can reject us without saying outright that it's because we're Arabs,' Raji told me. Few Palestinians were hired into senior positions in the private or public sectors. They could only fill such roles in the Arab branch of the Ministry of Education, for example, or at their local councils.

The village was full of frustrated graduates, waiting for interviews that never came. Raji's brother had graduated from the Technion, the Israel Institute of Technology. I found out that there were several subjects that Palestinians could not study, such as certain fields of physics, nuclear science, or pilot training, for example, on the pretext of 'security'. In employment, they were completely excluded from the defense and aviation industries, among others. To avoid having to look for an employer, many students were still turning to free professions, such as law, landscaping, dentistry, and other health professions where they could open their own practices.

A year after graduating in engineering, Raji's brother was still jobless. 'I can't believe, after all the studying I did, that I still have to take money from my father …' he told me. 'I feel like an ox, sitting at home, being fed. He worked night and day to put me through university!'

With no army number, it was very difficult to qualify for student loans, as well. My cousin had applied for a loan each year through his studies, without success, though he was a top student.

I asked him whether his classmates had found jobs. 'None of them are in touch,' he shrugged. 'Me and another guy were the only Arabs in our class. The others didn't really talk to us. He hasn't found a job, either. I called him and he said he's working as a waiter at the wedding hall in Kafr Yasif, to make some money.'

With this reality, it was a shock when I had to leave my job, for the second time. I found out another fact about Yarka: there was a large drug trade and a lot of inter-familial conflict. In December 1996, I arrived at the office to see police cars in front. The employees were standing outside, and they told me that someone had come in the night and poured gasoline around the building to burn it, but had been stopped. An investigation was underway.

I turned around and hitched a ride back home.

XIII

Thankfully, my aunt told me that an English teacher at Fassouta's school was on maternity leave and they needed a replacement. I had never taught before and had no teacher training, but I thought I'd give it a try. 'You'll be great!' the headmaster assured me. 'We don't have anyone fluent in English here.'

I walked into Grade 8 and asked for a simple sentence. The children had been studying the language since Grade 3. Silence fell over the classroom. I prompted them again and heard a few half-hearted words and phrases. I tried again, with different sentences. They had no knowledge of basic grammar or vocabulary. I was amazed. What had they been doing for five years?

Suddenly, I remembered my flatmates in Haifa as they had pored over their reading lists in agony, a big dictionary next to them. I had felt sorry for them. They had studied English as a third language, after Arabic and Hebrew. When they got to university, their Arabic was useless, unless they were studying it. Israeli universities taught in Hebrew and used English sources. The girls were lost. It took them hours to get through a simple article.

I looked at the children facing me now. We had three months until their teacher returned. It began as a battle. They did not take substitute teachers seriously. I was shaking, inwardly, but I took a fierce attitude and raised my voice. There was no other way, at least at the outset. I left school each day a bundle of nerves, unleashing my frustration at home. At night, I corrected stacks of exercise books and prepared lessons for the next day. Then I gritted my teeth and walked in again. I taught Grades 1, 3, 6, and 8. A few weeks down the line, I had managed, at least, to achieve relative calm in class, and we were working through the syllabus. I tried not to think of the number of children who had no clue what we were doing. They had never had a good base, and there was almost nothing to build on now.

English teachers in our community who had graduated from Israeli universities were inept, which seemed to explain the situation. Four years of exposure to a language they did not speak or practice did not lead to fluency. One day, another teacher approached me with an apologetic expression. He wanted to give his class a quiz, and he showed it to me. Then he asked me, bashfully, to check his sheet so he could mark the children's. As I corrected his answers, one after the other, my heart fell. Most of them were wrong.

By now, I had broken the ice with the children. Sometimes, I told English stories to the younger classes, and they loved it. They held their breath, little faces pinned on mine as I recounted the adventures of some tortoise or lion. I smiled to myself, remembering Ammo's stories to us as children. With the older ones, we talked about university and careers. Occasionally, I had to switch to Arabic, as I realized there was no setup in school to talk to them about these issues. Most of them were too shy to even speak up in class. They had been taught not to think creatively or express themselves. Their confidence was low and they blushed and stuttered when I asked them to speak.

I liked the children and saw an opportunity. Perhaps I could do this as a career, I thought. It was comfortable working in the village and not having to commute. I asked the teachers about the pay and conditions. The base salary was low, but if I did some continuing education courses, they told me, it would rise. There was also the difficult hoop to jump through of being hired by the Ministry of Education, necessary to secure a permanent position. Due to the challenge of finding jobs in other fields, a disproportionate number of Palestinians trained to be teachers; there was fierce competition and a great oversupply. But I was optimistic that, once they had seen my English, they would accept me. My fellow teachers were neutral. At the outset, they had just smiled politely and eyed me in suspicion, but they soon gathered I did not know anyone, was not a gossip, and was harmless. I also did not pose a threat to them, as they had no interest in teaching English.

Raji's sister, who was also a teacher, introduced me to a supervisor in the Ministry. He was in charge of a national extracurricular program to raise the level of English in schools. My first meeting with an Israeli interviewer was awkward. He addressed me in Hebrew and, when I said I could not speak it, he raised his eyebrows. I explained that I was a recent returnee from abroad. He nodded and did not seem inclined to ask further questions. Hearing my English, he kept the meeting short and assigned me to two Palestinian schools in the Galilee, pushing some forms across for me to sign. 'The idea is to do fun activities with the children, painting, stories, songs ...' he explained, 'to make them enjoy English more and be able to use it.' I noticed that he had a heavy accent, too. He told me that the program could further my chances of being appointed as a full-time teacher.

It was a disaster. I walked into the first school in Mazra'a and had a nasty shock. About fifty children were crammed into each room of the dilapidated building, with rickety furniture and no amenities or teaching materials. Classes were out of control. The second school, in Hurfeish, was just as much of a shambles. Children sat on worn, creaky furniture, drumming and singing in class. They were friendly and quietened down when their teacher and I walked in, but she told me their academic standard was low. The boys were expected to finish school and go to the army; the girls were raised to be housewives. The schools felt like farmyards intended to lock in the greatest number of cattle.

Such was my awakening to our education system. Palestinian schools had lower budgets and suffered shortages in everything: classrooms, study materials, and facilities. Exam grades were significantly lower than those of Jewish students.[6] Palestinian teachers were still appointed by approval of Israel's secret service. There was no such intervention for Jewish schools, even those in communities known for their incitement against Palestinians.

With segregated schools, Jewish and Palestinian children did not mix together, even when they lived a short distance apart. From a young age, Israelis learned that Palestinians were refugees, primitive farmers, terrorists, or absent.[7] Jewish students did not study Arab culture, while, in Palestinian schools, the curriculum was a near translation of the Hebrew one. Palestinian students found no mention of their history or identity. It was out of the question for a teacher to bring up Palestine in class; it would lead to the termination of his or her job, if not police investigation. The students covered the Torah, Jewish history, Israel's 'war of independence', and the victory of the Jews in 'redeeming their land'. Not surprisingly, they did not identify with anything they were taught and simply memorized it to pass the exams. The teachers were burnt out. Most of them gave up and just tried to get through the day for the salary.

My plan of teaching as a career quickly fizzled out. At the end of my assignment, I left with mixed feelings. I was going to miss the children, but I felt sorry for both them and their teachers.

XIV

I suggested to Raji that we go away for a few days. In the whirlwind of my return to Fassouta, I had not yet been to see Raja and Sawsan, my university friends in Ramallah. That weekend, Raji and I made the trip.

We were overjoyed to meet again. 'The only good thing about Oslo,' they laughed, 'is that we could see you again!' We thought back to our tearful goodbyes a few years earlier, in Britain. Who could have guessed that we would be here now?

My friends were stuck in the West Bank. Before the Accords, there had been movement restrictions on Palestinians in Gaza and the West Bank, although it was still possible to circumvent some of them. 'We simply got in the car and went,' they told me. 'To Haifa, to Jerusalem, to the beach in Jaffa ...' Now, the restrictions were increased. Israeli checkpoints were set up at all entry points to Israel, and Palestinians needed permits to cross. After that, they were barred from using the airport at Tel Aviv, just half an hour away. To travel abroad, they had to cross over to Jordan and fly from Amman, adding time and expense to their trip.

The Palestinian sovereignty provided for by the Accords was a mere façade. The identification cards and passports issued by the Authority needed Israeli approval, just as they had when issued by Israeli occupation forces. All border crossings were controlled by Israel.

Worse, the new Palestinian police force became a tool for security coordination with Israel, trailing and handing over those who engaged in resistance. No one could have imagined such a scenario. Objectors to the new setup found themselves excluded from the jobs and perks of the Authority or imprisoned.

'We're living a worse nightmare than before,' Raja told me. The agreements made Palestinians subservient to Israel, economically, politically, and in every aspect of life. When the Oslo Accords were signed, Israeli settlement activity was to cease immediately in the Palestinian territory, and, three years later, permanent status negotiations were to begin on significant issues, including the settlements, Jerusalem, the refugees, and borders, aiming for a full Israeli withdrawal at the end of five years.

But Israel had already thrown its commitments to the wind. Newly elected prime minister Benjamin Netanyahu was from the right-wing Likud Party, which had opposed Palestinian statehood and Israeli withdrawal from the occupied territory. His government continued seizing land to expand illegal Jewish settlements and construct Israeli-only bypass roads. Instead of stopping, Israel's settlement activities had multiplied.

The Oslo Accords were soon seen by Palestinians as bringing neither peace nor freedom, and tensions simmered between the Fatah-dominated Palestinian Authority and Hamas. Israel pressured Arafat to rein in 'terrorism', as it termed any act of resistance, and he, though reluctant, often complied.

My friends were angry and insecure in the new circumstances. They knew how different life in Israel was. The decades of occupation had left their own society damaged, unable to rise to the same standard of living. When I told them about my life and problems, they looked at me in disbelief. 'You're lucky ...' they said, dourly. 'Use the chance!'

12

STRANGER IN MY OWN LAND

Every Palestinian in front of me was not any more a human being like me; was an enemy, a potential terrorist, or wasn't there at all.

Yehuda Shaul
Co-founder of Breaking the Silence[1]

I

I had gone through three jobs in less than two years. I needed a solution.

Rummaging through a box, I found the Hebrew study pack that I had bought at the airport on our first visit. It had a book and four cassette tapes. With sudden resolve, I went to the small bookshop in the village and bought pens and notebooks, to the curious smiles of the owner, my mother's cousin. Back home, I opened the book and stuck the first cassette in the player. As the voice began, I recoiled. But I drew a deep breath and willed myself to try.

For three months, I locked myself up and studied, taking a mechanical attitude and pushing my feelings aside. The language seemed to be a simplified version of Arabic. By the end of that time, I could speak, read, and write basic Hebrew. I began to apply to software companies. Predictably, weeks went by with no response. Then, a call came from a large firm in Haifa. The lady spoke to me in Hebrew, and I was very nervous, but I managed to arrange the time of my interview.

On the day, when I found the building and passed security, I tensed up. So far, other than my brief meeting with the teaching supervisor, I had had almost no interaction with Israelis. When a pleasant young man met me at the door and shook my hand, I broke into a light sweat.

There were two other people in the room. I sat down, trying hard to stop the thought that I was meeting with Israelis, trying to block the images of the past, of my family, my history that suddenly flashed across my mind. They asked me many questions and, thankfully, I could answer some of them in English. Leafing through my CV, they enquired, in more detail, about my work in Cyprus. I was glad and took it as a sign of interest.

'Well, thank you,' the pleasant man finally smiled. 'Oh, and one more thing. Can we have your army number?'

I had a sinking feeling. 'Um, I don't have one ...'

'OK,' the smile remained, fixed in place. 'Thank you. We'll be in touch.'

I walked out in defeat. I had researched the company, prepared for the interview, bought a new outfit. I had dreams of relocating to Haifa and starting a good career; Raji and I had been excited about the opportunity, which would be better for his work prospects, too. But no one called, and neither did three more companies that I interviewed with. Fighting panic, I began to wonder what to do. Was it back to teaching? What about the computer science degree I had earned with merit, the money my father had spent in a top British university? Why was it so easy in Cyprus, and so difficult here?

I was on the porch one afternoon, hanging the laundry dejectedly, when the neighbor said hello. Rosette was in her fifties and was always cheerful. Her smile was contagious.

She had a job for me. I could not believe it. She worked as a cleaning lady for a Jewish family in Kfar Vradim, a nearby village, and her employer worked at a software company. 'I've told him about you, and he asked me to bring your CV!' she beamed.

I almost jumped up and hugged her. Rushing inside, I printed it out and gave it to her. The company was in a technology park in Tefen, an industrial zone about twenty minutes away. It was perfect. And it was different from the other meetings I had had. Her employer was an older man with a quiet demeanor. He perused my CV thoughtfully, asked me a few questions and seemed impressed. 'We need a software tester. I think you would do well on the team,' he smiled. There was no mention of an army number.

Like a dream, I went back for a second meeting, this time with HR, and signed the contract. It took me a few seconds to realize the salary was written in dollars, and I guessed it was because the company was a subsidiary of a US-based one. My heart leapt; the pay was more than twice what I had made in Cyprus! I stared at the figure, hope and doubt gnawing at me, and back at the lady. 'Um, can I ask you a question?' I blushed. 'This salary, is it in shekels or … dollars?'

'No, it's in dollars,' she smiled, looking slightly taken aback. 'But it's converted to shekels on payment.' She did not know that, in my village, entire families subsisted on less than half that amount.

I practically danced my way home.

II

It seemed like such a miracle that, for months, I could hardly believe it. The first thing I did was buy a car. My aunt, Muna, had a Datsun that she was not driving, and she gave it to me for next to nothing. Though it was very old, it changed my life. I did not have to stand on the road for hours and hitch rides anymore. At last, the insecurity and stress of the last two years were behind me.

It took me a few days to realize that, of about thirty staff, I was the only Palestinian. The managers lived mostly in Kfar Vradim, the affluent community nearby, while the others lived in Haifa, Karmiel, and other towns in the Galilee. My team included David, an Israeli of British origin who had grown up near Tel Aviv, and two Russian testers, both recent immigrants. Vladimir lived with and supported his elderly mother and young brother. Natasha was a single mother with two children. They both lived in Haifa and often complained about the huge tax, almost half of their salaries, that they had to pay. When I got my first paycheck, I noticed that I had not had the same deduction, though we earned the same amount. It turned out that I had a tax break because Fassouta was near the northern border and was considered a high-risk area. I was receiving a tax benefit from Israel, I realized, for living in my village, close to Lebanon—the 'danger zone' where I was born and spent ten years of my life!

But this incentive, I discovered, was not meant for me. It was part of Israel's program to 'Judaize the Galilee', bringing more Jews to live there in order to break up the Palestinian majority. Despite this, Palestinians continued to make up more than half of its inhabitants, living in their villages that had survived the Nakba.

I made a great start at work, so relieved was I to be back in the world of an international company. My team members were quiet and kind, and quickly accepted me into their midst. A friendship grew with David. We both loved British culture and took lunch breaks together, laughing in the kitchen as people looked at us quizzically. I also became close to Lisa, the human resources officer. It was a curious friendship. She was in her fifties and I was twenty-four, younger than her daughter. But we were delighted to chat in English. Lisa was Jewish and had emigrated from Britain as a teenager and married a local Israeli. She liked gossip and small talk, but she was simple and kind, with a motherly demeanor. She turned up daily at my door, after making her tea in the kitchen nearby, for a quick chit-chat. Sometimes, it was not so quick, and I would glance worriedly in the direction of my manager's office and mutter: 'I'd better get to work …'

Lisa, startled, would then look at her watch. 'Oh, dear me, look at the time! Must be off now! Ta ta, love!' Then she would rush off, leaving me grinning in her wake. I was happy to have people to connect to, like this; they were the only ones I could talk to about the wider world, the parts of my life before our return.

The company's handyman, Moshe, was of Moroccan origin and was friendly to me from day one. A few weeks into the job, he stood in the doorway of my small office, coffee cup in hand. 'You're doing great, Fida! The CEO has heard excellent reports about your work!'

I smiled. Everyone knew that Moshe tried to look important by posing as the trusted, right-hand man of senior management. Lisa liked to refer to him as 'the sidekick'. I held back a laugh and said: 'Thanks, Moshe!'

He grinned. I was about to turn back to my screen, but he studied me for a few seconds and added, rather thoughtfully: 'You're not like other Arabs, eh? You've made something of yourself.'

I paused.

'I tell you, you Christians …' he continued, sticking his head in a little closer and lowering his voice. 'You're different. We have no problems with you!'

Each time I saw him in the corridor, or driving the company car around, I was reminded that reality lay outside the polite, manufactured environment that I worked in. I had a constant feeling that I was 'lucky', somehow singled out, to be there—as though I had no right to such a job. Other than my team and Lisa, the remaining employees did not talk to me much. One software developer made efforts to have longer chats with me. He was a runner and we talked about nutrition and exercise. But I could never quite overcome my intimidation at working with Israelis. I often overheard them talking about 'milu'im', the army reserve duty that they were summoned to for a few weeks each year. On Thursday afternoons, at the end of each work week, we were all called up to the large conference room for Kabbalat Shabbat, a receiving of the Jewish Sabbath. Cakes and pastries were laid out on the large mahogany table, and everyone ate and chatted before breaking up for the weekend. There were discussions about the recent Oslo Accords and the relationship with the Palestinians. I was silent and extremely uncomfortable. I could not help wondering, as I gazed around the room, how many of my colleagues had served in Lebanon during the invasion. I wondered what they would say, how they would react, if I told them my story.

Moshe continued to be friendly, but I noticed that he was very insecure. He went over and above his duties at work, trying to position himself as the go-to man for any issue that needed solving. Lisa always joked about it, but, one day, she spoke seriously. 'It's not easy for him. He's a Mizrahi, there's a lot of baggage there ... And he holds a lower position, which feeds into that.'

I had no idea what she was talking about. From my father, I began to find out that Israeli Jews were not one people, but 'tribes'. They were divided into two main groups: Ashkenazi and Sephardi/Mizrahi. The Ashkenazim had emigrated from the West; the others, from North Africa and the Middle East. The Ashkenazim dominated in wealth and control, settled in the center of the country, and lived in better neighborhoods. They looked down on the Sephardic and Mizrahi Jews, especially those who had come from Arab countries. Those 'eastern' Jews were pushed out to live in poorer areas. Their numbers grew to more than half the Jewish population, but they would never have more than two ministers in government, and would never hold an important ministerial post. They also remained the poorest among the Jews in Israel. The political establishment demanded that they renounce their Arab identity and tried to eliminate their culture. They had to dress, educate their children, and think like the Ashkenazim in order to get ahead. In time, the Sephardim/Mizrahim moved to open hatred of the Arabs and Palestinians to try to prove themselves. The more they distanced themselves from Arab culture or even married Ashkenazim, the more they could raise their chances of success in Israeli society.

I began to understand Moshe. At home, too, my grandmother told me about Mordechai, from neighboring Elqosh. He had emigrated from Iraq and found his way to the Deir, as she still called it, where he raised chickens. He brought fresh eggs to sell in Fassouta, and, with his fluent Arabic, struck up friendships with people. 'He would always reminisce about his house and properties back in his country,' my grandmother told me. 'He could never forget. "Um Nour," he said, "we had it good there, we really did. I had my house, my orchards, and trees; we never wanted for anything. Why did they bring us to this desolation? We lost everything to come here and be looked down on!"'

III

Like Mordechai, the people of Elqosh kept chickens, grazed cows, and grew vegetables and fruit. They popped into Fassouta to do some small trade and see the doctor or dentist. Each day, as I drove back and forth, the houses of Deir el-Qasi, which my father had shown us, stared back at me. Which was worse? I wondered. To have one's home destroyed, or to have it remain, for others to live in?

Driving on, I passed the site of Suhmata. All that remained were desolate olive trees, with some stones jutting out that had survived the bulldozers. Most of its people were in Lebanon, but some had managed to stay, and they lived in nearby villages. Tens of them had settled in Fassouta, and I met several families there. Again, I wondered which was more painful: being totally removed and far away, or having to pass by the site of their village and see its ruins?

Sixty years on, not only my grandmother, but everyone in Fassouta, mentioned those villages as though they were still there: 'I'm near Suhmata,' or 'I'm passing through the Deir ...' they said, in everyday parlance. They spoke about men and women they knew and memories between them and Fassouta before 1948, including intermarriages with Suhmata, which had had both Christians and Muslims.

My little cousins had just arrived from England to start their new lives in Fassouta, as we had done. My uncle, Geris, took us all on a drive to show us the path by which he had escaped to South Lebanon, all those years ago. Miraculously, we had all managed to return, but the refugees had not. At work, while walking outside at lunch breaks, I stopped and looked over the horizon, thinking of them. They were barely an hour away. It was only through a fluke of fate, I realized, that I was not in some refugee camp with them.

When I went back to the office, I had to silence these thoughts. There, I was just an employee in a software company, with projects, deadlines, and internal politics. There was an impenetrable wall between me and my colleagues. They had their homes, their jobs, their lives; few stopped to think of where the land that they lived or worked on had come from. It was this jarring sensation, of being in a huge graveyard while everyone else ignored the tombstones, that began to eat away at me, and that would eventually break my sad attempt to integrate.

At home in Fassouta, I could not find anyone who would understand. They were all born there, grew up there and knew nothing else except that reality. It was my problem; I was the misfit. And so, it seemed, were my cousins. Their return came to an abrupt end. In September 1997, my uncle enrolled them at the village school. They were welcomed by teachers and students alike, many of whom were our relatives. But, after the first day, my cousins came home in shock. They had heard the teachers yelling, seen the chaos and rowdiness. It was nothing like they had been used to, in London. My uncle told them to be patient and reminded them of how difficult it was when they had first moved there. But this was a starkly different reality, and they could not cope. 'Either you bring me my other school, or you send me back there!' the little one, Shadi, insisted.

My uncle and his wife thought about it. They knew that the children would have a far better education in England. 'I don't want them to grow up here, like cattle,' my uncle admitted to me, painfully. Finally, he and his wife decided that she would take them back, while he would stay in the village and travel to see them whenever he could.

For him, to go back to London was out of the question; he had waited for years to come home. He began to build his house on the same plot of land he had dreamt about, all those years before, in Beirut. He remained a PLO employee, working with the Planning Center in Gaza.

With that, he would never live with his family again; he would go back and forth to visit them, but his children would make a life for themselves in England, far from his home in Fassouta. Ammo felt his old pain, that he could never make a plan, never had a solid basis to plan from.

IV

One day, Lisa appeared at my office for our usual chat. I looked up gratefully from my screen. But she was flustered. 'I'm a bit worried about driving home these days,' she blurted out.

'Why?' Lisa lived in Atzmon, a Jewish community in the Galilee.

'Because of the recent troubles. Some Arabs have been throwing stones along the road.'

Arabs, I noticed, not Palestinians. The state had labored to negate our identity and had not used the word 'Palestinians' until after the Oslo Accords in 1994, and, even then, only to refer to Palestinians in the West Bank and Gaza, not to its own citizens. Even my father had used 'The Arabs' in the title of his book, all those years ago—so strong was the taboo on referring to ourselves as Palestinians.

It was the first time that Lisa had ever mentioned us. 'Troubles?' I echoed.

'A few Arab boys were working in Atzmon for a while, but some people were upset and made them leave. And for a few days now they've been throwing stones at our cars as we pass. It's really stressful!'

'Why were they fired?' I asked.

'Oh, you know …' she looked uncomfortable, waving her hand. 'Some people just don't want Arabs working in the community.'

'Oh.' I swallowed. Many Jewish communities did not allow Palestinians to work in them, and most did not allow them to live there, either. One of my cousins was a handyman at a kibbutz, but the likes of him were few. Most of these communities had a vetting procedure through an 'admissions committee', the decision of which was final. Some even began to require their applicants to swear loyalty to Zionist principles. A few Palestinians had gone to court to protest, but it was rare that they won.

Similarly, it was unthinkable for a Jew to live in a Palestinian village; those who did, to make a point, were usually welcomed by the Palestinian communities and largely shunned by their own. But they were, again, very few.

I looked at Lisa and wondered what her take was on this. But she was so agitated, she seemed oblivious to my thoughts. 'I'm calling my husband to be on standby, in case I need help. I'll do that before I leave!'

I nodded and she said a hasty goodbye and was gone. On my way home, I thought about her words as I passed Kfar Vradim, with its rows of neat villas, lush gardens, fountains, and wide pavements. The difference between Palestinian and Jewish communities, often lying next to each other, was so marked that anyone could immediately tell them apart. Palestinian villages had evolved over hundreds of years, before modern zoning and municipal planning. The new Jewish communities were built in a planned, methodical way, their homes neat copies of each other, like neighborhoods in the West. They seemed to have dropped from the sky, in place of the destroyed villages, and I only saw ugliness in all the beauty and order, because my mind unwittingly turned to how they came about.

But there was another reason for the stark difference. Fat state budgets for Jewish communities ensured that they would offer a standard of living to attract immigrants. Hundreds of Jewish localities had been built by Israel since its establishment, but not one new Palestinian village or town was created, and the existing ones were suffocated. Fassouta had 11,000 dunums within the jurisdiction of its local council, yet only a few hundred were approved by the government for building expansion. In every Palestinian village I visited, I saw the same picture, or worse: neglected, overcrowded ghettos, narrow streets full of potholes, a lack of amenities, no parks or public spaces, and a heavy, depressed atmosphere.

In the village, I was embarrassed to tell people about my work. I felt almost guilty for slipping through the net that would not let them through. My uncle, Nour, had worked in construction for thirty-five years and built half the state, in his words, but had endured racism, low pay, and harsh conditions. 'Very few Jews work in construction, you know why?' he told me. 'Because it's hard work, and dirty work, and you lose your health and don't see your family, and no one wants to do it. But we need work. We had our lands, they're gone. Even my kids, they go to university and end up working with me. They can't find work in the areas they studied.'

My heart broke as I looked at his withered face. 'You work at a good place, with decent hours,' he continued. 'Hold on to your job, you're very lucky that they keep you!'

'I think it's mostly my English, Uncle,' I murmured.

'English, French, whatever … Just hold on to your job! You get up at a normal time, dress nicely, work in a clean office all day. I've been up at dawn all my life, worked in heat and cold, been covered in sand and cement and slept in every dirty barracks this country has!'

I felt heavy the next morning as I stared into my screen. Lisa popped by to say hello, but I replied without much spirit. She did not seem to notice. 'Yesterday, some guys from the kibbutz called the police and they went after the boys! They weren't there this morning,' she said, in relief.

I decided to invite her and her husband to my home.

Raji was skeptical. With the exception of the few 'mixed' cities, Palestinians and Jews led segregated lives. We did not know how they lived, how they thought, any more than they did about us. References to Palestinians in the news were usually about 'terror'. I suspected that Lisa, and others in the office, thought I was some good 'exception'.

I was determined to break this wall. I prepared some of our tasty, traditional dishes, set the table and waited for her and her husband. It was the first time that I met him. He seemed somewhat dry and aloof, but I thought he would warm up when we got talking.

He did not. They liked the village and the food, but the conversation was strained and took a great deal of effort, nothing like the chatter and laughter I shared with Lisa at the office. Each topic I brought up received a lukewarm response, and they thanked us and left as quickly as possible.

I cleared the plates afterwards, feeling puzzled and deflated. Raji did not say much. At work, Lisa apologized, telling me that her husband had served in a high-ranking position in the Israeli army and was uncomfortable visiting an Arab home.

V

In the spring, my cousin gave us tickets to a concert for Land Day, the annual commemoration of 30 March 1976, when Israeli forces killed six Palestinians in demonstrations protesting the seizure of land. The concert was held in Kibbutz Kabri, half an hour's drive from Fassouta. Amal Murqus, a gentle singer, began with these sobering words: 'Our gathering today is a reminder of our life of contradictions. We are singing in a kibbutz, yet our songs are in commemoration of Land Day, on the remains of the Palestinian village of Kabri.'

The ghosts continued to haunt me. In the summer, Raji took me to Ayalon Canada Park, a popular picnicking spot near Jerusalem. It was huge, full of trees and ponds, and I was oblivious to its reality until I overheard a group of people near us. 'This park was built on the remains of three villages,' one of them was saying. 'In the 1967 war, the Israeli army destroyed Yalu, Imwas and Beit Nuba, and expelled their people.'

Thousands of pine trees were planted over the remnants of the villages. The evergreen trees were chosen over indigenous ones because they concealed the rubble, year-round. They also grew quickly, ensuring that people could not return.

I had to keep blocking these painful thoughts out in order to carry on in my small world. At Easter, I helped my mum to color the eggs and make date cookies. I loved the holidays, for the rituals spelled Palestine and our belonging to it, as though, for a brief while, I could forget the distress I felt. The mass was held in the small hours of the morning as we shivered and rubbed our hands together in church, which soon warmed up when we crowded inside. Afterwards, we spilled out into daybreak, wishing each other a happy holiday and scattering about the tiny roads to go home. A warm glow filled my heart.

The next day, we dressed in new clothes and did the rounds of family visits. The holidays were sweet, with everyone offering chocolates, brandy, and sugar-sprinkled cookies. By lunchtime, we barely had an appetite, but barbeques were lit up all over the village. During Lent, many families abstained from meat and dairy, and no one fired the grill. On Easter Sunday, the delicious smell of sizzling goat and pork drifted around the streets. We had spent the winter months huddled up, taking shelter from the biting wind that whipped across the mountains and seeped into our bones. Few people could afford central heating; we gathered around electric heaters or fireplaces, warmed by pots of chamomile and sage tea as we toasted cheese sandwiches and chestnuts. Now, the flowers were in bloom and our step was lighter.

Quickly, the summer was upon us, a season when we mostly lived outside. Families and neighbors gathered on porches and under trees, eating sunflower seeds and watermelon and gossiping about the latest news and weddings. There were also food storage rituals for winter. We boiled and ground freshly harvested wheat to make bulgur. Over several weeks, a large cauldron was taken from home to home and placed over a fire all day, to give the large sacks of wheat that were emptied into it time to cook. The women sampled some seeds from time to time, chewing them thoughtfully to see that they had reached just the desired state and no more, so as not to turn into mush in the grinding. Finally, the cauldron was removed from the fire by two or three men and tilted over a large sieve for the water to drain. The wheat was then spread out on large sheets on the roof. Birds pounced on it, gleefully, but they could only eat so much. It took several days for the wheat to dry so it could be taken to the stone press. We kept the same rituals from my father's childhood in the village: after the wheat was removed, delicious sweet and savory flatbreads were baked on the fire.

There were vegetables and herbs to store for the cold months, when they were out of season. Women gathered to pick mloukhieh, a leaf eaten in stews. The custom was to go from family to family, helping each other. I sat with them, grasping bunches of the soft twigs, picking the dark green, slightly coarse leaves and piling them in bowls as we chatted. Next came okra, or bamieh, which had to be cleaned from its stub, washed, and dried for storage, and was a favorite in a tomato stew with goat meat. We collected wild thyme and plucked its tiny leaves, our hands smelling of the herb for hours after, then ground it and added sesame and sumac to make za'atar. For a treat, we picked carobs and made thick, sweet syrup. I was gaining weight, unable to resist all this.

For a while, I seemed to fit in. There was something warm and cozy about strolling down the road for coffee with an aunt, being invited into homes, chatting with a cousin at the grocery store. I still felt people's looks of curiosity, heard them asking each other who I was, nodding and dissecting me with their eyes. Rania visited me when she came to see her parents in the village. I became close to another cousin, as well, and to a neighbor, who was from Mi'ilya and had married in Fassouta. But I felt like a lone ship at sea. Hebrew was everywhere, including, to my dismay, in our dialect. Our identity was a warped mutation between Palestinian and Israeli; we were a minority struggling to survive, while trying to hold on to its own fabric. I noticed that we referred to Israel as '*al-blad*', in Arabic—the country. We could not say 'Palestine', but, often, we avoided saying 'Israel', too. There were no links to the Arab world; they had been cut off by decades of prohibition. I struggled to understand this community and to fit in.

VI

As my third Christmas in the village drew near, Rania and I decided to go shopping for new outfits. I took her in my old car and we chattered happily, listening to Arabic tapes. But our carefree mini-reality faded, as it always did, the minute we entered the mall. We walked into a shop and felt that familiar nervousness associated with speaking our language. As we looked around, our voices dropped. Seeing an assistant, I pointed to a dress and, switching to Hebrew, asked her for the right size to try. 'Last items!' she snapped and walked away.

I turned away, uncomfortably, but we were not surprised by the response. Israeli society simmered over a hotbed of violence that spilled over into daily life and the smallest situations. Initially, I thought it was just some individuals. Maybe the clerk at the post office was having a bad day, or the shop assistant was tired. But there was a thick atmosphere of tension just waiting to snap. People were often sullen. They did not smile. When settling a dispute, they frequently raised their voices and behaved with a sense of entitlement.

'Do you still want the dress?' Rania's voice jolted me back. A more cheery-looking assistant had come up to help, and we were grateful.

I tried it on. 'Wow!' the assistant exclaimed, as I came out of the fitting room. I knew she wanted to sell, but I smiled, nonetheless. Then, she added: 'You're so beautiful, one would never think you were an Arab!'

I gave back the dress and walked out with my cousin. It was not possible to live for even one day without being reminded that we were us and they were them—and that we may never be accepted as equal to them. In most of my interactions with Israelis, I felt a thinly veiled hostility, cautious suspicion, or, in the best case, an attitude of grudging tolerance of us, the natives, towards whom they were being generous in allowing us to stay on our land.

As we lined up for burgers, I glanced curiously at the Jewish family near us, crowding at the shawarma stall. I wondered how it was that Palestinians did not seem to exist in this country, but our food was so sought after. The shawarma had a kosher label, too. We were bending over backwards trying to integrate, but the state would have been happier if we just worked our falafel and shawarma stalls and faded into the background after that.

To add to my irritation, I was beginning to notice that much of our culture had been appropriated by Israeli Jews, who were immigrants from many countries and had no unifying culture of their own. Our staple foods, such as falafel, hummus, and shakshuka, were marketed as 'Israeli food'. The intricate designs of our kufiyyeh and thobe, the Palestinian traditional dress, popped up on scarves, handbags and jewelry. Much of Israeli music sounded Arabic, with the distinctive darbuka drum accompanied by Hebrew lyrics. Even the Hebrew curses were versions of ours.

They had taken not just the country, but everything else, too.

VII

At work the next day, I asked Vladimir for a blank CD from his office supplies. 'They're in my top desk drawer. Help yourself,' he smiled, heading past me to a meeting.

I opened the drawer. Moving some stuff around, I saw they were at the back. Then, I noticed a small, wooden cross. I picked it up, briefly, and put it down again, in confusion. Why was he keeping a cross in his belongings?

Many Russian immigrants to Israel in the 1990s were not Jews, it turned out.[2] Some came to the country by marriage to Jews; others claimed to be Jewish to escape difficult conditions in the ex-Soviet Union. I was startled to see some of them wearing crosses at the mall or on the beach. That was bold, I thought.

I did not mention it to Vladimir. It was none of my business.

Later that day, I came out of a meeting in which Natasha had barely said a word. I followed her into her office. 'What's wrong?' I asked. She was usually quiet, but she had seemed more down in the dumps lately.

'Nothing,' she replied, with a tight smile. 'I'm OK.'

'No, you're not,' I smiled. 'Is something bothering you at work?'

'No ...' She sat down, sighed, and her eyes clouded over. 'I'm just a little ... lonely.'

'Lonely? You don't have friends?'

'I do, but they're all in the Russian community, and most of them have problems like mine.'

'Well, what about others? Have you tried?'

'I don't feel welcome. It's suffocating, you know, because all the Russians stick together, and if I try to make friends with others, like mothers at my children's school ... Well, I don't feel welcome.'

'Maybe it's just the beginning,' I tried to comfort her, realizing how bizarre the situation was.

'It's so expensive, too!' she fumed. 'I can barely make ends meet. The kids are growing all the time, they need new things. I need to pay for their books, clothes, outings ... I struggle just to get to the month's end.'

'Their father?' I asked. Natasha was not open about her personal life. She must have been having a really bad day to blurt it out like this.

'He doesn't care. He's not here,' she said, flicking her hand.

'I'm sorry ...' I ventured. It was an odd exchange, too, because Natasha seemed to have no idea of who I was or who the Palestinians were. She was swamped in her problems and seemed to be more overwhelmed by her move to Israel than I was. The only time her eyes lit up is when she spoke about anything Russian. I had a feeling she would leave, again, perhaps when her children were older.

A new programmer joined us that month. Tamar was my age, but taller, darker, and with silky, black hair down to her waist. Hair was the first thing we spoke about.

Tamar was an Indian Jew whose parents had immigrated to Israel twenty years before. Her fiancé was a Jew of German origin. The couple loved each other, but their relationship was strained due to tension between their families. Tamar was struggling, as it was clear that her boyfriend's family was not too pleased with his choice. Her parents were reacting in hurt pride, wondering why their daughter could not marry one of their own and not subject them to this indignity. The couple began to fight. 'Nothing I do is good enough!' Tamar exclaimed. 'I wish we could marry and live alone and not have to deal with his family or mine!'

Black immigrants, mostly Jews from Ethiopia, had it tough, too. They were referred to as 'kushim', a derogatory term meaning curly African hair. Scandalous reports filled the Israeli media about their treatment. They were pushed to live in segregated areas and given the most menial jobs, and their children did not attend schools with white people.

Palestinians were on the bottom of the social ladder. The older generation remembered the years of military rule and oppression. They had lived under a thick blanket of intimidation. For decades, they had stopped referring to themselves as Palestinians. Instead, we had a great oxymoron of a label: 'Israeli Arabs'. People in Fassouta reacted either with bewildered silence or acute discomfort when I mentioned Palestine. Even when we spoke of our inferior standing, they only saw it from the angle of work and their immediate problems. They had to be part of the Israeli system in order to survive. For the younger generation, born after the creation of Israel, this system was all they knew.

The village became suffocating to me. On top of that, my job was boring; the great start I had been so grateful for had wilted as I found myself in monotonous software work and began to realize it was not for me. I struggled in my marriage, my inner discord growing by the day. My relationship with my extended family was also changing. The overjoyed welcome we got after we arrived had become chance encounters in the street, polite, hasty greetings, and invitations to visit that were often quickly forgotten. But one could not be a guest forever.

Mum had settled back in, and she often dropped in to see me. My uncle, Geris, had asked for leave from the PLO and decided to run for head of the local council in the village. In 1998, he won the elections jointly with another candidate and they split the five-year term between them. In 1999, after four years of going back and forth to Gaza, my father moved, too, to East Jerusalem. Arafat wanted to reestablish the Palestine Research Center there. A building was found, with a top-floor apartment that Dad could live in, and a few staff were employed to get things up and running again. Mum began to accompany him, sometimes, and spend her time between there and the village.

Everyone was finding their way, and I still had to find mine.

VIII

I groped for solutions in the only area I felt I could change: my work. With a degree in computer science, my options were limited; for the humanities, which I wanted to go into, I had to start all over again. Business seemed to be a middle ground. I applied for an MBA at the University of Strathclyde in Glasgow and got a scholarship for tuition fees. But I could not afford to go abroad, so I enrolled to study by correspondence. The first box of books arrived in January 2000. I was not sure how I was going to keep up around my job, but I spoke to my manager, Danny, and he was supportive. I had changed department, and, like my previous boss, Danny was always calm, no matter how many deadlines loomed. It made it easier to juggle work and my studies. But I did not have a moment to spare. I worked from nine to five, came home to cook and do housework, then sat down with the books. Evenings and holidays were crammed. In some ways, I was running away from my situation, from having to think.

Raji helped with some housework. Soon, I began to hear voices of disapproval. 'A man hanging laundry?' my grandmother exclaimed. The neighbors tut-tutted when they saw him through the kitchen window, doing the dishes. Thankfully, neither of us paid much attention. My bigger problem was the interruptions. The village had an 'open door' policy, I joked ruefully to Danny. Anyone could knock on the door at any time of day or evening to visit. My aunts or cousins often showed up to chat, exchange recipes and have the odd bit of gossip. It was great, but I had to study, and I needed space.

I talked to Raji about renting an apartment in Nahariya. It was only a half hour from Fassouta and the same distance from my work as the village. It was also closer to his work in Haifa. He was reluctant, for we would have to pay rent, but I told him it would only be until I finished my degree. I also wanted to get out of the village, try something new. We drove around the town, looking for rental signs. On a building near the beach, we were stunned to see a handwritten notice: *'No dogs, no Arabs.'*

We stood there, staring at it. It was not new. The ink had faded, and the cardboard was worn at the edges. It had been hanging there for some time, I thought.

We drove through the nearby streets and stopped to ask at apartment buildings, but they told us openly that they did not rent to Arabs. There was no apology and it was said unabashedly, like a simple fact. We left the area, thinking it would be too expensive, anyway. On the outskirts of town, we stopped at a group of buildings that we had often driven past. They were brand new and still being finished, and were very different from the cramped, ugly structures that filled the country. The location was perfect, halfway between the village and Nahariya. We would be near our work, our families, and the city at the same time. We parked and quickly found the office.

'Yes?' the janitor enquired, cautiously.

'Good morning!' Raji said, as brightly as he could. 'We're looking for an apartment to rent!'

His accent gave him away. She looked uncomfortable. We were used to this, so we just smiled and pretended not to notice. She fiddled with a bunch of keys and escorted us out of the office, towards one of the buildings. 'We have one here ...' she said.

One? The compound was almost empty, I thought.

I was a little disappointed when she opened the door. The apartment was bright and new, but it was very small. 'Do you have anything bigger?' I enquired.

'No, this is all that's available.'

At least it was closer to Fassouta, I told myself, suddenly feeling disappointed that we could not find a place near the beach. 'How much is the rent?'

'Uh, I need to ask you something, first. Where are you from?'

This being Israel, we did not think of the inappropriateness of the question. 'Fassouta. It's a village about twenty minutes from here. Near Ma'alot,' Raji ventured, in reference to the Jewish town near us. Mentioning other Palestinian towns would have been useless.

'Right ...' she nodded, frowning. 'I need to ask you, then, to bring two references with your application, then I'd have to check with the neighbors.'

'The neighbors?'

'I have to be straight with you ... I don't think the owners want to rent to Arabs. And the neighbors might give you trouble. But I'll try to push your application through and see what happens. Do you have references, anyone we can ask about you?'

We turned on our heels and walked out.

In some ways, it was easier if one wanted to buy. Some Jewish homeowners did not care and sold to anyone who paid. But this sometimes upset other neighbors. One of my cousins and her husband had no land to build on, and they bought a small apartment in Haifa with a mortgage, which his modest income was just enough to pay back. I went to visit her in the tiny place and felt sorry for her three, small children cooped up in it. This was the best they could do, though, and she tried to make it a good home. I casually asked how the neighbors were. She told me that several Jewish families had sold their apartments and left after her family and two other Palestinian families had moved in.

'Are you serious?' I gaped.

'Yes. They were gone very quickly.'

The segregation was entrenched by the state and accentuated each side's fear and suspicion of the other. Intermarriages were practically non-existent. Many Israeli Jews opposed them as 'miscegenation', and there was no civil marriage in Israel. Couples of mixed religions had to go abroad to get married, usually in Cyprus, and apply for the marriage to be recognized in Israel on their return.

My brother was living in a shared apartment in Haifa. He had graduated a year before from the London School of Economics. Despite the university's standing, he could not find a good job in Israel. He worked with small Palestinian NGOs, but the pay was low and there were no prospects. 'I'm thinking of going back to England,' he told me.

We were having coffee at my house. 'It would be nice to leave ...' I nodded.

'Why don't you apply to Canada?'

'What?'

'It's accepting immigration. I saw it on their government's website. Just go online and fill out a few forms to see if you qualify.'

Canada. It was a faraway place and I did not know much about it, but it was probably similar to the United States, I mused. Cyprus and England needed work permits to move back there. It could not hurt to try the Canada option, if it was formal immigration. I found the website and did the pre-assessment. I had all the needed points!

The information was encouraging. The country needed professional workers and accepted thousands of immigrants each year.

Jobs were plentiful and the standard of living was among the highest in the world. The conditions for acceptance were easy: knowledge of English or French, a good education, and some work experience. I spoke to Raji and he got excited. 'You mean, they have a lot of work there?' he asked.

Yes, I told him, that was what the website said. He could probably find a good job and establish a career.

We went to the Canadian Embassy in Tel Aviv. The clerk took our forms and told us it would take up to two years to get an answer.

Two years? My heart sank. I had to find a way out, in the meantime.

IX

Tension was rising in the country. After seven years of the 'peace process', none of its promises had been fulfilled. Negotiations dragged on, with no end in sight. In June 2000, Israeli prime minister Ehud Barak put forth an unacceptable proposal: the division of the West Bank into three parts, keeping the Jewish settlements in place and preventing the establishment of a Palestinian state. A month later, US president Bill Clinton called Barak and Arafat to a peace summit at Camp David. The aim was to reach a final agreement, but the offer was not viable for the Palestinians. The issues of borders, Jerusalem, dismantling of settlements, and refugees were all unresolved. The Clinton administration was quick to blame Arafat for the failure of the summit, and the Israeli government insisted there was no 'partner for peace'. Arafat began to understand that the Israelis did not intend to follow through on the Oslo Accords. In private, he began to tell his confidants: 'They tricked us!'

On 28 September 2000, despite warnings from Palestinian officials, Israeli Likud party leader Ariel Sharon charged into the grounds of al-Aqsa Mosque (the Temple Mount) in Jerusalem, with a delegation of his right-wing party and hundreds of members of the security forces. Sharon occupied a particularly painful place in Palestinian memory due to his involvement in the invasion of Beirut, the Sabra and Shatila massacre, and his lifetime record of violence against Palestinians. Their fury erupted. In the ensuing riots, the Israeli police killed seven civilians. It was the outbreak of the second uprising, al-Aqsa Intifada. The violence spread as the police confronted unarmed protestors. In two days, twenty Palestinians were killed, including twelve-year-old Mohammed al-Durra, who was shot in Gaza as he crouched behind his father in terror.

Palestinians in Israel took to the streets. The security forces suppressed them with live ammunition and rubber bullets. Thirteen young men were killed in the Galilee.

Israeli forces moved in to reoccupy the Palestinian territory, in violation of the Oslo Accords. This time, the intifada was armed, and Palestinian factions resorted to suicide bombings in Israel. Quickly, the uprising took a much deadlier turn.

I was taking the train to Tel Aviv to sit my Master's exams at the British Council. Scores of soldiers were on board, with their guns, and talk of the clashes was everywhere. I sank in my seat, trying to revise my notes.

I stayed with my father at his apartment in East Jerusalem. The Research Center was up and running, though with a small staff—even smaller than that in Cyprus. It was risky to place Palestinian institutions in the city, Arafat knew, but he wanted to make a point of sovereignty and of East Jerusalem being the capital of a future Palestinian state. For my father, it was business as usual, but I was worried about him. The clashes were everywhere. Palestinians were at a low; it was much worse to have their hopes dashed after the wave of optimism that had marked the peace accords. 'I knew, I suspected,' Dad told me, solemnly, 'that Israel would not follow through. As soon as the right wing came back to power, I knew.'

X

It had taken me a year to finish the first term of studies, and I was exhausted. I had saved some money and I decided to go to Scotland to finish the degree. Raji was supportive. He had seen my struggle trying to juggle everything, and he told me to go.

I resigned from my job. My colleagues wished me well but were sorry to see me leave. At this point, I was skeptical about my friendships at work. Another Palestinian had joined, a young graduate of the Technion. He flatly refused to talk about anything relating to us or the situation. I understood. The price we had to pay for success was to be seen as 'cooperative', not to bring up such issues or to be politically involved. Other colleagues were civil to us, but, as the tension thickened in the country, the taboos on our conversations were reinforced. It was remarkable, I discovered, how we could open up about work, family, health, relationships, all sorts of personal issues, but how there was a silent agreement never to broach certain topics. The intifada raged, the death toll climbed, but the thick wall of silence remained, so loud it was deafening.

My friendship with Lisa ended abruptly. She came to me one day and blurted: 'Why do people cause trouble? What's the point of clashing with the police, who are trying to keep law and order? Why can't we all just live and let live?'

As much as I loved her, I could not keep silent any longer. After she left, I found myself writing a long email. I explained our feelings of loss and alienation, our anger and frustration. I sent it to her and went home.

Raji gasped. 'What! Are you crazy? Do you want to be arrested?'

'Why would they do that?' I asked, in sudden alarm.

'Because you can't write things like that! God knows how she could use it against you! She can give it to the police and accuse you of harassing her! Do you want us running after you in the courts?'

My eyes widened in fear. 'But, she wouldn't do that ...' I began, feebly.

He cut in. 'Is this woman still at the office?'

'What?' I looked at my watch. 'Yes. She usually leaves at about six. Why?'

'We're going back. Come,' he motioned, grabbing the car keys.

'What?'

'You have to go back! And apologize, and get her to delete the email!'

'Aren't we blowing this out of proportion?' I asked. But, seeing him so agitated, I panicked, too. He drove me straight back. The office was quiet. Most people had left. I went upstairs to her office, my heart pounding. 'Hi, Lisa,' I ventured.

She turned around, surprised to see me. Her face was deeply flushed.

'Hi, Fida. I got your email.'

'Lisa, I'm sorry ...' I began.

'It's OK ...' she said. But it did not look OK at all. She went on, her voice terse. 'Fida, I think you should consider psychological counseling.'

'What?'

'You have a lot of anger issues and you definitely need to speak to someone to sort them out.'

I bit back my rage and nodded, tears of humiliation glistening in my eyes. 'Can you please delete it?'

'Yes, no problem.' I saw her delete it on her screen. Then she looked at me and attempted a smile. I just nodded and left.

We did not speak again until a few weeks later, when I said good-bye. She wished me the best, but it was a hollow farewell. It hurt to think of how close we had been, yet, in the most important way, she had never understood me.

I was touched by a gesture from Danny. He had been very supportive over the last year. Twice, before my exams, he had actually sent me home to study. Now, he gave me a card. He wrote that he was very proud of me for taking this step, which required a lot of courage, and wished me the best.

I gazed at the words with a lump in my throat. But, as soon as I left the building, reality hit like a ton of bricks. I kept Danny's card, put everything behind me and flew to Glasgow.

13

NOWHERE TO TURN

From the point of view of hits, I have the most. In my battalion they would say: 'Look, here comes the killer.' When I came back from the field, they would ask, 'Well, how many today?' You have to understand that before we showed up, knees were the hardest thing to rack up. There was a story about one sniper who had 11 knees all told, and people thought no one could outdo him. And then I brought in seven—eight knees in one day. Within a few hours, I almost broke his record.

Israeli sniper
Gaza Strip[1]

I

My stress and agitation at Ben Gurion Airport began before its series of entry checkpoints and nerve-wracking procedures. They began with its very name. David Ben-Gurion was the founder and first prime minister of Israel, one of its pioneers of violence and racism against Palestinians and certainly not someone I wanted to remember each time I flew. But his name, and the names of the founders of Zionism and of Israel's most notorious war generals, were given to major streets in every Israeli city.

I took a deep breath as I was pounced on by the first agent. She asked me where I was going, flicked through my passport and told me to stand in line. This line did not lead to the check-in counter. It led to security, the first stop in a series of stations. I waited for 45 minutes until it was my turn. Two more agents pounced. 'Hello, Madam,' said one, in Hebrew. 'I'm here to ask you some questions for security purposes.'

Did I pack my own bags?

When did I pack them?

Did anyone give me anything to take with me?

Did I make any stops between leaving home and arriving at the airport?

Do I have firearms, ammunition or any sharp objects?

My bags then went through the scanning machines and were cleared. But, as they came out on the conveyor belt, the agents put a yellow sticker on each of them, which alerted security at the next stop. This was only done to Palestinian passengers and to some foreigners, not to Israeli Jews.

The same agents popped up again, and one of them took me aside. She opened my passport, and I almost saw her gaze fixate on my place of birth, Lebanon.

'Where do you live?' she asked, flicking through the pages.

'Fassouta.'

'Where?' she finally looked up at me.

'Fassouta. In the Galilee.'

'Where in the Galilee?'

'Near Ma'alot.'

'How long have you lived there?'

'Six years.'

'And before that?'

'Cyprus.'

'What were you doing in Cyprus?'

'I went to school.'

'Your family was with you?'

'Yes.'

'What does your father do?'

'He's a lawyer.'

'Why are you going to England?'

'Scotland. I'm going back to university.'

'What will you study?'

'Business.'

'Where?'

'Strathclyde University.'

'Where …?'

'Strathclyde. In Glasgow.'

'Do you have any papers to prove this?'

'Yes.' I produced my acceptance letter, which she inspected.

'Do you still have family in Lebanon?' I knew this would come up.

'No.'

'Do you have contact with anyone in Lebanon?'

'No.'

'You don't have family or friends there still?' They also repeated their questions, presumably to catch people off-guard.

'No.'

'When did you leave there?'

'1983.'

'You have no relatives or friends still living there?'

'No. I don't.' I willed myself to stay calm.

'What family do you have in Fassouta?'

'My husband, and all my family.'

'Meaning?'

'My father, mother, and brother.'

'You have other family there? Uncles, aunts?'

'Yes.'

'Why didn't you mention them?'

I blinked. 'I thought you were talking about my parents.'

'Was anyone else with you in Lebanon?'

'No.' I opted to leave out my uncle's story.

'What do you do for work?'

'I was a software tester.'

'Where did you work?'

'In a company in Tefen, an industrial park.'

'What is the name of this company? Do you have their contact details?'

'Yes.' I produced a card, which was still in my purse. She scrutinized it and gave it back to me.

'What did you do there?'

'I worked as a software tester.' *As I just told you.*

'What does your husband do?'

'He works in construction.'

'Your father?'

'He's a lawyer.'

'And your mother?'

'She's at home.'

'And your brother?'

'A student.'

It went on and on. If I was wanted for a criminal offence, I would have been called to the police and charged, not questioned randomly at the airport. This was, supposedly, only about the safety of the flight. The other agent joined her and they began repeating the questions. I took a deep breath and said: 'You've already asked me that.'

'We just want to make sure that you haven't forgotten anything.'

That was highly unlikely, given that we had gone over them about five times. My answers trickled down to monosyllables. Finally, the first agent said: 'Please follow me.'

We arrived at a special search area. I was told to wait until a counter freed up. There were ten counters, at which agents were rummaging through people's luggage. I stood and waited, looking at the expressions of those around me. The Palestinians showed silent agitation or anger; the foreigners, complete bewilderment.

Eventually, the agent beckoned me to an empty slot, where I was asked to haul my bags onto the metal table and open them. A gloved man began taking out each item, feeling it, and putting it aside. He passed a small detector around all my toiletries. Then he passed it around the inside of my bags, unzipped each pocket in them, and did the same. The bags were left empty, as they were when I had taken them out to pack the night before. My hairdryer and alarm clock were set aside for further scanning.

Jewish passengers sailed past on their way to the check-in counters. The agent suddenly said: 'We want to open this, to scan it.'

'What?' I frowned. It was a bag of ground Arabic coffee. 'If you open it and put detectors in it, you'll ruin it! Might as well throw it away.'

He appeared to consider this and said: 'OK, we'll scan it from outside.'

'You're already done that,' I snapped. But it was whisked off.

It took another twenty minutes as I sat and waited. For this reason, Palestinian passengers always came to the airport several hours before their flights. Once the agents were done, they piled my things back in the bags and asked for my help in closing them. The bag of coffee, my hairdryer and clock reappeared, with yellow stickers on them. My stuff was all jumbled; there was no time to fold and put it back properly and I began cramming it into the bags, as the gloved people watched and offered to help. But, when they touched my things, they incensed me even more. I looked up at the agent as I tried to zip up my bag, conscious of time ticking and that I really had to rush to the gate now. 'Why do you do this?' I demanded. It was a struggle to keep the anger from my voice.

He was taken aback for a second, then the automatic expression returned. 'For your security, Madam.'

'So why don't you do it to everyone?'

'We do.'

'No, you don't! You don't do it to Jewish passengers!'

He had no answer.

As simple as that. He said nothing.

The first agent returned and escorted me to the check-in counter. She stayed with me right through to passport control and to my gate. I wanted to shop at the duty-free zone, but she was not letting me out of her sight. At the gate, I sat down to wait, and she stood a short distance away, chatting with the clerk at the desk. I got up to the vending machine to get a bottle of water. Thirty seconds later, the agent bore down on me. 'Why did you leave your seat?'

'To get this!' I said, lifting the bottle.

'Please tell me if you need anything and I will get it for you. Stay in your seat.'

Only when we were called and I gave my boarding pass to the clerk and began to walk down the passageway to the plane, did they leave me alone.

II

At Heathrow, before taking my transfer flight, I began to breathe more easily. I felt mildly surprised when people were nice or courteous, realizing how novel this was to me now.

I arrived in Glasgow to a snowstorm. I had forgotten the British winters, and I had a very abrupt reminder: the January days ended in the early afternoons as sheets of rain pelted down and frost covered the sidewalks. My class had more than thirty student nationalities. It was just as demanding as my year of correspondence, but the experience was much richer than that of my first degree. We were not fledglings out of high school; everyone was older, with work and life experience. I was back in the tradition of the British pub, finding comfort in its warm lunches to escape the bitter cold and smiling at the trip down memory lane.

I lived in student halls, downtown, with four flatmates. The two Chinese girls kept to themselves and had a large crowd of Asian friends. I became close to Angela, a Colombian exchange student. She was a devout Catholic with sweet, broken English, who was always cooking soup. We were entertained by our fourth flatmate, Anjana, an Indian who told us tales of being set up with future husbands through palm and card readings, and we spent hours in the kitchen, laughing and drinking wine as our course assignments piled up.

But I soon found that my savings would run out faster than I had thought. Raji could not support me on his meager salary. As a student, I was allowed to work for a certain number of hours per week. I had an idea, and I printed out my CV and went to the computer science department at the university.

I explained to the receptionist that I was looking for work, and, to my surprise, she told me to take a seat and wait. A few minutes later, she returned with a professor, who invited me back to his office. It turned out he was running a European Union project and needed a coordinator for a few hours per week.

It was perfect. I walked back to the dormitory, not believing my luck. He even arranged to loan me a computer from the department so I could work from my room. It was a godsend, for I was able to do my assignments, as well, without the hassle of going to the computer room on campus. At the time, few students had laptops.

Being in a normal country lifted my spirits, filled me with joie de vivre and hope. I was appreciated as a human being, and I felt relaxed and surrounded by opportunities to thrive. Raji gave me snippets of news over the phone but I was not interested. As far as I was concerned, the place had ceased to exist until I returned.

Yet, even as I dreaded the moment, the months flew by and I soon found myself on a plane back home. There was no space for a quiet transition. Six months earlier, in March 2001, Ariel Sharon had come to power as Israeli prime minister and begun his term with a military campaign in the Palestinian territory. Hamas and other Islamic factions continued their suicide attacks in Israel, which blamed Arafat and retaliated with disproportionate force against Palestinian towns and villages. Hundreds of homes were demolished; thousands of dunums of agricultural land were seized. The territory suffered frequent closures and curfews. Food and medicine ran short. Education, healthcare, and other services were heavily disrupted. The death toll was climbing at a rate five times higher among Palestinians. It was the bloodiest period of fighting since the 1948 war.

In the village, I was really depressed. I had no money and my job prospects were dismal. There was no word from the Canadian Embassy and we had no idea how much longer it would take. It was coming up to two years. Raji enrolled in an evening marketing course in Haifa. 'I need a decent job,' he told me. 'I can't do this anymore.' Twice a week, he commuted to his classes after work and came home at midnight, exhausted.

My father's work also took a hit. The Israeli authorities closed a number of Palestinian institutions in East Jerusalem, chief among them the Orient House and the Palestine Research Center. They sealed the Center with red tape, with all the computers, office equipment and documents inside. The staff had just finished preparing the first reissue of *Palestine Affairs* when they found themselves unable to access the building. My father then went to work in Ramallah. He spent much of his time in al-Muqata'a, Arafat's headquarters.

In December 2001, Israel announced that Arafat's movements from Ramallah were solely at its discretion. Israeli tanks and military vehicles besieged al-Muqata'a. At Christmas, he was prevented from leaving to participate in the mass at Bethlehem, as he did every year. Two months later, Israeli helicopters fired missiles at a building in al-Muqata'a compound. In March, helicopters and naval gunships destroyed al-Muntada, Arafat's headquarters in Gaza. He remained under siege in Ramallah.

In Israel, the atmosphere was charged with tension. I spent days on the couch. I had never felt so low or listless. I did not want to face the world or make any decisions. I did not even want to go out to the village to buy milk.

Then, a large white envelope came in the mail. We had been accepted for immigration to Canada.

III

After the initial high, we realized we had a serious obstacle. We needed 11,000 dollars in savings in order to get our visas. This was a requirement to support ourselves during our move and setup. The offer was valid for two years, otherwise we would lose the option. I panicked. I had to find a job, and fast!

My previous workplace had long filled my position and did not have any vacancies. I spent every day at the computer, sending applications to any jobs I could find. For months, there was not a single response. I had hit total desperation when I saw a posting for brand managers in an online marketing company. They needed fluent English, and I got a call.

I drove to Karmiel, about an hour away, and met the marketing manager, Samantha, and her subordinate, Tom. She had immigrated from Britain a few months before. He had come from Australia. We chatted in English; they seemed impressed and asked me to start a few days later. Relief washed over me as I went home. I prepared, mentally, for the reality of being in an Israeli workplace again, telling myself it would be temporary.

But, when I started, it was worse than I thought. People were cold and unfriendly. I tried to strike up conversations with my colleagues, and a few kept their smiles, even after finding out that I was Palestinian. But most of them turned away. Groups of employees passed by every day on their way to the lunchroom. No one asked me to join them. It was as if they did not see me. When I greeted them, I got no reply. At the coffee machine, they looked at me with blank faces and turned their backs. If Tom had not spoken to me from time to time, I would have thought I was invisible.

Then, one of my teammates, a blonde girl with shining blue eyes, came up to me. Sofia was a Swede who had come to the country in her teens and married an Israeli. She was gentle and serene, and we liked each other immediately.

Karmiel was built on land confiscated from three Palestinian villages: Deir el-Assad, Bi'neh, and Nahaf. I tried to push this fact from my mind, but it popped up as I drove to the town each morning and again as I left it in the afternoon. Karmiel was touted as a model of new development. It was awarded the Beautiful Israel Prize and the Kaplan Prize for Management and Services. When it was first built, Palestinians were prohibited from living in it—my father had faced a police officer with this fact as he was being driven to exile in Safad, all those years ago. Like Upper Nazareth, Karmiel was part of the project to 'Judaize the Galilee', as was Ma'alot, near Fassouta.

Yet, life had its own turns. All of these towns, built to be fortresses of 'Judaization', ended up with a quarter to a third of Palestinian residents. Young Arab couples, facing housing shortages in their own communities, began to buy homes from their Jewish owners.

The new company where I worked was largely staffed by recent immigrants, mostly young, zealous Zionists from the United States, Canada, and Britain who had performed 'aliyah' to fulfil their dream of living in 'the Jewish state'. I was amazed at how they had barely been in the country for a year, but they were already Israelis. Two weeks into the job, Samantha called me to her office. She smiled as I sat down. 'I'm very happy with your work, Fida. I'm sure you'll be a great asset to the team!'

'Thanks, Samantha.'

The smile shrank a bit. 'I just wanted to ask how things are going, personally.'

'Sorry?'

'I mean, do you fit in with the others? Are you feeling OK here?'

'Yes.' I briefly imagined telling her how I really felt.

'I just thought this may be overwhelming for you, with the different culture ...' she continued, fiddling with her pen. 'And I don't want any problems to develop between people.'

I blushed. So I had been called in to discuss the 'problem' of my being Palestinian, I gathered. 'It's fine,' I said, keeping it short.

'I'm just aware that you may have different political views ...'

I stared. This woman was British. How could she question me about this *at work?*

'Samantha, I'm aware that everyone here is Israeli, and I'm also aware that people have different views. That's fine. I'm here to work.'

To my astonishment, she launched into a political monologue, telling me that I did not appreciate their point of view, that it was important to understand that Israel's security was always at risk, that they lived in a difficult climate and were surrounded by enemies—who seemed, I felt, to include me. I stared, open-mouthed. She was waiting for me to reply. Bristling, I answered that Israel had no qualms about maintaining its oppression of Palestinians and using violence for years with no end in sight. She looked at me pointedly and, holding her pen still, delivered her final blow.

'But you Arabs have the concept of jihad ...'

I drew a sharp breath. *You Arabs?*

Amazingly, she did not appear to notice. I strained to keep my voice normal. 'Samantha, jihad is a religious concept, but in its more general, everyday use, it means to defend one's country and people.' An alarm bell was ringing loudly in my head that this was no topic to launch into at work!

'Right, right,' she said, shuffling some papers in front of her. When she looked up again, her smile was more fixed. 'Well, good luck with the job, and let me know if you need anything!'

I nodded and walked out, tension clamping my stomach. When I returned to my desk, an instant message popped up on my screen. 'Is everything OK?'

It was Sofia. 'Yes,' I messaged back. She asked if I wanted to have lunch. We walked down to the cafeteria and she introduced me to Eva, a Hungarian Jew who had immigrated and had also married a local. Eva was very funny. She was a cynic who made fiery comments about everything and was politically incorrect on every level. I laughed with them and did not mention the exchange with Samantha.

Still, they were my only small circle. Each morning, as I walked into the office and greeted the secretary, Jen, I received no reply. I found myself telling my new friends. 'Jen will simply not talk to me. It's embarrassing. I don't know whether I should just walk past her and not say anything, but I can't do that, either! She's right at the front of the office!'

Jen was a recent immigrant from Canada. I noticed that she was very friendly and all smiles with everyone, though her Hebrew could best be described as awful. With me, she would not exchange a single word.

Eva explained. 'You've created a big problem for her.'

'What?'

'You were educated abroad, your English is fluent, you hold a higher position than hers, you make more money than she does, and she can't handle it. You're not the Arab she's been told about, the backward, illiterate savage who lives in a tent and keeps camels. She doesn't know what box to put you in.'

The Russians, too, scowled and refused to talk to me. *Fine*, I thought, remembering my two friends at Tefen and wondering at the difference. In time, though, I noticed that the Russians here were like that towards everyone. They stuck together at breaks, smoking and speaking their language. Their Hebrew was terrible, with a thick, heavy accent that they could not seem to get rid of. I noticed, too, that the others generally avoided them, and it was then that I felt sorry for them. They must have been going through similar feelings to mine, I thought, wondering where they had landed and how to cope with life in this frigid, forbidding place. They probably would not have come here if they had had a decent life elsewhere.

But all my sympathy was useless. During my whole year at the company, the Russians refused to speak to me. The only exception was Victor, the network administrator, who was friendly and always had time for a laugh. I liked him and occasionally walked over to his side of the building to chat.

Around us, things were getting worse. On 27 March 2002, Hamas carried out a suicide bombing at the Park Hotel in Netanya, near Tel Aviv, killing thirty Israelis and wounding 140. Two days later, Israel launched 'Operation Defensive Shield', a massive incursion into the West Bank with about 20,000 soldiers, 500 tanks, and dozens of fighter planes and bulldozers.[2] In Ramallah, tanks rolled into al-Muqata'a, which had been under siege for six months. They destroyed its surrounding wall and shelled parts of the compound. Armored carriers crushed cars in their path as soldiers stormed through, and a hail of mortars and gunfire fell on Arafat's building. The next day, dozens of foreign nationals entered al-Muqata'a in a show of solidarity. About 400 Palestinians and foreign nationals were besieged with him, amidst the intermittent shelling.

Israel redeployed its military forces in the West Bank in full, reversing the Oslo Accords and all the agreements since, and devastating the Palestinian Authority. The army invaded Palestinian cities, killing hundreds of people, arresting thousands, and destroying infrastructure. Israeli media portrayed the Palestinians as terrorists, and the damage done to them was never exposed. The army used Palestinian civilians as human shields, forcing them to knock on doors for house searches, check suspicious subjects, and stand in the lines of fire from militants. Medical teams, ambulances, journalists, and human rights workers were also attacked.[3]

On 2 April, Israeli troops besieged the Church of the Nativity in Bethlehem, where Palestinian militants had taken refuge and some 200 monks lived. Tanks were deployed near Manger Square, opposite the church, and snipers took up positions on the roofs of surrounding buildings. They were instructed to fire at anyone they saw inside the church, using laser beams to seek out targets.

One day later, Israeli forces began a full-scale assault on Jenin refugee camp, which lasted for nine days, razing large areas and turning houses into rubble. More than fifty Palestinians were killed.[4] Each night, I went home to watch the horrors on the news. Al

Jazeera showed detailed coverage. I had headaches and nightmares. At work, I could barely focus on anything. I did not want to see or talk to anyone. I just wanted to crumple in a heap of tears.

An American colleague, Greg, sat a few desks away from me, in his Levi's and baseball cap. He chuckled to Ted, another American: 'We're creaming them, man. They don't stand a chance!'

I looked up. We worked in a large, open-space hall, and I could hear them. They had arrived in the country a few months before. I could not say anything. I remembered the incident at Tefen, with Lisa, and the climate then was nothing like what it was now.

On 9 April, it was 'Yom HaShoah' in Israel, the annual Remembrance Day for victims of the Holocaust. In the morning, sirens sounded throughout the country, and everyone stopped what they were doing and stood for two minutes in silence. Drivers halted, and some got out and stood on the roads. The country came to a standstill.

I was at work, staring dimly into my screen. I had barely slept all week. The killing and rampage were happening a short distance away, and I felt utterly helpless, consumed with pain and rage. At times, I could not breathe fully and had to get away from the TV, which the village and entire Palestinian population seemed to be glued to in misery.

Suddenly, a high-pitched sound broke the silence. Everyone rose to their feet. It was the memorial siren.

At that moment, I could not get up.

I just could not.

Blood rushed through my veins, my heart pounding, and I felt sick. All I saw were flashes of coverage: the blood, the mutilated bodies, the women screaming and tearing their hair, the rubble, the funerals with body after body wrapped in Palestinian flags.

My legs refused to move. I stared at my screen and felt the eyes of every person in that room boring into me. For two minutes, they stood, but I was in a trance. They sat down again and there was silence. Everyone resumed tapping their keyboards. I continued working, or staring into space, until lunch break.

'You didn't stand up,' Sofia said, gently.

I looked at her. After a few moments, I found my voice. 'They're killing my people as we speak. As they stand to remember their dead, they're making more of mine.'

IV

Again, there was the wall of silence. As long as we stayed away from 'political talk', we could pretend to maintain a civil atmosphere. My colleagues would make the odd remark and answer each other, as though I was not there. I discovered that, to the average Israeli, the Palestinians did not really exist as a people; we were a formless mob of terrorists. These immigrants were told that Israel had waged a glorious 'war of independence' and regained its land 'promised' by God to the Jewish people. The 'Arabs' were simply driven away and no one had to worry about them, and, anyway, 'they had twenty-two countries they could go to'.

Even among my friends, the comments surfaced. I was always reminded, in some way or other, that the friendship could never be complete. Sofia visited me at home, once. But, when I invited Eva, she blurted out: 'Good heavens, I can't possibly drive to an Arab village! The streets, the chaos! How do you do it?'

In Ramallah, the campaign against Arafat intensified. He and those besieged with him suffered water and electricity cuts, shortages of food, and a lack of air due to overcrowding. The Israeli army continued to destroy the buildings of al-Muqata'a, leaving only the two where the besieged took shelter. They were encircled by tanks, pointing their guns at the windows. Finally, after international pressure, the army withdrew from the compound on 1 May. Israeli prime minister Ariel Sharon forbade Arafat from leaving the Palestinian territory unless he had no intention of returning. The cities and refugee camps of the West Bank were surrounded by Israeli troops. On 10 May, they ended their five-week siege of the Church of the Nativity, killing seven Palestinians.[5]

Weeks later, the army invaded Ramallah, again, and attacked Arafat's headquarters, killing one of his guards. My father was stuck in the city and could not leave for several days. Israel had designs for a much larger blockade. The government approved the construction of a separation barrier: a massive, concrete structure with trenches, barbed wire and watchtowers that ran around the West Bank.

I was at my desk, in my usual daze, when the voice of the company's owner broke the silence. 'Hi, guys!'

351

I looked up to see him in full army uniform, gun slung over his shoulder. My stomach lurched. I could not hide a fleeting spasm on my face. I looked back at my screen and continued typing.

He looked in my direction and said: 'Sorry if I'm intimidating anyone.'

I felt myself stiffen. He stood for a few minutes and chatted with the others, then left. I was not sure if he meant to appear like that to make a point, or if it was the casual coincidence that it seemed like. It did not matter. By this point, I was seriously thinking about quitting—money and savings be damned.

But I knew that finding another job was close to impossible. And I had one goal: to save the money needed for our exit. Raji's salary was spent on living expenses, and mine was saved, though we sometimes had to dip into it as his earnings diminished. He had finished his marketing diploma and was looking for better work, without success. His work with his father was suffering. Their construction projects dwindled as the situation in the country worsened. Each month, we made our calculations to see how much longer we would need. I was very tense and kept having outbursts, but he told me to be patient.

At the same time, we both battled the prospect of leaving our families. Mum had suffered from diabetes and hypertension for years, and her health was failing. Raji's parents were old and tired, their life a stream of endless toil. Our decision to leave weighed so heavily on us that we could not share it. We felt guilty keeping our plans from them, but we knew they would try to talk us out of them. 'Anything could happen; let's wait until we actually put the money together and decide to go, before we tell them,' Raji said, morosely.

I told Sofia and Eva. Their faces fell. 'Isn't it a drastic decision? Are you sure?'

I nodded. Sofia said: 'I understand. We don't want you to leave, but I totally understand.'

For the first time, I told them more about my life: who my father was, what had happened in Beirut, how we had ended up in Israel. They listened, trying to hide their shock. 'I'm thinking of writing a book,' I finished.

But Eva, whose expression had changed, looked at me and said: 'Why, do you think your life is so interesting that people will want to read about it?'

I tried to hide the hurt I felt, taking it as the casual joke that it sounded like. They smiled and went back to their desks. From that point, I shut down and spoke as little as possible. Most of the others still seemed ill at ease in my presence, and I was tired of trying. They shuffled awkwardly when speaking to me, keeping the conversation short. Many continued to walk past me, averting their eyes and staring straight ahead.

I was surprised when an instant message popped up on my screen. It was Dave. He worked in another team and sat at the far end of the hall. He was a loner, always behind his computer, and he did not come down to the cafeteria for lunch. I knew he was American, but I had noticed that he made a concerted effort not to hang out with the others, especially Greg and Ted, who sat next to him, babbling ceaselessly. 'Is there a "mute" button? I sure as heck could use it!' he typed.

I grinned, and we struck up a conversation. Then we went out for coffee on the balcony. Dave was interesting, warm, and empathic. 'I can't connect to these people,' he confided in me.

He had been in the country for a year, and he had a lot of questions, which I did my best to answer. Until his arrival, he told me, he had not been aware of the Palestinians in Israel, or at all. 'I read that Arab villages face a lot of discrimination; is that true?' he asked.

I looked at his innocent, almost childish face, at curious odds with his large frame. Then I began to tell him. It was a difficult leap for me, the first time I was talking to an Israeli who actually wanted to listen—seven years after I had come to the country. I could tell it was difficult for him, too. I had to walk a fine line; if I said too much, I felt he would recoil. We took more breaks and continued talking. It frustrated me, having to hold back and only give little snippets. It also really depressed me that people who had made the decision to immigrate simply *did not know*. I wanted to come out with everything, tell him the whole story, but the topic made him uncomfortable and he always said: 'We should get back to work ...'

A few weeks later, he did not come to the office. He was absent the next day, as well. I found out from Eva that he had been called to army service, and would leave work in the coming weeks.

He reappeared that afternoon, greeted us all and sat down at his desk. A while later, we went outside for our coffee and I asked him if everything was alright.

'Yes, Fida. But I couldn't come to work yesterday. I found out that I had been called to service, and I was worried that you'd be upset. I didn't know what to tell you.'

I was stunned. I told him it was fine, that he should do what he had to do. But the words were sour in my mouth, even as I was moved by his thoughtfulness.

The army and security apparatus were Israel's mania—they could not be questioned or criticized. Every newscast seemed to have some mention of the army. There were army radio channels. Military trucks and jeeps intermingled with traffic. The army provided study loans and careers. For Jews, refusing to serve meant being ostracized in society. Some became depressed and left their service. There were cases of suicide. There were also those who would not serve, on principle, but they were few. In a system that viewed army performance as a precondition for all personal progress, those refusers were punished by the state. They were often imprisoned, and they could lose their study loans and be refused employment. They also faced a social stigma, even from family and friends. Dave was clearly not up to it, this eager newcomer with shining eyes and burning idealism. He wanted to make a good start to his life in the country. I did not judge him, but I could not help feeling alienated. A chasm opened up between us, and, eventually, the friendship petered out.

The Israeli rampage in the Palestinian territory crushed Arafat's efforts to declare a unilateral ceasefire. On 19 September 2002, after another suicide bombing in Tel Aviv, the Israeli army laid siege to al-Muqata'a for the third time and largely demolished it. Arafat refused an order to hand over twenty Palestinians who were inside, and a rumor spread that the army would storm his office. Thousands of Palestinians broke the imposed curfew and poured out towards his headquarters. The army opened fire, killing two and wounding dozens, but the protests spread to other Palestinian towns and refugee camps. Ten days later, the tanks and bulldozers rolled away, leaving only one building of the large compound standing: the block housing Arafat's office, where he and his aides were confined, in tough conditions, on the second floor.

Greg and Ted kept talking about 'battering them' and gleefully boasting of Israel's 'victories'. Other employees were silent or

60. Elias Jiryis (Abu Sabri) visiting Sabri and the family in Cyprus, 1984.

61. Wardeh Jiryis (Um Sabri) at Sabri's home, Fassouta, 2008.

62. Wardeh Shaheen (Um Nour), Fassouta, 2009.

63. Road sign to Fassouta, two miles before reaching the village, 2015.

64. View at entrance to Fassouta village, 2019.

65. Sabri picking lemons from the garden of his home in Fassouta, 2012.

66. Fida pointing to Fassouta on a map of Palestine from 1948, al-Shurouq bookshop, Ramallah, 2017.

67–8. Fida stands at al-Zaqaq, the old center of Fassouta, with cobbled roads and homes dating back many decades.

69. Bell tower, St. Elias Church, Fassouta, 2017. The church is more than a century old.

70. Mass in St. Elias Church, Fassouta, 2017.

71. Fida in Rawabi city, West Bank, 2014.

72. Tomb of Mahmoud Darwish at the Mahmoud Darwish Museum, Ramallah, 2014.

73. Site of Iqrit village, the Galilee, with only the church remaining, 2012.

74. Temporary structures set up by the youth in Iqrit. Graffiti: *I shall not remain a refugee; we shall return.*

75. The northern border with a road leading to Lebanon, photo taken from Fassouta, 2018.

76. View of part of Fassouta village, 2018.

77. View of Fassouta village, 2018.

78. Fida helps her family pick olives in Fassouta, October 2015.

79. Mousa pruning an olive tree in Fassouta, October 2015.

80. Geris picking olives in Fassouta, October 2015.

81. Fida and Sabri in front of an olive tree at home in Fassouta, 2017.

82. Fida and Mousa, Ramallah, 2009.

83. From left to right, Geris, Fida, Muna, and Sabri at Muna's (Elias and Wardeh's) house in Fassouta, 2017.

84. Fida and Geris in Fassouta at Muna's (Elias and Wardeh's) house, 2017, with a view of the Galilean mountains and the northern road to the border with Lebanon.

85. From left to right: Sabri, Muna, Fida, and Geris at Muna's (Elias and Wardeh's) house, 2017. Family photos hang on the wall behind them.

86. Sabri and his three brothers playing cards while two of their sons look on. From left, clockwise: Sabri, Mousa, Subhi, Geris, Shakeeb (George's son), and George.

87. Fida and Mousa with Sabri on his eightieth birthday, 4 December 2018, Mi'ilya.

88. Fida wearing thobe, Palestinian dress, at the launch of her second Arabic book, *al-Khawaja*, at the Mahmoud Darwish Museum, Ramallah, 2014, with the Palestinian flag behind her.

muttered a few bits of news to each other in somber tones. Things were so tense they were like a taut wire about to snap. I was having lunch in the cafeteria, sitting at the end of a long table that we all shared, when my ears picked up a heated discussion taking place further down. It became louder and more intense. Suddenly, one of the girls snapped: 'I think our government is making a huge mistake!'

Everyone paused. All eyes turned to her.

'I think we should go in there and blitz everything,' she said. '*Everything*. People, cats, dogs, trees, the air! Just wipe the entire area clean. That will solve the problem!'

Dave was sitting right there. He did not say a word.

V

Desperate to leave, I made a last scramble and asked to release the funds in my retirement plan. They were small, for I had only worked a few years, and I had to pay a chunk in tax for withdrawing them before maturity. But we were finally able to put the needed money together. I rushed to print the bank statement and made an appointment at the Canadian Embassy.

At the interview, the woman looked through our papers and asked us: 'What line of work do you hope to do in Canada?'

We told her. It seemed she was more interested in hearing our English. She smiled, placed the stamps on our passports, and said: 'Canada needs people like you. I'm sure you'll do very well!'

At home, we had to break the news. 'Canada?' Mum gasped.

There was little I could say to make it better. 'You were so excited when we came back; you were the one who pushed for it!' she faltered, sudden tears in her eyes.

My father was somber, and, years later, would declare: 'I hate those countries, the ones that open their doors for immigration and take our young people!'

My in-laws were devastated. It was just as well that we had left the announcement until shortly before we left.

Only one person was not surprised. My uncle, Geris, had been head of the local council for two years. He struggled with the corruption around him. 'Since the days of military government, they divided people and taught them that each man was for himself,' he told me. 'No one cares about the public interest of the village. Everyone wants favors, tax breaks, jobs!'

When he pushed back, he found himself ostracized. Yet, he was hopeful. He wanted to run for the next round to try and make things better. But the villagers did not want him. They were content in their system, he realized; who was this newcomer from abroad to change it? In an almost unbelievable precedent, two families that were historically at odds with each other, and had divided the whole village in each round of elections, now united against his electoral list.

A week before election day, he received a call from the Israeli security services: 'It's finished. Don't bother.' They had pulled their weight to make sure he was ousted. It was well known that they interfered in elections in Palestinian communities, but he felt it was more than that: it was in revenge for his resistance activities, all those years ago. Of that, he was certain.

'Do what you need to do, and get out,' he said to me, tiredly.

What remained was some paperwork for us to complete with the Israeli national insurance department. We filled out the forms and I took them to Nahariya. As usual, I emptied my pockets, gave my bag to the security guard, and entered through a metal detector. By now, I was used to this.

Inside, I took a ticket and waited. At a booth in front of me, a young man finished his turn and got up. He began talking on his mobile, in Arabic, and I could not help overhearing. 'I don't know, I didn't really get it … She asked me for a form, but I didn't understand. Can I give her the phone to talk to you?'

After a pause, he went back to the booth and asked the clerk if he could give her his mobile for a minute, so she could explain to his employer, who was on the line, which documents he needed to bring.

'No! I don't speak to anyone on phones!' she snapped.

I stared. He opened his mouth to say something, but she added, loudly: 'I told you what needs to be done! I'm done talking!'

She waved him away and gestured to the next person in line. I was livid. The man, red-faced, began to walk away. He stopped and looked around him, helplessly, for a minute. I slumped in my seat, not wanting to meet his eyes, or show him that I had seen his humiliation.

14

ESCAPE

I'm not asking if we've forgotten how to be Jewish, but if we've forgotten how to be human.

Reuven Rivlin
Israeli president[1]

I

On 26 March 2003, I looked at the visas in our passports and checked, again, that we had everything. Four suitcases sat in the living room with the bits of our life that we could cram into them. Our house filled up with people to say goodbye. We had wanted a quiet exit, but it was not to be, and the bigger the affair, the more pained and guilty we felt. Finally, we got in the car with Dad, who was driving us to the train station in Nahariya. I turned back to wave goodbye, and my last image was of Mum, standing on the balcony, watching us speed away.

It was one of the hardest moments of my life. My eyes filled with tears. I wondered, for the hundredth time, if we were not making some huge mistake, leaving behind our aging parents whom we would not see again for a long time.

It was equally painful to say goodbye to Dad. He had never interfered in our decisions, mine or my brother's, but I knew he was very unhappy with this move. Still, he wished us well. I felt numb with sadness as we continued to the airport. Raji, too, was very quiet.

As the scenery sped past, I thought back to my family's return. I had been on top of the world. I was going home, at last! Now, I was so far from that point I felt I had no home at all, anywhere. What had first seemed like a miracle had turned out to be a nightmare. In eight years in Israel, I had never felt happy, nor free.

We braced ourselves for the airport procedure. But, when we told them we were emigrating, everything changed. 'May I see your visa?' the agent asked, in a cheery voice.

We showed her.

'You're going there for good?' she eyed us for confirmation.

'Yes,' we nodded. To our shock, she folded the passports, returned them to us, and waved us straight to check-in. No one touched our bags. We queued up in confusion, waiting for them to be on our tail. But, for the first time, ever, we sailed straight through. Finally, Raji said to me: 'They're only too glad to see Arabs leave ...'

Again, I felt I was replaying the past. My father had told me that he had felt the same reaction from the policeman who had given him his exit permit from Israel, all those years ago under military rule.

On the plane, nervousness began to sink in. Raji's cousin, Elias, lived in Kitchener, about an hour from Toronto. He was meeting us at the airport. It was good to know we had someone to help us settle in.

Our first shock was the snow. It was the first time we had seen such a thick blanket of it. We were in mid-March, and Elias told us it would be more than a month before it cleared. 'You'll get used to it,' he laughed, escorting us to his small car.

Elias worked at a convenience store owned by his uncle and lived with his uncle's family to save on rent. He took us to a bed and breakfast for a few days. The place was lovely, a large, Victorian-style home with quaint furniture. Its proprietor was an old English lady who was very proper about her tea. She served everything with timed precision and joked about the coffee needing exactly four minutes to brew. We spent a few hectic days doing our paperwork and looking for a place to live. Elias introduced us to a Palestinian couple from Nazareth. There were vacant apartments at the building they lived in, and we found one that we liked.

From the early days, we felt an aura of quiet and calm. There was an organized, tranquil atmosphere, with no tension, no stress in the air as in Israel. On our first trip to the mall, Raji and I stood at the entrance, wondering where security was. It took us a few moments to realize there was none, and we walked in, sheepishly. 'So, this is what the normal world is like!' he said.

The apartment was empty, but we were careful with the money we had brought. We only bought a mattress and some basic kitchenware while we began to look for work. This turned out to be the hardest part. Despite the promises on the immigration website, finding jobs as new immigrants was really difficult. We sent tens of applications and made endless calls, but the most we could find were low-paid shifts in grocery stores or factories. Raji began to work at the store with Elias, for minimum wage. I could not find a job. In three months, our savings were gone, and he had a very low income that barely covered our expenses. Then, he found work at a factory that assembled mobile phones. The pay was only slightly better, but he took it in his stride, though he was fighting his misgivings.

We continued to apply for jobs and took turns encouraging each other. But, as weeks turned into months, we missed home tremendously and asked ourselves, daily, what we were doing. We had not anticipated that it would hit us so hard. The question plagued us from the moment we got there: did we really want to leave our families and live so far away? 'We should have answered that before we came!' Raji said. I saw more in his eyes, but he did not want to say it: I had wanted the move desperately, more than he did, and had nagged day and night to make it happen. But now that we were there, we both fought a crushing voice of doubt.

Our new friends reassured us. 'We all went down this path. Sometimes, we still do. But it's better here. You'll find your way. It's full of problems, *al-blad*—we left it for a reason!'

I noticed, again, that Palestinians referred to Israel as 'the country'. Syrians, Egyptians, Jordanians all called their countries by name, but we did not.

As I willed myself to keep trying, a phone call from Mum shattered my world. Dad had contracted a rare, vicious virus and was in hospital in Haifa. He had to have surgery, and he had lost one of his eyes, to save his life. 'What?' I screamed and broke down, wailing uncontrollably.

Raji grabbed the receiver and spoke to her, then rushed to my side. 'He'll awaken in a few hours, she told me, and you can talk to him! Calm down!'

'I want to go home! Now!' I sobbed.

'You will … Don't worry …' he fumbled for words. We had no money at all. He had had to borrow twenty dollars from his cousin until he got his weekly pay.

My father awoke from the anesthetic and spoke to me. He told me he was alright, not to worry, and that they would operate on his other eye to remove a cataract that had long been bothering him, so he could regain his vision. He urged me not to make the trip back. 'There's no need, sweetheart, really; I'm fine!'

I waited by the phone. They were horrible days. I paced up and down our apartment, crying. Raji was on night shift and was exhausted. He tried to reassure me, but I was consumed by heartbreak, guilt, anger. 'I hate that country!' I screeched. 'If things had been normal there, nothing would have forced us into this hardship!'

Thankfully, Dad had the surgery and regained full sight in his other eye. He called me from hospital. 'I got up and walked around for the first time in a week, and I stood at the window. I can see as far as Mount Carmel! Don't worry!'

I was shaken for weeks, also by the realization that we had had no money to make the trip. Only my first year in Israel had been this frightening. I joined Raji at the factory. For the first time, I stood at a production line. It was the most excruciating work I had done, standing for hours in the same place, repeating the same movements. The factory was a depressing repository of dozens of people like us: recent immigrants from many countries who had come to Canada to better their lives. Row after row of laborers toiled on, all holders of first- and second-class degrees and years of work experience. Many had left good jobs and stable financial situations for the promise of better opportunities and social freedom, or to escape oppressive regimes. A sense of bitterness and despair filled the air.

Sofia, my friend from work, sent frequent emails to ask how I was doing. Eva surprised me; she called every few weeks. They were a huge support.

Raji and I waited for better news from home, but there was none. On 4 October 2003, we were startled by an unusual call from his parents. There had been a suicide bombing at Maxim, a beachside restaurant in Haifa, killing twenty-one people and injuring dozens.[2] Among the dead were two restaurant staff from Fassouta: Hanna Francis, 39, and Sharbel Matar, 23. It was a shocking blow to the village. Hanna was my mother's cousin, and was going to get married that summer. Instead of a wedding, his fiancée flew in from Australia for his funeral. Sharbel's parents had died young, and he had been supporting his three sisters.

The beach restaurant was frequented by Palestinians and Jews, and was seen as a symbol of coexistence in Haifa. Islamic Jihad claimed responsibility for the attack. The suicide bomber, twenty-eight-year-old Hanadi Jaradat, was from Jenin, in the West Bank. She was due to qualify as a lawyer a few weeks later. Her fiancé, brother, and cousin had been killed by Israeli forces.

Raji and I knew we simply had to go on. There was nothing to go back to.

II

At the end of the year, we moved to Mississauga, a suburb of Toronto, in the hope of finding better work. I left my work at the factory, but Raji continued to commute to the job in Kitchener while I widened my search. The employment office advised me to register with an agency, which sent me on temporary assignments. I stood at bus stops in the freezing weather and tried to find my way to the companies around Toronto, which needed me for a few days or weeks. The work was no more than typing or shelving, the pay was low, and rent was more expensive. I desperately looked for any resources that could help, and I found a Palestinian community center nearby.

The director, Issam, welcomed us and listened to our story. When we told him we had come from Israel, he stared at us in disbelief. 'You mean, you were living in your village? In the Galilee?' He was a refugee, and most of the newcomers he saw were refugees, as well. We were shocked to discover that he originated from Suhmata, a mere ten-minute drive from Fassouta. 'It's a small world,' he smiled, sadly.

Issam's father, Ahmad (Abu Maher) al-Yamani, was born in Suhmata. During the Nakba, he was exiled to Lebanon with his family. He became a leader in the Arab Nationalist Movement and, later, helped to establish the Popular Front for the Liberation of Palestine (PFLP) and held key positions in the PLO.

Issam grew up in Bourj el-Barajneh refugee camp, in Beirut. After the Israeli invasion in 1982, he ended up in Canada with his wife and children. Twenty years later, although his family had long since acquired Canadian citizenship, he had not. His application continued to be rejected, as he had been a member of the PFLP, which was on Canada's blacklist. After a long legal battle, he received a deportation order, but it could not be carried out because no country would accept him. He had no other citizenship and only Palestinian refugee documents. He was stuck in Canada, where he could not work, nor receive any social benefits. The community center paid him his salary in cash.

'All I want is to be allowed back to my homeland, to feel some dignity in life,' he said. 'I just want a tiny room to live in, there, and nothing else from the world.'

I squirmed, suddenly feeling how lucky I was, somehow. 'How did you get there, then leave?' he asked me, incredulously.

'Because … Life is very hard there, Issam.'

'Hard?' He shook his head. 'Even if it was hell, you should have stayed! What are you doing here?'

We began to explain, but he did not seem convinced. 'Listen, I'll be straight with you,' he said. 'It's very difficult to find jobs in your professions here, as new immigrants. Many people spend years in this loop and never come out. We can help point you to the employment agencies and government resources, but we can't do much else.'

Our hearts sank. But, when I called my father, later, I could sense his smile on the phone. 'Abu Maher is my friend. I used to see him at the National Council sessions; he always talked to me about Suhmata and Fassouta. I told him, too, that when we returned and ran for elections, I would run against him, and win!'

'What did he say?' I smiled.

'He always said: "Of course you'll win! All of Fatah would vote for you!"' Dad laughed.

We saw Issam at an event in the community center a few weeks later. There was a small audience of about twenty people, most of them older Palestinian men. They all had the same look. 'As though time stopped after the Nakba,' Raji whispered. I had never seen a group of people look so out of place, as they sat in that room, listening to a political lecture, a flag of Palestine hanging desolately in the corner.

III

Sifting through the job boards, I saw a quality assurance position advertised in Kitchener. I applied, out of desperation, though I did not expect to be called. To my shock, a call came three days later. Raji and I went back for my interview. Finally, a year after our move, I was accepted for a professional job.

We had to break the lease on our apartment in Mississauga and pay the penalty. Then, we rented another place in Kitchener. Raji was relieved to move back and not have to make the long commute. He seemed to be getting on well in the factory and had been promoted. The company where I began to work had a mix of nationalities and reminded me of my years in the UK. I made friends and was relieved to see a few success stories: immigrants who had found better jobs, bought homes, and begun good lives.

Raji and I relaxed, somewhat, created a small social circle, and tried to live with the constant sense of homesickness that plagued us. We had come halfway around the world, only to end up with a circle of friends from back home. We searched fervently for any connection to it, shopping at overpriced Arabic grocery stores and paying too much at Middle Eastern restaurants. Clearly, neither of us was really up to assimilation in a new society. If it were not for the hardship back in Israel, we would never have taken this step.

Slowly, too, as I stopped firefighting, the pressing issue that I had forced myself to ignore rose to the surface. I was still unhappy in the marriage, and, though we had come closer through the shared difficulties of our move, it had not changed anything for me. I needed to make a decision, and I was stalling.

IV

Back home, my father had recovered. He kept working in Ramallah, as much as he could in the dire situation of the intifada. But Arafat struggled with sickness and extremely difficult conditions under his siege. Finally, he broadcast a message: 'They want me a captive, a fugitive, or a dead man, but I say: a martyr, a martyr, a martyr!'

In October 2004, after thirty-four months of siege, his doctors announced he was gravely ill. He was finally flown out of Ramallah to Jordan, then to a military hospital in Paris. He fell into a coma and died on 11 November, at the age of seventy-five.

A French Army guard of honor held a brief ceremony for him, and President Jacques Chirac stood by his coffin. The next day, Arafat's body was flown to Cairo for a military funeral. Throughout the West Bank and Gaza, mourning prayers sounded from the mosques. Finally, he was buried in Ramallah, after Israel refused his will to be buried near al-Aqsa Mosque, in Jerusalem. Tens of thousands of Palestinians attended his funeral. My father and brother were among them.

Dad was deeply saddened. He considered Arafat to be the father of modern Palestine. Without him, he felt, Palestine would not have returned to the world stage after the Nakba.

He had seen Arafat three days before his flight to Paris. The leader had been his director for twenty-six years. 'Rest in peace, Chairman,' he thought, as thousands of Palestinians bade him farewell. 'We shall go on.'

Years later, an autopsy[3] conducted by a team of French, Swiss and Russian experts suggested that Arafat had died of polonium poisoning. Samih Shbib, my father's colleague at the Research Center, who was privy to the exhumation, told my father that they had found 'black heaps' and not bones in the grave, which the experts said strongly suggested poisoning. Many fingers were pointed at Israel, after its siege and the statements by Israeli officials before and after his death.[4] They consistently denied the allegations. To Palestinians, he did, indeed, die a martyr.

A temporary mausoleum was built over his tomb, so it could still be moved to Jerusalem at a later date. On the minaret of a mosque on the mausoleum plaza, a laser light pointed to the holy city, just a few miles away.

Palestinians had mixed feelings towards Arafat. They admired him for what they saw as his principled stances, and they sometimes defended his mistakes as being the result of the very difficult political environments, brought on by the Arab regimes, that he had to navigate. Those regimes had been complicit with Israel in leaving him to his slow death. But many Palestinians were angry with the corruption of his Fatah circle and the blunders that the post-Oslo Authority had made. Arafat had kept power through co-optation and suppression. However, for the Palestinian cause, he had clear boundaries he could not cross, concessions he could not make. He had resisted Israeli and American pressure until the end. It was understood that, ultimately, he paid for this with his life.

V

With our better financial means, Raji and I could finally plan a visit back home. It had been almost three years. I was worried about Mum. Dad tried to reassure me, but I could tell she was not well. At Christmas 2005, we booked a trip back. They were thrilled. My uncle, Geris, told me on the phone: 'I was going to go to London to see the kids, but I'm postponing it to see you!'

I called my friends from work. Sofia was going to Sweden, but Eva was home, and she told me to call her as soon as I arrived. 'I can't wait!' she laughed.

I also told Issam, our friend from the community center, and asked him if he wanted anything. A flicker lit up his eyes. 'No, thanks,' he muttered. His voice caught as he told me to have a good trip. I felt sad and almost guilty for telling him, for casually doing something that he wanted to do more than anything in the world, but could not.

When we arrived, though, I was in for a nasty shock. I saw Mum and could not believe my eyes. She had aged rapidly, barely resembling herself three years before. Her face was hollow with sickness, and she was moving with difficulty, using a walking stick. Though she was overjoyed to see us, her voice was hoarse with pain and discomfort.

I had not been there to see this. It hit me like a ton of bricks. When Raji and I went to our apartment, I sat on the bed and burst into tears. I thought of the distance, the uncertainty in Canada, the sacrifice or selfishness of leaving our parents. I pondered life there and felt the heaviness of life in Israel, but, suddenly, it did not matter. All that mattered was that, in making the move, we had had to leave very important things behind. I felt torn and guilty, thinking I should never have gone anywhere.

The next day, I asked about my uncle Geris.

'He's not here,' Mum said, quietly. 'He's been arrested.'

'What?'

'The police came and took him, and they won't let anyone see him.'

'What?' I looked at her in bafflement. 'I spoke to him on the phone last week!'

'Yes, this was just two days ago. They sent a huge force and took him in the middle of the night.'

A convoy of armored jeeps and a helicopter had shattered the silence of the early morning hours. The police and special units had raided his home, woken the neighbors, and spread fear and confusion. No one could understand why so much force was needed to arrest a man in his late fifties, who lived alone, had recently been head of the village council, and was retired. A simple phone call to summon him would have been enough, he later told me.

The police said he was being held on 'security grounds'. My father did not know what was going on. No one was allowed to see him. The arrest was kept secret by the Israeli military censor until *Haaretz* won a court order allowing publication. It took ten days for my father to be able to see him, as his lawyer, and find out his charges. The security service had accused my uncle of communicating with an enemy state, Iran, and being recruited by its intelligence to spy on Israel.

After leaving the village council in 2003, my uncle had briefly returned to work for the PLO Planning Center, which had become the Ministry of Planning under the Palestinian Authority. He then took early retirement. In 2005, his longtime Lebanese friend in Cyprus suggested they work together to reissue my uncle's political and economic journal, *al-Malaf*, which he had published when he had lived on the island. His friend told him that he had potential funding, and my uncle went to Cyprus to see him. But, when he heard that the funders were Iranian, he said no.

My father assured me that it would be alright; Ammo was not guilty of anything; it was all just to cause him hassle and would fizzle out into nothing. But I went to visit Eva with a heavy heart. I wanted to cancel, but Mum told me there was no sense in sitting around. None of us could see my uncle, and we were waiting.

Eva lived in Lavon, a small Jewish community less than an hour's drive from Fassouta. It was my first visit to her home, and I pushed aside the memory of her reluctance to come to mine. I drove past the sign and saw an electric gate. Jewish communities were nearly always gated, though I had never heard of any attacks against them. Abirim, near Fassouta, also had a gate. Each time I took a walk along my favorite road out of the village, I ended up at the forbidding barrier and had to turn back. The borders of Fassouta folded naturally into the surroundings; we had no fences or gates.

I drove up, slowly, to the entrance. A guard sat in a little cubicle, and I stopped and called Eva, then waited for a minute while she called him to open the gate. I drove through and took the turn she had described, feeling deeply out of place. But, when she met me outside her door, I hugged her, happily. We laughed, delighted to see each other, and she invited me in to meet her small family.

Her husband was pleasant, and her little son peeked at me shyly from the corner of the living room. She had made dinner, and we ate and had some wine. Afterwards, she and I chatted alone. But, strangely, I could not feel relaxed. I looked around her spacious home, amidst expanses of beautiful forest, and thought of the people in my village struggling to find small plots to build on. I thought of Issam, in Canada, and the millions of refugees who could not come home. The thought had hit me as soon as I had driven into the community, and it would not budge. But I could not express any of this to Eva. I did not tell her about my uncle, either. I focused on Canada and thanked her for her support, which had really helped me through a difficult time. She told me the gossip from my old workplace and shared some of the daily routine of her life. I had really missed her, but I left with an unsettled, morose feeling.

Raji and I had so many visitors: every friend and relative came to see us. It was exhausting, and I wanted to spend time with my parents. I tried to see Mum as much as possible, and my heart ached each time. She was taking an awful lot of medicine and seemed to be getting worse, by the day. A few nights before we left, Raji and I joined my parents for a game of cards. Mum had enjoyed this tremendously in Cyprus; it had been one of our summer rituals. But, now, the diabetes had really weakened her eyesight. She lifted the cards up very close to her face to see, insisting on having a good time with us. I held back my tears, and, that night, I told Raji I would have to come home. He nodded, gravely. 'It's just one year till we get the citizenship,' he muttered. 'Let's finish it, then see what to do.'

I could not see my uncle before we flew back. No one was allowed to see him except my father. I returned to Canada with a heavy heart.

VI

Things took a downward turn faster than we had anticipated. Mum's eyesight deteriorated rapidly, and Dad told me she was set for surgery in April. I had to fly home, again, and, thankfully, my manager was understanding when I asked for unpaid leave.

Dad picked me up from the airport. He was tired and drawn, and, though he tried to be positive, he had shown little resistance to my coming over. I got the feeling it was a lot worse than he was telling me.

It was six in the morning when we arrived at the hospital in Nahariya and parked in the almost empty lot. 'These are not visiting hours, of course,' he said. 'But we'll tell the nurses that you're her daughter and have just arrived from abroad.'

We made our way into the still hospital and up the elevator. The patients were asleep, and a few nurses manned the stations. Dad said a few words to one of them and she nodded. We went in to see Mum.

He shook her awake, gently, and told her she had a visitor. As she awoke, confused, she looked to the side, and my heart dropped into an abyss.

I realized she could not see.

'Hello, Mum …' I said, bending down to kiss her, and a sudden, huge smile broke out on her face.

'Fida!' she said, still between sleep and wakefulness. I held her hand tight and told her it would be OK, and that I was coming back in a few hours. Dad and I left, in order not to disturb the other patients, while she looked in our direction, but not at us.

I tried, as hard as I could, to hold myself together on our way home. 'She has cataracts,' Dad explained, 'like I did. They're making the condition worse. The doctors will remove them, and she'll be better.' But, as soon as I went into the shower, I broke into sobs. I felt much worse than I had at Christmas. Everything flooded my mind in sharp succession: the decision to leave, the hours I spent counting at Karmiel, my heartbreak at saying good-bye, Mum's standing on the porch as we drove away. I cried myself into a fitful sleep, waking up at noon. Then, Dad and I went back to the hospital.

I helped Mum get into a wheelchair and took her with the nurses to the operating room. A few hours after the surgery, they removed the bandages and she could see, somewhat. I almost cried again, in relief. But I knew we were on a steep slope, and that I was coming home for good, soon.

VII

They kept her in hospital for two days. My father had to attend a court hearing for my uncle, and I decided to go with him. I had not seen Ammo in three years.

The court was in downtown Haifa, near where I used to work. It overlooked the port on one side and old, crumbling houses on the other. They had been deserted since the Nakba. I was surprised that the state had not swallowed them up, yet. When we arrived at the large building, I stopped short at the security process. After living in Canada for three years, I had grown unaccustomed to it. The day before, I had popped into the mall and momentarily forgotten, and I had to suddenly stop and turn back, red-faced, after a guard yelled at me.

My father and uncle were already inside the court building. Uncle George had gone back to university and recently qualified as a lawyer. Aunt Muna and I hurried up to them, and we went up to the sixth floor. We were all tense. Dad told me he had barely slept that night.

We arrived at room 605. Here, my uncle's hearing would be held. My father and uncle disappeared to prepare, along with a third lawyer, a friend of Ammo, and I was left outside with my aunt. She seemed to know the routine. 'Come,' she motioned. 'Let's not go in now; they haven't brought him yet. Did you eat this morning?'

I had to smile. It was a never-changing fact that every time any of my aunts saw me, they felt compelled to feed me. She opened her bag and gave me a za'atar sandwich, telling me she had baked the bread. Then, she passed me a cucumber. I had no appetite, and had only managed a few sips of coffee before we had left. But, to allay the nausea I felt, I forced myself to eat. At the first bite, the familiar taste was so comforting that I almost wanted to huddle up to my aunt. I suddenly looked at her, missing my teenage years when she had visited us in Cyprus and I had done that. I smiled, and she said, eagerly: 'There's more! Finish that piece!'

Sitting there, in the spot of sunlight from the window, the full weight of the situation hit me. Four months after my uncle's arrest, he had been presented with a list of fake charges and not allowed out on bail because he allegedly posed a threat to the security of the state. 'Security' was the term used in Israel to justify any practice, usually a breach of rights, against Palestinians. My uncle was somewhat 'luckier' as he was an Israeli citizen; Palestinians in the West Bank and Gaza fared much worse. Thousands languished in Israeli prisons under administrative detention, held for months or years without trial.[5] Others had double or multiple life sentences, their only hope being some exchange deal or political solution that could bring about their release.

I shuddered, thinking of Ammo. My brooding was interrupted when Aunt Muna looked at me sheepishly and took something out of her purse. She left me in charge of her bag and disappeared to the smoking area.

Alone in the quiet of the corridor, my thoughts drifted, again—to childhood, this time. I thought of my mother and how we had lost her in Lebanon. Then I thought of my uncle. A hard lump formed in my throat. *Stop!* I told myself. *He'll probably be out soon and this will be behind us!*

'We're going in!'

Startled, I looked up to see my aunt beckoning me to the courtroom. My other aunts had arrived. We filed into the room and sat on the wooden benches.

He was led in by two uniformed guards.

He saw me and a flash of happy recognition lit his face. I stood up and dashed towards him but felt a cold, hard arm in the way. The guard stopped me. I pushed forward, again, but he was intent on pushing me back. I held out my arm. Ammo reached out and we held hands for a tiny second before the push returned.

As the hearing began, I was only half-aware of my surroundings. I was staring at my uncle, in his brown prison uniform, searching for signs of his state. He had lost a lot of weight. The long beard he had grown was alien; I had never seen him with one before. He scratched it repeatedly and ran his hands through it as he listened to the proceedings. His arms were white, much lighter than those of his brothers, because he had not, I realized, been in the sun for several months. His eyes were tired, but intent; he followed each word and whispered to my father, Uncle George, or the third lawyer at periodic intervals. The rest of the time, he sat, head trembling in a tiny, nervous tic that he had had for years. It was barely perceptible and most people did not notice it, but it made my heart ache because it was so … him.

About an hour into the hearing, he rested his head in his hands and leaned forward, shielding his eyes. I wanted, in any way possible, for him to be out of this situation. I looked at the huge Israeli flag in the courtroom, the three judges presiding, the prosecutors. My father had requested the policeman who had arrested my uncle and a representative of the security service to appear for testimony. The policeman said: 'We've tapped this man's house phone, computer, and mobile phone for nine months, but we've found nothing.' He presented a recording of a phone call in which my uncle was heard rejecting the Iranian's offer.

So why are you holding him? I asked silently, angrily. Eventually, they had dropped the spy charges but kept holding him on others, without any proof. Worse, these other charges were kept secret and not revealed to him or his lawyers, on the pretext of state security. This was common practice with administrative detainees. My father explained to the court that my uncle was very secular, belonged to the centrist block of the PLO, and believed in a peaceful resolution to the conflict. There was no way he would get involved in espionage, certainly not for an Islamic state.

I turned to Ammo again. He looked at me and my aunts—his sisters—sitting on the bench and he gave us a small wave. His eyes caught mine and I smiled, as big a smile as I could, and gave him a thumbs-up sign. He raised his hands in a gesture of helplessness, but smiled back.

I noticed that, from time to time, the guard would lean across to him and ask him something, and Ammo would reply, presumably with details of what was happening in the case. It was the same guard who had pushed me back. Shortly before the hearing ended, the guard changed. The new one was Palestinian, an Israeli citizen who worked in the state security apparatus. He allowed us to come close to Ammo and stepped to the side. I saw it in his eyes: this could have been his own father, uncle, brother.

I rushed up to my uncle and kissed him, squeezing his hand. We could only talk for half a minute. 'How long are you here for?' he asked.

'Only two weeks.'

'What will you do later, are you coming back?'

'I don't know.'

'Don't come back here, there's nothing for us in this country!'

'What will you do, Ammo? Will you go back to London after this is over?'

'When this is over. If I leave here, first ...' he attempted a smile. My aunts clamored around him and I had to step aside. But I could not bring myself to step out of the court. I waited for everyone and kept looking at him in the precious little time left.

It was only at the end, after he was led away, that I went to the bathroom and burst into tears. I was doing this a lot, lately. When I joined my aunts, outside, their faces were somber. We said our muted goodbyes and went home.

VIII

At last, Mum seemed to be better. We chatted about life in Canada and I told her about Issam, that I wanted to visit Suhmata and take a few photographs for him. She reminded me that my uncle George's wife was from Suhmata. By curious coincidence, my uncle dropped in to see my father that evening and told me that they were going, the next day, to the annual commemoration of the village.

Mum encouraged me to go. 'Get some soil for your friend.'

On Nakba Day, 15 May, internally displaced refugees visited the sites of their destroyed villages. Those 'present absentees', about a quarter of the Palestinians in Israel, could not claim their land, nor any of their properties that had survived. Their children had been born after the Nakba, but their parents told them of their roots. Together, they made the journey each year.

Crowds of people arrived at the site of Suhmata on that crisp spring morning. The Israeli police had sent four cars, and a few policemen were standing around, looking bored, as though they knew the drill and just wanted it to be over. The procession gathered at what used to be the village entrance. I stood with Um Afif, my uncle's mother-in-law. I told her that I had come to hear about Suhmata and take some soil for my friend. She held my arm. 'Come, dear!'

We joined the others as they began their march, holding pictures and banners. I noticed the absence of a Palestinian flag. To carry it would be to risk a lot of trouble.

374

Um Afif and I were soon lagging behind, as she took her time to explain. 'Here was the mukhtar's house,' she began.

I only saw a patch of grass.

'Right there, they used to bake the bread,' she added, pointing to a shrub.

'And here,' she continued, as we walked, 'was the main road of the village. Up there was our neighbor's house ...'

There was nothing, save for a tiny fragment of wall. Only a few bits of stone, scattered about, were telltale signs that another life had existed here. My stomach lurched. I kept gazing at her, then at where she was pointing to as she spoke breathlessly, willing me to imagine, to go back in time with her. Here was so-and-so's house. Here, everyone gathered for holidays. There was the mosque, those were the remains of the church, and here ...

Tears made their way down the old woman's cheeks. She clutched, feebly, onto my arm. 'Here was ... our house,' she croaked.

The lump was back in my throat. I held her arm tighter and patted her hand. She took out her small handkerchief and dabbed her eyes, the creases on her withered face deepening, her expression transfixed in time and place. Um Afif had been twenty-four years old in 1948. She remembered everything. She knew how their home used to be, how they lived in it, their neighbors, the village, an entire community that was expelled.

Around us, spring was in full bloom. Nakba Day fell near Easter. Um Afif told me how the celebrations used to be, in the village that was no more.

We stood for a while, lost in thought. Then, I gently steered her back to catch up with the others. Everyone had gathered in the middle of the site, where a few people spoke of the history of their village and affirmed their right of return.

I thought of Issam, and how his right of return would, likely, never be realized. I bent down, scooped some soil into a small bag, tied it, and put it in my handbag. Then, I took some pictures. I hesitated. Did I really want to show him tiny pieces of walls, the mass of mountain wilderness?

But I owed him to bring back whatever I could. And Issam knew what to expect; he had seen pictures of Suhmata on the internet. I looked at the tens of people starting to gather their things. Um Afif and I slowly returned to the car. My uncle saw me and patted my back. There was nothing to say.

IX

On the flight back, I was overwhelmed. On top of my worries about Mum and Ammo, I knew that my marriage had to end. I had been playing a waiting game for years, waiting for us to travel, waiting to settle in Canada, waiting until I could support myself ... And now, with everything going on back home, I suddenly felt how short and fragile life was. I arrived and immediately talked to Raji. It was not the first time we had had the conversation. For weeks, we grappled with the idea of divorce. Finally, we tried to do it in as civil a way as possible. A few months later, in the summer of 2006, we signed our divorce papers, and Raji moved out of the apartment to another in Kitchener.

Our families were in shock. My father, though very disturbed, supported my decision. But everyone else was against it, and they interfered in every way. There was no divorce in Fassouta; the Catholic church did not grant it, and it was not socially acceptable. Our relatives talked to my parents. My phone started ringing off the hook. The only calls I answered were Mum's, and she was devastated. She saw it as a scandal. They were very difficult weeks as I tried to explain. Dad was a huge help.

It was a sad time of reflection, and I began thinking of whether to go home after getting the citizenship. I knew the hubbub in the village would die down, eventually, and I was not sure I wanted to stay in Canada, alone and far from my family. But another war stopped me short. In July 2006, Hezbollah kidnapped two Israeli soldiers near the Lebanese border. Israel responded with an invasion of South Lebanon. Hezbollah began to launch rockets into northern Israel in return. I was worried sick. Fassouta was right in the middle, and Israeli tanks were stationed at the entrance of the village to fire into Lebanon. I kept calling my parents. 'We haven't slept for weeks!' Mum told me. 'It's been nonstop. The babies and children are freaked out. No one can sleep.'

I spoke to Dad and heard shrill whistles behind him. He told me it was the sound of missiles. Some had fallen near the village, but, mercifully, in empty areas. One rocket had hit the school, which was closed, due to the summer holidays. There were no public shelters in Fassouta, unlike the Jewish communities around us. Mum told me she was hiding in the shelter in the house whenever the sirens went off. In Israel, to get a building license, each house was required to have one room of reinforced concrete to act as a bomb shelter. It was unthinkable to my friends in Canada, when I told them.

The north of Israel came to a standstill. Haifa was a ghost town. My cousins, coming home from work in Tel Aviv, told me there was no one on the streets.

One of my friends, a Palestinian Canadian, was frantic. She and her brother were in Canada, her father was working in the Gulf, and her mother and sisters were visiting relatives in Lebanon when the war broke out. In Kitchener, she made frenzied calls to report them for evacuation by the Canadian government. I sat with her and we watched the news, people going through this horror for the umpteenth time. At the scenes of destruction, my memories of childhood came flooding back. Israel bombed indiscriminately, without any thought for civilian life. On 29 July, warplanes fired missiles at the village of Qana, hitting a building in which sixty-three people had sought shelter. At least fifty-four, including twenty-seven children, were crushed to death when the building collapsed. Rescue teams could not reach them until the next morning because of the shelling. The scene on TV was indescribable. A dazed man held a cat up to the camera and shouted: 'My wife and sons have all died. All that's left is the cat!'

My friend and I had to turn the TV off. She paced up and down with the phone, trying to get through to her family. The horror continued until 14 August, killing 1,300 people.[6] It destroyed the infrastructure of South Lebanon and left thousands homeless.

Alone in the apartment I used to share with Raji, I suddenly felt the need to distance myself from the whole region, the entire mess. In November 2006, we finally got our citizenship. He left Canada and returned to Fassouta. I battled with what to do. The divorce was still searing the family. I had understood their reaction in the beginning, but now I was furious at the extent of their meddling. 'It's my life!' I said to Mum, and decided not to go back at Christmas. I flew to see my brother and cousins in London.

X

When I returned to Canada, in early 2007, I coasted along in my job for a few months, adjusting to life alone. My emotions were haywire and often contradictory. I would be terribly homesick, then I would feel that I was not making use of the opportunity I had been given in Canada. I would be relieved that the divorce was over, only to battle loneliness, insecurity, and the frightening question of where to go next. I knew that the alienation I had felt in the village was a huge reason why I could not keep the marriage going, and why I could not really assimilate.

In December, I flew back to Fassouta for Christmas. My uncle was finally free. He had been forced to take a plea bargain. Once the prosecution had secured his detention until the end of all proceedings, they had lengthened the process as much as they could to keep him imprisoned. His lawyers had requested his release, even house confinement, while the case was being deliberated, but they had been rejected. They had appealed to the Supreme Court and had also been turned down.

There was nothing to incriminate him, no contact whatsoever with 'foreign agents', nor any illegal activity. But forty-six court hearings were held as his imprisonment continued for two years, repeatedly extended on 'security grounds'. It was a strategy clearly aimed at revenge, at humiliating and exasperating him and his family, and to use him as a deterrent for anyone involved, or thinking of being involved, in any activism or struggle. It also won the Israeli security apparatus points for bringing this 'dangerous criminal' to justice, as the media eagerly smeared him.

All of it crumbled, though. After an infuriating amount of wasted time and fabrication, he was found not to have endangered the security of the state in any way. But it was not the end. The prosecutors told him they would need another six months to present their conclusions, and then they would take the case to the Supreme Court, even if he was found innocent. This would take two to four years. My uncle knew that they could keep him imprisoned for a long time. Finally, he agreed to plead guilty to one of the charges and receive a reduced sentence, equal to the period he had already been in prison. Eighty-one days went by after his planned release date until he was finally set free.

I saw him and, though he was happy and relieved, anger and bitterness engulfed him. 'That's two years of my life for something I didn't do!' he said. 'Two years of worry, fear, wondering what my fate was going to be.'

He was still reeling from his imprisonment, so I could not ask him about his plans. The first thing he wanted to do was to see his children, but he was not allowed to leave the country for one year, and he had to report to the police once a week. The children would have to come and see him. He also intended to go to court for compensation, for the extra time he had been held. I hugged him and told him it was all over. But he shook his head. I had never seen him so weary.

I spent time with him and my parents, and saw a couple of my friends. When I returned to Canada, it struck me, with a pang, how much of a stranger I had felt. I had lost the connections and little details of their lives. During my visits, I lived with them, shared their daily routines, caught up on small bits of news. Then it was all severed again when I returned. The weekly calls from home felt more like quick news bulletins.

While other immigrants focused on finding better jobs, buying homes, and cementing their new lives, I faltered in my tracks. I could not get away from the feeling that I had had every day in Canada, a feeling that I was going home.

My friends went berserk. 'Are you crazy? Go back where? To Israel?'

'Didn't you run away from there?'

'No one in their right mind goes back to that country! And anyway, what will you do for a living? You know how insane it was. Look at how well you're doing here!'

They were right, I told myself. Anxious and muddled, I decided I needed a change. I had to get out of small-town Kitchener. In February 2008, I found another position and moved back to Mississauga. My brother came to visit me. He had gone back and forth to the UK a few times, working in various jobs, then returned to Ramallah, where he had previously lived while my father was there. Neither of us seemed able to settle, or to have a home, anywhere. He was thinking about moving to Canada, but he went back to Ramallah and seemed confused.

I also realized that Mississauga was a residential suburb, a larger version of Kitchener. That summer, I met Dalia, a Palestinian from Gaza who directed an NGO in Toronto. She recruited me to a position there. 'I'm finally moving to the big city!' I told Lori, one of my friends. She had grown up in Toronto.

'That's great!' she enthused. 'But I hope you have luck with finding an apartment. It's expensive.'

It was. Rents were in the range of one thousand dollars, more than half my earnings. To work in a human rights NGO, I had had to take a pay cut. I was also still dealing with the adjustment of surviving on one salary, not two. But the job was the most meaningful I had ever found, and I was impatient to move. After one day of searching, I found a place on St. Clair and Bathurst, downtown. I signed the contract and came home jubilantly to tell Lori.

She laughed for a long time into the phone.

'What?' I asked, in confusion.

'Fida, there are six million people in Toronto ...'

'And ...?'

'You had to go and find a place in that spot.'

'What's wrong with it?' I began to panic. The street had seemed quiet, and the apartment was the best I could find for under a thousand dollars.

'It's a Jewish area.'

I started to laugh, too. 'It's OK. On my first night, I'll make a cake and go around to the neighbors!'

Lori was still laughing.

XI

Sure enough, on my first morning in the new neighborhood, I drove down Bathurst Street and my eyes skimmed over something before my brain registered: *Hebrew signs.*

I sat bolt upright behind the steering wheel. Driving down, I passed several signs of schools and community centers in Hebrew. At a traffic light, I saw a large poster: 'Israel needs you! Support its settlements!' Underneath the text, I was shocked to see the sign of the Jewish Agency. As I saw more, it clicked: the Jewish Canadian immigrants that I had met in Israel had come from places like this.

I remembered Jen, the secretary in Karmiel. For a few seconds, I had a jarring feeling of being back. I resolved to avoid that part of the street.

Life in Toronto was overwhelming, the leap from small town to big city. But there was so much to do, and I quickly made a new circle of friends. The city was three-quarters immigrant, and I did not stick out in any way. It felt so good to be free, to be *equal*.

When I heard about a planned Toronto Palestine Film Festival, I was on board. I met the group and volunteered to help. The first round was held in October 2008 and had a good turnout, despite our nervousness. Standing at the theatre entrance, wearing my festival T-shirt and taking people's tickets, I felt a surge of pride.

In December, I booked my Christmas visit to Fassouta, feeling more buoyant this time. But Mum had kidney failure and had started dialysis. I sat with her in hospital during one of her sessions and knew that my fears were materializing. I also knew, with cold certainty, that I could not move back to live in Israel.

Suddenly, another option presented itself.

XII

When my father told me he was going to Ramallah, I decided to accompany him. Mousa was still working there. Raji and I had discussed the option of moving there, in the past, but he had always balked at the idea. It was not his kind of environment, he had said. Now, it emerged as a possible solution for me.

As we neared the city, a horrid view stopped me short. 'Dad! Is this the Separation Wall?' I gasped.

'Yes.'

The huge, ugly structure rose up to our left, stretching ominously for miles ahead. It was the first time I had seen it, and it was completely different from hearing about it, far more shocking and harsh. Like a snake, it twisted and turned, severing the horizon.

We came to a halt at a large checkpoint. Scores of cars piled up, honking and trying to wedge in. 'This is Qalandiya,' my father said. But the last I remembered, from my visit in 1997, was the open road from Jerusalem. 'They've closed everything,' he explained. 'Now, it's like going from one country to another.'

It took us about an hour to cross, as the traffic crawled forward through the metal barrier. 'Do you go through this every time?' I asked him.

He nodded. 'Well, I don't come here often, anymore. Only to see friends.'

Inside the city, life seemed to be normal, as I remembered it from my previous visit. We spent a lovely evening with Samih Shbib, my father's colleague from Beirut and Cyprus, and his family at their home. Afterwards, I went for a drive with his daughter, Bayan, and her husband. I told them I was thinking of moving. They encouraged me. 'With your English, you'll find work in no time!'

I thought about it on my trip back to Canada. It made sense. I could be near my parents, without having to live in Israel. Mum's situation could not wait; I would have to wrap things up in a few months, at most.

No sooner had I landed than I was hit by news of a massive Israeli strike on Gaza. On 27 December 2008, on the pretext of stopping rocket attacks by Hamas, Israel launched 'Operation Cast Lead'. My friend and NGO director, Dalia, darted into my office as soon as I arrived at work. Her family were there and she could not get through to them, she told me. I looked at her in shock and helplessness. She was calling everyone, asking for help from whoever she could reach. Two days later, she came to tell me that her father's cousin and his wife had been killed. They had left their three small children with their grandmother and gone out to run an errand when a rocket fell and killed them both. 'My parents are going to the funeral,' she said, tightly. 'If they can hold one.'

For three weeks, the invasion continued, killing and injuring thousands. Gaza suffered an unbelievable amount of destruction. Its infrastructure was ruined. The tiny strip was one of the most overcrowded places on earth. Most of its people were refugees from 1948.

We were helpless, powerless to do anything as we followed the news in horror. Protests erupted around the world. My friends and I went to a large demonstration in Toronto. A few minutes before we began, a group of pro-Israel demonstrators showed up on the other side. My friend saw one of them carrying an Israeli flag and shouted: 'Child murderers!'

'You haven't seen anything yet!' he yelled back.

The Canadian police moved, quickly, to separate us. We marched to the Israeli Consulate, chanting and holding Palestinian flags. People around me shouted, others wept. Lori marched next to me with her two children.

Weeks later, Dad called to tell me that part of Mum's foot had been amputated because of the diabetes. I quit my job, gave notice on my apartment, and booked my flight home.

15

IN SEARCH OF PALESTINE

The deterioration is first and foremost a result of the illusion that the government's inaction on every front can actually freeze the situation in place, the illusion that 'Price Tag' is simply a few slogans on the wall and not pure racism, the illusion that everything can be solved with a little more force, the illusion that the Palestinians will accept everything that's done in the West Bank and won't respond despite the rage and frustration and the worsening economic situation, the illusion that the international community won't impose sanctions on us, that the Arab citizens of Israel won't take to the streets at the end of the day because of the lack of care for their problems.

Yuval Diskin
Israeli security service[1]

I

I landed in Tel Aviv and, taking a deep breath, walked into the terminal. As I queued up, a woman nearby spoke loudly to her husband. 'What? We were in front of them in the line! Why are they ahead of us now?'

'Because the kids lagged behind! How many times have I told you to have them ready when we leave the plane?'

'What do you want me to do? Can't you see the number of people around? We should say something. They shouldn't be in front of us!'

Their voices rose with that familiar sense of entitlement. She started arguing with the couple in front of her, who argued back, and we had a scene.

Welcome home, I thought.

Mum was bedridden. The first thing I noticed was a huge wad of plaster covering the front of her right foot. 'She lost her toes to gangrene,' Dad told me. 'I've been cleaning it and applying medicine, as they told us to do. She'll be alright. It's already healing.' It was time for the daily ritual. But, when he came to remove her plaster, I could not watch. I had to step away.

I took my suitcases to my room and began to unpack, but I stopped and sat down on my bed in pain and disbelief. I had to pull myself together. She needed support, not panic.

Social services had provided someone to help. I met her that afternoon. Camelia lived nearby and came to see Mum daily. She helped her with her shower and to move around. They knew each other from when they had worked at a clothing factory, years before Mum had left for Cyprus. 'In fact, I found her her husband!' Mum chuckled. 'He was our neighbor, and I introduced them!'

'Yes, and I wish you hadn't!' Camelia retorted. We all shared a laugh. I was happy to see Mum in light spirits, and I asked the lady to take a seat, this time, while I made coffee. Mum was very social and loved people, and I knew it helped and distracted her.

Camelia was from Pequi'a, nearby, and had married in Fassouta. Abu Saleem, my parents' friend in Lebanon who had loved us so much, was her uncle. 'What a small world,' I murmured. I told her how we had often stayed at his house, as children, and how he always ate standing up.

We made a few more changes for Mum. I wheeled the TV stand into her room and moved the dressing table to the side. The more urgent need was to help her walk. Dad and I went to the hospital and rented a walker for her from the medical services unit. She was wobbly at first and had to use it sparingly. But her foot was healing well. Twice a week, the ambulance came to take her for dialysis in Nahariya and brought her back. Camelia did the housework and helped her wash and change. The days settled into a routine.

I had to find a job. I had left Canada in debt. My work in Toronto had not covered my expenses, and I had paid for two flights home within three months. I called Bayan, my friend in Ramallah, whom I had seen at Christmas. She was an actress at a theatre, and she told me they needed an executive director. 'Send me your CV!'

Mum was upset. 'You're going away, again? Why don't you find work here?'

I reassured her I would visit. 'I'll be much closer now, only a drive away. I really don't want to work here, again, Mum,' I added, desperately.

My father and uncle were all for it. Ammo was very frustrated. He had filed a suit for compensation for his extra time in prison, but had only received a fraction of the sum granted in similar cases. The matter should have been decided in one hearing, but, even on this count, it took several court sessions. The ruling was given despite the written agreement that the prosecution had violated. 'The law is in their hands,' he told me, bitterly. 'And it's very elastic. They can evade justice in any way they see fit.'

Despite his ordeal, though, he did not have the heart to leave. A journalist came to interview him and asked him what his plans were. 'This is my home,' Ammo replied. 'I have no alternative but here. I dream of a secular, democratic country, where everyone lives in peace and equality.'

His family had settled in London. But he could not hack it. 'There's nothing for me, there,' he told me. 'It's not my culture, my home. Why should I choose voluntary exile? Haven't I been a fugitive long enough?'

I was accepted to the job in Ramallah. Despite Mum's protests, I packed and set off, telling her I would be back to visit as soon as I could.

II

At first, I was oblivious to the new reality. My heart fluttered when I saw the Palestinian flags on rooftops and in front of official buildings. I gazed at government ministries with a sense of pride; here were hints of Palestinian sovereignty, a fragment of Palestine. All was not lost! There were no Hebrew signs. People were friendly and welcoming. It was almost like coming to a different country.

The logistics took surprisingly little time. I stayed with my friends while I found an apartment and bought some furniture. Within a couple of weeks, I sat on the balcony of my new home, marveling at the speed with which everything had fallen into place.

At the theatre, I asked the artistic director if there were any nearby parks to walk in. She looked at me, her face a mixture of amusement and disbelief. I heard the employees chuckling behind her. 'Parks?' she smiled. 'Where do you think you are, Fida?'

As it turned out, I had no idea. My first shock came with my trip back to the village. I took a service taxi to the Qalandiya checkpoint and went down to cross it on foot. Cars with Palestinian license plates were not allowed into Israel, and I had to take an Israeli bus or taxi after crossing the checkpoint. These 'yellow plates', as they were called—in contrast to the Palestinian cars, which had green and white plates—were usually driven by Palestinians from East Jerusalem, who had an Israeli ID and residency.

I carried my bag and walked into the pedestrian terminal. Going through a turnstile, I saw tens of people lined up. I stood with them. A metal detector beeped as they filed through it, placed their belongings on a conveyor belt, and waited to cross another turnstile. A light above shone red. Every few minutes, it turned green, and the steel rattled to let one or two people in, like cattle. I had never seen such a sight. An Israeli soldier shouted instructions through a loudspeaker in Hebrew, which most Palestinians in the West Bank did not understand. The crowd stood, patiently, endless waiting etched on their faces. I felt sorry for the elderly, who looked exhausted. The stench of sweat and stale cigarette smoke was suffocating. It felt like there was no air to breathe. A few people pushed and shoved, wanting to escape the confined space and get out. Those near me squeezed tighter, almost choking me.

The light seemed to be red for a long time. I asked the woman standing next to me. 'They often do that, they close it for as long as they want,' she said. When it finally shone green and we neared the turnstile, she practically pushed me through so she could wedge in behind me.

I approached one of the counters and showed the soldier my ID. She looked at it, then at me, and frowned, asking what I was doing there. 'Working,' I said, in Hebrew. She tapped her keyboard for a while, slid the card back at me beneath the glass partition, and summoned the next in line. I walked the length of the distance past metal bars and emerged through the final gate. Now, I was on the other side.

A service taxi was parked a few yards away. 'Jerusalem?' I asked, and hauled my bag in. I waited for the car to fill up, thinking of the thousands of people who had to go through this every day to get to work, school, or family on the other side. Anyone who was 'suspect', for any random reason, or even had a relative considered to be a 'security threat', could be barred from entry.

The taxi took us to the bus terminal in the old city. My brother had told me what to do, and I walked up a hill for ten minutes to find a taxi to the central station in West Jerusalem, where I waited for a bus to Haifa. After a two-hour journey, I changed buses to Nahariya, and, there, I took a service taxi to Ma'alot. Then, my father came to pick me up. It took five hours and seven changes to cover a three-hour journey. 'This is insane!' I fumed. 'If this was a normal country, there would simply be a train from Ramallah to Nahariya!'

The trip back was equally exhausting. I did it two more times, then I bought a car. Camelia helped me find an old Daewoo that was not too high on mileage. I paid for it on credit, hoping I could pay it off from my new job. In relief, I began my drive back.

III

I got off the highway and began the ascent towards Ramallah. But I made a mistake. Near Ofer, an Israeli prison, was a sign to the city.

Some years before, the entrance and exit from Ramallah had been from there, before the Qalandiya checkpoint was built a few miles down. No one had bothered to take down the sign. I mistakenly turned left.

I stopped, abruptly, when I saw the prison. Israeli flags fluttered atop the intimidating structure, its watchtowers bearing down. Flustered, I looked around, wondering where I had gone wrong. An Israeli soldier came up to me. I pulled down my window and asked her: 'Ramallah?'

'Not from here!' she scowled, swinging her gun to the front of her body.

'Where is the entrance to Ramallah?' I repeated, fighting panic.

'Not here! Not here!' she shouted and waved me away.

I did a U-turn and stopped at a safe distance away, then called Dad on my mobile. He was stressed, too, not knowing where I was. Then, he understood. 'Relax!' he said. 'It's OK. You want the next left turn, the one to Atarot. Stay on the line.'

I revved the car back onto the highway and drove further down, my heart pounding. Then, I saw the sign to the Jewish industrial zone. Ramallah was not signposted. I turned left, went through two roundabouts, and finally saw the checkpoint ahead. 'I'm here, Dad,' I said, exhaling in relief.

Entering was another hurdle. Slowly, painstakingly, cars wound their way around the maze of concrete. Qalandiya was the largest and most notorious checkpoint in the West Bank. Drivers jostled on the roads, which twisted into a chaos of suffering. Soon, we came to a complete standstill. Old beggars stood nearby, in the beating sun. There were a few vegetable stalls, their produce absorbing a steady stream of car fumes. The checkpoint was jammed more often than not. It could take an hour, sometimes two, to cross the few hundred yards into Ramallah.

After finally maneuvering through, the first sight was a jungle of buildings. The Kafr Aqab area was a suburb of Jerusalem, severed from it by the Separation Wall. Its residents kept their Jerusalem ID and social benefits, but found themselves living on the other side of the Wall. The area became a no-man's land in terms of municipal services. Garbage piled up, potholes filled the streets, sewage over-flowed, and, even worse, tall buildings went up with very little oversight. Housing demand was high, for Palestinians could lose their Jerusalem ID if the Israeli authorities found out that they had left the Israeli-defined Jerusalem jurisdiction and were living elsewhere. Thus, most of them did not move to nearby Ramallah but stayed in the crowded, dirty ghetto. Nearby, the inhabitants of Qalandiya and al-Am'ari refugee camps suffered the same conditions, but they held Palestinian ID and were under the care of UNRWA. Two worlds, in less than a square mile.

I drove through these areas as quickly as I could. Ten minutes later, inside Ramallah, everything changed. The city was a bubble. Modern buildings filled the skyline, expensive cars roamed the streets, and patrons crowded into posh cafés and restaurants. 'A five-star occupation,' was the common saying. There were plays, concerts, festivals, even bars that held frequent parties. The difference between the inside of the city and its outskirts was staggering.

It did not take long for me to understand the engine behind it all. At the theatre, I managed the administration and also worked in fundraising. The money came from international donors. There were funds for everything: state building, capacity development, women, children, prisoners, human rights, health, education, art, and culture. The NGOs were the new kings. Millions of dollars poured in to sustain the post-Oslo framework. It felt wrong, the use of our suffering for money. The donors dictated their own agendas. There was a lot of funding for 'peace building' and 'non-violent resistance', while Israel continued to pound the Palestinians, daily. The system also held people captive through mortgages, car loans, and credit cards, which banks readily gave out. The population that had staged two uprisings seemed largely to have been 'tamed'.

I was among the lucky ones. The funding system relied on proposals and reports, all written in English. Those who knew the language well could get good jobs. My salary was better than my last one in Canada. I also found some Arabic–English translation work on the side. Despite the difficult environment, I thought of my years of struggle in Israel and felt, in Ramallah, a curious homecoming. But many around me struggled with unemployment and poverty. There were few jobs outside the public or service sectors, both of which paid little. A few weeks after I started, we hired a financial officer. His salary was less than half of mine, but was standard for such positions. 'I consider myself lucky,' he smiled, when we spoke more about it. 'Most men in my village don't make this kind of pay.'

Our administrative assistant had a college diploma, and I could not understand how he survived on his salary, which was a little more than my rent. 'My wife is Belgian,' he told me. 'We're applying to move there.' Travel was an exit route for many frustrated young people.

As I tried to settle down, though, my worry about my parents was growing. I had thought I would be close enough, in Ramallah, but I could only visit them every two or three weeks. Mum was not happy or convinced. Even in my car, it was a seven-hour journey there and back. The exit was as horrible as the entry. Lines of cars piled into the long stretch of Kafr Aqab. Some people without cars stood near the checkpoint and beckoned to the drivers, to see if one of them could pick them up and save them from going through the pedestrian crossing. The traffic crawled forward, bumper-to-bumper, cars squeezing to within inches of each other to push through. My foot was on the brakes as I clutched the steering wheel and leaned forward so I would not hit anyone or be hit. Loud honking filled the chaos. About 500 yards before the exit, a concrete barrier separated the lanes. From that point, we were stuck. If fighting or stone-throwing broke out in the nearby camp against the Israeli soldiers at the checkpoint, we had no way to turn back. Twice, I had to duck in my seat as bullets began to fly overhead, asking myself, in horror, where I had moved to.

In the last stretch of road, small children tapped the car windows, offering candy or tissues. Young men peddled coffee and housewares, or carried small cloths to wipe the windshields for a few shekels. Surrounded by dust and exhaust fumes, I kept my windows closed. To the right, the ugly Separation Wall loomed, covered with human rights graffiti and pictures of Palestinian leaders who had been killed or were in prison.

As we drew nearer, I felt even more tense. Many Palestinians had been shot and killed at the checkpoints, and none of the soldiers were ever brought to trial. Should anything happen, we would be stuck for hours in the ensuing fear and traffic freeze. Each time, I prayed for a smooth crossing, my eyes darting around nervously.

Finally, at the checkpoint, the soldiers stopped each car, looked at all the passengers' IDs, and searched the vehicle. It was nerve-wracking, with the guns a few inches away. Most of the soldiers were fresh out of high school, doing their army service. Sometimes, they asked the drivers to step out of their cars, to suffer the added indignity of being questioned and hassled by teenagers.

It took anywhere between forty-five minutes to an hour and a half, sometimes more, to cross. The minute I was through, I felt like I was on another planet. Driving down the smooth, modern highways, I choked on my anger. Israelis lived in oblivion to all of this. They were worlds away.

I used a toll road to avoid traffic. Highway 6 passed near Palestinian towns and villages in the Triangle, on land that some owners had been forced to sell. Apart from industrial plants, there were few Jewish communities along the route. Half-way through, there was a large service station. Here, I made the mental switch to being in Israel and speaking Hebrew. As I continued north, each stop I made, every flag I saw reminded me of my years there and the suffocation I had felt. In the village, I hid from it all, but I still had to deal with it when I went to hospital with Mum.

Back in Ramallah, I took off that hat and put back on the Palestinian one. I was lucky in my freedom of movement. In the West Bank, Palestinians could not get from one city to another without going through Israeli checkpoints. The landscape was dotted with Jewish settlements, built illegally on Palestinian land. They had their own network of roads, many of which were forbidden to Palestinians. The roads, of course, were also built on stolen land.

IV

Three months after my move, a theatre in Hebron invited us to watch one of their plays. It was my first visit to the city, which bustled with light industries and shops. Its people were known dynamos of Palestinian commerce. Before the play began, the director took us on a tour to the Cave of the Patriarchs (Ibrahimi Mosque), a landmark that was sacred to both Muslims and Jews. Inside, I was shocked to see metal fences keeping the two groups apart. The mosque had been the site of the mass murder in 1994 by a Jewish settler, Baruch Goldstein.

We walked in the old town. In 2009, at the time of our visit, Hebron had more than 200,000 Palestinians, with settlements of a few hundred Jews right in the middle of it. They were guarded by hundreds of Israeli soldiers. The settlers attacked Palestinians and prevented them from getting to their homes and businesses. We walked down Shuhada Street, which used to be one of the main thoroughfares of the city. Abandoned stores lay shuttered on either side. In some areas, settlers had taken over the top floors of homes and buildings. I was surprised to see large nets and canvases hanging overhead, and asked the theatre director what they were. 'The Palestinians living in the bottom floors put them up to protect themselves, because the settlers hurl garbage down at them,' he said.

I looked up at the nets and saw rotten food, used diapers, and bags of waste. The canvases were used to protect people from dirty water, which the settlers also threw down. Walking on, we saw a few homes that they had completely taken over. They were surrounded by metal fences and electric gates. Children in Jewish religious clothing peered at us from behind the thick wire mesh. 'Can you imagine?' the director said. 'They take the kids to school and bring them back in armored cars.'

I wondered what kind of upbringing this was, how these children would grow up. He seemed to read my mind. 'They'll do exactly what their parents are doing—make our lives hell,' he winced.

On the way back, we were very quiet. When I got home, though we had not walked much, exhaustion seeped from my body. I made a cup of tea and checked my email. There was a message from Sofia. She had gotten divorced and moved back to Sweden, and was coming for a visit. 'Shall we get together, perhaps with Eva?' she suggested. 'Maybe do lunch in Karmiel, for old times' sake!'

I looked at the message, folded my laptop, and lay on the couch. Somehow, I could not bring myself to write back that night.

V

I told my colleague, Amin, about our trip. 'My uncles had a huge problem this weekend,' he countered. 'They went to pick the olives and the settlers attacked them!'

Each year, the olive harvest began in October and lasted about a month. Amin's family lived in Burin, a village near Nablus. They suffered frequent attacks from the nearby settlers of Yitzhar. 'They stole the bags of olives that my uncles had picked and beat them up!' Amin told me. 'The guards of the settlement joined in, then other settlers came, and they were armed. My uncles had to leave!'

The attacks had become a ritual. Settlers burned farmland, stole trees, and damaged crops. Israeli authorities uprooted thousands of olive trees each year to make way for more settlement. Palestinian farmers also faced closures and could not get to their lands. Then there was the Separation Wall. Most of its route snaked through the West Bank, by design, annexing a tenth of its land. It sliced through Palestinian communities, cutting people off from their families, schools, jobs, and from land that they had worked for generations. Without access, Amin explained, many landowners were forced to abandon lucrative farming, which needed year-round cultivation, and replace it with olive trees, which took less care. Yet, even olive trees grew sick and gave a smaller yield if they were not tended to. Harvesting was also made difficult by the thorny weeds, which the farmers could not get to regularly and remove.

During the harvest, Palestinian families traditionally worked together, from great-grandparents to their grandchildren. But the Israeli authorities refused to grant permits and often allowed only the landowners, who were usually the oldest and least able-bodied, to access the land.

I could not say much to Amin. His anger was palpable. The settlers were protected by the army, which turned a blind eye to their attacks and even joined them. There was little the farmers could do as they watched their land and crops withering away.

VI

A few days later, I drove north to Karmiel to meet the girls. I was very happy to see them, but, from the first moment, everything felt different. They were the same; I was not. 'So, how's Ramallah?' Sofia asked, with a smile.

'Good,' I said. I did not know where to begin.

'You work in a theatre, you said?'

I started to tell them about my job and a little about the city. Eva cut in. 'Tell me, what is it like? Is it a normal place, with houses and cars and everything?'

'No,' I smiled. 'We live in tents, and each of us has a camel tied out front.'

Sofia burst out laughing. 'How can you ask her that?'

Eva blushed. 'Well, I didn't know ... I've never been there.'

'You'll just have to come visit,' I said.

'What? No! I can't!'

'Why not?' Both of us looked at her.

'It's dangerous! Israelis are not supposed to go there!'

In fact, there was a big, ugly sign at the entrance of Ramallah prohibiting Israelis from entering. They could still come in through the roads to the Jewish settlements, but few of them wanted to. The exception, of course, was Palestinians with Israeli citizenship, thousands of whom had moved to Ramallah to escape the same oppression I had felt.

Again, I felt the huge distance between us. I told Sofia and Eva about the occupation. I had to keep my patience as I toned it down, just as I had done with Dave, because I realized they would never understand—and, unlike Dave, they were not interested. I felt my old resentment that I had tried so hard to ignore. We moved on to other topics as I felt the chasm widening.

I gave Eva my number and called her several times, but she stopped calling me back. Sofia and I continued to meet when she visited, but I was finding it more and more difficult not to talk about the situation, and feeling angry at the disinterest, when I did.

It was not much better in the village. By now, I had understood that there were three types of people there, and among Palestinians in Israel, generally: those who were active and spoke out, risking danger and harassment; those who understood, but kept quiet because they were worried for their livelihoods; and those who went above and beyond to assimilate, almost negating their identity to 'fit' a docile image. My old neighbor in Fassouta, to whom I was very close, could not fathom why I was living in Ramallah. 'What are you doing there?' she demanded, each time she saw me. I tried to explain, but she kept brushing it away. 'You had a great salary here; you could come back tomorrow and be rid of all that stress!'

I finally lost my patience and explained that I could not, after my experience, work in Israeli companies again.

'Why?' she asked, heatedly. 'You're still into Palestine and all that?'

I had never seen her so het up. I was used to people in the village sticking their nose, sometimes bluntly, into everyone's business, but her tone was unusually aggressive. 'I'll tell you something,' she added. 'My brother is in the army, and while you're sleeping soundly at night, he and others like him are protecting us!'

'From whom?' I asked, weakly. I had not known she had a brother in the Israeli army.

'From the terrorists across the border!' she blurted.

'I was born across that border,' I told her. There was a heavy silence.

Fassouta had not changed, I knew, in my few years away. But, the more I saw, the more limited it became, in my eyes.

VII

The first Christmas, after my return, was a sad affair. Mum could hardly move. The dialysis had debilitated her and she was developing further complications. She told me to prepare dinner and I did it with a heavy heart. I finished cooking and called Mousa and Dad. They told me to take the food into her room, to make it easier. We sat around the bed, put a small table between us, and tried to be cheerful, but all of us were down. Two days later, she had to go back to hospital, and we spent New Year's Eve without her. She was in hospital more often than not and needed care that we could not give her at home. My father began to enquire about transferring her to a longer-term facility, where she would be more comfortable. 'Go back to your work,' he told me. 'I'll take care of it.'

The next few weeks were turbulent, and my mind was with her. I kept following up with Dad, but her condition was too unstable to move her elsewhere. Three days before Easter, he called me. 'Can you come a bit earlier?' he asked. Mousa had just left for London to start a new job.

I was set to go to the village the next day, but I hurriedly packed and left straight after work. By the time I arrived, an ambulance had taken her back to hospital. 'We'll go see her tomorrow,' Dad said.

The next day was her fifty-seventh birthday. We spent the morning with her and talked to our family doctor, who was the head of department and was treating her. He revealed there was little they could do. 'It's in God's hands,' he finished.

I felt lightheaded. Dad and I walked out of his office, shaken. We did not share this with Mum. The visiting hours were over, and I told her I would come back to be with her in the afternoon, during her dialysis session. Dad and I kissed her and left, saying little on the way.

In the village, the church bell began its sad chimes for Good Friday, and I felt an ominous heaviness. But I kept telling myself she would be OK. The doctor had told us that no one knew; she could still live for many years, even in her condition. I tried to hold on to that. I fixed a quick lunch, which Dad and I ate without an appetite. Then, I lay down a little. My mobile rang. 'What are you doing?' Mum asked.

I told her I was resting until visiting time, when I would come to see her.

She started to cry. 'I don't think I'm going to make it till Easter,' she wept.

'What?' I sat up, desperately. 'Mum, you'll be fine! Dad and I are going to transfer you somewhere better, and you'll be fine, I promise!'

'I'm going to my dialysis now. Don't be late,' she sniffed.

I lay back on the bed with a heavy heart. I must have nodded off for a few minutes. The next thing I knew, Dad was rushing through the door and shaking me awake. They had just called from the hospital. She had died of a heart attack.

VIII

The world crashed, stopped, blurred into nothingness. For a week, the house filled with people. I could not stop crying. I cried for everything: for her, for Mama Hanneh, for our scattered lives. I was crushed with pain and guilt. I should have returned from Canada much earlier, I kept telling myself, should have stayed in Fassouta. I felt that I had let down a woman who had loved me and my brother and done everything she could to raise us as her own.

I suggested to Dad that I move back with him, but he refused. His brothers and sisters were near, and he could manage very well by himself, he told me. Camelia stayed on to do the housework. 'You're doing well in Ramallah, stay there,' he said. 'What will you do here, go back to work in Israeli companies? Have you forgotten what it was like?'

No, I had not. And my alienation had grown, tenfold, since I had known life 'on the other side'. On the journey back, carrying my pain, I was so incensed at the inhuman jam at the checkpoint that I lost my patience and charged ahead, wanting to get in front of a large truck that was squeezing me out. I miscalculated. He moved forward at the same time, ramming my car in the side. A pedestrian began to yell: 'Slow down! You've hit your car!' as a thick stream of tears blurred my vision. I did not bother to get out and ask the truck driver for his insurance details. I would live with the big dent in the side; my car was so old that I knew its days were numbered. The trips across the checkpoint had all but finished it off.

At the theatre, everyone gave me their condolences. I began to feel an overwhelming emptiness. The phone would not ring any-more with Mum's calls. I would not be following up on her situa-tion with Dad, planning trips to see her, feeling happy on the days that she looked better. It had all happened so fast, when I had felt she would still be around for years.

IX

I tried to get on with work. Amin and I were supposed to finish the accounts of a major production, but he was distracted. 'We went to visit my brother, in Ofer,' he told me, suddenly.

'What?' I had not known he had a brother in prison.

'Security charges …' he sighed. 'They said he threw stones.'

His brother was a victim of administrative detention. The Israeli army went into towns, villages and refugee camps at all hours, searching homes and arresting people, including children. 'He's been inside for six months. They won't put him on trial,' Amin said.

'Does he have a lawyer?' I asked.

'Yes. But it's my mother I'm worried about. She's crying all the time.'

I had heard horror stories of the treatment of detainees. They were kept for hours in the sun or cold, denied basic amenities and family visits, and had very poor medical care. They were transferred to courts, clinics, or other prisons in a metal, cage-like vehicle known as the 'bosta' (like a postal truck), which could barely accommodate one person in a sitting position. Their hands and feet were cuffed through the journey, and they could be shackled for more than twelve hours a day, without food or water.[2] They staged many hunger strikes to protest their conditions. Many of the chronically ill died of neglect. It was on the news all the time.

'How often do you get to see him?' I asked Amin, as he stared into space.

'Not often. We keep going and they turn us back. He seemed to be doing OK when I last saw him. But he's younger, and I worry about him.' He looked up at me. 'They do all kinds of things to get "confessions". That's what worries me.'

The system stopped at nothing. It used torture, sexual abuse, threats against family members, and even sexual threats against female relatives to force the detainees to 'confess'. On the flip side, it gave them money or promised shorter sentences in return for collaboration. Thousands of Palestinians had been snared in this way, co-opted into Israel's secret service.

'The lawyer is working on it,' said Amin, matter-of-factly. There were no fair trials or due process in the military courts. All the lawyers could do for the desperate families was to try to reduce the victims' sentences.

'I hope he comes out soon,' I replied, feeling the same helplessness I had felt at every turn since coming to Ramallah. Amin went back to his office. Every Palestinian family seemed to have a story of suffering. More than half the people I had met, in less than a year, had either been in prison or had a family member there. Many had relatives or friends who had died in the conflict.

The more I saw, the more discord I felt in my work. International aid kept us alive, but our subjugation deepened every day. Writing applications for funding felt mercenary and degrading. At the end of the year, I resigned and did some freelance translation. Then, one of my parents' friends introduced me to the director of a public media outlet. 'They're looking for someone to edit English news,' she told me.

In many countries, a government position was a good job. The public sector provided security, financial incentives, and a comfortable work environment. Under the Palestinian Authority, the picture was entirely different. 'I'll have to contract you as a consultant in order to pay you properly,' the director said. 'If I hire you as a permanent employee, the salary would be too low.'

We had our meeting at his office, on the top level of a five-storey building. The large mahogany desk, quality carpets, and huge flag behind him belied what he was saying. The pay he could offer was still low, even with the arrangement he had proposed, but it was the most he could do, so we agreed that I would work part time. This seemed to suit him, and I could continue with some translation on the side. Despite the limited setup, I walked out in excitement. It was the first time that I was really looking forward to a new job, the first time I would do something so directly related to Palestine.

I started in January 2011. Immediately, I was hit by that feeling of listless bureaucracy that pervades government departments in poor countries. The news staff were on the second floor. The editor-in-chief welcomed me warmly and told me that they had been looking for a good English editor for some time. I understood, tacitly, that I had good standing as I had been sent by the director, which made me slightly uncomfortable, but I knew I would prove myself soon enough. He took me to the English room, introduced me to my co-editor and left.

The whole floor was depressing, with bare-bones furniture and fading paint on the walls. Dozens of employees punched in each day, but many spent their days drinking coffee, smoking, and chatting, for lack of work to do. The Authority was the largest employer, and thousands of jobs had been created so people could earn a living and support their families, in an economy strangled by Israeli occupation. The Arabic department was next to us and was far larger. Some of the staff glanced at us, but they kept to themselves, as though they did not have the energy to meet anyone new.

In the English room, things seemed a little different. I worked with five women, all fresh graduates. They were eager to do well, hoping for long-term positions. I felt a stab of pity as I looked at their keen faces. We did two weeks of training, then I went to the editor-in-chief with ideas and plans. 'Just do the work you've been hired to do,' he grunted, smoking heavily. Several PLO old-timers sat around his office, exchanging meaningless chatter. They looked at me curiously, their eyes lighting up for a second, then going blank

again. I nodded and went back to my desk. It took little time for me
to become demotivated, too.

Slowly, I got to know more of the Arabic staff. For the first
time, I saw the real poverty that many people lived in. They had
their budgets tightly worked out, right down to a few shekels for
transport and a falafel sandwich at work. Each expense frightened
them, whether it was heating bills, their children's university fees,
or a sudden illness, for government care was severely lacking.
Many shopped in cheap outlets or street markets, waiting for the
end of day when stall owners gave out the remaining produce for
next to nothing.

The girls I worked with counted on their meager earnings to
cover their expenses and help their parents. Still, they had ambition.
One wanted to improve her composition and write features.
Another wanted to do a Master's. The other two were obsessed
with cameras and hoped to become field journalists. The last, who
had the toughest home circumstances, had humbler dreams. 'I want
to buy some new clothes and eat at a restaurant,' she told me, shyly.
'It would be so nice ...'

X

At a cultural event in Ramallah, I met Trees, a Dutch lady who was
married to a Palestinian from Sakhnin, in the Galilee. She invited
me to visit her. She and Ali Zbeidat, her husband, lived in a house
that had belonged to his family for generations, but the authorities
claimed that it was built on land belonging to Misgav, the Jewish
regional council.[3] The house was under threat of demolition, and
the couple fought a battle in Israeli courts for more than ten years,
paying thousands of dollars in fines and legal fees. Finally, Ali was
sentenced to time in prison or to community service, for failing to
evacuate his own home.

A tenth of the Palestinians in Israel were in the same situation,
living in homes that were classified as illegal, or in unrecognized
communities. After the founding of the state, about forty-five
Bedouin villages in the Naqab (Negev) and the Galilee were not
recognized. They received no water, electricity, infrastructure, or
public services. Although the state denied the Bedouin's ownership

of their land, it recognized them as owners if they decided to sell it.[4] To get them to move away, it built several 'legal' townships in the Naqab, and about 100,000 Bedouin moved there. Jewish settlements were off-limits to them.

An equal number of Bedouin stayed on their land, even though their unrecognized status meant they lived in appalling conditions. Some villages, such as al-Araqeeb, were demolished dozens of times, only for their people to rebuild their shacks. They could not practice self-sufficient agriculture, as they had always done. The government enforced severe grazing restrictions, and those who moved to the townships rarely got permits to keep livestock. They did not receive subsidized water, which the state gave to Jewish agricultural collectives. Slowly, the Bedouin's way of life was eroded, and they struggled in poverty.[5]

While Palestinians in Israel could still, as citizens, fight the system from within—though they had very few wins—those in the West Bank had no such luxury. In their walled-off confines, the right of return seemed no more than a pipe dream. In February 2011, the Minister of Culture in Ramallah hosted a well-known poet, Ahmad Dahbour, who suddenly broke into sobs on stage, describing his family's exodus from Haifa during the Nakba. Tears filled my eyes. I knew how remote and illusory the dream of return really was. In Israel, the government had just passed a new Nakba Law, which threatened to cut off public funding for any organization that taught about the event, or marked Israel's Independence Day as a Palestinian day of mourning.

XI

A few months later, we were told that our salary payments would be delayed. 'Israel is withholding the taxes,' my co-editor told me. According to the Oslo agreements, the Israeli government collected custom tariffs, on behalf of the Palestinian Authority, on goods that were destined for Palestinian markets but had to transit through Israeli ports. The sums, amounting to tens of millions of dollars, were transferred to the Palestinian Authority each month and made up two-thirds of its revenue.[6] The Authority used them to pay its nearly 150,000 employees, who supported a significant portion of the population. But Israel had withheld these funds several times, in the past, in order to apply political pressure, or as a form of mass punishment when Palestinian resistance broke out. The funds were held up in 2000, after the outbreak of the Second Intifada, and again in 2006, when Hamas won the parliamentary elections.

This time, in May 2011, Israel suspended the transfers in response to a reconciliation deal between Fatah and Hamas. Weeks dragged on, with no payments in sight. One morning, an older colleague from the Arabic department stormed into our office. 'I'm tired!' he burst out. 'I have five children to feed, and two of them are studying at university. How long will we be at their mercy to survive?'

One of the girls left our team. Morale was low, and work suffered. The crisis was eventually resolved, only for another one to hit. Tired of the negotiations track that the United States kept pushing while Israel continued building illegal settlements and trampling Palestinian rights, the Palestinians decided to take their cause to the international arena. In September 2011, President Mahmoud Abbas submitted Palestine's application to join the United Nations. A month later, while this was in process, Palestine was granted full membership of UNESCO. The United States announced that it would suspend its payments to the organization, and Israel suspended the tax revenue payments to the Palestinian Authority. Salaries were delayed, again.

At this point, I found work in consulting and gladly left my depressing spell in 'government' work.

XII

Working with the public, private, and civil sectors, I began to see how deeply the Israeli occupation damaged our economy. Universities were mostly restricted to students from their own localities, due to the movement restrictions. Private sector companies could not grow at will; their imports, exports, and manufacturing facilities were limited by Israeli constraints. Tens of thousands of Palestinian laborers were pushed to work in Israel, earning less than Israelis and having no social benefits. The public projects I worked on showed the humiliating controls that the Authority was under. The 'interim' situation that had followed the Oslo Accords had become the status quo, with no Palestinian state in sight.

Still, I settled down in Ramallah—perhaps because it was by choice and I could leave at any time, perhaps because the alternative was even more suffocating. At curious odds with the political situation, or, perhaps, because of it, the culture scene was thriving. There was an incredible number of films, plays, concerts, and book events. Each year saw multiple festivals organized by the municipality and various NGOs. It seemed to be the only outlet for the prevailing frustration.

I admired people who stuck it out, who saw no alternative to staying in their country and labored to make it better. As I had done in Fassouta, I envied those who were born and brought up in Ramallah. They knew no other reality, and they fought to survive, every day. I visited the village often, as much as to see my family as to get away, but I could not think of returning to Israel.

Yet, most Palestinians in Ramallah looked on my Israeli ID with envy. When I said I was from the Galilee, they grew wistful. Many had visited before the Oslo Accords and the closing off of the Palestinian territory. But most of the younger generation had not. 'It's very beautiful there, isn't it?' they asked, longingly.

The sea was also a short drive away, yet most of them had never seen it. On some weekends, I endured the grueling exit from Ramallah to go swimming in Tel Aviv. Yet, I never fully enjoyed it. It felt wrong to be able to do something so simple that my friends could not. I never told them I had gone. At the beach, the scene of normality sliced through me. Crowds of Israelis and tourists milled around, swimming and enjoying themselves. No one thought of the millions of people, just an hour away, who were barred from doing the same thing.

Gaza, a little south along the coastline, had been under Israeli blockade since 2007, after Hamas had come to power. The strip had turned into an open-air prison.

On my drive back to Ramallah, the settlements loomed, alien and condescending. I drove past the rows of houses and thought of their residents cozied up inside.

The aftermath of the Nakba followed me, everywhere I went. In April 2012, Mousa Assi, my uncle's friend from the days of resistance, passed away at sixty-four years of age in Fassouta. After the discovery of their Fatah membership, in 1970, Mousa and George

Matar were imprisoned for eight years. Ali and Nimer Shaqqour, who were cousins and worked with them, received longer sentences, but they managed to flee the country. Israeli intelligence used extremely cruel methods of interrogation. One was the intense shaking of a person until his brain suffered temporary damage and he began to hallucinate. Mousa was tortured until he lost his mind. He was discharged a year before the end of his sentence due to his psychological illness. His family spent years treating him, to no avail. He had lost any awareness of himself or those around him, and died without knowing who or where he was.

XIII

Two months later, the Israeli government ran an advertising campaign to encourage the employment of its Palestinian citizens in Israeli workplaces.[7] One of the ads asked: 'What's wrong with an Israeli Arab in your office?' Underneath, it provided the answer: 'Nothing!'

Israel continued to refer to its Palestinian citizens as a 'demographic problem', and some members of government regularly called for their expulsion through 'demographic transfer'—forced displacement, or another Nakba—to neighboring Arab countries or to a future Palestinian state, in order to achieve the 'ethnic purity' of the 'Jewish state'. Those calls were made publicly, without shame or reprisals. Right-wing governments continued to gain power in Israel, ministers agitating against Palestinians had rising support, and racist laws continued to pour forth. It was commonplace to speak of the 'Jewish state', oaths of allegiance to such a state, and the threat of stripping Israeli citizenship for alleged disloyalty, a practice unheard of in other countries. Public bodies, such as local councils, were forbidden from political criticism, with the threat of losing their funding. A bill allowed libel suits and criminal charges against anyone who criticized Israel; another law limited the freedom to call for a boycott of any Israeli entity; and an anti-infiltration law handed down prison sentences for helping asylum seekers and refugees. NGOs and activists that worked for peace and justice were facing a rise in arrests, interrogations, and police violence.[8]

The laws effectively barred marriage between Palestinians in Israel and those in the West Bank and Gaza, as well. Suhad, my friend, was from Nazareth and had married a Palestinian from Ramallah. Her husband was not allowed to live with her in Nazareth. They had spent years applying for temporary residency for him. Under Israeli law, marriage did not confer Israeli citizenship to a Palestinian spouse. When Shadia, my uncle Geris' wife, had arrived from the UK, she had also been refused naturalization in Israel, as she was of Palestinian origin. The law did not apply to other foreign spouses brought into Israel, who could apply for a naturalization process, similar to that in other countries.

Suhad had to live in Ramallah with her husband. Their three children had Israeli ID. When she took them to Jerusalem to access medical care, her husband could not accompany her. Nor could he go when she took them to visit her family. 'Sometimes, I feel like I'm divorced,' she told me. 'People even look at me strangely.'

Many such couples lived apart, with the one from Israel visiting the one in the West Bank.[9] Suhad had made the move, but she gave up a good job in Nazareth and missed her family and network of support. Her trips back and forth were draining and took a toll on her relationship. 'I'm torn between two places, two lives, just for marrying the man I want,' she said.

XIV

In the summer of 2012, trouble was brewing, again, in Gaza, where the blockade had led to untold loss and suffering. On top of the suffocating controls, Israel restricted fishing, an industry that supported thousands of families. The army attacked Gazan fishermen, confiscated their boats, and damaged their equipment. Hamas increased its rocket attacks and the army responded with raids. On 14 November 2012, Israel assassinated Ahmed Jabari, chief of the military wing of Hamas, and launched 'Operation Pillar of Defense' on the Strip.

It was less than four years since the last onslaught, when I had demonstrated with friends in Canada. Now, I was watching the scenes, again, but they were barely an hour away. No one was allowed into Gaza except the staff of international organizations, aid workers, and journalists. Dozens of Palestinians were killed and hundreds injured. On 21 November, a ceasefire was announced. The Israeli strikes left another wave of massive damage in Gaza, and the blockade was not lifted.

A week later, on 29 November, the United Nations General Assembly admitted Palestine as a state, within the 1967 borders, and granted it non-member observer status. I stood with my friends in al-Manara Square, the center of Ramallah, watching the large TV screens that had been set up. Crowds of people cheered. We did what Mahmoud Darwish had said: cultivate hope.

But there was little to go on. In the news, images of dead young men, wrapped in Palestinian flags and accompanied by hundreds of mourners, were routine, as were scenes of homes being bulldozed in front of their sobbing residents. Olive trees were violently uprooted by settlers. Children were run over. Prisoners died in hunger strikes. The notion that we were trying to live our lives and make the most of a terrible situation rang hollow. We were all burying our head in the sand, until our turn came.

In June 2014, three teenage settlers went missing near Hebron. Israel claimed that they were abducted by Hamas. For two weeks, the army stormed cities and villages in the West Bank, blocked roads, and closed charitable institutions and universities. Hundreds of Palestinians were arrested, many of whom had been freed in a prisoner exchange deal three years earlier. Four were killed in the clashes. In Ramallah, angry crowds hurled stones at a Palestinian police station, enraged at the security coordination with Israel. Palestinian police stayed off the streets and did not interfere when the Israeli army came in. We lived in spiraling fear, for the army's actions were accountable to no one.

Two weeks later, the bodies of the Israeli teenagers were found in a field, west of Hebron. They had been shot soon after the kidnapping.[10] The army's campaign escalated in the West Bank. Hundreds of Israelis rioted in Jerusalem and attacked Palestinian passersby, who had to be extricated by the police. Prominent right-wing Israelis, including rabbis, posted messages of hate and incitement on social media. Soldiers called for revenge; ministers and politicians called for 'war on the snakes' and genocide.[11] Jewish crowds at football matches chanted: 'Death to Arabs!'[12] One

Facebook page showed two, smiling Israeli girls with a caption: 'Hating Arabs is not racism, it's values!'[13]

In Shu'fat, a Palestinian neighborhood of East Jerusalem, a family was walking on the main road when a car stopped beside them and someone grabbed their ten-year-old boy and tried to abduct him. His mother fought with the assailants and the child managed to wriggle free. But, in the early hours of the morning, a group of Jewish settlers kidnapped, tortured, and burned alive another boy, Mohammed Abu Khdeir.[14]

16

CULTURE OF HATE

Abu Khdeir's murderers are not 'Jewish extremists'. They are the descendants and builders of a culture of hate and vengeance that is nurtured and fertilized by the guides of 'the Jewish state': Those for whom every Arab is a bitter enemy, simply because they are Arab; those who were silent at the Beitar Jerusalem games when the team's fans shouted 'death to Arabs' at Arab players; those who call for cleansing the state of its Arab minority, or at least to drive them out of the homes and cities of the Jews.

No less responsible for the murder are those who did not halt, with an iron hand, violence by Israeli soldiers against Palestinian civilians, and who failed to investigate complaints 'due to lack of public interest.' The term 'Jewish extremists' actually seems more appropriate for the small Jewish minority that is still horrified by these acts of violence and murder. But they too recognize, unfortunately, that they belong to a vengeful, vindictive Jewish tribe whose license to perpetrate horrors is based on the horrors that were done to it.

Haaretz editorial[1]

We were in the Muslim holy month of Ramadan. At 3:45 in the morning on 2 July 2014, sixteen-year-old Mohammed stood near to his house in Shu'fat, waiting to eat the pre-dawn meal with friends. A car stopped next to him and a few men dragged him into it. 'Dad, dad, save me!' he screamed as it sped off. His family immediately called the police. The four settlers, two of them minors, took him to the Jerusalem Forest, where they beat him repeatedly with a crowbar. With each blow, their ringleader shouted out the name of an Israeli victim of violence, including the three murdered teenagers.[2] The attackers then threw petrol on their victim, forced him to swallow it, and burned him alive. His charred body was found by the police an hour later. The results of the autopsy found soot in his lungs, showing that he had inhaled the burning material.

Thousands of mourners gathered for the funeral in East Jerusalem, sparking two days of violent clashes. Eleven other Palestinians were killed and dozens wounded. Mohammed's cousin, fifteen-year-old Tariq, was abducted and savagely beaten by the police. 'And they hit me, and they kept hitting me and then I fell asleep and then I woke up in the hospital,' he said.[3] An Israeli Instagram page showed his horribly swollen face with an image of a pig next to it. When his dead cousin's family went to court, a group of settlers spat at them.[4]

Throughout the ordeal, tension was again rising in Gaza. On 8 July, Israel launched 'Operation Protective Edge', the third onslaught in six years. In two days, it dropped 400 tons of bombs on the strip.[5] The strikes targeted civilian areas, claiming that militants were hiding in homes, schools, and hospitals. Moshe Feiglin, deputy speaker of the Knesset, called on the Israeli government to cut off electricity to Gazan hospitals.[6] Some soldiers posed with guns on social media with the caption: 'Let us just spray!'[7] In the West Bank, the 'Price Tag' campaign of violence, which had been ongoing for six years, peaked. Settlers attacked Palestinians, threw stones, burned mosques, defaced churches, vandalized cars, and uprooted trees. In Jerusalem, there were more attempts to kidnap children. Israeli universities, hospitals, and mobile phone companies suspended Palestinian employees for posting support for Gaza on Facebook. When Palestinian citizens in Israel called for a general strike to protest the Gaza war, Israeli foreign minister Avigdor Lieberman called on Jews to boycott Arab restaurants and shops, saying the state should transfer hundreds of thousands of its Palestinian citizens to the West Bank and strip them of their Israeli nationality.[8] Members of the Knesset who objected were thrown out of sessions.

In seven weeks, Israel launched 6,000 strikes on Gaza. Tens of thousands of homes, schools, hospitals, and businesses were destroyed, and the infrastructure was devastated—again.

Israel said it was protecting Israelis from Hamas. The Israeli death toll was sixty-seven soldiers and six civilians. Thousands of Palestinians were killed or maimed.[9]

II

I packed my bag and ran away to Fassouta. Half-way through, at the service station on Highway 6, I could not bring myself to stop and buy coffee. Terror and grief raced through me. I kept charging north. Near Haifa, I almost got a speeding ticket.

When I got home, Dad was sleeping. I put my things down and headed for a walk. I took the road out of the village, which ended at Abirim, the Jewish community near us.

I picked up my pace, footsteps pounding the asphalt. This path was always surreal to me, so remote and idyllic that it seemed removed from the rest of the country. Small olive groves lay on each side, fringed with pine trees and wild shrubs. In the distance, the mountain slopes were a brilliant green, giving way to the shimmering sea.

A couple made their way up the road, two dogs in tow. I often saw them on my walks. They were dressed in hippie style that looked starkly out of place in the Galilean setting. 'Shalom,' they said, and walked past, deep in conversation. Another man followed, his shaggy dog trailing behind. I saw him often, too. We did the cursory nod.

We lived so close together, yet there was no sense of a shared space, only a wary tolerance in which we mostly ignored each other. There was very little visiting or mingling.

At the end of the road, I had to turn back. I had reached the gate. I suddenly remembered Eva. Since I had given her my mobile number in Ramallah, years ago, I had not heard from her again.

The way back was slower, as I had to climb the hill. At the top, I paused, panting. A car suddenly stopped by my side and two men ambled out. One of them carried a map. 'Excuse me, do you know where the Crusader fortress is?' he asked, in English.

They seemed to be Jewish Americans, from their accents and the kippahs they wore. 'Uh, no,' I faltered. 'I know it's somewhere around here, but I haven't been there.'

'OK, because it says it's through there,' he said, pointing to a nearby sign on what seemed to be an abandoned gate.

Suddenly, I was afraid. The attempts to kidnap Palestinians and the torture and murder of that poor boy flashed through my mind. I was conscious of being alone on that stretch of road, with these people only a few feet away and their car behind them. 'I'm sorry,' I said, beginning to walk on. 'You can continue up to the moshav,' I pointed at Abirim, 'and ask there.'

The man thanked me and said: 'Have a good walk!'

I strode ahead, hearing him on his mobile behind me. My steps were faster than usual and I hoped to see anyone from Fassouta, of the usual crowd who came walking. But the road was strangely deserted. I heard the car start up behind me and my heart beat faster. Finally, when the hum of the engine had faded, I allowed myself to look back. They had gone. I turned again and hastened my steps. The village was not far, I told myself.

Twenty minutes later, they passed me, again, and the driver called out, jubilantly: 'We found it!'

I smiled, feeling relieved that I was near the village. 'You've put me to shame ...'

'Want a ride?' he grinned.

'No,' I attempted a laugh.

'Well, I'm only joking. I wouldn't give you one, even if you said yes!' He gave me a thumbs-up, smiled and drove on.

No one would have guessed what was happening a mere three hours away.

III

In March 2015, during elections, Israeli prime minister Benjamin Netanyahu rallied his supporters with a warning: 'The right-wing government is in danger. Arab voters are heading to the polling stations in droves. Left-wing NGOs are bringing them in buses.'[10]

The turnout of Palestinian citizens had always been low, out of hopelessness and despair. Their few parties could gain limited seats and could not hope to impact government policies. In 2014, the government tried a different route to stop them from entering the Knesset. It passed a Threshold Law, raising the proportion of votes needed to win a seat. The threshold was too high for each of the four Palestinian parties to clear. But the move backfired. They came together to form 'the Joint List', which became one of the largest blocs in parliament.

Unlike the Zionist parties, the List had a mandate of peace, equality, and justice for all citizens. Palestinians were one-fifth of the population, yet they were were never allowed to be part of a government coalition. They could not have a say in the affairs of the 'Jewish state', nor to contest its nature. It was unthinkable for Jews to imagine a non-Jewish prime minister. Palestinian members of Knesset were loudly attacked during sessions, and, with the success of the Joint List, we knew that more racist laws would be fired at them.

A few weeks later, I had a medical appointment in East Jerusalem. My doctor was in the heart of the old city. I usually dreaded these visits, for the area bore witness to decades of abuse and neglect. The pavement was worn; garbage was piled high in the dumpsters. There was little investment in housing, infrastructure, or public services. Most of the buildings were in a race against time. When they finally crumbled, the intended result was for the occupants to move away. West Jerusalem, of course, was a thriving hub for its Jewish residents.

The health center was so old that it reminded me of black-and-white movies. It housed several clinics and a lab. Rows of people waited with their babies and infants. We were a young society; more than half were children. There was a severe shortage of schools in East Jerusalem. Unemployment was high and drug use

416

was rampant. I looked at the little ones and wondered what kind of future they had ahead.

'Ah, Fida!' the doctor smiled. Dr. Kamal was in his early sixties and had practiced in England. As a Jerusalem resident, he did not have Israeli citizenship and could not vote in general elections. He had suffered under state policies all his life, and he was not hopeful at the recent outcome, with the Joint List. 'I hope they can do something, but I doubt they'll get very far,' he muttered.

After the appointment, I was in no hurry to struggle through the checkpoint on my way back. I strolled through the nearby market. Some shops were no bigger than my living room. The government had found another way to squeeze Palestinians out of the city: it had classified a third of their land as 'open, scenic areas' and declared an unusually high number of national parks in it, which had nothing of archaeological or natural importance.[11]

I stopped at a clothes shop. The owner was quick to come out on the pavement. 'How much are these?' I asked, pointing to a pair of pajamas.

'Thirty,' he said.

'And these?'

'Twenty-five.'

I did not have the heart to haggle. The prices were so low that I wondered how he made a living. I paid for the first pair, took them, and walked away, remembering that I had seen the same ones in Nahariya for 50 shekels.

On an impulse, I left the bag in the car and decided to visit the Church of the Holy Sepulcher. I had not been there in years. Walking to the end of Salaheddine Street, I felt a nervous tension at the row of parked police cars. The authorities had encouraged thousands of settlers to move into the heart of Palestinian neighborhoods. They attacked people and drove them out of their homes, with the help of the police and security services. The settlers were untouchable. They had become major supporting blocs of Israel's right-wing governments, which allocated disproportionately high funds for illegal settlement.[12]

The church was a short distance away, through Damascus Gate. Soldiers stood at the gate, guns gleaming in the sun. Looking up, I saw another soldier standing guard atop the city walls. Quickly, I walked through the arch of the gate and into the alleyways beyond.

I loved the atmosphere of the old market. Palestinian peasants crouched at floor stalls, selling fresh produce. Young boys wheeled carts around with bread and pastries. Inside, there was little light in the covered archways. The cobbled paths wound into a maze of shops that sold everything. Clothes, shoes, and jewelry jostled with food, spices, and souvenirs as locals and tourists ambled down the ancient alleys. The owners sat in front of their stores. They had little business. Again, I wondered how they survived. Most Palestinians in East Jerusalem lived in poverty.[13]

As I walked down, some men passed me hurriedly, dressed in Jewish religious garments. They marched with a sense of purpose in the direction of the Wailing Wall. They did not seem perturbed or to feel any danger, for they knew they were under full police protection. The Wall constituted the eastern border of the Noble Sanctuary of al-Aqsa Mosque. Jewish settlers and the police often attacked Muslim worshippers, and riots broke out.

On that day, curiosity got the better of me and I wanted to see the Wall, which I had never been to. I followed the signs. As I got closer, I noticed that the Palestinian stores on either side were bolted with large locks. They had been forced out of business, I gathered. Up ahead, I heard loud chanting. A group of young men came into view. At the start of each Hebrew month, a Jewish ceremony was held in the Muslim Quarter of the old city, with the police standing guard.[14] As I stared, men in religious clothing danced between the shuttered Palestinian shops, pounding on the closed doors. They held hands and spun around, chanting hymns in Hebrew. It was loud and over-bearing, like a war dance. A sudden tension thickened the air and Palestinian passersby kept a distance. I turned around and scurried back, abandoning my whim to see the Wall.

The church was a five-minute walk away. Groups of foreign pil-grims stood in the large courtyard with their tour guides. The tour-ism sector had been heavily diverted to serve the Jewish sector. Most of the tourists were bussed in by companies from Israel to see the sites, then taken back to Israel to eat, sleep, and shop. More and more hotels and stores in East Jerusalem were closing down, buck-ling under high taxes and trickling business.

In the dim interior of the church, I lit a candle, looking at the throngs of people around me. Some were lost in devotion. They

418

knelt, eyes closed, lips moving in silent supplication. It seemed so detached, somehow, from the calamity outside. I left and walked back to the car with a heavy heart. Before the founding of Israel, Jerusalem had been a religious destination and a thriving hub of Palestinian politics, commerce, education, and culture. Now, it had lost that standing, chopped up and cut off from its environs, like a sick man left to die.

IV

On 31 July 2015, at 2:00 am, two men smashed the windows and lobbed firebombs into two houses in Duma, a village near Nablus. One of the families was visiting relatives, but the Dawabsheh family was home. Their neighbor and relative heard screams and ran out. He saw two masked men standing over the family as they burned.[15] The men fled the scene, while the neighbor and his family tried to help the victims. They managed to bring their four-year-old son, Ahmed, out to safety. But his baby brother, eighteen-month-old Ali, was burned alive.

The wall of one of the houses was sprayed with Hebrew graffiti: 'Revenge!' and 'Long live the Messiah!', next to a Star of David.[16]

Both Sa'ad and Riham, the parents, died of their injuries. Only Ahmed survived, with serious burns over most of his body.

Weeks later, Israeli TV showed a video of a wedding in which friends of the assailants were celebrating the murder. They held up a photograph of the baby, Ali, and stabbed it as they danced around, waving knives, pistols, rifles, and Molotov cocktails, and chanting songs of revenge from the Old Testament.[17] At a court hearing of the assailants, Jewish extremists taunted Ali's uncle and grandfather: 'Where's Ali? Ali's on the grill!'[18]

Two months after the Dawabsheh attack, Hadeel al-Hashlamoun, an eighteen-year-old girl, was killed at an Israeli checkpoint in Hebron when two soldiers shot her at close range. Reports said she was holding a knife, but witnesses countered that she had not come close to the soldiers. They shot at her feet and she fell to the ground. They could have arrested her, but they continued to shoot, riddling her body with multiple bullets.[19]

The Palestinian Authority's response was to 'strongly condemn' these murders and call on the international community for help.

Palestinians were angry at their leadership, which was elitist, self-serving, impotent, and disconnected from their daily struggle. The split between Fatah and Hamas continued. Both were rife with corruption, and both cracked down on political dissent and refused to hold free elections. Foreign donors dictated the political figures in power and gave bloated budgets for Palestinian security services in order to protect Israel. The Authority escalated its crackdown on any resistance. Anger and despair spilled over, especially among youth, and we were in the midst of a new phenomenon.

It was not a mass uprising, this time. Young people, some in their early teens, acted of their own accord, often on the spur of the moment. They found their way to Jewish areas and stabbed Israelis with knives, machetes, or even scissors. The attackers were almost always killed.

Palestinian society had mixed reactions to the attacks. They were tragic, lone expressions of rage that brought their perpetrators home in coffins. Every few days, I was horrified to see another face on the news, another youngster who had lost the chance at life.

With every bout of violence, Palestinian self-questioning intensified. Twenty years of the failed 'peace process' had worn people out, and they had vivid memories of both uprisings, with a sense of despair that it had all led to nothing. There was no third intifada on the horizon. By March 2016, the knife attacks began to die down.

My avoidance of West Jerusalem had turned into terror. When I had to go for a medical follow-up, I was nervous every step of the way. To make things worse, I was given an appointment with a specialist in a Jewish Orthodox neighborhood. I drove over, found street parking, and got out my car to find the place. As I peered at the building numbers, a man suddenly came up to me. 'Are you looking for something?' he scowled.

I shook my head and walked away, stomach clamping in tension. There had been many attacks in the area, and the city was one of the main hotspots of the conflict. In the health center, I felt like a pariah and could not wait to leave. It was obvious that I was the only non-Jew, and people stared. I took my mobile phone out of my bag and kept my eyes fixed on it until I was called in.

I did not know whether to laugh or cry when the doctor diagnosed my ailment: 'It's most likely stress.'

V

I turned the water faucet in my kitchen. Nothing.

In Ramallah, we suffered shortages of water. The Jewish settlements surrounding us had plenty to water their lawns and fill their swimming pools, most of it stolen from Palestinian sources, while we had constant cuts. The last one had completely emptied my cisterns and those of the neighbors.

The announcement was that a major pipe had burst, and the Israeli water authority, which needed to make the fixes on its side, was stalling. Fed up, I escaped to Fassouta for a while, hoping the issue would be resolved when I returned. Dad's house, and all houses in Israel, did not have water cisterns. They had a constant supply of water.

When I returned, a week later, I tried again. Still, nothing. I climbed up on the roof. The large cisterns were empty. I checked with the neighbors. The water 'had not come', they told me. I went down to the supermarket and bought two packs of mineral water.

On my way upstairs, the neighbor stopped me. 'There's a man with a truck who comes around to fill your cisterns, if you want,' he said. 'I had to call him, because I have four kids and this was just unbearable. But it's expensive. He charges 200 shekels.'

That was three times my monthly bill, for a single filling. 'Thanks, but I'll manage,' I told him. I carried the bottles up the stairs and began to heat water in the kettle so I could empty it into the bucket and wash.

Before I could stop the thought, I remembered my childhood in Beirut. Then, too, the Israelis had cut off the water.

I filled the bucket, part hot and part cold, carried it to the bathtub, and placed it gingerly on the side. History, I thought, had a way of repeating itself.

VI

I was woken by a sudden noise just before dawn. There were rushed footsteps on the stairs, loud knocking, muffled cries, and the sound of steps clamoring down. I was too scared to open the door and did not dare to look out the window. In all likelihood, it was the Israeli army, breaking in to arrest someone. There had been a wave of incursions, and a recent one had been on our street, two buildings down.

I waited until things were quiet and went back to bed. But I could not sleep. Finally, in the morning, I heard voices on the stairs and rushed to open the door. 'They've taken Samir!' my neighbor said. She was standing with his wife, who was crying.

'Why?' I asked. The man worked at a pizza restaurant.

'No one knows,' the neighbor answered. Army break-ins were routine. Sometimes, the arrests were made in the day, but the jeeps often came in the middle of the night. The soldiers stormed homes, gathered people at gunpoint, and grabbed whoever they wanted. Children, even young ones, were often taken. The jeeps then rushed out of the city. If they were seen and chased by the youth, the soldiers threw stun grenades to clear the way.

I left the apartment to see my friends. They told me that the army had been in different places in town. No one felt safe or out of their reach. When I came home, I had barely sat down when I was startled by very loud bangs. I jumped up and tried to look out the window without getting too close. Clouds of heavy smoke rose in the near distance. Three Israeli army jeeps raced away as ambulances sped to the scene, sirens blaring. Then, I smelled it. They had used tear gas. I rushed to close the windows, but the choking stench had seeped into the house. My eyes began to well up and a burning sensation filled my throat. I was gripped by a cough and ran to the kitchen, the furthest room away. I grabbed my phone and called a friend, who lived right where I had seen the commotion. 'They were downstairs!' she said, in terror. 'Use onions! And keep the windows closed!'

VII

On 6 December 2017, US President Donald Trump formally recognised Jerusalem as the capital of Israel and announced plans to move the US Embassy there from Tel Aviv. Since 1948, the US, and virtually every country in the world, had refused to recognize Jerusalem as the Israeli capital, deferring recognition of the city's status until a final peace agreement. International law and most of the world consider East Jerusalem, illegally annexed by Israel in 1967, to be occupied territory. Palestinians were angry; their hopes of having East Jerusalem as the capital of their future state were dashed. Dozens were killed in protests.

Some months later, on 19 July 2018, the Israeli parliament passed a new 'Nation-State Law', which held that Israel is 'the national home of the Jewish people' and that only Israeli Jews have the right of self-determination in it. The law stated that all of Jerusalem was the capital of Israel, made Jewish settlement a national priority, and downgraded the status of Arabic as an official language, though 'its speakers have the right to language-accessible state services'. The law did not include the words 'democracy' or 'equality'.

Protests again broke out. Several appeals were made to the Israeli Supreme Court. Yet, nothing about the law came as a surprise, and none of it was new. The things it had codified had existed since Israel's birth. Adalah, a legal rights group for Palestinians in Israel, listed more than sixty-five Israeli laws that discriminated against them, in all areas of life.[20] On whatever side of the Separation Wall we lived, we paid the price, every day, for not being Jewish.

Over that raging summer, the US State Department canceled most aid payments to the West Bank and the Gaza Strip, and to UNRWA, the UN Palestinian refugee program. At the same time, President Trump rolled out his 'Peace to Prosperity' vision for the Middle East. The 'deal of the century', as it was dubbed, laid the blueprint of a Palestinian state as scattered pieces of territory under complete Israeli control. While 'negotiating' with the Palestinians for over two decades, Israel had increased its illegal settlers from 200,000 to nearly 700,000, almost a quarter of the population of the West Bank. The aim was to squeeze Palestinians into Bantustan-like population centers surrounded by Jewish settlements, walls, fences, security zones, and bypass roads. Under the plan, there would be no Palestinian state or anything resembling a sovereign entity, but ongoing Israeli occupation, phrased in different terms. The United States recognized Israel's illegal settlements and gave it the green light to formally annex a third of the West Bank.

In 2020, the coronavirus pandemic threw into sharp relief the discrimination against Palestinians in the West Bank and Gaza

Strip; Israel refused to share its abundance of vaccines and withheld millions of dollars, again, from the taxes that it collected on behalf of the Palestinian Authority. In East Jerusalem, Israel continued demolishing houses. While everyone was being told to stay home, those families suddenly had no homes to stay in. The Israeli Health Ministry focused its testing on the Jewish parts of the city and discriminated against the Palestinian residents. Palestinians formed committees to take care of themselves, but the police arrested officials who were in charge, harassed young volunteers, and confiscated the food and aid that they were trying to deliver to needy families.

While businesses were closed all over the country, some Israeli construction sites kept going. Most of the workers were Palestinians from the West Bank, and they were ordered to remain in Israel for several weeks and not to go home if they wanted to keep their jobs. Many had to sleep on the streets or on construction sites. One worker had trouble breathing, and his employer suspected that he was infected. He was tossed out of an Israeli police car at the Beit Sira checkpoint, near Ramallah, and left feverish on the ground, barely able to walk. The officers got out of the vehicle, disinfected themselves and the seats, and drove off.[21]

During the Jewish Passover holiday, Israel sent thousands of workers back to the West Bank without testing them for the virus. Many returned through circuitous routes and tunnels. Panic hit as the Authority struggled to test and safely isolate them.

Thousands of Palestinian detainees were held in Israel, at very high risk of the disease. Several suspected infections of prisoners were reported, and an Israeli interrogator who questioned them was diagnosed with the virus.[22] But Israel refused to release them, as some countries had done with their prisoners.

In the West Bank, despite the movement restrictions and social-distancing measures, Israeli settlers were imbued with new energy for destruction. For weeks, they stole livestock, torched cars, attacked homes, and scared people by spitting on their doors, sending local health teams chasing to disinfect after them. In Hebron and Nablus, they turned sewage water onto Palestinian crops, drove farmers off their lands, and damaged hundreds of trees. The Israeli police joined them in their attacks, or made arrests, threw tear gas canisters, and fired rubber bullets at Palestinians trying to defend themselves. The settlers, some with firearms, assaulted Palestinians with clubs, axes, electroshock weapons, stones, and dogs.[23] It seemed to be in line with the annexation fever raging in the country.

The 'deal of the century' was flatly rejected by Palestinians, and, this time, the world condemned the US–Israeli plans. In Israel, there was opposition within the coalition government, and many army commanders and security specialists rejected the move, seeing it as a threat to Israel's security. In the face of this local and international opposition, Israel was forced to back down, at least publicly.

When the dust had settled, though, there was little to celebrate. De facto annexation had long since taken place.

In May 2021, a wave of attacks by Israeli settlers on the al-Aqsa Mosque, and an Israeli eviction order for six Palestinian families in the East Jerusalem neighborhood of Sheikh Jarrah, led to an escalation in violence and another eleven-day military onslaught on Gaza. The war destroyed hundreds of homes and businesses and killed at least 256 Palestinians, including sixty-six children. On the Israeli side, there were thirteen deaths, including two children.

On 19 October, Israeli defense minister Benny Gantz designated six leading Palestinian civil society organizations (CSOs) as 'terror organizations', outlawing them and putting them at risk of reprisals.

In April 2022, a fresh wave of provocation by Israeli settlers and incursions into the al-Aqsa Mosque caused another outbreak of deadly violence.

And on 11 May 2022, Shireen Abu Akleh, a veteran Palestinian journalist, was killed by the Israeli army as she covered yet another incursion into Jenin refugee camp. Shireen was one of the longest-serving and most renowned journalists in Palestine. She worked for Al Jazeera and had been watched on TV in every Palestinian and Arab home, providing relentless coverage of events since the Second Intifada.

In 2021, I was working for Al Jazeera in Ramallah. When Israel had blown up the building that housed the Al Jazeera and the Associated Press offices in Gaza, I had sent a message to Shireen telling her to take care of herself. In more than twenty years of coverage, she had escaped death dozens of times.

But, on that spring morning, a year later, as she wore her 'Press' jacket and helmet, a bullet from an Israeli sniper hit her in the neck and ravaged her brain and skull. Shireen fell, face down, her blood seeping into the soil of Palestine. The friends who dressed her for the funeral described how they had to hold her body up to do so, for the head was hollow in the back and there was nothing to hold in order to lift it.

At her funeral in Jerusalem, Israeli police closed off the roads leading to the church where the service was held and attacked the mourners as they carried her coffin, beating them with batons and kicking them. They smashed the windows of her hearse and tore out the Palestinian flag, confiscated all the other Palestinian flags at the procession, and forbade them from walking her through the city. Instead, she had to be taken by car to her final resting place.

Shireen was as much of a threat to Israel in her death as in her life—for her legacy, and that of my mother and of countless Palestinian martyrs, will live on.

My journey continues. But one thing is certain: wherever I go, Palestine will be with me.

EPILOGUE

The story I have recounted in this book is hardly surprising, given the nature of Israel. More than a quarter century after my return to my homeland, I still struggle to find my place. Is it as a 'citizen' in a state that discriminates against me and labors to negate my existence; a member of the Palestinian community in Israel that suffers as inferior citizens; or a Palestinian among my brethren in the Palestinian territory, whose lives are a story of suffering each day?

The cases of Palestinians killed that I have recounted in this book are only a glimpse; each day or two in the West Bank, another Palestinian is routinely shot by the Israeli occupying forces, another life is taken with no accountability. Tens of Palestinians have perished before and after Shireen Abu Akleh, and they continue to die. The Euro-Med Monitor, in April 2022, documented that Israel has killed five times as many Palestinians this year than it killed in the same period in 2021.[1] The United Nations documented 132 Palestinians killed in the West Bank from 2021 to mid-June 2022.[2]

Israel has long touted itself as 'the only democracy in the Middle East'. In fact, it is a religious ethnocracy in which the dominant classes are Orthodox Jews, both Askhenazi and Sephardic. Anyone falling outside these categories is discriminated against, including American Jews such as Progressives and Reform Jews, who are not allowed to freely worship in Israel and have no place in its religious courts and institutions. Refugees are also not welcome in Israel and periodic reports emerge on the difficulties and racism they face, whether those who come from African countries or, most recently, from Ukraine.[3]

As for Palestinians, they are the bitter enemy, to be suppressed and subjugated. To name only a few reports: in June 2020, Yesh Din, an Israeli human rights organization, released its legal opinion: 'The Occupation of the West Bank and the Crime of Apartheid',

427

where 'in this context of a regime of domination and oppression of one national group by another, the Israeli authorities implement policies and practices that constitute inhuman acts as the term is defined in international law'.[4] B'Tselem, another Israeli human rights organization, followed with a report in January 2021: 'A regime of Jewish supremacy from the Jordan River to the Mediterranean Sea: This is apartheid'. In this report, B'Tselem clearly stated that 'the entire area between the Mediterranean Sea and the Jordan River is organized under a single principle: advancing and cementing the supremacy of one group—Jews—over another—Palestinians.'[5]

Three months later, Human Rights Watch released a 224-page report, 'A Threshold Crossed: Israeli Authorities and the Crimes of Apartheid and Persecution'. By every definition under international law, it found that the deprivations enforced by Israel against the Palestinians 'are so severe that they amount to the crimes against humanity of apartheid and persecution'.[6]

The latest report, in 280 pages, came from Amnesty International in February 2022: 'Israel's apartheid against Palestinians: a cruel system of domination and a crime against humanity'. The report made it clear that Israel 'enforces a system of oppression and domination against the Palestinian people wherever it has control over their rights. This includes Palestinians living in Israel and the Occupied Palestinian Territories (OPT), as well as displaced refugees in other countries.'

Amnesty called on the International Criminal Court (ICC) to 'consider the crime of apartheid in its current investigation in the OPT' and called 'on all states to exercise universal jurisdiction to bring perpetrators of apartheid crimes to justice'.[7]

The reports stated what I already knew and lived through: wherever I am in this country, whether in Israel or the Palestinian territory, I suffer the policies of apartheid by the Israeli state. Israel is the only country in the world where apartheid still exists formally, through its Nation-State Law and other laws that explicitly uphold Jewish supremacy. In July 2021, its Supreme Court turned down fifteen petitions against this law, with a majority of 10 of its 11 judges. The sole dissenter was a Palestinian Arab judge.[8] Israel continues to brand itself as a 'Jewish state' and does not have a constitution—rather, a 'Basic Law', to which it periodically adds more laws based on ethnic supremacy.

Despite Israel's allegations that it seeks peace, it has rejected any peace offers or initiatives, even those made by other states. In 2002, the Arab League put forth the Arab Peace Initiative (also known as the Saudi Initiative). The Arab states offered Israel the normalization of relations with it, in return for a full peace agreement, ending the occupation, and an independent Palestinian state, with East Jerusalem as its capital.[9] The Organisation of Islamic Cooperation (OIC), with fifty-seven Islamic states, also adopted the initiative.[10] But Israel has not agreed, despite repeated attempts by the Arab League in 2007 and 2017. The 'ghetto', or exclusivist, mentality seemingly continues to dominate the state's thinking.

Meanwhile, any criticism of the state's practices is categorically branded anti-Semitic. The United States continues to back Israel, militarily, diplomatically, and financially.

The Nakba continues. It has not ended: not with the continuing slow eviction of Palestinians from their homes and lands; not with Israel's systematic seizure of their territory and relegating them to inferior status in an apartheid state; and not with the brutal violence meted out against them on an almost daily basis. Palestinians are routinely imprisoned, tortured, and killed. There is still no right of return for Palestinian refugees and no Palestinian state on the horizon. Our rights, peace, sovereignty, and dignity remain a long way away.

Yet, how long can this last against the winds of freedom, justice, human rights, and equality? In the words of the Tunisian poet, Abu Qasem al-Shabbi:[11]

'If the people want life, then fate will comply
The night will end, and the chains will be broken.'

NOTES

NOTE ON NAMES AND PLACES

1. Resolution adopted by the General Assembly [without reference to a Main Committee (A/67/L.28 and Add.1)] 67/19. Status of Palestine in the United Nations, A/RES/67/19, United Nations General Assembly, Sixty-seventh session, Agenda item 37, 4 December 2012.

INTRODUCTION

1. *My Promised Land: The Triumph and Tragedy of Israel*, Ari Shavit, Spiegel & Grau, New York, 2013, p. 38.
2. 'Deir Yassin: The Zionist Massacre That Sparked the Nakba', Brett Wilkins, Antiwar.com, 14 April 2018, https://original.antiwar.com/brett_wilkins/2018/04/13/deir-yassin-the-zionist-massacre-that-sparked-the-nakba/ (last accessed 27 May 2022).
3. *The Arabs in Israel*, Sabri Jiryis, Monthly Review Press, New York, 1976, p. 76.
4. *Tabo* was the system used during Ottoman rule of Palestine to register ownership of lands and issue title deeds for tax purposes. The British took over this system and expanded it during the Mandate.
5. 'The Hidden Question', Yitzhak Epstein, lecture delivered at the Seventh Zionist Congress in Basel, 1905, published August 1907.
6. 'The Balfour Declaration', British Library, published in the press on 9 November 1917.
7. *The Gun and the Olive Branch*, David Hirst, Nation Books, New York, 2003, second edition, p. 185, citing David Hacohen, *Haaretz*, 15 November 1969.
8. Jiryis, 1976, pp. 9–10.
9. *Palestine and Israel, A Challenge to Justice*, John Quigley, Duke University Press, Durham, NC and London, UK, 1990, p. 25.
10. 'United Nations Special Committee on Palestine: Report to the General Assembly', vol. I, 3 September 1947, p. 54.
11. 'British Mandate: A Survey of Palestine' (vols I, II, III), prepared by the British Mandate for the United Nations Special Committee on Palestine (UNSCOP) in 1946, prior to proposing the 1947 Partition Plan.

12. 'United States Proposal for Temporary United Nations Trusteeship for Palestine', Statement by President Truman, 25 March 1948.

13. *Enemies and Neighbors: Arabs and Jews in Palestine and Israel, 1917–2017*, Ian Black, Atlantic Monthly Press, Washington, D.C., 2017, p. 116.

14. 'Text of Plan Dalet' (Plan D), 10 March 1948, General Section, translated by Walid Khalidi, *Journal of Palestine Studies*, vol. XVIII, no. 1, 1988. Translated from *Sefer Toldot Hahaganah (History of the Haganah)*, vol. 3, ed. Yehuda Slutsky, Zionist Library, Tel Aviv, 1972, Appendix 48, pp. 1955–60.

15. *The Birth of the Palestinian Refugee Problem, 1947–1949*, Benny Morris, Cambridge University Press, Cambridge, 1987, p. 250.

16. *My Father was a Freedom Fighter: Gaza's Untold Story*, Ramzy Baroud, Pluto Press, London, 2010, Foreword by Dr. Salman Abu Sitta, p. xi.

17. *All That Remains: The Palestinian Villages Occupied and Depopulated by Israel in 1948*, ed. Walid Khalidi, University of California Press, Berkeley, 1991, p. 582. Other estimates put the number of expelled Palestinians closer to a million: *Atlas of Palestine, 1917–1966*, Salman H. Abu-Sitta, Palestine Land Society, London, 2010, p. 117.

18. 'Palestine refugees', UNRWA, https://www.unrwa.org/palestine-refugees (last accessed 30 October 2019).

19. 'Reflections on al-Nakba', Fawaz Turki, *Journal of Palestine Studies*, vol. 28, no. 1, Autumn 1998, pp. 5–35.

1. A HOMELAND IS LOST

1. *Arabesques*, Anton Shammas, New York Review Books, New York, forthcoming. Translated from the Hebrew by Vivian Eden.

2. 'Deir Yassin Remembered', www.deiryassin.org, 28 July 2018 (last modified), (last accessed 30 June 2018).

3. 'Deir Yassin …', Wilkins, 14 April 2018.

4. *To Be an Arab in Israel*, Fouzi el-Asmar, The Institute for Palestine Studies, Beirut, 1978, p. 12.

5. Baroud, 2010, p. 40.

6. 'The 418 Destroyed Villages of Palestine', *Palestine-Israel Journal of Politics, Economics and Culture*, cited in Khalidi (ed.), 1991.

7. El-Asmar, 1978, p. 13.

8. 'Jewish Soldiers and Civilians Looted Arab Neighbors' Property en Masse in '48. The Authorities Turned a Blind Eye', Ofer Aderet, *Haaretz*, 3 October 2020, https://www.haaretz.com/israel-news/2020-10-03/ty-article-magazine/.highlight/jews-looted-arab-property-en-masse-in-48-the-authorities-let-them/0000017f-e7d4-d62c-a1ff-ffff83bd0000 (last accessed 27 May 2022).

9. Ibid.
10. Ibid.
11. Morris, 1987, p. 255.
12. 'Folke Bernadotte and the White Buses', Sune Persson, *Journal of Holocaust Education*, vol. 9, issue 2–3, 2000, pp. 237–68. Also published in *Bystanders to the Holocaust: A Re-evaluation*, eds. David Cesarani and Paul A. Levine, Routledge, Abingdon-on-Thames, 2002.
13. Located in the center of Israel, the Triangle is actually a rectangular strip of land, thus named due to its proximity to the three Palestinian cities of Jenin, Nablus, and Tulkarm in the West Bank.
14. Jiryis, 1976, Appendix: 'Table 1, Jewish and Arab Population of Israel', p. 289.
15. Iqrit is also spelled Ikrit, Iqrith.
16. *Palestinians: The Making of a People*, Baruch Kimmerling and Joel S. Migdal, Harvard University Press, Cambridge, MA, 1998, p. 416.
17. United Nations General Assembly, A/RES/194 (III), 11 December 1948.
18. *Our Roots Are Still Alive: The Story of the Palestinian People*, Peoples Press Palestine Book Project, Institute for Independent Social Journalism, second edition, 1 January 1981, ch. 9.

2. THE ALIEN STATE

1. From 'Reflections on Al-Nakba', Mamdouh Nofal, Fawaz Turki, Haidar Abdel Shafi, Inea Bushnaq, Yezid Sayigh, Shafiq al-Hout, Salma Khadra Jayyusi and Musa Budeiri, *Journal of Palestine Studies*, vol. 28, no. 1, 1998, pp. 5–35. Copyright © Institute for Palestine Studies, reprinted by permission of Taylor & Francis Ltd, http://www.tandfonline.com on behalf of Institute for Palestine Studies.
2. *Det förlorade landet: en personlig historia [The Lost Land, a personal history]*, Göran Rosenberg, Albert Bonniers Förlag, Stockholm, 1996, p. 328 (English translation by Göran Rosenberg).
3. Jiryis, 1976, p. 246.
4. *Mansour Kardosh, Un juste a Nazareth*, Marion Sigaut, Collection: Les artisans de la liberté, Dirigée par Michel Cool, 1998; translated into Arabic by Fairuz Abboud and Jadallah Shehadeh, Arab Association for Human Rights (HRA), Nazareth, 2001, p. 41.
5. *Hapraklit (The Lawyer)*, Dov Joseph, The Jewish Agency, February 1946, pp. 58–64.
6. These land laws are presented in Jiryis, 1976.
7. 'Revealed from Archive: Israel's Secret Plan to Resettle Arab Refugees', Arik Ariel, *Haaretz*, 19 December 2013, https://www.haaretz.com/.

premium-israel-s-nixed-plan-to-resettle-arabs-1.5301726 (last accessed 5 May 2022).

8. *The Arabs Under Israeli Occupation Since 1948* (Arabic), Habib Qahwaji, Palestine Books, no. 38, Research Center, Palestine Liberation Organization, Lebanon, 1972, p. 189.

9. Ibid, p. 188.

10. 'The Uncounted: Citizenship and Exclusion in the Israeli Census of 1948', Anat Leibler and Daniel Breslau, *Journal of Ethnic and Racial Studies*, vol. 28, issue 5, September 2005, pp. 880–902.

11. *Haaretz*, 6 January 1949, cited in Jiryis, 1976, p. 259.

12. *Israel Government Yearbook* 5719, 1958, p. 235.

13. Moshe Carmel, commander of the Carmeli Brigade, about the looting in Haifa. Cited in 'Jewish Soldiers ...', Aderet, 3 October 2020.

14. 'United Nations General Assembly Resolution 302, A/RES/302 (IV): Assistance to Palestine Refugees, #5', 8 December 1949, 302 (IV).

15. Interview with Hasan Amoun, 25 April 2018, Deir el-Assad, conducted by Emtiaz Diab.

16. Jiryis, 1976, p. 82.

17. The Green Line: a demarcation line set out in the 1949 Armistice Agreements between Israel and its neighbors (Egypt, Jordan, Lebanon, and Syria) after the 1948 Arab-Israeli War (Nakba), and subsequently marking the border between Israel and the territory captured in the 1967 Six-Day War (Naksa), including the West Bank, Gaza Strip, and Golan Heights.

18. 'Iqrit and Bir Am: A Christmas Tale with a Moral', Richard Curtiss, *Washington Report on Middle East Affairs*, December 1987, https://www.wrmea.org/1987-december/iqrit-and-bir-am-a-christmas-tale-with-a-moral.html (last accessed 27 May 2022).

19. *Blood Brothers: The Dramatic Story of a Palestinian Christian Working for Peace in Israel*, Elias Chacour, Baker Books, Ada, MI, 1984, p. 91.

20. Ibid.

21. *Nakba and Staying On: The Story of Palestinians who remained in Haifa and the Galilee (1948–1956)* (Arabic), Adel Manna, Institute for Palestine Studies, 2016, pp. 202–3.

22. 'The ethical hollowness of Israel's liberals', Jonathan Cook, *Middle East Eye*, 26 January 2018, https://www.middleeasteye.net/opinion/ethical-hollowness-israels-liberals (last accessed 5 May 2022).

23. Jiryis, 1976, p. 92.

24. *Israel's Border Wars: 1949–1956*, Benny Morris, Aam Ufid, Tel Aviv, 1996, pp. 135–7.

25. Black, 2017, p. 150.

26. Morris, 1996, p. 273.

27. *Haaretz*, 3, 19 November 1959, cited in Jiryis, 1976, p. 258.

28. Jiryis, 1976, p. 80.

29. Interview in *The Jerusalem Post*, 7 March 1997, cited in 'Turning Palestine into Earth', Ibrahim Matar, *This Week in Palestine*, 29 May 2012.

30. Jiryis, 1976, p. 132.

31. 'The Legal Transformation of Ethnic Geography: Israeli Law and the Palestinian Landholder, 1948–1967', Alexandre (Sandy) Kedar, *New York University Journal of International Law and Politics*, vol. 33, no. 4, Summer 2001.

32. Qahwaji, 1972, p. 56.

33. El-Asmar, 1978, p. 81.

34. Jiryis, 1976, pp. 33–4.

35. In 1952, Israel replaced the Palestinian pound with the Israeli pound as its currency. This was the currency in use until 1980, when the shekel was introduced.

36. 'General's Final Confession Links 1956 Massacre to Israel's Secret Plan to Expel Arabs', Ofer Aderet, *Haaretz*, 13 October 2018, https://www.haaretz.com/israel-news/.premium.MAGAZINE-general-s-confession-links-massacre-to-israel-s-secret-plan-to-expel-arabs-1.6550421 (last accessed 5 May 2022).

3. RESISTANCE

1. *The Arabs in Israel*, Walter Schwarz, Faber and Faber, London, 1959, p. 15. Reuse permission kindly granted by Dorothy Schwarz.

2. Qahwaji, 1972, p. 495.

3. Israeli Communist Party statement, 12 March 1958.

4. Sigaut, 1998, translated by Abboud and Shehadeh, 2001, p. 44.

5. 'Abu Issam, Hanna Naqqara', *al-Ittihad*, 15 July 1966, cited in 'The Legal Structure for the Expropriation and Absorption of Arab Lands in Israel', Sabri Jiryis, *Journal of Palestine Studies*, vol. 2, no. 4, Summer 1973, pp. 82–104.

6. 'Military Rule, Political Manipulation, and Jewish Settlement: Israeli Mechanisms for Controlling Nazareth in the 1950s', Geremy Forman, *The Journal of Israeli History*, vol. 25, no. 2, 2006, p. 350.

7. '48 human beings were massacred—and we have forgotten them', Shirley Racah and Abed Kannaneh, +972 Magazine, 3 November 2013, https://www.972mag.com/48-human-beings-were-massacred-and-we-have-forgotten-them/ (last accessed 6 May 2022).

8. 'The Value of Security vs. the Security of Values: The Relationship between the Rights of the Minority and the Security of the Majority in

Israel', Ronnie May Olesker, *International Law and Organization*, Fletcher School of Law and Diplomacy, Tufts University, 2007, p. 318.

9. El-Asmar, 1978, p. 74.
10. Ibid., pp. 74–5.
11. Ibid., p. 72.
12. Ibid., pp. 76–7.
13. Jiryis, 1976, p. 109.
14. Jiryis, 1976, pps. 43, 110.
15. *Encyclopedia Judaica*, 1971, vol. 2, pp. 503–4.
16. *The Challenge of Ethnic Democracy: The State and Minority Groups in Israel, Poland and Northern Ireland*, Yoav Peled, Routledge, Abingdon-on-Thames, 2014, p. 110.
17. 'Sabri Jiryis: "Al-Ard Movement", a Palestinian Experience after the Nakba' (Arabic), Sabri Jiryis, interview on Arab48.com, 11 August 2017.
18. Qahwaji, 1972, p. 168.
19. Knesset Debates, 20 February 1963, pp. 1215–16.
20. Rosenberg, 1996, p. 327.
21. Defence (Emergency) Regulations, 1945, Article 94 (2).
22. Jiryis, 1976, p. 189.
23. Ibid., p. 190.
24. Al-Ard's Bylaws (Arabic); translation cited in el-Asmar, 1978, p. 77–8; Jiryis, 1976, p. 190.
25. Jiryis, 1976, p. 191.
26. Judgments 18, part 4: 670, Sabri Jiryis v. the Haifa District Commissioner, case 253/64, cited in Jiryis, 1976, p. 192.
27. *Haaretz*, 24 July 1964, cited in Jiryis, 1976.
28. Judgments 18, part 4: 677, Sabri Jiryis v. the Haifa District Commissioner, case 253/64, cited in Jiryis, 1976, p. 192.
29. Ibid., part 4: 680.
30. *Al-Ittihad*, 14 August 1964, cited in Jiryis, 1976.

4. EVERY PATH CLOSED

1. Meeting of the Mapai party secretariat on 1 January, 1962, cited in '"We Look at Them Like Donkeys": What Israel's First Ruling Party Thought About Palestinian Citizens', Adam Raz, *Haaretz*, 13 January 2018, https://www.haaretz.com/israel-news/.premium.MAGAZINE-what-israel-s-first-ruling-party-thought-about-palestinian-citizens-1.5730395 (last accessed 9 May 2022).
2. 'Nakkara, Hanna Deeb', *Encyclopedia of the Palestinians*, Philip Mattar, Infobase Publishing, New York, 2005, p. 330.

3. 'Israeli Supreme Court Doctrine and the Battle Over Arab Land in Galilee: A Vertical Assessment', Geremy Forman, *Journal of Palestine Studies*, vol. 40, no. 4, Summer 2011, pp. 24–44.

4. Jiryis, 1973, pp. 82–104.

5. Judgments 18, part 4: 670, Sabri Jiryis v. the Haifa District Commissioner, case 253/64, cited in Jiryis, 1976, p. 192.

6. 'Four Al-Ard members temporarily expelled from their homes' (Hebrew), *Haaretz*-Nazareth editorial, 5 September 1965.

7. 'What the Al-Ard Movement's men want: To negate the existence of the State of Israel, from the Knesset podium' (Hebrew), Shmuel Segev, *Maariv*, 6 September 1965.

8. *The Legal Status of the Arabs in Israel*, David Kretzmer, Westview Press, Boulder, CO, 1990, p. 24.

9. Judgments 19, part 3: 365, Ya'acov Yeridor v. the Chairman of the Central Elections Committee of the Sixth Knesset, Elections Appeal 1/65, cited in Jiryis, 1976, p. 194; *The Jerusalem Post*, 14 November 1965.

10. Peled, 2014, p. 110.

11. 'Sabri Jiryis: "Al-Ard Movement" …', Sabri Jiryis, 11 August 2017.

12. 'A Case Study in the Banning of Political Parties: The Pan-Arab Movement El Ard and the Israeli Supreme Court', Ron Harris, *bepress Legal Series*, Working Paper 349, 22 August 2004.

13. Jiryis, 1976, p. 195.

14. El-Asmar, 1978, p. 80.

15. Jiryis, 1976, p. 194.

5. BROTHERS IN ARMS

1. 'Spotlight on Arab Students', Butrus Abu Mana, *New Outlook*, March 1965, pp. 45–8; 'Arabs at the Hebrew University', Anis Abu Hanna, *New Outlook*, July–August 1958, pp. 54–6.

2. Yosef Harmelin, director of the Israeli General Security Service (Shabak), State of Israel, State Archives, 'Foundations of the Government's Policy Towards the Arab Minority in Israel', sheet no. 17068/5, 1965, document no. R0003dac 2–113–4–3–1, released 7 January 2021, p. 102.

3. 'November 8, 1966: Military Rule on Israeli Arabs Lifted', Odeh Bisharat, *Haaretz*, 16 June 2013, https://www.haaretz.com/jewish/1.5280516 (last accessed 9 May 2022).

4. Peled, 2014, p. 109.

5. Jiryis, 1976, pp. 64–5.

6. 'Palestine Refugees', United Nations, ch. 10.

7. 'Report on the Destruction of the Villages of Beit Nuba, Amwas and Yalu', Amos Kenan, 1967, cited in el-Asmar, 1978, p. 141.

8. *The Forgotten Palestinians: A History of the Palestinians in Israel*, Ilan Pappé, Yale University Press, London, UK and New Haven, CT, 2011, pp. 113–14.

9. Jiryis, 1976, p. 65.

10. Ibid., p. 254.

11. 'The 1967 War ... The Naksa Day', Yasser Arafat Foundation, 12 January 2016, https://yaf.ps/page-1141-en.html (last accessed 6 April 2022).

12. *Righteous Victims: A History of the Zionist-Arab Conflict, 1881–2001*, Benny Morris, Vintage, August 2001, p. 369.

13. 'Israel and the arson attack against Al-Aqsa Mosque', Ghazi Hussein, Middle East Monitor, 12 August 2015, https://www.middleeastmonitor.com/20150812-israel-and-the-arson-attack-against-al-aqsa-mosque/ (last accessed 10 May 2022).

14. El-Asmar, 1978, p. 66.

15. 'Support for the Hunger Strikers', *Haaretz*, April 1970, cited in el-Asmar, 1978, p. 206. The petition was signed by Yigal Burstein, film producer; Dan Ben Amotz, author; Arthur Goldreich, architect; Ili Gorlitsky, actor; Elisha Gat, architect; Uri Davis, student; 'Yebi', poet; Chanoch Levin, playwright; Uri Lifschitz, painter; Joseph Mundi, playwright; Y. Kipnis, actor; Amos Kenan, author; and Nahum Shalit, actor.

6. EXILE

1. 'Cry, the Beloved Country' (Hebrew), Ezriel Carlebach, *Maariv*, 25 December 1953 and 18 February 1983. English version by Ami Asher.

2. 'Where We Work', UNRWA, https://www.unrwa.org/where-we-work (last accessed 11 May 2022).

3. Luke 15:4.

4. *Anis Sayegh on Anis Sayegh* (Arabic), Anis Sayegh, Riad el-Rayyes Books, Beirut, 2006, p. 221.

5. Ibid, pp. 255–7.

6. 'Why Land Day Still Matters', Sam Bahour and Fida Jiryis, *Haaretz*, 30 May 2012, https://www.haaretz.com/opinion/1.5209824 (last accessed 13 May 2022).

7. Jiryis, 1976.

8. 'Assad and the Palestinians: from Tal al-Zaatar to Yarmouk', Ibrahim Halawi, The New Arab, 7 April 2015, https://english.alaraby.co.uk/analysis/assad-and-palestinians-tal-al-zaatar-yarmouk (last accessed 13 May 2022).

9. 'Palestinians Preparing to Open Office in Washington', Bernard Gwertzman, *The New York Times*, 20 November 1976.

7. HAPPY TIMES

1. 'Hanneh', Jamal Qa'war, *al-Ittihad*, 18 February 1983, p. 7. Author's translation.
2. *A History of Zionism* (Arabic), Sabri Jiryis, Research Center, Palestine Liberation Organization, Beirut, 1977.
3. 'On Political Settlement in the Middle East: The Palestinian Dimension', Sabri Jiryis, *Journal of Palestine Studies*, vol. 7, no. 1, Autumn 1977, pp. 3–25.
4. *British Mandate: A Survey of Palestine prepared in December 1945 and January 1946 for the Information of the Anglo-American Committee of Inquiry*, vols. I, II and III; *Palestine: Land Ownership by Sub-Districts, 1945*, Prepared on the Instructions of Sub-Committee 2 of the Ad Hoc Committee on the Palestinian question, Source: British Mandate Village Statistics, published by United Nations, August 1950; *Village Statistics 1945: A Classification of Land and Area Ownership in Palestine*, Sami Hadawi, Palestine Liberation Organization Research Center, Beirut, 1970.

8. THE DARK HOUR

1. 'After Nineteen Years: Sabra and Shatila Remembered', Ellen Siegel, *Middle East Policy*, vol. VIII, no. 4, Winter 2001. Reproduced with permission of the Licensor through PLSclear.
2. 'War of Three Months, and the Number that Could Not Be Eradicated' (Arabic), Faisal Hourani, *Palestine Affairs*, issue 129–30–31, August–September–October 1982, pp. 5–17.
3. 'Testimony from Ansar Camp' (Arabic), Sa'adoun Hussein, *Palestine Affairs*, issue 132–3, November–December 1982, pp. 17–40.
4. Ibid.
5. Ibid.
6. Ibid.
7. 'The Full Story of the Theft of the Palestine Research Center in Beirut' (Arabic), Faisal Hourani, *Romman Magazine*, 30 November 2017.
8. 'War Casualties Put at 48,000 in Lebanon', Jay Ross, *The Washington Post*, 3 September 1982, https://www.washingtonpost.com/archive/politics/1982/09/03/war-casualties-put-at-48000-in-lebanon/cf593941-6067-4239-a453-71bdcaf9eba0/ (last accessed 16 May 2022).
9. 'Arafat Demands 3 Nations Return Peace Force to Beirut', Henry Kamm, *The New York Times*, 17 September 1982.
10. *Beware of Small States: Lebanon, Battleground of the Middle East*, David Hirst, Faber and Faber, London, 2011, p. 156.
11. '30 Years Since The Sabra and Shatila Massacre', *The News Line*,

19 September 2012, https://wrp.org.uk/features/30-years-since-the-sabra-and-shatila-massacre/ (last accessed 16 May 2022).

12. 'The Commission of Inquiry into Events at the Refugee Camps in Beirut, 1983, Final Report', Yitzhak Kahan, Aharon Barak, Yona Efrat, 1983.

13. 'Testimonies by Survivors of the Massacre' (Arabic), *Palestine Affairs*, issue 132–3, November–December 1982, pp. 41–58.

14. Estimates on the number of dead vary from different sources. After the massacre, the Palestine Research Center sent its own investigation team, which conducted a field study in the camps. Its estimate, the lowest, lay between 350–400 victims; other estimates placed the number between 1,000–3,500.

15. *From Beirut to Jerusalem*, Thomas Friedman, Macmillan, London, 2010, p. 109.

16. 'Syrians Aid "Butcher of Beirut" to Hide from Justice', Fergal Keane, *The Daily Telegraph*, 17 June 2001, https://www.telegraph.co.uk/news/worldnews/middleeast/israel/1310100/Syrians-aid-Butcher-of-Beirut-to-hide-from-justice.html (last accessed 17 May 2022).

17. 'Remembering Janet Lee Stevens, a Martyr for Palestinian Refugees', Franklin Lamb, The Palestine Chronicle, 21 April 2010, https://www.palestinechronicle.com/remembering-janet-lee-stevens-a-martyr-for-palestinian-refugees/ (last accessed 17 May 2022).

18. Cited in '30 Years Since …', *The News Line*, 19 September 2012.

19. *Gate of the Sun* (Arabic), Elias Khoury, Dar el-Adaab, Beirut, 1998, p. 278.

20. 'Israeli Policy Towards the Camps in South Lebanon' (Arabic), Hanneh Shaheen, *Palestine Affairs*, issue 135, February 1983, pp. 120–6.

21. '18 Die in Bombing at P.L.O.'s Center in Western Beirut', Thomas L. Friedman, *The New York Times*, 6 February 1983.

22. 'Martyrs of the Research Center' (Arabic), *Palestine Affairs*, issue 136–137, March–April 1983, pp. 16–18.

23. Hezbollah: a Shia Islamic militant group and political party based in Lebanon and regarded as a resistance movement by much of the Arab world. Hezbollah first emerged in response to the 1982 Israeli invasion of Lebanon and receives financial and political support from Syria and Iran.

24. *The Lost Memory—Tale of the Tragic Fate of the Palestine Research Center* (Arabic), testimony by Samih Shbib, published by Palestine Land Society, London, and Muwatin, The Palestinian Institute for the Study of Democracy, June 2005.

25. 'The "Long-Arm" Policy: Israeli Revenge Operations in the 1950s' (Arabic), Hanneh Shaheen, *Palestine Affairs*, issue 136–137, March–April 1983, p. 53.

26. *Israel's Lebanon War*, Ze'ev Schiff and Ehud Ya'ari, Simon and Schuster, New York, 1984, p. 284.

9. SAFER SHORES

1. *Smoke of the Volcanoes* (Arabic), Samih al-Qasim, al-Muhtaseb Library, Jerusalem, 1968, p. 181. Author's translation.
2. 'Palestinians and Israelis Welcome Their Prisoners Freed in Exchange', David K. Shipler, *The New York Times*, 25 November 1983.
3. Baroud, 2010, p. 135.
4. 'Kuwait Expels Thousands of Palestinians', Steven J. Rosen, *Middle East Quarterly*, Fall 2012, pp. 75–83.

10. A MIRACLE OF SORTS

1. Golda Meir, interview with Frank Giles, *The Sunday Times*, 15 June 1969.
2. 'The Making of a Murderous Fanatic', Richard Lacayo, Lisa Beyer, Massimo Calabresi and Eric Silver, *Time Magazine*, 7 March 1994.
3. *Oud* (Arabic): a stringed musical instrument; *darbuka* (Arabic): a hand-held drum. Both widely used in the Middle East.

11. THE RETURN

1. Jiryis, 1976, p. xiii.
2. 'Mustafa Issa, Abu Firas, Ex-Governor of Ramallah, Passes Away' (Arabic), *al-Hadath*, 24 December 2018.
3. 'The Druze and Military Service', Samer Swaid, New Profile, https://www.newprofile.org/english/node/204 (last accessed 17 June 2021).
4. 'The "Center of Life" Policy: Institutionalizing Statelessness in East Jerusalem', Danielle C. Jefferis, *Journal of Palestine Studies*, issue 50, Summer 2012, pp. 94–103.
5. Ibid.
6. 'Second Class: Discrimination Against Palestinian Arab Children in Israel's Schools', Human Rights Watch, 20 September 2001, https://www.hrw.org/report/2001/09/30/second-class/discrimination-against-palestinian-arab-children-israels-schools (last accessed 19 May 2022).
7. *Palestine in Israeli School Books: Ideology and Propaganda in Education*, Nurit Peled-Elhanan, Library of Modern Middle East Studies, I. B. Tauris & Co. Ltd., London, 2012.

12. STRANGER IN MY OWN LAND

1. 'The Interview', FRANCE 24, Annette Young interviews Yehuda Shaul, 10 October 2013, https://www.france24.com/en/20131009-interview-yehuda-shaul-breaking-the-silence-israeli-army-palestinian-territories-occupation-idf (last accessed 22 July 2022).
2. *Improperly Jews*, Yair Sheleg, Israel Democracy Institute, p. 10.

13. NOWHERE TO TURN

1. '"42 Knees in One Day": Israeli Snipers Open Up About Shooting Gaza Protesters', Hilo Glazer, *Haaretz*, 6 March 2020, https://www.haaretz. com/israel-news/.premium.HIGHLIGHT.MAGAZINE-42-knees-in-one-day-israeli-snipers-open-up-about-shooting-gaza-protesters-1.8632555 (last accessed 20 May 2022).
2. 'Israeli Occupation Besieges President Arafat in al-Muqata'a' (Arabic), Al-Arabi Al-Jadeed, 11 October 2015.
3. 'UN Report Details West Bank Wreckage', Brian Whitaker, *The Guardian*, 2 August 2002.
4. 'Jenin: IDF Military Operations', Human Rights Watch, vol. 14, no. 3 (E), May 2002.
5. 'The Saga of the Siege', Matt Rees, Bobby Ghosh, Jamil Hamad and Aharon Klein, *Time Magazine*, 20 May 2002, https://content.time.com/time/subscriber/article/0,33009,1002452–2,00.html (last accessed 20 May 2022).

14. ESCAPE

1. 'The One-State Reality; Israel's Conservative President Speaks Up for Civility, and Pays a Price', David Remnick, *The New Yorker*, 10 November 2014, https://www.newyorker.com/magazine/2014/11/17/one-state-reality (last accessed 30 May 2022).
2. 'Suicide bombing of Maxim restaurant in Haifa', Israel Ministry of Foreign Affairs, 4 October 2003.
3. 'Yasser Arafat exhumed and reburied in six-hour night mission', Chris McGreal, *The Guardian*, 27 November 2012, https://www.theguardian. com/world/2012/nov/27/yasser-arafat-exhumed-reburied-night (last accessed 22 June 2022).
4. 'Sharon Hints That Arafat May Be Killed', Chris McGreal, *The Guardian*, 15 September 2004, https://www.theguardian.com/world/2004/sep/15/israel (last accessed 23 May 2022); 'The Murder of Arafat', Sam Bahour, CounterPunch, 3 August 2012, https://www.counterpunch. org/2012/08/03/the-murder-of-arafat-2/ (last accessed 23 May 2022).
5. '"We Arrested Countless Palestinians for No Reason," Says Ex-top Shin Bet Officer', Amos Harel, *Haaretz*, 17 February 2022, https://www. haaretz.com/israel-news/.premium.HIGHLIGHT.MAGAZINE-we-arrested-countless-palestinians-for-no-reason-says-ex-top-shin-bet-officer-1.10618087 (last accessed 23 May 2022).
6. 'Lebanon's pain grows by the hour as death toll hits 1,300', Robert Fisk, *The Independent*, 17 August 2006, https://www.independent.co.uk/

voices/commentators/fisk/robert-fisk-lebanon-s-pain-grows-by-the-hour-as-death-toll-hits-1–300–412170.html (last accessed 30 May 2022).

15. IN SEARCH OF PALESTINE

1. 'Ex-Shin Bet Chief: Israeli Illusions Fueled Blowup', J. J. Goldberg, *Forward*, 5 July 2014, https://forward.com/opinion/201468/ex-shin-bet-chief-israeli-illusions-fueled-blowup/ (last accessed 23 May 2022). Translated from the Hebrew by J. J. Goldberg.
2. 'The "Bosta", a Journey of Endless Pain', The Palestinian Information Center, 2019; *These Chains Will Be Broken*, Ramzy Baroud, Clarity Press, Inc., Atlanta, GA, 2019, p. 129.
3. 'Apartheid Targets Palestinian Homeowners inside Israel', Jonathan Cook, The Electronic Intifada, 10 March 2005, https://electronicintifada.net/content/apartheid-targets-palestinian-home-owners-inside-israel/5505 (last accessed 22 June 2022).
4. *The Palestinian Arab Citizens of Israel: Status, Opportunities and Challenges for an Israeli-Palestinian Peace*, Mossawa Center, June 2006.
5. '"Visible Equality" as Confidence Trick', Jonathan Cook, p. 140 in *Israel and South Africa: The Many Faces of Apartheid*, ed. by Ilan Pappé, Zed Books, London, 2015.
6. 'Israel's Illegal Freeze of Palestinian Tax Revenue', al-Haq, 6 December 2011.
7. 'Gov't ads encourage employment of Israeli-Arabs', Ilene Prusher, *The Jerusalem Post*, 6 August 2012, https://www.jpost.com/national-news/govt-ads-encourage-employment-of-israeli-arabs (last accessed 29 May 2022).
8. 'Tinderbox in Israel: Discrimination against Palestinians in the country is reaching frightening levels', Ann Crittenden, The American Prospect, 6 March 2012, https://prospect.org/culture/tinderbox-israel/ (last accessed 23 May 2022).
9. *The Palestinian Arab Citizens of Israel*, Mossawa Center, June 2006.
10. 'Israel's Kidnapped Boys Found Dead in Field', Josh Nathan-Kazis and Anne Cohen, Forward, 30 June 2014, https://forward.com/news/breaking-news/201064/israels-kidnapped-boys-found-dead-in-field/ (last accessed 23 May 2022).
11. 'Israeli lawmaker's call for genocide of Palestinians gets thousands of Facebook likes', Ali Abunimah, The Electronic Intifada, 7 July 2014, https://electronicintifada.net/blogs/ali-abunimah/israeli-lawmakers-call-genocide-palestinians-gets-thousands-facebook-likes (last accessed 23 May 2022).
12. 'Anti-Arab soccer fans rampage in shopping centre—but no arrests',

Catrina Stewart, *The Independent*, 24 March 2012, https://www.independent.co.uk/news/world/middle-east/antiarab-soccer-fans-rampage-in-shopping-centre-but-no-arrests-7584089.html (last accessed 23 May 2022).

13. 'Arab Boy's Death Escalates Clash Over Abductions', Isabel Kershner, *The New York Times*, 2 July 2014, https://www.nytimes.com/2014/07/03/world/middleeast/israel.html (last accessed 23 May 2022).

14. 'Burned Body of Arab Found in Jerusalem Forest', The Yeshiva World, 2 July 2014, https://www.theyeshivaworld.com/news/headlines-breaking-stories/244703/burned-body-of-arab-found-in-jerusalem-forest.html (last accessed 23 May 2022).

16. CULTURE OF HATE

1. 'Jewish Hate of Arabs Proves: Israel Must Undergo Cultural Revolution', *Haaretz* editorial, 7 July 2014, https://www.haaretz.com/opinion/.premium-a-vengeful-vindictive-tribe-has-spoken-1.5254664 (last accessed 23 May 2014).

2. 'Mohammed Abu Khdeir murder: Israeli man convicted of burning Palestinian teenager to death in revenge killing', Lizzie Dearden, *The Independent*, 19 April 2016, https://www.independent.co.uk/news/world/middle-east/mohammed-abu-khdeir-murder-israeli-man-convicted-of-burning-palestinian-teenager-to-death-in-revenge-killing-a6991251.html (last accessed 23 May 2022).

3. 'Palestinian American teen describes savage beating by Israeli police', Ali Abunimah, The Electronic Intifada, 6 July 2014, https://electronicintifada.net/blogs/ali-abunimah/palestinian-american-teen-describes-savage-beating-israeli-police (last accessed 23 May 2022).

4. 'The four year anniversary of the murder of Mohammed Abu Khdeir', International Solidarity Movement, 2 July 2018, https://palsolidarity.org/2018/07/the-four-year-anniversary-of-the-murder-of-mohammed-abu-khdeir/ (last accessed 23 May 2022).

5. 'Remembering the 2014 Israeli Offensive Against Gaza', Hana Hussain, Middle East Monitor, 8 July 2018, https://www.middleeastmonitor.com/20180708-remembering-the-2014-israeli-offensive-against-gaza/ (last accessed 23 May 2022).

6. 'Cut off Power to Gaza dialysis patients, Knesset deputy speaker urges', Ali Abunimah, The Electronic Intifada, 11 July 2014, https://electronicintifada.net/blogs/ali-abunimah/cut-power-gaza-dialysis-patients-knesset-deputy-speaker-urges (last accessed 23 May 2022).

7. 'Selfies in the Service of Hate', Asher Schechter, *Haaretz*, 3 July 2014,

https://www.haaretz.com/.premium-selfies-in-the-service-of-hate-1.5254300 (last accessed 23 May 2022).

8. 'Do We Belong? The war in Gaza fuels tensions between Israeli Arabs and Jews', *The Economist*, 26 July 2014, https://www.economist.com/middle-east-and-africa/2014/07/26/do-we-belong?fsrc=scn%2Ftw_ec%2Fdo_we_belong_ (last accessed 23 May 2022).

9. 'Key Figures on the 2014 Hostilities', United Nations Office for the Coordination of Humanitarian Affairs (OCHA), Occupied Palestinian Territory, 23 June 2015, https://www.ochaopt.org/content/key-figures-2014-hostilities (last accessed 23 May 2022).

10. 'Binyamin Netanyahu: "Arab Voters are Heading to the Polling Stations in Droves"', Mairav Zonszein, *The Guardian*, 17 March 2015, https://www.theguardian.com/world/2015/mar/17/binyamin-netanyahu-israel-arab-election (last accessed 23 May 2022).

11. 'National Parks as tool for constraining Palestinian neighborhoods in East Jerusalem', B'Tselem, 16 September 2014, https://www.btselem.org/jerusalem/national_parks (last accessed 23 May 2022).

12. 'Israeli Government Allocates Disproportionate Aid to Settlements, Study Finds', Hagai Amit, *Haaretz*, 20 November 2017, https://www.haaretz.com/israel-news/business/israel-allocates-disproportionate-aid-to-settlements-study-finds-1.5466853 (last accessed 23 May 2022).

13. 'Development for Empowerment: The 2014 Palestine Human Development Report, Poverty', UNDP.

14. 'Why are Israelis So Shocked by the "Wedding of Hate" Video?' Amira Hass, *Haaretz*, 28 December 2015, https://www.haaretz.com/opinion/.premium-why-so-shocked-by-wedding-video-1.5382719 (last accessed 23 May 2022).

15. 'Relative of Arson Attack Victims: I Saw Two Masked Men Standing by as They Burned', Amira Hass, *Haaretz*, 31 July 2015, https://www.haaretz.com/.premium-i-saw-two-masked-men-standing-by-as-they-burned-1.5381745 (last accessed 23 May 2022).

16. 'Family of Slain Palestinian Infant Clings to Life, Clashes in West Bank', Jack Khoury, Ido Efrati and Gili Cohen, *Haaretz*, 1 August 2015, https://www.haaretz.com/.premium-family-of-slain-infant-clings-to-life-amid-west-bank-clashes-1.5381810 (last accessed 23 May 2022).

17. 'State prosecutors admit losing original video of anti-Arab "hate wedding"', Stuart Winer, *The Times of Israel*, 22 October 2018, https://www.timesofisrael.com/state-prosecutors-admit-losing-original-video-of-anti-arab-hate-wedding/ (last accessed 23 May 2022).

18. 'Jewish extremists taunt "Ali's on the grill" at slain toddler's relatives', Jacob Magid, *The Times of Israel*, 19 June 2018, https://www.timeso-

fisrael.com/jewish-extremists-taunt-alis-on-the-grill-at-slain-toddlers-relatives/ (last accessed 23 May 2022).

19. 'The Execution of Hadeel al-Hashlamoun', Amira Hass, *Haaretz*, 3 November 2015, https://www.haaretz.com/opinion/.premium-execution-of-hadeel-al-hashlamoun-1.5417049 (last accessed 23 May 2022).

20. The Discriminatory Laws Database, Adalah, 25 September 2017, https://www.adalah.org/en/content/view/7771 (last accessed 23 June 2022).

21. '"The moment a worker is sick, they throw him to the checkpoint like a dog"', Suha Arraf, +972 Magazine, 24 March 2020, https://www.972mag.com/checkpoint-palestinian-laborers-coronavirus/ (last accessed 23 May 2022).

22. 'Analysis: Palestine is Occupied, Segregated, and About to Face COVID-19', Taya Graham, The Real News Network, 29 March 2020, https://therealnews.com/palestine-israel-occupied-segregated-pandemic-covid (last accessed 23 May 2022).

23. 'Israeli settlers exploit coronavirus to take over West Bank land with military backing: Violent attacks spike in April', B'Tselem, 23 April 2020, https://www.btselem.org/press_releases/20200423_violent_attacks_by_settlers_spike_in_april (last accessed 23 May 2022).

EPILOGUE

1. 'Israel killed five times as many Palestinians in 2022 than it killed in the same period in 2021 [EN/AR]', News and Press Release, Euro-Med Monitor, 15 April 2022, https://reliefweb.int/report/occupied-palestinian-territory/israel-killed-five-times-many-palestinians-2022-it-killed-same (last accessed 22 June 2022).

2. Protection of Civilians Report: 31 May - 13 June 2022, United Nations Office for the Coordination of Humanitarian Affairs (OCHA), 17 June 2022, https://www.ochaopt.org/poc/31may-13june-2022 (last accessed 23 Jume 2022).

3. 'Ukrainians Fleeing War Find an Unwelcoming Israel – if They're Allowed in at All', Bar Peleg and Liza Rozovsky, *Haaretz*, 5 July 2022, https://www.haaretz.com/israel-news/2022-07-05/ty-article-magazine/.highlight/no-food-no-employment-being-a-ukrainian-refugee-in-israel/00000181-c968-dafa-afdd-ff6a69320000 (last accessed 9 July 2022).

4. 'The Occupation of the West Bank and the Crime of Apartheid: Legal Opinion', Yesh Din, 9 July 2020, https://www.yesh-din.org/en/the-occupation-of-the-west-bank-and-the-crime-of-apartheid-legal-opinion/ (last accessed 23 June 2022).

5. 'A regime of Jewish supremacy from the Jordan River to the Mediterranean

Sea: This is apartheid', B'Tselem, January 2021, https://www.btselem. org/publications/fulltext/202101_this_is_apartheid (last accessed 23 June 2022).

6. 'A Threshold Crossed: Israeli Authorities and the Crimes of Apartheid and Persecution', Human Rights Watch, 27 April 2021, https://www. hrw.org/report/2021/04/27/threshold-crossed/israeli-authorities-and-crimes-apartheid-and-persecution (last accessed 23 June 2022).

7. 'Israel's apartheid against Palestinians: a cruel system of domination and a crime against humanity', Amnesty International, 1 February 2022, https://www.amnesty.org/en/latest/news/2022/02/israels-apart-heid-against-palestinians-a-cruel-system-of-domination-and-a-crime-against-humanity/ (last accessed 23 June 2022).

8. 'High Court rejects petitions seeking to strike down nation-state law', Amy Spiro and Toi Staff, *The Times of Israel*, 8 July 2021, https://www. timesofisrael.com/high-court-rejects-petitions-seeking-to-strike- down-nation-state-law/ (last accessed 22 June 2022).

9. 'Arab peace initiative: full text', *The Guardian*, 28 March 2002, https:// www.theguardian.com/world/2002/mar/28/israel7 (last accessed 23 June 2022).

10. 'Organization of Islamic Cooperation affirms its Constant Position on the Palestinian Cause', Organization of Islamic Cooperation, 24 August 2020, https://www.oic-oci.org/topic/?t_id=23777&t_ref=14148& lan=en (last accessed 23 June 2022).

11. 'The Will of Life' (poem, Arabic), Abu Qasem al-Shabbi. 16 September 1933. One of the most well-known works in modern Arabic poetry.